The Baker & McKenzie International Arbitration Yearbook 2011-2012

JURIS

Questions About This Publication

For assistance with shipments, billing or other customer service matters, please call our Customer Services Department at:
1-631-350-2100.

To obtain a copy of this book, call our Sales Department at: 1-631-351-5430
Fax: 1-631-351-5712 or 1-631-351-5430

Toll Free Order Line: 1-800-887-4064 (United States and Canada)

See our web page about this book:
www.jurispub.com

Printed in the United States of America
ISBN 978-1-937518-05-9

This is the fifth edition of the *Baker & McKenzie International Arbitration Yearbook,* an annual series established by the Firm in 2007. This collection of articles is comprised of reports on arbitration in key jurisdictions around the globe. Leading lawyers of the Firm's International Arbitration Practice Group, a division of the Firm's Global Dispute Resolution Practice Group, report on recent developments in national laws relating to arbitration and address current arbitral trends and tendencies in the jurisdictions in which they practice.

For this 2011-2012 edition, the topic of Section C of each chapter is public policy in international arbitration. Each jurisdiction reveals how public policy issues intersect with arbitration.

The aim of this *Yearbook* is to highlight the more important recent developments in international arbitration, without aspiring to be an exhaustive case reporter or a textbook on arbitration in the broad sense. It is hoped that this volume will prove a useful tool for those contemplating and using arbitration to resolve international business disputes.

JurisNet, LLC
71 New Street
Huntington, New York 11743 USA
www.jurispub.com

TABLE OF CONTENTS

Table of Contents

Table of Contents

Table of Contents

Table of Contents

Table of Contents

Table of Contents

FOREWORD

On behalf of Baker & McKenzie's International Arbitration Practice Group, it is a great pleasure to present you with the fifth annual edition of our *International Arbitration Yearbook*. Initially published by our European offices in 2007, the *Yearbook* has expanded to include developments in jurisdictions in Asia, Latin America and North America, and has become a valuable resource for clients and colleagues in the international business community.

Our 2011-2012 *Yearbook* covers thirty-seven (37) jurisdictions and is organized by country. As in past years, the first section (Part A) of each chapter describes important recent developments and trends in national legislation and practice affecting the conduct of international arbitration. The second section (Part B) reports on noteworthy case law in each country, and, in a feature that first appeared in the second edition of the book, a third section (Part C) focuses on an important current topic in international arbitration.

This year's topic is public policy in international arbitration. The chapters discuss scenarios of reliance on public policy, i.e., the circumstances under which a party can invoke public policy considerations in that jurisdiction as a means to invalidate an arbitration agreement, set aside an award or as a defense against recognition and enforcement of an award. Each jurisdiction looks at the modes and limitations of reliance on public policy and answer how and within which timeframe public policy considerations can be invoked, whether the defense has to be invoked with the tribunal and whether enforcement is affected if the award was vacated in its country of origin. We asked each jurisdiction to identify the mandatory rules that are considered to be part of public policy in their legal system and to explain whether a distinction is made between "domestic" and "international" public policy, and especially whether the breach of an "international" public policy can be invoked as a defense to enforcement.

The diversity and breadth of Baker & McKenzie is clearly displayed in these chapters. Overall, this *Yearbook* provides critical commentary about world-wide developments in this fascinating field of law that directly affects the risks and challenges of doing business locally and internationally and managing the disputes that follow.

As with past editions, this *Yearbook* does not aspire to be a guide to arbitration in a general sense, nor is it intended as a comprehensive case reporter. Instead, it is a selection of the most noteworthy developments in the countries on which we comment. We trust that these materials will be helpful to those who contemplate arbitration as a process for resolving disputes in international business transactions, especially with respect to choice of venue, as national courts play a critical role in enforcing arbitration agreements and awards, and supervising the arbitral process generally.

We welcome any comments you may have on the content of this edition and any suggestions about topics you would like to see included in future editions.

This publication would not be possible without the effort and diligence of our colleagues from around the world who drafted the chapters and our regional editors who reviewed their submissions.

We take this opportunity to specifically thank Vivianne Knierim, Michael Atkins and Laura Zimmerman of our New York office; Duy Binh Tran in our Ho Chi Minh City office; and Liz Williams in our London office for their invaluable contributions and assistance in preparing this year's book.

Nancy M. Thevenin
Executive Editor

ABOUT THE 2011-2012
B&M YEARBOOK EDITORS

Executive Editor:

Nancy M. Thevenin is Special Counsel in the New York office of Baker & McKenzie and the global coordinator of the Firm's International Arbitration Practice Group. She routinely advises on arbitration institutions, mediation, disputes boards and expertise proceedings, *ad hoc* cases and use of pre-arbitral referee procedures. Her experience includes handling international commercial mediation and arbitration under the auspices of the AAA, ICC and ICDR. Ms. Thevenin has handled disputes in various industries, including construction and engineering, financial services, commercial real estate and aviation, often involving issues concerning M&A, sales, distribution, licensing, technology transfer and leasing agreements. She currently serves as co-chair of the International Arbitration & ADR Committee of the International Law Section of the New York State Bar Association, vice-chair of the Arbitration Law Committee of the Inter-American Bar Association and executive committee member of the American Branch of the International Law Association. Before joining Baker & McKenzie, Ms. Thevenin served as deputy director of arbitration and ADR for North America for the ICC International Court of Arbitration in New York.

Regional Editors

Asia-Pacific:

Gerald Kuppusamy is a Senior Associate in the Singapore office of Baker & McKenzie. He advises clients on cross-border litigation and international arbitration in a wide variety of commercial disputes. He has represented clients in courts in Singapore and New York, and in arbitrations under the arbitration rules of the ICC, SIAC, NASD (now FINRA), AAA and in *ad hoc* arbitrations under UNCITRAL rules. He is a Fellow of both the Chartered Institute of Arbitrators and the Singapore Institute of Arbitrators.

Europe and Eastern Europe:

Jürgen Mark is a Partner in the Düsseldorf office of Baker & McKenzie and a member of the Firm's European Dispute Resolution Practice Group Steering Committee. His practice covers a wide range of domestic and international disputes involving litigation and arbitration in the areas of commercial and company law, product liability law and distribution law. He has handled complex litigation, as well as ICC, DIS and *ad hoc* arbitrations. Mr. Mark has also acted as arbitrator on arbitration panels for the ICC and DIS relating to corporate and post-M&A disputes, major construction projects, product distribution and product liability. He is a member of the German Lawyer's Association, International Bar Association, German Institution of Arbitration (DIS), London Court of International Arbitration, Swiss Arbitration Association, International Law Association, German Association for Intellectual Property & Copyright, German-American Lawyers' Association and Canadian-German Lawyers' Association.

Edward Poulton is a Partner in the London office of Baker & McKenzie and a member of the Firm's Global Dispute Resolution Practice Group. He focuses his practice on international arbitration, complex litigation, commercial and investment treaty arbitration and public international law. His experience ranges from contract and M&A disputes to more specialist claims in the banking sector and investment treaty claims. He has acted as advisor and advocate in many international arbitrations under the rules of the major arbitral institutions, and is currently serving as arbitrator under both the ICC and LCIA rules. Mr. Poulton's client base covers a wide range of sectors, including financial services, electronics, aviation and telecommunications. He is a member of the Law Society of England & Wales, ICC, LCIA, Young International Arbitration Group and Investment Protection Forum of the British Institute of International and Comparative Law.

Jeremy Winter is a Partner in the London office of Baker & McKenzie and a member of the Firm's Global Dispute Resolution Group. Mr. Winter advises on a wide range of construction and infrastructure projects and has experience doing so in over 30 different countries, particularly in Europe, the Middle East, the CIS and Africa. His experience includes a wide range of contractual disputes, with a strong focus on international arbitration. He has been increasingly successful in resolving issues before they must be handled through formal litigation or arbitration. As solicitor advocate, he is able to conduct cases in the high courts – including appeals from arbitrations and adjudications. Mr. Winter is a contributing author of *International Arbitration Checklists*, 2nd Ed. (Juris 2008) and *International Commercial Arbitration – Practical Perspectives* (CCLM 2001).

Mathias Wittinghofer is a Partner in the Frankfurt office of Baker & McKenzie and a member of the Firm's Global Dispute Resolution Practice Group. A member of the Chartered Institute of Arbitrators and double-qualified as a German attorney-at-law and a solicitor (England & Wales), Mr. Wittinghofer routinely handles international arbitration proceedings, most notably in the areas of post-M&A and banking and finance dispute resolution. He has handled a wide variety of disputes both before German state courts as well as in national and international arbitrations before all major arbitral institutions. His clients include international corporations, banks, private equity firms and other members of the banking & finance industry. Mr. Wittinghofer has published several articles and spoken extensively on the topic of international arbitration, and recently completed the theoretical training required to qualify as a *Fachanwalt für Bank- und Kapitalmarktrecht* (attorney specialized in banking and finance).

Urs Zenhäusern is a Partner in the Zurich office of Baker & McKenzie. Mr. Zenhäusern mainly handles commercial, transactional and intellectual property disputes before state courts and international arbitral tribunals. He has acted as sole arbitrator, chairman and secretary of arbitration panels and as counsel in domestic and international litigation and arbitration. He also advises clients on antitrust law and sports law, as well as on legal matters related to unfair competition and distribution, agency and licensing contracts. Mr. Zenhäusern is a frequent writer and speaker at seminars on litigation and arbitration law and intellectual property law topics. He is a member of the Swiss Arbitration Association, German Institution of Arbitration, International Bar Association, International Law Association, Licensing Executives Society, AIPPI and INGRES.

Latin America:

Grant Hanessian is a Partner in the New York office of Baker & McKenzie. Mr. Hanessian serves as co-chair of the Firm's International Arbitration Practice Group and chair of the Litigation/Dispute Resolution department of the New York office. He has more than 25 years of experience serving as counsel and arbitrator in disputes concerning contract, energy, construction, commodities, financial services, insurance, intellectual property and other matters. Mr. Hanessian is a member of the Commission on Arbitration of the ICC and the ICC Task Force on Arbitration Involving States or State Entities, as well as the American Society of International Law, American Bar Association, Association of the Bar of the City of New York, American Arbitration Association and London Court of International Arbitration. He is an editor of this publication and co-editor of the *Gulf War Claims Reporter* (ILI/Kluwer, 1998) and *International Arbitration Checklists* (Juris Pub., 2d ed., 2008).

Luis Peretti is a Senior Associate in the São Paulo office of Trench Rossi e Watanabe, which is the Brazilian firm associated with Baker & McKenzie. Mr. Peretti handles both international and domestic arbitration cases, including ancillary court proceedings. He has experience in arbitrations administered by the ICC and the largest Brazilian arbitration institutions. His experience covers disputes concerning resolution of construction, engineering, corporate, distribution and intellectual property agreements. He is a member of the ICC Young Arbitrators Forum and of the Young Chinese European Arbitration Centre (CEAC). He is also a member of the Brazilian Bar Association.

North America:

David Zaslowsky is a Partner in the New York office of Baker & McKenzie. Mr. Zaslowsky has practiced in the area of international commercial litigation and arbitration for more than 27 years. He has appeared in various federal and state courts (trial and appellate) throughout the country and has participated in arbitrations, both inside and outside the United States, before the AAA, ICC, ICDR, Iran-United States Claims Tribunal, HKIAC and NASD, as well as in *ad hoc* arbitrations. Mr. Zaslowsky currently serves on the ICC Task Force on Decisions as to Costs. He is included in the *Chambers USA Guide* for his expertise in International Arbitration. He is also on the roster of arbitrators for the ICDR and the AAA.

ABBREVIATIONS AND ACRONYMS

AAA	American Arbitration Association
BIT	Bilateral Investment Treaty
CIETAC	China International Economic and Trade Arbitration Commission
ECT	Energy Charter Treaty
HKIAC	Hong Kong International Arbitration Centre
JCAA	Japan Commercial Arbitration Association
IBA Rules	International Bar Association Rules on the Taking of Evidence in International Commercial Arbitration
ICC	International Chamber of Commerce
ICC Arbitration Rules or ICC Rules	Rules of Arbitration of the International Chamber of Commerce
ICDR	International Centre for Dispute Resolution (part of the AAA)
ICDR Rules	International Arbitration Rules of the International Centre for Dispute Resolution, 2003
ICSID	International Centre for the Settlement of Investment Disputes
ICSID Convention	Convention on the Settlement of Investment Disputes between States and Nationals of Other States
LCIA	London Court of International Arbitration
LCIA Arbitration Rules or LCIA Rules	Arbitration Rules of the London Court of International Arbitration, 1998

NAFTA	North American Free Trade Agreement
New York Convention	United Nations Convention on the Recognition and Enforcement of Foreign Arbitral Awards, 1958
Panama Convention	Inter-American Convention on International Commercial Arbitration, 1975
SCC	Stockholm Chamber of Commerce
SIAC	Singapore International Arbitration Centre
UNCITRAL	United Nations Commission on International Trade Law
UNCITRAL Model Law	United Nations Commission on International Trade Law Model Law on International Commercial Arbitration, 1985, amended in 2006
UNCITRAL Rules	United Nations Commission on International Trade Law Arbitration Rules, 1976
WIPO	World Intellectual Property Organization
WIPO Rules	World Intellectual Property Organization Arbitration Rules, 1994
ZPO	Zivilprozessordnung [German Code of Civil Procedure]

ARGENTINA

Gonzalo E. Cáceres[1] and Santiago L. Capparelli[2]

A. LEGISLATION, TRENDS AND TENDENCIES

A.1 Legislation

Despite repeated attempts to obtain congressional approval to adopt the UNCITRAL Model Law as the Argentine federal arbitration act, Argentina still does not have federal legislation specifically dealing with arbitration. Instead, the country's civil procedure codes contain arbitration regulations. Because Argentina is a federal country, each province has its own code of civil procedure that applies within that province. The National Code of Civil and Commercial Procedure ("CPCCN") applies to the Autonomous City of Buenos Aires (the capital) and in each federal court across the country.[3] Because the provincial codes tend to be consistent with the CPCCN as regards to arbitration, this report will only refer to the CPCCN.

---

[1] Gonzalo E. Cáceres is a Partner in Baker & McKenzie's Buenos Aires office, and has served as an arbitrator under the rules of the IACA and the ICC. He is a member of the Commercial and International Relationships Committee of the Buenos Aires Bar Association and for several years, served as an associate professor in commercial law at the School of Law of the University of Buenos Aires.

[2] Santiago L. Capparelli is a Partner in Baker & McKenzie's Buenos Aires office. He practices litigation, alternative dispute resolution, international and domestic arbitration and has represented parties in *ad hoc* arbitral proceedings, as well as in proceedings administered by the ICC and local arbitral institutions, such as the Buenos Aires Stock Exchange Market Arbitral Tribunal, the Buenos Aires Grain Market Arbitral Tribunal and the Private Center for Mediation and Arbitration.

[3] Código Procesal Civil y Comercial de la Nación, [National Code of Civil and Commercial Procedure], Law No. 17.454, Sept. 20, 1967, as restated in Decree 1042/1981, Aug. 18, 1981, *et seq.*

This section will discuss the relevant provisions of the CPCCN (A.1.1) and the most relevant international arbitration agreements to which Argentina is a party. These agreements are important because they provide rules in the absence of national legislation. These agreements include the International Commercial Arbitration Act of Mercosur (A.1.2); the Panama Convention (A.1.3); and the New York Convention (A.1.4). Finally, we will provide comments on recent legislative developments (A.2).

A.1.1. National Code of Civil and Commercial Procedure

Articles 1 and 737 of the CPCCN govern arbitrable issues. Controversies of a monetary nature (Article 1) that are subject to settlement by the parties (Article 737) are arbitrable. If both of these requirements are met, parties can submit their disputes to international arbitration, provided that the controversy is "international" (Article 1). However, the law does not provide express guidance for determining when a specific controversy is "international" for purposes of this provision. Nevertheless, the consensus is that "international" for the purposes of this provision, refers to cases relating to more than one legal system (e.g., parties with different nationalities; parties with addresses in different countries; or different locations of the goods or places where damage has occurred).[4]

The procedure under the CPCCN is obsolete, because it requires establishing a party's consent to arbitration in a document separate from the arbitration agreement itself. This document is called a *compromiso*.[5] A party agreeing to arbitration should

---

[4]   Antonio Boggiano, "*Aspectos internacionales de las reformas al Código Procesal Civil y Comercial de la Nación (1° parte),*" ED 90-880, cited by Julio César Rivera, "*Arbitraje Comercial,*" p. 32.

[5]   Similar in nature to the "Terms of Reference" described in Article 18 of the ICC Rules, http://www.iccwbo.org/uploadedFiles/Court/Arbitration/other/rules_arb_english.pdf.

legalize the *compromiso* before a notary public or the intervening court (Article 739). Unless the parties provide otherwise, the arbitration procedures, including receipt of evidence, will correspond to those in ordinary court proceedings (Article 751). The default provisions for whether a party can appeal an award are that, unless the parties waive their right to appeal or to file any other available remedy, these remedies remain available (Article 758). Thus, when a party wishes to waive its right to appeal an award, the party must provide clear language to this effect in the arbitration agreement or *compromiso*. Otherwise, the right to appeal remains available.

Courts in Buenos Aires usually uphold a party's waiver of its right to appeal. However, in *José Cartellone Construcciones Civiles S.A. v. Hidroeléctrica Norpatagónica S.A. o Hidronor*, the National Supreme Court decided that a party's waiver of its right to appeal should be disregarded when public policy considerations so recommend.[6] We will analyze this case in further detail below. As the defendant in that case was an Argentine public entity, it is debatable whether the *José Cartellone* doctrine can serve as precedent for future National Supreme Court decisions involving private parties.

Local procedural law provides that parties cannot waive their right to request an annulment of an award. Parties can file for an annulment only in the following circumstances: (i) when the tribunal issues the award outside the term granted to it; (ii) when the award resolves issues that the parties did not request to be adjudicated or if the award does not provide for the relief that the parties requested; or (iii) when the arbitrators failed to follow the procedures established by the parties.

---

[6] Corte Suprema de Justicia de la Nación [CSJN] [National Supreme Court of Justice], 1/6/2004, *José Cartellone Construcciones Civiles S.A. v. Hidroeléctrica Norpatagónica S.A. o Hidronor/proceso de conocimiento*.

A.1.2. International Commercial Arbitration Act of Mercosur

Absent any federal arbitration act in force in Argentina, the most important legislation dealing with international arbitration is probably the *Acuerdo sobre Arbitraje Comercial Internacional del Mercosur* (Mercosur Accord on International Commercial Arbitration), issued in Buenos Aires on July 23, 1998 ("Buenos Aires Convention").[7] Argentina, Brazil, Uruguay and Paraguay are parties to this convention.

The Buenos Aires Convention applies to disputes between parties that at the time of the execution of their agreement: (i) have their domiciles in signatory countries to the Convention (section 3(a)); (ii) have contact with at least one signatory party to the Convention; or (iii) have chosen the seat of the arbitration in a signatory country to the Convention (section 3(c)).

Contrary to the CPCCN, the Buenos Aires Convention's treatment of international arbitration is in line with most of the relevant international arbitration statutes (e.g., UNCITRAL Model Law). Among the issues contemplated therein, the Buenos Aires Convention explicitly allows—and mandates—a court to assist an international arbitration tribunal in the course of its proceedings (e.g., by issuing interim measures).

One final element to consider regarding this Convention is that absent an indication to the contrary, each party is responsible for paying its own attorney's fees and costs. Consequently, if parties subject to this Convention want to take a "loser pays all" or "costs follow the event" approach, they must provide specific language to that effect in their arbitration clause or in the *compromiso.*

---

[7] Incorporated into domestic Argentine law by Law No. 25.223.

A.1.3. Panama Convention

Argentina is also a signatory to the *Convención Interamericana sobre Arbitraje Comercial Internacional* or Panama Convention. Again, given the absence in Argentina of specific legislation dealing with international arbitration, this Convention is relevant because it stresses the court's powers (and obligations) to enforce international arbitration clauses, provided that such disputes are of a commercial nature and a written arbitration agreement exists. When this arbitrability threshold is met, the Convention also mandates the local courts to assist international arbitration tribunals.

A.1.4. The New York Convention

Finally, Argentina is a signatory to the New York Convention, adopted by Law No. 23.619. Argentina made two reservations to this Convention that affect whether an Argentine court will recognize and enforce a foreign arbitral award: (i) that the award is issued in a country that is a signatory to the Convention; and (ii) that the underlying dispute is considered to be of a commercial nature under Argentine law.

A.2 Draft Legislation

There are currently several draft bills of law before the National Congress that aim to enact specific legislation on arbitration. Two of them are under consideration in the House of Representatives by a commission created for that purpose,[8] and meetings are being held within that commission to request the opinion of many renowned institutional arbitration and local bar

---

[8] N°. 3301-D- 2011, presented by Congressman Tunessi *et al.*, contemplating domestic and international arbitration, and N° 0009-D-2011, recommending the adoption of the UNCITRAL Model Law.

representatives. Hopefully, this matter will finally become part of the political agenda and Argentina will soon have this very important legislation.

B.   CASES

B.1   Enforcement of the Arbitration Agreement

On October 19, 2010, the National Court of Appeals on Commercial Matters decided *Camaedu S.A. et al. v. Envases EP S.A. et al.*[9] The controversy related to a lease agreement executed between the lessor, the lessee and a guarantor. A controversy arose between the plaintiff (lessor) and the guarantor and the former resorted to the judiciary, arguing that the guarantor was not a party to the arbitration agreement (which was an agreement "separate" from the lease agreement). The guarantor, in turn, contended that by executing the agreement it should also be bound by (and be considered a party to) the arbitration provision. The first instance court ruled against the plaintiff and referred the parties to arbitration. The court of appeals affirmed.

The court of appeals decided that the parties did not intend to exclude the guarantor from the arbitration agreement (therefore providing for proof of intent that *all* of them would arbitrate any dispute related to the lease agreement), and the guarantor was sued for claims arising out of that lease agreement. Consequently and although the court of appeals did not explicitly rely on the "severability" doctrine, its decision was nevertheless consistent with this principle.

---

[9]   Cámara Nacional de Apelaciones de la Capital Federal (CNCom) (National Court of Appeals on Commercial Matters) Section C, 10/19/2010, *Camaedu S.A. et al v. Envases EP S.A. et al.*

B.2 Autonomy, Scope and Validity of the Arbitration Clause

On March 1, 2011, the Federal Court of Appeals in Civil and Commercial Matters in Buenos Aires decided *Smit International Argentina S.A. v. Puerto Mariel S.A.*[10] The parties executed a charter party agreement with an arbitration clause, and this agreement was eventually terminated by the defendant. The plaintiff sued requesting that the court compel the defendant to arbitrate. The First Instance Federal Court granted a motion to defer consideration on the matter until a final ruling was entered on whether the arbitration provision survived termination of the agreement (as the defendant had argued that it did not). The Federal Court of Appeals reversed by majority with one of the appellate judges dissenting.

The decision discussed several important topics in arbitration, such as the autonomy of the arbitration clause, and found that upholding arbitration agreements is part of Argentine public policy. To that effect, the court concluded that despite the fact that Argentine law does not yet have specific legislation regarding the autonomy of arbitration agreements, it is a widely accepted principle that is contemplated in draft bills that are currently being discussed in Congress. Further, the court noted that properly considered, it would not be necessary to "fill any legislative gaps" on this matter, but to provide for proper interpretation of other existing legislation such as the New York Convention and the Buenos Aires Convention. Finally, the court went on to say that the defendant's contention limiting the scope of the arbitration agreement only to determine factual issues was baseless and contrary to the party's intent to submit "all disputes" to arbitration.

---

[10]   Cámara Nacional de Apelaciones en lo Civil y Comercial [CNac. Civ. Com. Fed.] [Federal Court of Appeals in Civil and Commercial Matters] Section III, 3/1/2011, *Smit International Argentina S.A. v. Puerto Mariel S.A.*

Justice Farrell dissented, arguing that the majority's reference to legislation providing for the autonomy of the arbitration agreement relates to "international" cases and not domestic ones such as the instant case. He stressed that there is no provision in Argentine law providing for the autonomy of the arbitration clause. As a result, he contended that this issue should be resolved by general principles of contract law (which, he believed, would mandate resolving the dispute against the plaintiff's position).

In our view, this is a very important decision because it reinforces fundamental notions about the autonomy of an arbitration agreement, while providing guidance for construing the scope of these agreements.

B.3 Annulment of Award for Defects While Constituting the Arbitral Tribunal

On May 14, 2010, the National Commercial Court of Appeals decided *American Restaurants Inc. v. Outback Steakhouse Int.*[11] The defendant filed an action to vacate an award rendered by a sole arbitrator, who acted pursuant to an arbitration clause that called for ICC proceedings. Under the arbitration clause, each party had the right to appoint arbitrators for a three-person tribunal, and the two party-appointed arbitrators were to appoint the chairman. If any party failed to nominate an arbitrator or the two appointed arbitrators were unable to nominate the chairman, then the party-appointed arbitrators were to request the ICC to select the chairman. In the instant case, American Restaurant appointed its arbitrator and so did Outback Steakhouse. However, the latter died before a chairman could be elected. Thus, instead of asking the ICC to provide further nominations,

---

[11] Camara Nacional de Apelaciones de la Capital Federal [CNCom] [National Commercial Court of Appeals] Section C, 5/14/2010, *American Restaurants Inc. v. Outback Steakhouse Int.*

American Restaurant's party-appointed arbitrator decided that proceedings should go forward with him as sole arbitrator. Outback Steakhouse declared that to be against the selection process that the parties agreed to and decided that it would not participate further in the arbitration. The sole arbitrator appears to have issued an award without executing a Terms of Reference and it was unclear whether the ICC was further involved in the case. In any event, after being served with this award, Outback Steakhouse filed an action to have it vacated. The court of appeals accepted the request and vacated the award.

The decision to vacate the award was based on the conclusion that the arbitrator's conduct resulted in an "essential failure" in the course of the proceedings (section 760 of the CPCCN). As additional basis for this decision, the court noted that the sole arbitrator failed to execute the Terms of Reference provided for in the ICC rules and failed to set forth a procedural timetable, thereby failing to abide by the ICC procedures selected by the parties.

C. PUBLIC POLICY IN INTERNATIONAL ARBITRATION

C.1 Does Public Policy Affect Arbitrability?

Perhaps because of its lack of precise boundaries, the notion and effects of public policy have served as the basis for extensive debate in Argentine doctrine and case law. One of the misconceptions in that debate was that issues of public policy are not arbitrable. There is no basis in Argentine law that would support such a conclusion. As stressed above in section A.1.1, the only requirements that a private party must meet if it wants to arbitrate a dispute are: (i) that the dispute is subject to settlement under argentine law;[12] and (ii) that the dispute is of a commercial nature.[13] If a party wants to submit a dispute to arbitrators seating outside Argentina, additional requirements would apply: (iii) the dispute must be considered "international;" and (iv) Argentine courts do not have exclusive jurisdiction over the dispute.[14]

If all the above requirements are met, a dispute is arbitrable under Argentine law (and it can even be submitted to arbitrators seating outside Argentina). No reference to public policy would therefore affect the arbitrability of such disputes.

Regrettably, there have been a few occasions where local courts used "public policy considerations" as a means to interfere with arbitration. A brief description of such decisions follows, but in our view, none of these cases represent the general approach of the judiciary in Argentina.

C.1.1. *CRI Holding Inc. Sucursal Argentina v. Compañía Argentina de Comodoro Rivadavia Explotación de Petróleo S.A.*

On October 5, 2010, the National Commercial Court of Appeals decided *CRI Holding Inc. Sucursal Argentina v. Compañía Argentina de Comodoro Rivadavia Explotación de Petróleo S.A.*[15] The case related to the plaintiff's request to compel arbitration, executing all relevant acts in order to constitute the

---

[12] Sections 736 and 737 of the CPCCN provide that all matters that are subject to settlement are subject to arbitration.

[13] Section 1 of the CPCCN provides that matters of a monetary nature can be referred to arbitration.

[14] Section 1 of the CPCCN provides that a party can only refer disputes to arbitrators seated abroad when both requirements are met.

[15] Cámara Nacional de Apelaciones de la Capital Federal [CNCom] [National Commercial Court of Appeals] Section C 2/18/2011 *CRI Holding Inc Sucursal Argentina v. Compañía Argentina de Comodoro Rivadavia Explotación de Petróleo S.A.*

tribunal and set forth the issues to be included (and resolved) in the award. Both parties executed an agreement to jointly operate a mining company in Argentina. When a dispute arose, the defendant rejected the request to pursue arbitration and the first instant court concurred for two reasons. It found that (a) the arbitration agreement was no longer binding on the parties, and (b) the issues that the plaintiff wanted to submit to arbitration contravened public policy. The court of appeals analyzed only the latter argument and confirmed.

The court of appeals found that the agreement evidenced an attempt to supersede the relevant provisions of Argentine law regulating mining companies, which is against public policy. Consequently, the court concluded that the plaintiff's request should be rejected based on an alleged "longstanding case law from the Supreme Court." This is clearly incorrect, as it has been noted by commentators that none of those Supreme Court cases resolved the legal issues of the instant case.[16] To summarize, it is clear that the court of appeals erred in this case by declaring that public policy affects arbitrability and there is no Supreme Court case supporting its decision.

C.1.2. Would public policy affect waiver of the right to appeal the award?

On June 1, 2004, the Supreme Court decided *Jose Cartellone Construcciones Civiles S.A. v. Hidroeléctrica Norpatagónica S.A. o Hidronor S.A.,*[17] declaring that waiver of the right to appeal should be ignored when the relief granted in the award rendered that award contrary to public policy. In that case, the award ordered Hidronor (a state-owned company) to pay interest

---

[16] Rivera, Julio Cesar "Arbitrabilidad; Cuestiones regidas por leyes de orden público," *La Ley*, 28/2/2011, 7.

[17] Full citation in A.1.1, *supra*.

at what was considered by the Supreme Court to be abusive rates. Thus, as abusive interest rates would violate public policy, the Supreme Court found that waiver of the right to appeal can never be made to produce such a result. Regrettably, the Supreme Court improperly considered the substance of the arbitrator's decision through the procedural framework of an annulment request, "harming," quite unnecessarily in the process, the validity of the party's right to waive the appeal of the award.

The consensus is that this Supreme Court decision was entered in particular circumstances and against a public entity such as Hidronor S.A. Therefore, it seems unlikely that the *Jose Cartelone* doctrine would apply in further Supreme Court or lower court's decisions. On the contrary, appellate court rulings issued after *Jose Cartelone* resolved the same legal issue in the proper fashion (departing from *Jose Cartelone*),[18] and even explicitly criticized this Supreme Court decision.[19]

C.2 Public Policy and Enforcement of the Award

On November 5, 2002, the Commercial Court of Appeals decided *Reef Exploration Inc. v. Compañia General de Combustibles S.A.* in which it granted the plaintiff's request for recognition and enforcement of an award issued by the AAA.

A particular element of this case was that during the arbitration proceedings, a Buenos Aires court issued an injunction against

---

[18] Cámara Nacional de Apelaciones de la Capital Federal [CNCom] [National Commercial Court of Appeals], Section D, 2/21/2008, *Nemesio, Antonio y otros v. Teledigital Cable S.A.*, *La Ley Online*, AR/JUR/1008/2008 and other cases cited.

[19] Cámara Nacional de Apelaciones de la Capital Federal [CNCom] [National Commercial Court of Appeals], Section D, 2/7/2011, *Sociedad de Inversiones Inmobiliarias del Puerto S.A. v. Constructora Iberoamericana S.A.*

the continuance of the arbitration. The arbitral tribunal ignored the injunction, and eventually issued an award. The first instance court rejected the recognition and enforcement of the award on the basis that to do so would be against the defense set forth in section 517 of the CPCCN, i.e., that the decision of the arbitral tribunal would be against another ruling issued by a local court (in this case, the mentioned injunction). The court of appeals reversed and accepted the plaintiff's request for enforcement and execution.

The rationale of the court of appeal's ruling was that the injunction was not mandatory for the arbitral tribunal, and would only have been effective if the arbitral tribunal would have accepted it. Further, the court of appeals noted that the lower court's decision to grant the injunction was erroneous in that it ignored the party's agreement to arbitrate all disputes. Finally, the court of appeals indicated that nothing in the award would affect local public policy. On the contrary, it noted that the respect of party autonomy (and specifically, the agreement to arbitrate) are principles of Argentine public policy with which the instant award complied in full.

AUSTRALIA

Leigh Duthie[1] and Sarah Lancaster[2,3]

A. LEGISLATION, TRENDS AND TENDENCIES

A.1 Legislative Framework

Australia is a signatory to the New York Convention, which (together with the UNCITRAL Model Law) has been implemented in Australia through the International Arbitration Act 1974 (Cth) ("the IAA"). The IAA also gives effect to the ICSID Convention.

In addition to the IAA, which covers the field for international arbitration, each State and Territory in Australia has its own (largely uniform) domestic arbitration legislation. New uniform domestic arbitration legislation is currently being implemented by all the States and Territories. That new legislation, like the IAA, is based on the UNCITRAL Model Law.

---

[1] Leigh Duthie is a Partner in Baker & McKenzie's Melbourne office, with over 15 years' experience acting for major Australian and international corporations and government agencies in relation to complex claims arising from infrastructure projects, defects in plants, and faults in heavy mining machinery. Mr. Duthie's experience includes appearing before all major Australian courts, as well as expert determinations, special referee procedures, and domestic and international arbitrations.

[2] Sarah Lancaster is a Senior Associate in Baker & McKenzie's Sydney office with over 10 years' experience in dispute resolution gained in London and Sydney. Ms. Lancaster's practice incorporates international arbitration and complex commercial litigation, with a particular focus on resource and telecoms disputes. She is a council member of the Australasian Forum for International Arbitration.

[3] The authors would like to thank Pouyan Afshar, Tom Bridges and Annalise Haigh of our Sydney office and Cara North and Jacob Chylinski of our Melbourne office for their assistance with this chapter.

A.2 Amendments to Australia's Legislative Framework

In last year's *Yearbook*, we reported on the implementation, in 2009 and 2010, of amendments to the IAA. In summary, some of the key amendments to the IAA were to:

- incorporate the updated 2006 version of the UNCITRAL Model Law;

- expand the definition of "arbitration agreement" to include agreements made by way of electronic communication, as well as verbal agreements (where the contents of the agreement are subsequently recorded in any form);

- remove the ability of parties to opt out of the Model Law in international commercial arbitrations;

- enhance the court's power to act in aid of arbitration proceedings—for example, to order a party to produce documents or provide evidence—while ensuring that the court may not unnecessarily interfere in those proceedings;

- promote the ease of enforcement of foreign arbitral awards; and

- introduce opt-in provisions on confidentiality.[4]

In early March 2011, the government appointed the Australian Centre for International Commercial Arbitration ("ACICA") as the sole default appointing authority for the purpose of Articles 11(3) and 11(4) of the Model Law.[5] The practical effect of this appointment is that where parties have not provided a procedure for appointing an arbitrator or where the appointment procedure fails, parties to an international arbitration in Australia will be able to quickly arrange for the appointment of an arbitrator

---

[4] In Australia, unlike in many common law jurisdictions, there is no implied duty of confidentiality in arbitration.

[5] International Arbitration Regulations 2011.

through ACICA, rather than having to make a more costly application to a court.

As reported in last year's chapter, all Australian States and Territories recently agreed to adopt a new Commercial Arbitration Bill to more closely align the domestic arbitration framework with the UNCITRAL Model Law and the IAA. New South Wales was the first to enact the new Commercial Arbitration Act, which received assent on 28 June 2010 and came into force on 1 October 2010. The new Act also came into force in Victoria on 17 November 2011 and in South Australia on 1 January 2012. In addition, as of the time of writing, the new Commercial Arbitration Act has been adopted (although it is not yet in force) in Tasmania and the Northern Territory, while Queensland and Western Australia have introduced similar bills into their parliaments, which we expect to be enacted shortly.[6]

A.3   Investor-State Arbitrations

In April 2011, the Australian Government announced that it would no longer seek the inclusion of investor-state dispute resolution procedures in trade agreements with developing countries, where to do so would confer greater legal rights on foreign businesses than those available to domestic businesses, or would otherwise constrain the ability of Australian governments to make laws on social, environmental and economic matters in circumstances where those laws do not discriminate between domestic and foreign businesses.[7]

The practical effects of this policy statement, and whether it will result in the inclusion of fewer investor-state arbitration provisions in treaties with developing countries, remain to be seen.

---

[6]   The Act has not yet introduced a similar bill.

[7]   *See* http://www.dfat.gov.au/publications/trade/trading-our-way-to-more-jobs-and-prosperity.html#investor-state.

The April announcement included a statement that: "The Government has not and will not accept provisions that limit its capacity to put health warnings or plain packaging requirements on tobacco products . . ." On 27 June 2011, Philip Morris Asia Limited served on the Australian Government a Notice of Claim under Article 10 of the Agreement between Hong Kong and Australia for the Promotion and Protection of Investments, in relation to the Australian Government's proposed tobacco plain-packaging legislation, which became law on 1 December 2011.[8] Philip Morris served a formal Notice of Arbitration on 21 November 2011, to which the Government of Australia responded on 21 December 2011.[9] One of the key arguments advanced by the Government is that Philip Morris acquired its shares in the relevant Australian subsidiary in full knowledge that the Australian Government had already announced its intention to introduce plain packaging legislation. The arbitration will be conducted under the UNCITRAL Rules and a presiding arbitrator is expected to be appointed in early 2012.

A.4   Trends

The recent changes to the IAA and the Commercial Arbitration Acts make Australia a very attractive choice as the seat for regional arbitrations, particularly when viewed together with the facilities available (such as the Australian International Disputes Centre, which opened in Sydney in August 2010) and the increasing number of experienced international arbitration practitioners, many of whom have moved from other arbitration centers, such as London and Hong Kong.

---

[8]   A copy of the notice of claim can be found on the Attorney General's website at www.ag.gov.au./www/agd/agd.nsf/page/8F5B65DEBCAED226CA25796D006B 4857

[9]   *Ibid.*

In addition, Australia's leading international arbitration institution, ACICA, issued updated rules on 1 August 2011. Those rules now incorporate emergency arbitrator provisions, providing parties in need of emergency interim measures of protection a quick and efficient alternative to seeking such relief from the courts.

The growing importance of Australia as an arbitration venue has recently been recognized by a number of arbitral institutions. In May 2011, the Chartered Institute of Arbitrators held its Asia-Pacific Conference 2011 in Sydney, and in August 2011, the ICC held a series of seminars on international arbitration in Australia in Melbourne, Canberra, Sydney and Perth.[10] These conferences reflect the growing importance of Australia as a center for international commercial arbitration.

B. CASES

Australian courts have rendered a number of significant decisions in relation to international arbitration in the last twelve months. We summarize some of them below.

B.1 *Gordian Runoff*: Standard of Reasons in Arbitral Awards

Last year we reported on the decision in *Gordian Runoff Ltd. v. Westport Ins. Corp.*,[11] in which the NSW Court of Appeal held that all that was required for an arbitral award to be a reasoned award was a "statement of reasons for making the award, not a statement of reasons for not making a different award."[12] In

---

[10] These seminars followed the ICC's first visit to Australia to speak on international arbitration in 2010.

[11] [2010] NSWCA 57. It should be noted that this is not an international arbitration case under the IAA.

[12] *Ibid.* at [218].

other words, although the tribunal had to explain succinctly the basis for the conclusions in its award, the arbitrators were not obliged to explain why they had rejected alternative arguments. In reaching that conclusion, the NSW Court of Appeal departed from the recent decision of the Victorian Court of Appeal in *Oil Basins Ltd. v. BHP Billiton*,[13] which effectively held that reasons, of a judicial standard, had to be provided in awards.

On 5 October 2011, the High Court (Australia's ultimate court of appeal) handed down its decision on the appeal from the NSW Court of Appeal in *Gordian Runoff*.[14] The High Court stated that the suggestion in *Oil Basins* that an arbitrator's reasons should be of a judicial standard placed an "unfortunate gloss" upon the terms of the (now superseded) Commercial Arbitration Act. The majority agreed, however, with the conclusion of the Court of Appeal in *Oil Basins* that the nature of the reasons required in an arbitral award will depend on the nature of the dispute and the particular circumstances of the case.

The majority of the High Court held that no wholly satisfactory formula could be found to flesh out the requirement for reasons contained in the Commercial Arbitration Act. They therefore applied the test from *Bremer Handelsgesellschaft GmbH v. Westzucker GmbH (No 2)*,[15] which the parties agreed was the applicable standard. Under *Bremer*, "all that is necessary is that the arbitrators should set out what, on their view of the evidence, did or did not happen and should explain succinctly why, in light of what happened, they have reached their decision and what the decision is."

---

[13]   [2007] VCA 255.

[14]   *Westport Ins. Corp. v. Gordian Runoff Ltd.,* [2011] HCA 37.

[15]   [1981] 2 Lloyd's Rep 130 at 132-133.

In *Gordian Runoff*, a particular statutory provision was a critical element in the arbitrators reaching the award after a hard-fought and lengthy arbitration. Under those circumstances, the High Court held that the arbitrators had been "obliged to explain succinctly why the various integers in that complex statutory provision were satisfied,"[16] which they had failed to do. The High Court therefore allowed the appeal.

As reported in last year's *Yearbook*, a number of parties sought leave to appear as *amici curiae* in the case, including the Commonwealth Attorney-General, ACICA, and the Chartered Institute of Arbitrators Australia. The High Court granted them leave to appear. In their submissions, the *amici curiae* asked the High Court to distinguish the requirements for giving reasons under the Commercial Arbitration Act from the position under the IAA, which does not allow appeals on questions of law and affords very limited scope for challenging arbitral awards. The *amici curiae* submitted that all that should be required in an international arbitration was a statement of reasons to demonstrate whether the arbitrators had addressed the dispute submitted to arbitration.

The High Court declined to address this issue, restricting its decision to the (now superseded) Commercial Arbitration Act. Accordingly, determination of the standard of reasons for an award under the IAA must await another occasion. In the meantime, this decision provides a useful guide as to the standard of reasons that international arbitration tribunals seated in Australia should strive to meet.

---

[16] *Westport Ins. Corp. v. Gordian Runoff Ltd.*, [2011] HCA 37, per French CJ, Gummow, Crennan and Bell JJ, at [55].

B.2 *IMC Aviation Solutions v. Altain Khuder*: Enforcement against Non-Party

In its August 2011 decision in *IMC Aviation Solutions v. Altain Khuder*,[17] the Supreme Court of Victoria, Court of Appeal overturned a lower court's decision and set aside an order for the enforcement in Australia of a Mongolian arbitral award against IMC Solutions. The court held that IMC Solutions was not a proper party to the arbitration and that the enforcement order should not have been made.

The underlying arbitration arose out of a dispute between Altain Khuder, a Mongolian mining company, and IMC Mining, a company registered in the British Virgin Islands, regarding an operations contract for an iron ore mine in Mongolia. Altain Khuder had commenced arbitration proceedings against IMC Mining in Mongolia pursuant to the contract. The arbitral tribunal in Mongolia rendered an award in favor of Altain Khuder, ordering IMC Mining to pay the company approximately USD 6 million. Yet the tribunal also ordered IMC Solutions, an Australian company affiliated with IMC Mining, to pay these damages "on behalf of" IMC Mining— notwithstanding that IMC Solutions was not a party to the arbitration agreement and did not participate in the arbitration. The award, which did not explain the basis of the tribunal's jurisdiction over IMC Solutions, was verified by the Mongolian court.

Altain Khuder subsequently applied for enforcement of the award in Australia. The first instance court ordered enforcement of the award and dismissed objections by IMC Solutions that it had not been a party to the arbitration agreement. In doing so, the court noted that the onus of resisting enforcement was a

---

[17] [2011] VSCA 248.

heavy one, particularly in light of the pro-enforcement policy regarding international arbitration awards. The court held that IMC Solutions had not discharged this burden and found, on the evidence, that IMC Solutions had been represented at the preliminary hearing before the arbitral tribunal and had agreed that the tribunal had jurisdiction to hear and determine the dispute. It further found that both the tribunal and the Mongolian court had determined that the tribunal had jurisdiction over IMC Solutions and that neither IMC entities had sought to challenge those determinations at that time. The court therefore rejected IMC Solutions' argument that the arbitration agreement was not valid under the law of Mongolia (being both the governing law of the contract and the law of the seat).

The court also dismissed the other arguments raised by IMC Solutions to resist enforcement of the award, including its argument that it had not had proper notice of the proceedings. It found that IMC Solutions was, in effect, the alter ego of IMC Mining or was estopped from asserting otherwise.

IMC Solutions appealed. The appellate court held that when seeking to enforce an arbitral award, the initial evidential onus falls on the award creditor to satisfy the court, on a *prima facie* basis, that: (a) an award has been made by a foreign arbitral tribunal granting relief to the award creditor against the award debtor; (b) the award was made pursuant to an arbitration agreement; and (c) the award creditor and the award debtor are parties to the arbitration agreement. The court found that this evidential onus would be discharged where the award expressly stated that it had been made in favor of the award creditor against the award debtor pursuant to an agreement naming those parties.

The Court of Appeal held, however, that where, on the face of the agreement and award, the person against whom the award was made was not a party to the arbitration agreement, the award creditor bears an additional evidential onus to adduce further evidence to satisfy the court that the *prima facie* evidential requirements were met. Provided an award creditor could discharge this burden, the legal onus then shifts to the award debtor to persuade the court to refuse enforcement on the basis of one of the grounds specified in the IAA.[18]

On the facts of this case, the Court of Appeal concluded that IMC Solutions was not a proper party to the arbitration agreement and that the judge at first instance should not have made an order enforcing the award.

Further, the court concluded that it was entitled to consider and determine whether the tribunal had properly assumed jurisdiction over IMC Solutions, and found that it had not. The court determined that it had discretion to allow the appeal on the basis that it would be contrary to Victoria's public policy to allow enforcement of an award made against IMC Solutions without notice, that being a breach of the rules of natural justice.

The Court of Appeal also emphasized that at all stages of the enforcement process, the court must act judicially and not "robotically" in its approach and must exercise its judicial function in satisfying itself that it has jurisdiction to enforce an award—notwithstanding that the enforcement of foreign arbitral awards should involve only a summary procedure.

---

[18] Sections 8(5) and (7) of the IAA. The process for enforcement of foreign arbitration awards (including whether it can be sought *ex parte*) varies between States within Australia. We do not address this aspect of the judgment here.

B.3 *TeleMates v. SoftTel:* Challenge to Jurisdiction of Arbitrator

TeleMates v. SoftTel,[19] one of the first cases decided under the revised IAA, emphasizes the need for parties to bring applications within the time limits specified in the IAA, and reflects the increasingly pro-arbitration approach of the Australian courts.

TeleMates and SoftTel, an Indian company, disputed whether an agreement between them had been validly terminated. The agreement contained an arbitration clause providing that the parties must refer any dispute to arbitration and that such arbitration should proceed in accordance with the rules of the Institute of Arbitrators & Mediators Australia ("IAMA"). SoftTel commenced arbitration proceedings and asked that IAMA appoint an arbitrator in accordance with its rules. IAMA appointed an arbitrator and TeleMates objected, arguing that under the arbitration clause, arbitration could only be commenced by agreement and that TeleMates had not agreed to the commencement of the proceedings.

The arbitrator appointed by IAMA heard the parties' arguments and then made an interim award confirming that he had jurisdiction to deal with and resolve the parties' dispute.

TeleMates applied to the Supreme Court of New South Wales to challenge the arbitrator's competence and appointment. The court found that TeleMates' application, notwithstanding the way it was framed, was in fact a challenge to the arbitrator's finding that he had jurisdiction to determine the parties' dispute. Under the IAA (and, in particular, Article 16(3) of the Model Law), any such challenge had to be made within 30 days of the decision on jurisdiction. TeleMates' application was made

---

[19] *TeleMates (previously Better Telecom) Pty Ltd. v. Standard SoftTel Solutions Pvt Ltd.*, [2011] NSWSC 1365.

outside that period. Accordingly, the court held that it could not intervene and dismissed TeleMates' application.

B.4 *Uganda Telecom v. Hi-Tech:* **Enforcement of Foreign Award**

In *Uganda Telecom v. Hi-Tech*,[20] Uganda Telecom, a Ugandan corporation, applied under Section 8 of the IAA for enforcement of a Ugandan arbitral award in Australia against Hi-Tech, an Australian corporation. The underlying dispute arose out of a telecommunications contract between the parties that contained an arbitration clause that did not specify a seat or the procedural rules.

Uganda Telecom commenced arbitration proceedings in Uganda under the Arbitration and Conciliation Act ("the UAA").[21]

Before commencing the arbitration, Uganda Telecom had sent a letter notifying Hi-Tech of its desire to arbitrate, stating that if it did not hear back from Hi-Tech within seven days, it would apply to the Centre for Arbitration and Dispute Resolution in Kampala ("CADER") for appointment of an arbitrator. The letter was sent via email to the Chief Executive Officer of Hi-Tech, Mr. Yahaya, and delivered by DHL to the office of Hi-Tech. Hi-Tech failed to respond to this correspondence and the arbitration was conducted with the participation of Uganda Telecom only.

The arbitrator made an award in Uganda Telecom's favor, which Uganda Telecom then sought to enforce in Australia. Hi-Tech raised a number of arguments seeking to resist enforcement, all of which were rejected by the court.

First, Hi-Tech argued that the award should not be enforced because the arbitration agreement was invalid under the laws of

---

[20]   *Uganda Telecom v. Hi Tech Telecom Pty Ltd,.* [2011] FCA 131.

[21]   Cap 4 Laws of Uganda, 2000 Revised Edition.

Uganda.[22] Hi-Tech argued that the clause did not deal with "the seat of arbitration, the identity of the arbitrator(s), the number of arbitrators, the service of documents by which arbitration was initiated, the manner in which any disputes concerning the appointment of the arbitrator(s) should be resolved and the rules that were to apply to the arbitration."[23] Hi-Tech also submitted that the arbitration agreement was void because it did not specify the law that was to govern the arbitration. The court rejected these arguments, holding that the omissions, which focused on "alleged omissions from [the arbitration agreement] rather than on ambiguities or uncertainty in the language [of the arbitration agreement],"[24] were all covered in detail by the UAA.

Further, Hi-Tech submitted that it had been unable to present its case in the arbitration proceedings in Uganda and/or that the award should not be enforced on grounds of public policy, because Mr. Yahaya had been unable to travel to Uganda as he had been fearful of his life and had thought he would not receive a fair hearing in Uganda. Hi-Tech also argued, however, that it had never been made aware that the dispute had been referred to arbitration.[25] In light of these inconsistent arguments, the court rejected these arguments.

Finally, Hi-Tech submitted that "the amount of general damages awarded by the arbitrator in the Award was arrived at by [an] erroneous reasoning process involving mistakes of fact and law,"[26] which gave rise to a public policy defense. The court also

---

[22]   s 8(5)(b) of the IAA.

[23]   [2011] FCA 131, [64].

[24]   [2011] FCA 131, [69].

[25]   The Australian court found, however, that the letter from Uganda Telecom to Hi-Tech indicating its intention to refer the matter to arbitration, had been delivered to, and received by, Mr. Yahaya of Hi-Tech.

[26]   [2011] FCA 131, [125].

rejected this argument, finding that Section 8(5) of the IAA does not permit a party to resist the enforcement of a foreign award on the ground of error of fact or law, and that the enforcement of the award would not be contrary to Australian public policy.

B.5 *Wilson & Partners v. Robert Nicholls*: Arbitration and Court Proceedings

In *Wilson & Partners v. Robert Nicholls*, [27] the High Court of Australia ruled for the first time on the interaction between contemporaneous arbitral and court proceedings. In a unanimous decision, the High Court held that it is not an abuse of process to commence and maintain court proceedings merely because an arbitration has already been commenced against some related parties.

The underlying dispute involved claims by MWP, a foreign law firm, that three Australian employees had diverted business opportunities for personal benefit. MWP commenced arbitration proceedings in London against the "principal" and, two months later, commenced proceedings in the New South Wales Supreme Court against two of the employees who had allegedly acted as "accessories" to the relevant breaches. Importantly, the accessories could not have been joined as respondents to the London arbitration as they were not party to the arbitration agreement, and the principal had declined MWP's invitation to consent to be joined as a party to the New South Wales proceedings. The two proceedings therefore followed their separate courses.

There was substantial, but not exact, overlap between the allegations made in both proceedings. The arbitrator and the court, however, ultimately reached materially different

---

[27] *Wilson & Partners Ltd. v. Robert Colin Nicholls & ors*, [2011] HCA 48.

conclusions. The arbitrator (who rendered his award after judgment was delivered in the court proceedings) found that the principal was liable to MWP for some, but not all, of the alleged acts. The court, however, found the two accessories liable for knowingly assisting in the principal's alleged breaches. The accessories appealed, arguing that the court proceedings had constituted an abuse of process.

The New South Wales Court of Appeal allowed the appeal. While the judges adopted varying approaches in their analyses, they appear to have all proceeded from a common assumption that any liability of the accessories was limited by the nature and extent of the relief MWP sought and obtained against the principal in the arbitration.

The matter was appealed to the High Court, which held this assumption to be erroneous and found that the nature and extent of relief sought from the accessories was not in any way limited by that obtained from the principal in the arbitration proceedings. The High Court also held that the mere existence of a relationship between claims made at a trial in Australia, and those made previously at an arbitration in London, did not challenge the findings of the arbitrators, because no arbitration award had been made before the court judgment.

This decision of the High Court represents an important clarification of the interrelationship between contemporaneous court and arbitral proceedings and acknowledges the reality that engaging in arbitration can result in multiple proceedings brought under the same factual circumstances with potentially different results. The High Court, however, did not reach any conclusion as to whether it would have constituted an abuse of process if MWP had continued to pursue the accessories in court after an award by the arbitrator finding that the principal was not liable.

C. PUBLIC POLICY IN INTERNATIONAL ARBITRATION

C.1 Introduction

Public policy considerations generally arise at two stages in international arbitration proceedings: first, at or shortly after commencement of the arbitration, with one party arguing that the arbitration agreement is invalid or the dispute is not arbitrable; and second, and more commonly, at the stage of enforcement of a foreign award.

Similar to many other jurisdictions, Australia has not yet clearly delineated the scope of "public policy" and its application to international arbitration agreements and awards. The 2010 amendments to the IAA and several recent cases provide some guidance as to whether a party might have public policy arguments in a particular case.

C.2 Public Policy at the Stage of Recognition and Enforcement

Section 8(5) of the IAA provides that the court may refuse to enforce a foreign arbitral award on a number of grounds, including where a party can prove that the arbitration agreement is not valid under the law expressed in the agreement to be applicable to it or, where no such law is expressed to be applicable, under the law of the country where the award was made.[28] Further, Section 8(7) of the IAA provides that the court may refuse to enforce an award if it finds that:

- the subject matter of the difference between the parties to the award is not capable of settlement by arbitration under the

---

[28] Section 8(5)(b) of the IAA.

laws in force in the State or Territory in which the court is sitting; or

- to enforce the award would be contrary to public policy.

Doubt about what amounts to public policy, and whether that public policy is the policy of Australia or international public policy, has given rise to debate amongst both academics and practitioners.

Following the announcement by the Australian government in late 2008 of its forthcoming review of the IAA, there was some hope that the government might take the opportunity afforded by the review to clarify its position, by including in the IAA an express reference to international public policy and by listing what Australia considers to be a violation of substantive fundamental principles of public policy, as distinct from procedural public policy violations.[29] While the Australian Government did not go this far in the 2010 amendments to the IAA, it introduced a new Section 8(7A) as follows:

To avoid doubt and without limiting paragraph (7)(b), the enforcement of a foreign award would be contrary to public policy if:

1. the making of the award was induced or affected by fraud or corruption; or

2. a breach of the rules of natural justice occurred in connection with the making of the award.

This clarification is helpful and recognizes the growing awareness of the risk of fraud or corruption that necessarily accompanies the continuing globalization of commerce.

---

[29] *See, e.g.*, Nottage and Garnett, "Top 20 Things to Change in or Around Australia's International Arbitration Act," 6 *Asian International Arbitration Journal*, 1-43 (Kluwer Law International 2010).

The new provision is, however, expressly non-exhaustive, with the result that the precise scope of public policy will need to be delineated by the courts.

For some time, the leading case in Australia on the public policy defense to enforcement was the case of *Resort Condominiums.*[30] While the court in that case referred to other decisions indicating that public policy should be narrowly construed, it held *obiter* that the scope of public policy (which it considered to be Australian, and not international, public policy) was surprisingly wide and could include the fact that orders made by a foreign arbitral tribunal were not ones that a Queensland court would make (for example, an award for injunctive relief that did not include a cross-undertaking as to damages).

Subsequent cases have adopted a slightly different approach and clarified the position. In *Corvetina Technology Ltd. v. Clough Engineering Ltd.*,[31] the court recognized that there was a clear balancing exercise to be performed between, on the one hand, the need not to frustrate the object of the New York Convention (namely, to facilitate the enforcement of foreign awards) and, on the other, the need to preserve to the Australian court the right to apply its own standards of public policy when deciding whether to enforce a foreign award. The court in *Corvetina* also suggested that it was possible for a party to raise, as a public policy defense, an argument that the contract containing the arbitration clause was illegal, notwithstanding that this argument might already have been raised during the arbitration itself.

More recently, the court again considered the scope of the public policy defense in *Uganda Telecom*,[32] which post-dated the

---

[30] *Resort Condominiums v. Bolwell*, (1993) 118 A.L.R. 855.

[31] [2004] NSWSC 700.

[32] Discussed *supra* Section B.4.

amendments to the IAA. In that case, the court clarified that errors of fact and law in an award are not a violation of public policy within the meaning of Section 8(7)(b) of the IAA and that it was not against public policy for a foreign award to be enforced without examining in detail the correctness of the reasoning or the result reflected in the award. On the contrary, the court emphasized that the public policy defense should be narrowly interpreted and that Australia's public policy was to enforce arbitral awards wherever possible, remaining consistent with the objective detailed in the new Section 2D of the IAA, and giving effect to Australia's obligations under the New York Convention. The court also clarified that the complaint raised by Hi-Tech as to the arbitrator's assessment of damages could and should have been raised during the underlying arbitration proceedings, with the result that Hi-Tech was now precluded from raising it as a defense to enforcement.

Following the amendments to the IAA and the case of *Uganda Telecom*, parties are likely to be able to invoke the public policy defense to enforcement in reasonably narrow circumstances and would be well-advised to raise any relevant arguments during the course of the arbitration, rather than waiting until an application is made in Australia to enforce the award.

C.3   Public Policy and Arbitrability

The Australian courts have also considered a number of cases where one party has raised public policy at a much earlier stage of the proceedings, arguing that the arbitration agreement is inoperable or should not be enforced on public policy grounds. Those cases have largely concerned disputes in which one party raises a statutory claim that it feels would be better addressed by the Australian courts.

We discussed in the 2008 *Yearbook* a number of cases considering the arbitrability of claims under the Trade Practices Act 1974 ("the TPA"),[33] which proscribes misleading and deceptive conduct in commerce. In summary, the approach of the Australian courts has been to recognize that the TPA is a public policy statute,[34] although they have reached inconsistent conclusions about whether TPA claims are capable of settlement by arbitration or should fall to the courts for decision. The Federal Court clarified the issue in 2006 in *Comandate*,[35] where it recognized that not all claims under the TPA may be arbitrable, with arbitrability depending on the precise nature of the claim (for example, whether the claim involved an allegation of conduct that deceived or misled the public, rather than just the other contracting party) and the relief sought under the statute. In reaching this conclusion, the Federal Court recognized that the common element in non-arbitrable claims (such as those concerning intellectual property, antitrust, securities transactions, and insolvency) was a level of public interest sufficient to render it inappropriate that they be resolved by private resolution instead of by the national court system.[36]

In addition to claims under the TPA, certain claims under the Corporations Act 2001 (Cth) may not be capable of settlement

---

[33] Superseded by the Competition and Consumer Act 2010.

[34] *Clough Engineering Ltd. v. Oil & Natural Gas Corporation Ltd.,* [2007] FCA 881, discussed at pp. 8-9 of the *Baker & McKenzie International Arbitration Yearbook 2008.*

[35] *Comandate Marine Corp. v. Pan Australia Shipping Pty Ltd.,* [2006] FCAFC 192, discussed at p. 9 of the *Baker & McKenzie International Arbitration Yearbook 2008.*

[36] For further discussion on *Comandate* and the arbitrability of claims under the TPA, see Leanne Rich, "The Arbitrability of TPA Claims: To Stay or Not to Stay?," 18 *TPLJ* 7 (2010). Leanne is a senior associate in Baker & McKenzie's Sydney office.

by arbitration. Those that are not arbitrable would include a claim for the winding up of a company, one seeking rectification of the share register of a company, or a claim whose statutory remedy would involve the imposition of a fine or term of imprisonment on a director. By contrast, if the proceedings were to involve a claim and relief akin to that available at general law (for example, access to corporate information), then Australian public policy would not prevent that claim from being resolved by arbitration.[37]

The Australian courts have also recognized that it would be against public policy to enforce an arbitration agreement in respect of certain insurance disputes, as the result of a provision in a 1902 statute, which provides that an arbitration agreement in an insurance contract does not bind the insured, unless entered into after the dispute arose.[38] The court applied this provision in *HIH Casualty & General Insurance Ltd. (in liq) v. Wallace*,[39] holding that the arbitration clause in the parties' agreement was inoperable. The court reached this conclusion because the relevant agreement was governed by the laws of New South Wales. Importantly, however, the court also stated that it would have reached this conclusion no matter which governing law applied, as the provision was part of the mandatory law of the forum.[40]

There has been little consideration by the courts in Australia of the relationship between arbitrability and any possible illegality in the underlying transaction or agreement. In *Comandate*,[41] the

---

[37] *See* Leanne Rich, *ibid*, and *ACD Tridon v. Tridon Australia*, [2002] NSWSC 896.

[38] Section 19, Insurance Act 1902 (NSW).

[39] (2006) 204 FLR 297.

[40] At ¶ 35, *ibid.*

[41] *Op. cit.*

court clarified that the doctrine of separability is part of Australian law, with the result that an arbitration clause will be upheld unless the alleged fraud or corruption affected the arbitration agreement itself and not just the underlying agreement.

While it remains best practice to raise the question of illegality at the earliest possible opportunity during the underlying arbitration, the Australian court indicated in *Corvetina Technology Ltd. v. Clough Engineering Ltd.*,[42] that, in principle, it was open to a party seeking to rely on illegality to resist enforcement of an award, notwithstanding that the illegality had been raised before, and decided by, the arbitrator.

---

[42]   [2004] NSWSC 700, ¶ 14.

AUSTRIA

Stefan Riegler[1] and Heidrun E. Preidt[2]

A. LEGISLATION, TRENDS AND TENDENCIES

On 1 July 2006, Austria became a "Model Law Country." Now, five years after the implementation of the new Austrian arbitration law,[3] practice shows that it is not yet perfect. In particular, the following issue is subject to concern and has already been raised with the legislature:

Pursuant to Section 616(1) of the Austrian Code of Civil Procedure ("CCP"), the challenge procedure against an Austrian arbitral award is governed by the regular rules for contentious litigation. Thus, an award may be challenged before a state court of first instance whose judgment may then be subject to appeal before the Court of Appeals and, under certain circumstances, the Austrian Supreme Court ("OGH").

While in practice these proceedings are relatively swift and rarely lead to the annulment of an award, the Austrian arbitration community has nevertheless requested that the legislature adapt rules similar to those of other comparable arbitral venues[4] by

---

[1] Stefan Riegler is a Partner in Baker & McKenzie's Vienna office. He acts as counsel before state courts and arbitral tribunals and is increasingly serving as an arbitrator. He has authored several articles and publications, including *Arbitration Law of Austria: Practice and Procedure* (Juris 2007). He is a founding member and former chairman of the Young Austrian Arbitration Practitioners.

[2] Heidrun Preidt is a Law Clerk in Baker & McKenzie's Vienna office.

[3] Austrian arbitration law forms an integral part of the Code of Civil Procedure, Part VI, Section 577 *et seq.*

[4] For example, Switzerland, which provides for one stage of appeal, and Germany and France, which provide for two stages of appeal.

skipping at least one stage of appeal, ideally providing for a direct recourse to the OGH.

B.   CASES

B.1   Lack of an Arbitrator's Signature on the Arbitral Award Does Not Violate Public Policy

In its decision dated 13 April 2011 regarding the enforcement of a foreign arbitral award, the OGH addressed whether the lack of one of the arbitrator's signature on the arbitral award violated Article IV(a) of the New York Convention and Austrian procedural public policy according to Article V(2)(b) of the New York Convention. It held that according to Section 606 CCP, the signatures of a majority of the arbitral tribunal would be sufficient, as long as the reasons for the lack of such a signature were noted on the arbitral award and confirmed according to the rules of the respective arbitral institution. The purpose of those provisions is to guarantee the enforceability of the arbitral award, not only if an arbitrator is absent, but also if he/she simply refuses to sign the award and tries to obstruct the proceedings. The OGH held that it is neither possible nor necessary to review the cause of the lack of a signature. It further concluded that the lack of a signature does not violate Article IV(a) of the New York Convention or any principles of *ordre public*.

Further, the OGH clarified that there is no requirement to attach an arbitrator's dissenting opinion to the arbitral award. The dissenting opinion does not constitute an integral part of the arbitral award, and the failure to attach it does not violate public policy.

The OGH also found that there was no violation of public policy on the additional grounds submitted, namely that (i) there were no joint personal deliberations held between the arbitrators;

(ii) the arbitral tribunal did not vote with respect to the final decision; and (iii) the opinion of one arbitrator (who later issued a dissenting opinion) was overruled in the final award. In particular, it reasoned that the institutional arbitral rules do not stipulate in which form deliberations of the arbitral tribunal have to take place, and if they do take place, whether all arbitrators have to be present. As a principle, deliberations might be held via telephone or videoconference or even in writing. Even bilateral discussions between arbitrators are allowed as long as the third arbitrator is not excluded. As there was no indication, either in the submission of the parties or in the dissenting opinion of the arbitrator, that the arbitrator was *de facto* excluded from the decision-finding process, the OGH concluded that the lack of personal meetings to deliberate before rendering the award did not constitute a violation of Article V(2)(d) of the New York Convention nor was it a violation of procedural public policy.

B.2 A Substantive Review of the Arbitral Award Is Inadmissible

In its decision dated 19 January 2011, the OGH dismissed an action to set aside an arbitral award that allegedly violated public policy due to the arbitral tribunal's purported erroneous factual and legal assessment of the case. In that case, the claimant argued that the arbitral award violated Austrian *ordre public*, because the arbitral tribunal erroneously evaluated the claim thereby wrongfully deciding upon the validity of an assignment and the procedural costs. Further, the claimant—for the first time—objected to the validity of the arbitration agreement, alleging that it was not validly concluded between the claimant and the assignor. This objection was dismissed as it violated the prohibition against submitting new facts (*Neuerungsverbot*). With respect to the asserted violation of public policy, the OGH held that the notion of public policy should be used reluctantly and a mere inequity in the result would not suffice to violate public policy. The substantive objections made by the claimant would require the court to undertake a review of the arbitral award, which was not stipulated by law, and was thus inadmissible.

B.3 The "Duly Certified" Copy of the Arbitral Award

In enforcement proceedings of a foreign arbitral award, the OGH dealt with whether a copy of an arbitral award, which was certified and signed by an arbitrator but lacked a certified confirmation of his function or certification of the authenticity of his signature, violated the formal requirements of Article IV(1)(a) of the New York Convention. According to this provision, the party requesting recognition and enforcement of an arbitral award must submit, together with its request, a duly certified original or copy of the award. If a copy is provided, it has to be duly certified that the copy corresponds to the original. The OGH confirmed prior decisions in which it held that certifications made according to the law of the country where the award was rendered were sufficient. The OGH also confirmed that, if permitted by the respective institutional arbitral rules, certification by a neutral person, such as the presiding arbitrator or the secretary of the arbitral institution, is sufficient.

Further, the OGH held that such certification requires a stamp and the signature of the representative of the arbitral institution. The requirement that the authenticity of the signatures of the arbitrators on the original need to at least be indirectly certified is complied with if expressly provided for in the arbitral rules or if the arbitral institution has the duty to send the arbitral award to the parties, and if the original (from which a copy is made) remains with the arbitral institution. The duty of the arbitral institution to send a duly certified arbitral award to the recipients implies the duty to examine the authenticity of the arbitrator's signatures. According to the ICC Rules, the Secretariat has to deliver the original award to the parties and retain all remaining originals with the Secretariat. The ICC Rules also provide for the certification of arbitral awards and any copies thereof by its General Counsel. In the present case, the OGH concluded that the formal requirements of Article IV(1)(a) of the New York Convention were fulfilled as both copies of the award were certified by the General Counsel of the ICC. Further, the issue of the illegibility of the certifying person's signature is resolved, if the function and name of the person is provided for in the stamp of the institution.

C. PUBLIC POLICY IN INTERNATIONAL ARBITRATION

C.1 Scenarios of Reliance on Public Policy

A party can seek to set aside an arbitral award (rendered by an arbitral tribunal situated in Austria) in an Austrian state court on the grounds that the award violates public policy. In proceedings to set aside the award, Austrian law distinguishes between procedural (Section 611(2)(5) CCP) and substantive public policy (Section 611(2)(8) CCP). Violations of procedural public policy only cover fundamental breaches of procedural principles that are not covered by other provisions of Section 611 CCP. A party must invoke the violation of procedural public policy. Violation of substantive public policy, on the other hand, which concern the fundamental values of the Austrian legal system (see below C.3), may be considered by the court *ex officio*. Section 613 CCP ensures that a violation of substantive *ordre public* that had not earlier been discovered or remedied, might be addressed later on in "other proceedings, like enforcement proceedings."

A party can file an appeal against a decision to recognize and enforce a foreign arbitral award that allegedly violates procedural or substantive public policy. The enforcement procedure is regulated under Section 614 CCP, basically referring to Sections 79 *et seq.* of the Enforcement Act ("EO"), which are in fact overruled by the provisions of the New York Convention as well as those of the European Convention of 1961.

After the reform of 2006, Austrian arbitration law does not allow actions before a state court to determine the invalidity of an arbitration agreement due to the violation of public policy, neither prior to nor during the arbitral proceedings. It lies within the competence of the arbitral tribunal to decide upon any objection against the validity of the arbitration agreement.[5] Further, the Austrian legislature excluded certain matters of fundamental public interest from the jurisdiction of arbitral tribunals. Thus, these matters lack objective arbitrability. Arbitral awards that decide matters lacking objective arbitrability are set aside (Section 611(2)(7)) or refused recognition and enforcement, if invoked by a party or by the court *ex officio*.

In 1993, the OGH held that under the European Convention of 1961, setting aside an arbitral award in the country of origin due to the violation of public policy will not prevent the enforcement of the award in Austria.[6] In fact, this decision effectively limits Article V(1)(c) of the New York Convention, which stipulates

---

[5] The inadmissibility of such an action is based on the wording of Section 578 CCP, which stipulates that courts can only have jurisdiction over the matters expressly provided for by the CCP, which does not provide for such an action.

[6] OGH, 20 October 1993, 3 Ob 117/93; 23 February 1998, 3Ob 115/95; *see also* OGH, 26 January 2005, 3Ob 221/04b. The OGH applied Article IX of the European Convention and concluded that "the plain reading of Article IX shows that the setting aside of an arbitral award for violation of the public policy of the Contracting state where the award was rendered does not appear among the grounds exhaustively listed in Article IX of the European Convention as justifying a refusal of recognition and enforcement of an arbitral award."

that the setting aside of an arbitral award in its country of origin may be a ground for refusal of enforcement. Nevertheless, any circumstances justifying the setting aside of the arbitral award in the country of origin can be invoked in enforcement proceedings in Austria.[7]

C.2 Modes and Limitations of Reliance on Public Policy

Only a domestic arbitral award can be challenged in Austrian courts. An action to set aside an arbitral award due to the violation of public policy must be filed within three months after the arbitral award is served. In principle, this time limit cannot be extended. Even a request for the correction of an arbitral award (Section 610 CCP) does not extend the time period for filing an action to challenge the award. Only in exceptional circumstances, such as where a party is unable to file the challenge within the prescribed time limit due to an unexpected and unavoidable event, might the party request the reinstatement of the time limit (*Wiedereinsetzung in den vorigen Stand*).

The time limit to appeal a decision of the enforcement court that had granted leave for the enforcement of the foreign arbitral award is one month. Such appeal must be based on the grounds listed in the New York Convention or the European Convention of 1961. This time limit can be extended to two months if the appellant does not reside in Austria and the appeal was its first opportunity to participate in the enforcement proceeding (Section 84 (2)(1) EO).

C.3 What Constitutes "Public Policy"?

There is no distinction made between domestic and international public policy under Austrian law. According to case law, an

---

[7] OGH, 26 January 2005, 3Ob 221/04b.

arbitral award is contrary to substantive public policy if it violates basic values of the Austrian legal system, such as principles of the Constitution, the European Convention on Human Rights, or of criminal, private and procedural or public law. Implicit in the notion of public policy is the protection of the legal system as a whole rather than any one party to the proceeding.

The violation of mandatory law does not automatically constitute a violation of public policy.[8] The notion of public policy is narrower than the mere violation of mandatory law: each violation of public policy also constitutes a violation of mandatory law, but not vice versa. A mere inequity in the arbitral award must be accepted and cannot be challenged based on an asserted violation of public policy.

C.4 Review of Alleged Breaches of Public Policy

Case law demonstrates that the OGH is generally reluctant to set aside arbitral awards based on alleged violations of public policy. The OGH has repeatedly held that the public policy clause constitutes an exceptional rule that must be used reluctantly.[9] Thus, courts may not annul an arbitral award due to the incorrectness of its result or a violation of mandatory law. The relevant benchmark to determine whether the arbitral award conflicts with the Austrian legal system is whether the award is based on legal considerations that are incompatible with the

---

[8]   OGH, 1 April 2008, 5Ob 272/07x; in contrast to the old law, the challenge ground of violation of "mere" mandatory provisions that must be applied irrespective of the parties' choice of law (but that do not form part of the *ordre public*) was not retained after the reform of Austria's arbitration law (save for consumers and employees pursuant to Sections 617 and 618 CCP) (*see* Riegler in Riegler *et al.*, Section 611, *Arbitration Law in Austria: Practice and Procedure*, 2007, ¶ 87).

[9]   OGH, 24 September 1998, 6Ob 242/98a; 24 August 2011, 3Ob 65/11x.

domestic legal order.[10] It is not sufficient that the right or legal relationship contradicts public policy; rather, the enforcement of the award must be unbearable to the Austrian legal system.

As regards the scope of review, the OGH has repeatedly highlighted that a *révision au fond*[11] of an arbitral award is not permitted. There is no legal basis for an Austrian court to undertake a factual or legal review of the arbitral award[12] where a violation of *ordre public* is asserted. Above all, the prohibition against a *révision au fond* also means that the court may not review how the arbitral dispute should have been decided.[13] In fact, the court has to limit itself to a determination of whether the result of the arbitral award violates fundamental values of the Austrian legal system. For such determination, it is in principle not the way or the reasoning that is decisive, but the result of the arbitral award.[14] As the OGH held in 1998: "The incompatibility [with the legal system] *must be **obvious**. The factual and legal review of the foreign title [arbitral award] can in no case be reviewed from scratch."[15] (Emphasis and brackets added.)

---

[10] OGH, 24 August 2011, 3Ob 65/11x.

[11] OGH, 26 January 2005, 3 Ob 221/04 b; see also 5 May 1998, 3 Ob 2372/96 m; 20 November 1996, 3 Ob 2374/96 f; 18 September 1991, 1 Ob 582/91; 24 August 2011, 3Ob 65/11x.

[12] OGH, 26 January 2005, 3 Ob 221/04b; 24 August 2011, 3Ob 65/11x.

[13] OGH, 1 April 2008, 5Ob 272/07x.

[14] OGH, 26 January 2005, 3 Ob 221/04 b; 8 June 2000, 2 Ob 158/00 z; 5 May 1998, 3 Ob 2372/96 m; 20 November 1996, 3 Ob 2374/96f.

[15] OGH, 23 February 1998, 3Ob 115/95.

AZERBAIJAN

Gunduz Karimov[1] and Jamil Alizada[2]

A. LEGISLATION, TRENDS AND TENDENCIES

A.1 General

The governing arbitration statute in Azerbaijan is the Law of the Republic of Azerbaijan *On International Commercial Arbitration* (the "Arbitration Law"), dated 18 November 1999. Azerbaijan is also a party to the New York Convention, the Washington Convention and the European Convention.

Additionally, the Civil Procedure Code of the Republic of Azerbaijan (the "CPC"), effective 1 September 2001, contains provisions on the enforcement and recognition of foreign arbitral awards.

A.2 Types of Arbitration

Azerbaijani law distinguishes international arbitration from domestic arbitration and currently recognizes international arbitration only as a dispute resolution mechanism between foreign and Azerbaijani nationals or companies.

---

[1] Gunduz Karimov is a Partner in Baker & McKenzie's Baku office specializing in dispute resolution, intellectual property and compliance matters. Mr. Karimov graduated from Baku State University and received his LL.M. from Indiana University in Bloomington. A member of the Azerbaijan Bar Association and a registered trademark attorney, Mr. Karimov is also vice-dean of the School of Law of Baku State University.

[2] Jamil Alizade is an Associate in Baker & McKenzie's Baku office. He graduated from Moscow State Institute of International Relations (MGIMO) and Maastricht University with degrees in intellectual property law and knowledge management. Mr. Alizade joined Baker & McKenzie in September 2011.

Section 1(1)(3) of the Arbitration Law permits "International Commercial Arbitration" where:

- the parties to an arbitration agreement have, at the time of the conclusion of that agreement, their places of business in different states; or

- one of the following is outside the state in which the parties have their places of business:

  (a) The seat or legal place of arbitration as specified in the arbitration agreement;

  (b) Any place where a substantial part of the obligations of the commercial relationship is/were to be performed or the place with which the subject matter of the dispute is most closely connected; or

  (c) the parties have expressly agreed that the subject matter of the arbitration agreement relates to more than one country.

As stated above, the Arbitration Law governs only international arbitration, whereas domestic arbitration between local entities is not defined under Azerbaijani law. The CPC permits parties to settle disputes through *ad hoc* arbitration with the consent of the parties. It does not, however, provide for any mechanism or procedure for such arbitration. To date, there has been no domestic arbitration between local entities.

A.3 Regulation of International Arbitration

The Arbitration Law applies only if the place of arbitration is Azerbaijan. Parties may appoint independent arbitrators of any nationality. The arbitral proceedings may be conducted in any language chosen by the parties. All documents and materials pertaining to the dispute (except for those matters that must be exclusively resolved under Azerbaijani law, as indicated in Section A.5 below), and procedural law may be chosen by the parties, and, in general, the parties may stipulate other terms of the arbitration.

The Supreme Court of the Republic of Azerbaijani (the "Supreme Court") is the authority that controls and supports international arbitration proceedings in Azerbaijan. The Supreme Court has the right to (i) appoint arbitrators if the parties have not agreed on them; (ii) consider the parties' objections with respect to the arbitrators; (iii) annul an arbitrator's mandate for reasons provided in the Arbitration Law; (iv) assist an arbitral tribunal in gathering evidence; and (v) annul an arbitral award.

The Supreme Court can annul an arbitral award issued in Azerbaijan where one of the parties demonstrates that:

(a) one of the parties to the arbitration agreement did not have the legal capacity to enter into the agreement to arbitrate, or the agreement is otherwise invalid under applicable law;

(b) one of the parties was not notified of the appointment of the arbitrators or the date of the arbitration hearing, or could not present its case for other reasons;

(c) the arbitral award concerns a dispute or issues not regulated by the arbitration agreement; or

(d) the structure and procedure of the arbitral tribunal did not comply with the arbitration agreement, or in the absence of such agreement, with the Arbitration Law.

If the Supreme Court determines that the dispute is not subject to arbitration under Azerbaijani law or that the arbitral award is contrary to the sovereignty and laws of the Republic of Azerbaijan, it has the right to annul the award.

A.4 The International Commercial Arbitration Court

The International Commercial Arbitration Court ("ICAC") is a local institution established on 11 November 2003 to resolve international commercial disputes in Azerbaijan. It was founded by a non-governmental organization of the same name funded through various grants. The ICAC has its own official regulations, arbitrators and schedule of fees.

Pursuant to its Charter, the ICAC considers commercial disputes within 120 days. The Charter provides for a dispute to be brought before the arbitral tribunal if it is the subject of a written agreement, either in an independent arbitration agreement or as an arbitral clause within a contract.

The registration fee, which is paid at the time of filing the statement of claim, is USD 300 and is not refundable. The arbitration fee must be paid in advance. It must be paid in the national currency—Azeri Manat ("AZN"), if the claim amount is expressed in AZN. If the claim amount is expressed in any foreign currency, the arbitration fee should be paid in U.S. dollars. The ICAC also provides for special rules governing the reduction of the arbitration fee, its apportionment, extra expenses and payment procedure.

Arbitration proceedings are generally held in Baku—the capital of Azerbaijan. The parties can, however, agree to hold the hearing at any place within the country. In that case, payment of additional expenses incurred in connection with the arbitration hearing being held outside Baku is borne by the disputing parties. The parties can select any arbitrator, which facilitates having skilled professionals in dispute resolution. Further, although arbitration proceedings are conducted in the Azerbaijani language, the parties may also choose to have the proceedings conducted in another language.

Recognition and enforcement of ICAC arbitral awards is regulated primarily by the New York Convention. Azerbaijan ratified the New York Convention on 9 November 1999. Azerbaijan is also a party to a number of bilateral and multilateral international treaties that ensure the recognition and enforcement of ICAC arbitral awards in most countries of the world.

A.5   Protection of Foreign Investment

Under the Law of the Republic of Azerbaijan *On Protection of Foreign Investment*, dated 15 January 1992 (the "Investment Protection Law"), foreign investment is defined as investment of any property or proprietary right, including intellectual property rights, for the purposes of realizing profit from the investment. Generally, Azerbaijani law recognizes the right of foreign investors to arbitrate with state agencies both locally and internationally. Disputes between foreign investors and state agencies may be resolved by arbitration if the parties have agreed to arbitration or if so provided under an international treaty to which Azerbaijan is a signatory.

Whether Azerbaijani legal entities with foreign investment may choose arbitration outside Azerbaijan is unclear. Theoretically, international arbitration is possible between a wholly foreign-owned company incorporated in Azerbaijan and a local entity with a local investment. Under Article 42 of the Law of the Republic of Azerbaijan *On Foreign Investments* of 1992 (the "Foreign Investment Law"), any dispute between foreign-owned companies and local entities may be resolved either by a court or by domestic or international arbitration if there is an arbitration agreement between the parties. The Foreign Investment Law also provides that disputes between foreign investors and Azerbaijani state bodies or legal entities concerning the amount of damages may be adjudicated by an arbitral tribunal if the parties have agreed to arbitration. While the language of Article 42 is vague, the CPC does not specifically grant Azerbaijani legal entities the right to arbitrate. Accordingly, absent guidance from the Supreme Court, it is unclear whether two Azerbaijani legal entities (one with local investment and the other with foreign investment) can choose international arbitration.

In addition, Azerbaijani courts have exclusive jurisdiction to hear certain types of disputes. Pursuant to CPC, Azerbaijani courts' exclusive jurisdiction extends to:

(a) disputes relating to property rights over immovable property including claims concerning the lease or pledge of the property—if such property is located in Azerbaijan;

(b) disputes relating to invalidation of decisions, recognition of validity or invalidity, or dissolution of a legal entity whose legal address is in the Republic of Azerbaijan;

(c) disputes relating to claims concerning the validity of patents, trademarks or other rights—if registration or application for registration of these rights has taken place in the Republic of Azerbaijan;

(d) a judgment or order on compulsory enforcement measures requested and enforced in the Republic of Azerbaijan;

(e) disputes relating to claims against carriers arising out of transportation contracts; and

(f) disputes relating to termination of marriage between citizens of the Republic of Azerbaijan with foreigners or stateless persons—if both spouses have their place of residence in Azerbaijan.

B. CASES

B.1 General

Arbitration practice in Azerbaijan is generally limited to obtaining recognition by the Supreme Court of foreign arbitral awards. The Supreme Court may refuse to recognize a foreign arbitral award on the grounds listed in section A.3 above. Additionally, recognition of a foreign arbitral award may be rejected if (i) the award has not entered into force with respect to the parties or was annulled by a court or arbitral tribunal in another country; or (ii) the enforcement of the award contradicts the sovereignty and laws of Azerbaijan.

B.2 Recognition of Cases in 2010

In 2010, the Supreme Court received ten arbitral awards for recognition. Six of them were recognized. One arbitral award was not recognized on the grounds that it breached the laws of Azerbaijan. Another arbitral award was not considered by the Supreme Court, as it had not been duly translated into the Azerbaijani language—it was subsequently returned to the Ministry of Justice of the Republic of Azerbaijan. The consideration of the two other arbitral awards was left for the following year.

B.3 Recognition of Cases in 2011

In 2011, the Supreme Court received eight arbitral awards for recognition; among them, the following were recognized:

(a) the case between the St. Petersburg Traktorniy Zavod CJSC and Caucasus MTZ LLC, decided under the arbitration rules of the International Commercial Arbitration Court under the Russian Chamber of Commerce in the Russian Federation;

(b) the case between Melco Maritime LLC and Inter-Alyans LTD, decided under the LCIA Rules;

(c) the case between Golden Phoenix LLC and Iki Ulduz LLC, decided under the arbitration rules of the International Commercial Arbitration Court for the Chamber of Commerce in the Republic of Ukraine;

(d) the case between SAQA ATASH LLC and Ekoloji Inshaat LLC, decided under the arbitration rules of the Interregional Specialized Economic Court of the Mangistau region of the Republic of Kazakhstan.

The following two cases were not recognized by the Supreme Court due to their contradiction to Azerbaijani laws:

(a) the case between Enerqoprom—Novocherkassky Elektronny Zavod CJSC and Azerbaijan Aluminium OJSC, decided under the arbitration rules of the International Commercial Arbitration Court for the Russian Chamber of Commerce in the Russian Federation;

(b) the case between Baki-Alnas Servis LLC and Shelfgaztehnologiya LLC, decided under the arbitration rules of the International Commercial Arbitration Court for the Russian Chamber of Commerce in the Russian Federation.

The case between Belşina OJSC and Azerşina CJSC, decided under the arbitration rules of the Mogilev Economic Court in the Republic of Belarus, was returned to the Ministry of Justice, as the relevant documentation was not duly translated into the Azerbaijani language; the consideration of another dispute between Baki-Alnas Servis LLC and Shelfgaztehnologiya LLC, decided under the arbitration rules of the International Commercial Arbitration Court for the Russian Chamber of Commerce in the Russian Federation, was adjourned to 2012.

B.4   ICAC Cases

Although the practice of the ICAC remains limited, it is noteworthy that companies doing business in Azerbaijan or with Azerbaijani counterparties have started referring their disputes to arbitration. Since 2009, when the ICAC started operating at full capacity, it has considered a number of cases that involved the participation of Azerbaijani and foreign companies. However, due to the confidentiality of arbitration, the names of the companies are kept secret.

In 2011, the ICAC considered the case of poor quality products received by an Austrian company from an Azerbaijani individual. However, the ICAC rejected the case as the Austrian company failed to adduce proper evidence to support its claim.

Another case, which is currently pending, involves the non-payment of certain amounts due for industrial machinery received by an Azerbaijani company from its Russian counterparty. We understand from the ICAC that a decision is expected in 2012.

C.   PUBLIC POLICY IN INTERNATIONAL ARBITRATION

The concept of public policy is expressed in different forms and in various laws regulating the rules of private international law. Thus, the CPC provides that international letters of requests (or letters rogatory) issued by foreign courts shall not be executed if the execution is contrary to the sovereignty of the Republic of Azerbaijan and the general principles of law. The CPC further provides that the recognition and enforcement of decisions of foreign courts and arbitral tribunals is possible if they are not contrary to the legislation of the Republic of Azerbaijan and legal order and are mutually guaranteed. The compulsory enforcement of the decisions can be waived on similar grounds.

Article 4 of the Law of the Republic of Azerbaijan *On Private International Law*, dated 6 June 2000, provides that foreign legal provisions are not applied in the Republic of Azerbaijan if they contradict the Constitution and any regulations adopted through a referendum. We are unaware of any legal provisions that have been contested as contradicting the Constitution and relevant regulations.

Under Article 34 of the Arbitration Law, an arbitral decision can be annulled by the Supreme Court if it determines that the arbitral decision is contrary to the Constitution of the Republic of Azerbaijan.

Although the laws provide a theoretical basis for public policy arguments, to date we are unaware of any disputes considered in Azerbaijan where a party invoked public policy considerations.

BELARUS

Alexander Korobeinikov[1]

A. LEGISLATION, TRENDS AND TENDENCIES

A.1 Domestic Legislation

The Belarusian law *On the International Arbitration Court*[2] (the "International Arbitration Law") was enacted on 9 July 1999. The International Arbitration Law is based on the UNCITRAL Model Law and since 1999, no amendments have been made to it. The International Arbitration Law regulates arbitration proceedings in commercial disputes between both local and foreign entities, as well as the status of international arbitration courts. Under the general rules provided in Article 4 of the International Arbitration Law, all commercial disputes may be resolved by arbitration unless other legislation provides to the contrary. There is, therefore, no specific list of non-arbitrable disputes in the International Arbitration Law, although such information can be found from a review of other legislation.

There are now two international arbitration courts in Belarus: the International Arbitration Court at the Belarusian Chamber of Commerce and Industry; and the Chamber of Arbitrators at the Belarusian Union of Lawyers.

---

[1] Alexander Korobeinikov is an Associate in Baker & McKenzie's Almaty office and a member of the International Arbitration Practice Group of the Firm's Global Dispute Resolution Practice Group.

[2] The Law of the Republic of Belarus *On the International Arbitration Court* No. 279-Z, dated 9 July 1999 (as amended).

In addition, in 2009, the law *On Commodity Exchanges*[3] provided arbitration as a means of resolving disputes arising from stock exchange transactions. For that purpose, the Belarusian stock exchange established an arbitration commission, which acts under rules approved by the stock exchange.

In 2011, the Belarusian Parliament adopted the new law *On Domestic Arbitration Courts*[4] (the "Domestic Arbitration Law"), which is intended to regulate domestic arbitration and will come into effect in January 2012. While the main provisions of the Domestic Arbitration Law are based on UNCITRAL Model Law principles as well as on principles arising from the existing International Arbitration Law, there are some significant innovations. The key points to note are as follows:

(i) The new law regulates the establishment and registration of domestic arbitration institutions and their arbitrators and *ad hoc* arbitrators. Any violation of these rules will lead to the invalidation of an award.

(ii) An arbitration agreement that does not contain either the name of an arbitration institution or the procedure for composing an *ad hoc* arbitral tribunal will be considered null and void. Although it is not entirely clear, it seems likely that based on these provisions, the Belarusian courts may take a very conservative approach when examining the validity of an arbitration agreement.

(iii) An arbitration clause does not survive in the case of accessioning obligations under the main contract. In

---

[3] The Law of the Republic of Belarus *On Commodity Exchanges* No.10-Z, dated 5 January 2009.

[4] The Law of the Republic of Belarus *On Domestic Arbitration Courts* No. 301-Z, dated 18 July 2011.

addition, state authorities cannot be a party to an arbitration agreement.

(iv) The new law also places restrictions on the types of disputes that can be arbitrated. In particular, an institutional arbitration court cannot arbitrate disputes with its founder. Furthermore, arbitrators do not have jurisdiction over disputes affecting the rights and obligations of third parties that are not parties to the arbitration clause.

(v) Finally, the law allows state courts to set aside an arbitral award if facts that would have been important to a proper review of the case, come to light that were, at the time, unknown to the arbitral tribunal and one of the parties. Although such a provision is unusual in arbitration legislation, it was probably adopted under the influence of the state courts, which enjoy the same power under Belarusian procedural legislation.

It is fair to say that many of the provisions of the Domestic Arbitration Law are generally unclear, and we believe that their application will need to be clarified by the courts.

In addition to the laws identified above, arbitration in Belarus is also regulated by the relevant provisions of the Commercial Procedural Code and the Civil Procedural Code. The Civil Procedural Code contains rules regarding the arbitration procedure and the enforcement of domestic and foreign arbitration awards relating to non-commercial disputes. The Commercial Procedural Code sets out the rules applicable to the enforcement of both domestic and foreign arbitral awards for commercial disputes, as well as the procedures for court-ordered mediation. In October 2011, the Plenum of the Supreme Commercial Court adopted the resolution *On Certain Issues Relating to Reviewing Disputes with Foreign Persons by*

Commercial Courts[5] (the "Resolution"), which provides guidance for commercial courts considering the validity and enforceability of arbitration agreements. The Resolution also imposes on the court an obligation to disclose to a respondent the right to file an objection against the court's jurisdiction if there is an arbitration agreement between the parties. The Resolution, in general, is a good example of the increasingly pro-arbitration approach of the Belarusian commercial courts.

A.2 International Treaties

Belarus is party to a number of international and regional treaties related to arbitration, including the New York Convention, the European Convention and several CIS treaties.[6]

It should also be noted that although certain investment treaties ratified by Belarus refer to ICSID, it is not entirely clear whether Belarus is bound by the ICSID Convention. According to information from ICSID, Belarus signed and ratified the ICSID Convention in 1992;[7] nevertheless, Belarusian authorities often state that Belarus has yet to formally ratify it.

A.3 Trends and Tendencies

Over the past few years, arbitration and mediation have become increasingly popular as alternative methods of resolving commercial disputes. Additionally, state authorities are promoting

---

[5] The Resolution of the Plenum of the Supreme Commercial Court of the Republic of Belarus *On Certain Issues on Reviewing Disputes with Foreign Persons by Commercial Courts* No. 30 dated 31 October 2011.

[6] Although Belarus was a member of the Soviet Union until 1991, it has maintained the right to be party to international treaties since the 1940s.

[7] *See* http://icsid.worldbank.org.

arbitration and court-ordered meditation to reduce the amount of claims filed with the state courts.

In 2010, approximately 30% of commercial disputes initiated in Belarusian courts were resolved by court-ordered mediation. Furthermore, in the first half of 2011, all 16 claims relating to the enforcement of foreign arbitral awards reviewed by the courts were granted.

The process of court-ordered mediation is established by the Commercial Procedure Code and is used as a means of resolving commercial disputes once a legal action has been initiated before the state court. Mediation may be ordered by the judge upon the request of one of the parties, or by the court's own initiative at any stage of the proceedings, including the appellate and enforcement stages.

The mediator must have the required qualifications and can either be selected from the relevant court's staff or from the list of mediators approved by the Supreme Commercial Court. If the mediation is successful, the parties must conclude a settlement agreement, which must be approved by the court.

B.   CASES

While court decisions relating to the enforcement or setting aside of arbitral awards have generally been in line with international practice, the Belarusian courts have comparatively limited experience in dealing with arbitration-related cases and, from time to time, render controversial decisions.

Recent cases in which Belarusian courts have addressed arbitration issues are summarized below.

B.1 Arbitration Clause Providing for Disputes to Be Resolved by Arbitration Is Effective Notwithstanding Differences between Russian and English Versions of Clause

In 2010, a Czech company (the "Seller") initiated legal action in the Minsk City Commercial Court against a Belarusian company (the "Buyer") seeking collection of debts arising out of a sale and purchase contract that existed in both English and Russian and included an arbitration clause. The Buyer asked the court to dismiss the claim on the basis that the contract contained an arbitration clause. The Seller objected, arguing that the arbitration clause was inoperative and incapable of being performed. In particular, the Seller referred to differences between the Russian and English versions of the arbitration clause.

Under the Russian version, the parties agreed that if they failed to amicably resolve any disputes arising out of the contract, such disputes would be resolved by arbitration under the ICC Rules in Geneva, Switzerland. By contrast, the English version of the arbitration clause stated that any disputes arising out of the contract must be resolved by arbitration in accordance with amicable settlement rules, and the seat of arbitration was to be defined in accordance with Swiss legislation (the Swiss Labor Code).

Although both the English and Russian versions of the arbitration clause contained a special provision excluding the jurisdiction of the state courts, the Seller argued that as the parties had not agreed to the applicable rules or the seat of arbitration, the Minsk City Commercial Court should consider the claim on its merits.

In August 2010, the Minsk City Commercial Court dismissed the claim and held that both the English and Russian versions of the arbitration clause clearly demonstrated that both parties had intended to resolve any disputes through arbitration. Issues relating to the applicable arbitration rules and the seat of arbitration should therefore be addressed in the arbitration proceedings, and the differences between the English and Russian versions of the arbitration clause did not render the clause unenforceable. Both the Minsk City Commercial Court of Appeal and the Cassation Collegium of the Supreme Commercial Court (the "Cassation Collegium") subsequently upheld the decision of the Minsk Commercial Court.

B.2 Reference to Resolving Disputes in an Arbitration Court is Sufficient to Render the Arbitration Clause Valid

A Czech company (the "Seller") filed a claim with the Minsk City Commercial Court to enforce an award of the arbitration court issued in 2009 at the Czech Chamber of Commerce and the Czech Agrarian Chamber against a Belarusian company (the "Buyer"). The Buyer objected to the claim on the ground that the arbitral tribunal did not properly inform it about the arbitration proceedings, because the summons was sent to the Buyer without any Russian translations, which is required under the agreement *On Legal Support and Legal Relations on Civil, Family and Criminal Cases*[8] (the "Agreement") executed in 1982 between the USSR and the Czechoslovak Socialist Republic.

The Minsk City Commercial Court granted the claim, stating that the Agreement relates only to activities of the national courts and could not be applied to arbitration proceedings.

The Buyer appealed the Minsk City Commercial Court's decision to the Cassation Collegium. In addition to its earlier argument, the Buyer also argued that there was no arbitration agreement between the parties that referred to the arbitration court at the Czech Chamber of Commerce and the Czech Agrarian Chamber.

---

[8]   Belarus and the Czech Republic acceded the rights and obligation of the USSR and the Czechoslovak Socialist Republic under this Agreement.

The Cassation Collegium upheld the decision of the lower court and rejected the Buyer's new argument. The Cassation Collegium noted that the arbitration clause between the parties did not contain any reference to the arbitration court at the Czech Chamber of Commerce and the Czech Agrarian Chamber and, instead, simply stated that all disputes arising out of the contract must be reviewed by the arbitration court located in the country of the Seller's registration. However, the Cassation Collegium also noted that in 2008, when the Seller tried to initiate legal action against the Buyer in the Minsk City Commercial Court, the Buyer objected to the commercial court's jurisdiction on the basis that the parties had agreed to an arbitration clause. The Cassation Collegium further noted that the Buyer had not raised its argument against the jurisdiction of the arbitration court at the Czech Chamber of Commerce and the Czech Agrarian Chamber in the earlier court proceedings. While it is not entirely clear, it seems that all of these facts led the Cassation Collegium to conclude that the Belarusian company had abused its procedural rights, and therefore, its arguments could not be supported.

It is interesting to note that very short arbitration clauses of this type are not uncommon in Belarus because Belarusian companies often use templates of contracts that have been prepared in accordance with Russian law. Under Russian law, the term "arbitration court" is used to refer to the state courts resolving commercial disputes (like the commercial courts in Belarus). Therefore, in most cases where the arbitration clause refers to an arbitration court without making reference to particular rules or institutions, the parties intend to resolve the dispute in the state commercial court. However, due to their increasingly pro-arbitration approach, the Belarusian courts often ignore this particular feature of Belarusian commercial contracts.

C. PUBLIC POLICY IN INTERNATIONAL ARBITRATION

C.1 Legal Framework

Under Belarusian legislation, the concept of public policy arises both in the conflict of law rules (the substantial component) and in the procedural rules regarding the enforcement of foreign judgments and arbitral awards (the procedural component).

The substantive component of Belarusian public policy is set out in Article 1099 of the Civil Code of the Republic of Belarus (the "Civil Code"),[9] which provides that "foreign law shall not be applied in cases where its application is contrary to the fundamentals of the legal order (the public policy) of the Republic of Belarus, as well as in other cases, directly provided for by the legislative acts. In these cases, the law of the Republic of Belarus shall be applied."

Additionally, the Civil Code applies the concept of "supramandatory" rules. This concept means that mandatory provisions of Belarusian law will be applied in relation to foreign parties, notwithstanding any conflict of law rules or any contrary agreement between the parties (Article 1100(1) of the Civil Code). However, as of the time of writing, neither the legislature nor the courts have provided an entirely clear list of these supramandatory provisions. Consequently, these rules have been interpreted widely by the courts as discussed below.

The procedural component of Belarusian public policy is stated in Article 1 of the International Arbitration Law and it mirrors the substantive definition set out in Article 1099 of the Civil Code.

---

[9] Civil Code of the Republic of Belarus No. 218-Z dated 7 December 1998 (as amended).

C.2   Application of the Concept of Public Policy by Belarusian Courts

As previously mentioned, the statutory provisions regarding the substantive component of Belarusian public policy are not entirely clear and have been interpreted widely.

For example, in 2005-2007, the Supreme Commercial Court reviewed a number of cases regarding the invalidation of contracts between Belarusian and foreign companies. Despite the fact that all of the contracts contained governing law provisions stipulating to foreign law as the applicable governing law, the Supreme Commercial Court held that provisions of Belarusian laws regarding the validity of agreements were mandatory provisions that had to be applied under Article 1100(1) of the Civil Code.

The Supreme Commercial Court's decisions in these cases have been criticized by scholars and practitioners as politically motivated and the practical application of Article 1100(1) of the Civil Code remains unclear. The recent Resolution of the Plenum of the Supreme Commercial Court unfortunately fails to address this issue.

In relation to the application of the procedural component of public policy, it seems that the Belarusian courts are very reluctant to apply it to refuse enforcement of foreign arbitral awards. We are aware of only one such case during the last six years.

In 2005, the Supreme Commercial Court refused to recognize and enforce an arbitral award issued by the International Commercial Arbitration Court at the Russian Federation Chamber of Commerce and Industry in favor of an American limited liability company ("A") against a Belarusian company ("B") on the basis that enforcing the arbitral award would violate

Belarusian public policy. After the issuance of the award, B initiated bankruptcy proceedings and the Supreme Commercial Court concluded that because the company was subject to bankruptcy proceedings, any recognition and enforcement of the arbitral award would violate the rights of other creditors of the company, including the State.

BELGIUM

Arne Gutermann,[1] Joeri Vananroye[2] and Koen De Winter[3]

A. LEGISLATION, TRENDS AND TENDENCIES

A.1 Recent Legislation

There have been no legislative changes in the arbitration law of Belgium since the overview provided in the 2010-2011 edition of *The Baker & McKenzie International Arbitration Yearbook.*

A.2 Validity of the "Hybrid Arbitration Clause"

One trend that deserves to be discussed is the so-called "hybrid clause," which offers contracting parties the choice of bringing their dispute, at the moment of its occurrence, either before an arbitrator or before an ordinary judge.

---

[1] Arne Gutermann is a Partner in Baker & McKenzie's Brussels office. He heads the EMEA and Belgian Trade & Commerce Practice Group of Baker & McKenzie. Mr. Gutermann's areas of expertise include all forms of commercial contracts, general contract law, mergers & acquisition contracts and commercial litigation and arbitration. He is a regular speaker at conferences regarding Belgian contract law and co-author of *Distribution and Agency Laws in Europe* and *Standard Business Contracts under Belgian Law*, an English reference guide for standard commercial contracts under Belgian law.

[2] Joeri Vananroye is an Associate in Baker & McKenzie's Brussels office and a member of the International Arbitration Practice Group of the Firm's Global Dispute Resolution Practice Group, as well as member of the Corporate Finance Practice Group. Dr. Vananroye is also a visiting professor in the corporate law program jointly organized by the universities of Brussels (HUB) and Leuven (KULeuven).

[3] Koen De Winter is a Partner in Baker & McKenzie's Antwerp office and heads the office's Dispute Resolution Practice Group. During his 30-year professional career, he gained extensive experience in domestic and international litigation and arbitration on a large variety of commercial matters.

Three main types of hybrid clauses can be identified: (i) the reciprocal hybrid clause—offering the choice of jurisdiction to both parties to the dispute; (ii) the unilateral hybrid clause—allowing both parties to bring their dispute before an arbitral tribunal, while offering only one party the choice to also seize an ordinary judge, but only as long as no arbitral procedure has been launched by the other party; and (iii) the absolute unilateral hybrid clause—allowing both parties to bring their dispute before an arbitral tribunal, while offering only one party the choice to also seize an ordinary judge, even if an arbitral procedure has already been launched by the other party.

At first, Belgian legal doctrine and case law only reluctantly embraced the hybrid clause. In line with the majority of foreign jurisdictions, however, over the years, Belgian law has come to recognize the validity of the hybrid clause as a matter of principle insofar as the clause respects all principles of public policy and mandatory law, and the general conditions of validity for arbitration clauses.[4]

Some reservations still exist regarding the enforceability of an absolute unilateral hybrid clause. For example, seizing an ordinary judge could, under some circumstances, constitute an "abuse of right" in cases where the other party has already launched an arbitral procedure. If a judge finds that such "abuse of right" has taken place, he can decline jurisdiction.

---

[4]   G. Jakhian and F. Henry, "La validité de la clause hybride en arbitrage," *JT* 2011, 701-709.

B. CASES

B.1 Invalidity Due to Conflicting Reasons in Award

Pursuant to Articles 1704.2(i) and (j) of the Code of Civil Procedure, an arbitral award can be set aside if it lacks a motivation for the decision or if it contains conflicting provisions. A 13 January 2011 judgment of the Belgian Supreme Court gives a broad interpretation of these grounds for invalidity.[5]

In this judgment, the Supreme Court sided with the Brussels Court of Appeal, which had implicitly held that an arbitral award can also be invalidated in the case of *conflicting reasons* in the award. Clearly, this somewhat "formalistic" approach by the Supreme Court can have far-reaching consequences. Amongst others, it substantially increases the risk that an otherwise perfectly defendable arbitral award is invalidated by an ordinary court. Indeed, since *any* contradiction in the reasoning behind an arbitral award can now potentially lead to an invalidation of that award, this may result in a significant increase in proceedings to set aside awards by the losing party in the arbitral proceedings, even where the outcome of the initial arbitral award was perfectly justified.

It remains to be seen whether this trend, which further widens the ordinary courts' discretionary power to invalidate arbitral awards, will continue.

B.2 Invalidity because of Conflict with Public Policy

Recent case law regarding the invalidity of an award based on public policy is discussed in part C.2.

---

[5] Cass. 13 January 2011, *JT* 20111, 492, *TBH* 2011, note G. de Foestraets, *TBH/RDC* 2011, 496 (report K. Cox).

C. PUBLIC POLICY IN INTERNATIONAL ARBITRATION

C.1 Scenarios of Reliance on Public Policy

A party can invoke public policy considerations in proceedings to invalidate a Belgian arbitral award (Article 1704.2(a) of the Code of Civil Procedure) or as a defense against recognition and enforcement of an award (Article 1710.2 and 1723, 2°of the Code of Civil Procedure).

C.2 Rules that Constitute "Public Policy"—Recent Examples

By a judgment of 21 January 2011, the Belgian Supreme Court (*Hof van Cassati/Cour de Cassation*) confirmed once again that the right to a fair trial (expressed in, *inter alia*, Article 6.1 of the European Convention on Human Rights of 4 November 1950) is a matter of public policy.

In this case, which had already been ongoing for more than twelve years, the plaintiff sought to obtain a declaration from the court that the arbitral award handed down by the Antwerp Chamber of Commerce and Industry on 8 April 1999 was invalid because the right to a fair trial had not been observed. It was the second time that the Belgian Supreme Court was presented with this case. The first time, the Antwerp Court of Appeal dismissed the plaintiff's action to set aside the award, finding that although the arbitrator heard a witness in the absence of one of the parties, the right to a fair trial had not been violated because the absent party could not demonstrate that the arbitrator had taken the witness' testimony into account in his arbitral award and that the testimony had an effect on the arbitral award. The Belgian Supreme Court, however, quashed the Antwerp Court of Appeal's judgment by ruling that the violation of the right to a fair trial constitutes sufficient grounds to invalidate an arbitral award, even when such violation has no effect on the arbitral award.

The case was then referred back to the Ghent Court of Appeal, which, in line with the Supreme Court's judgment, invalidated the arbitral award. In so doing, it dismissed the plaintiff's argument that the violation of the right to a fair trial had to be raised during the arbitral procedure and that such belated submission of this ground for annulment was contrary to the principle of good faith. The plaintiff appealed to the Supreme Court once again, arguing that "each action of a party that consists of concealing an irregularity in the arbitration procedure and any subsequent invocation of that irregularity as grounds for invalidating that arbitral award in case it is unfavorable to it, is contrary to the execution of an arbitral agreement in good faith." In its judgment of 21 January 2011, the Belgian Supreme Court dismissed this argument on the basis that the right to a fair trial must be regarded as a matter of public policy and as a consequence cannot be waived by a party. Moreover, violations of public policy rights can be invoked in every stage of the proceedings, from the arbitral proceedings up to the enforcement or set aside proceedings before an ordinary court. According to the Supreme Court, rules of due process, which include rules to avoid dilatory procedural maneuvers, cannot prevail over fundamental human rights.

Note that Article 1704.2(g) of the Code of Civil Procedure already provides for the invalidation of an arbitral award for the violation of the right to a fair trial. This provision stipulates that, if the parties have not been given an opportunity to defend their rights and to present their arguments, or if any other mandatory rule of law with respect to arbitration proceedings has not been observed, the arbitral award can be invalidated by a court, though only to the extent that such failure has had an effect on the arbitral award. By its judgment of 21 January 2011, the

Supreme Court seems to suggest that a violation of the right to a fair trial, which would normally fall under Article 1704.2(g) of the Code of Civil Procedure, now falls under Article 1704.2(a) of the Code of Civil Procedure, thus circumventing the "effect-test" of Article 1704.2(g) (i.e., that a failure to observe the right to a fair trial must have had an effect on the arbitral award). This effectively seems to make Article 1704.2(g) of the Code of Civil Procedure meaningless as a ground for invalidating an arbitral award.

C.3 Review of Alleged Breaches of Public Policy

Belgian courts generally take a narrow approach when applying public policy as a ground for annulment and non-enforcement. The mere fact that a judge would have come to a different conclusion in applying a rule of public policy is not sufficient to set aside the arbitral award if the results of the award itself do not violate public policy.

A decision of the Court of Appeal of Ghent illustrates that the review by the courts should never come down to a full review of the merits of the arbitral award.[6] In that case, the losing party was found liable for violation of a non-compete provision in a share purchase agreement. This non-compete provision did not contain any explicit time limit. Under Belgian rules, a non-compete provision is null and void unless it is for a limited and reasonable time period. This rule is considered to be a rule of public policy. Traditionally, Belgian judges, when confronted with a non-compete provision without a time limit, do not infer a reasonable time limit, but instead strike the provision altogether.

---

[6]   Court of Appeal of Ghent, 3 December 2007, P&B / R.D.J.P. 2008, 131, RW 2008-09, 503.

The arbitrator in that case took a different approach. He found the non-compete provision to be implicitly limited to a period of five years and upheld the provision as valid because it was for a reasonable and limited time period. The party that was held liable challenged this decision on the grounds that it violated a rule of public policy, namely, that non-compete provisions must be for a limited and reasonable period of time; otherwise, they are void.

The Court of Appeal of Ghent rejected the challenge to the validity of the arbitral award. The court held that, when reviewing the award, a judge should not himself scrutinize whether the non-compete provision is valid under the rules of public policy. (As stated before, such review would probably cause a Belgian judge to find that the provision was not valid.) It is the arbitral award itself that has to be scrutinized against that rule of public policy. The court found that whatever the contractual provision stated, the arbitral award limited the non-compete undertakings to a limited and reasonable time period and that outcome could not be challenged as contrary to public policy. The court held that it was not the task of the judge to review whether the interpretation given by the arbitrator (i.e., that the clause was *implicitly* limited to five years) was an error of judgment.

A case heard before the Brussels Court of Appeal on 22 June 2009[7] takes a similar approach. At stake was a violation of EU competition rules. Since the decision of the European Court of Justice in *Eco Swiss v. Benneton* (case C-126/97), it is widely accepted that Articles 81 and 82 of the EC Treaty (now Articles 101 and 102 of the Treaty on the Functioning of the European Union) must be regarded as a matter of public policy. As a result, national courts must annul arbitral awards that are contrary to the

---

[7] This case was reported in the 2010-2011 edition of this *Yearbook*, p. 173.

European competition rules where domestic rules of procedure require it based on the failure to observe national rules of public policy. A disputed issue is the extent to which the reviewing court should scrutinize an award on its compliance with competition law. Are the national courts required to take a maximalist ("intrinsic") approach by determining whether the arbitrators have correctly applied the antitrust rules, or must they only conduct a limited, minimalist ("extrinsic") review to determine whether the arbitral award itself (i.e., the outcome) is a violation of public policy?

In its decision of 22 June 2009, the Court of Appeals of Brussels confirmed that the court before which the award is challenged "should not verify the accuracy of the arbitrators' reasoning and cannot substitute its own evaluation of the case with that of the arbitral tribunal," and that the grounds developed by a party pursuing "a complete revisiting of the merits of the case by asking the judge to reassess the consequences of the nullity of a contract in a manner different than the arbitrators' appraisal" are not in line with the mandates of public policy.

BRAZIL

Joaquim T. de Paiva Muniz,[1] Luis Alberto Salton Peretti[2] and Leonardo Mäder Furtado[3]

A. LEGISLATION, TRENDS AND TENDENCIES

Minas Gerais, a Brazilian state rich with agricultural commodities and minerals, *inter alia*, enacted State Law nº 19,477 on 12 January 2011: the Minas Gerais Arbitration Act ("MGA"). The act regulates arbitration proceedings in which the state of Minas Gerais or one of its instrumentalities is involved as a party.

The MGAA comprises two sorts of provisions. First, it includes an express statutory authorization allowing the State of Minas Gerais, its instrumentalities or other public entities to refer disputes to arbitration.[4] Second, it includes provisions detailing the proceedings to be instituted and specifies the options available under the Brazilian Arbitration Act ("BAA").

---

[1] Joaquim T. de Paiva Muniz is a Partner in Baker & McKenzie's office in Rio de Janeiro and a professor of business law and arbitration, teaching graduate courses at Fundação Getúlio Vargas (FGV). Mr. Muniz is Chairman of the Arbitration Commission of the Rio de Janeiro Bar (OAB/RJ) and coordinator of the arbitration courses of the Rio de Janeiro Bar, including a *lato sensu* graduate course. He is also Chairman of the Rio de Janeiro section of the Brazilian Institute of Corporate Law (IBRADEMP) and author of many articles on international arbitration and Brazilian corporate law, including co-author of *Arbitration Law of Brazil: Practice and Procedure* (Juris 2006) and *Arbitragem Internacional e Doméstica* (Forense 2009).

[2] Luis Alerto Salton Peretti is an Associate in the São Paulo office and his practice focuses on commercial arbitration and litigation.

[3] Leonardo Mäder Furtado is an Associate in the São Paulo office and his practice focuses on commercial arbitration and litigation.

[4] Article 2 provides that the state, its instrumentalities and other public entities may opt to refer to arbitration to resolve disputes regarding waivable patrimonial rights.

As regards the statutory authorization to arbitrate, it is still debated in Brazil whether public entities require an express authorization to arbitrate disputes as a corollary of the legality principle.[5] Commentators are divided between those who believe that public entities do not need any express authorization since the BAA includes a broad authorization to arbitrate,[6] and those who believe that a special authorization is required when public parties are involved.[7] In this sense, the MGAA follows a rather extensive string of statutory authorizations enacted by federal statutes.[8]

As regards the proceedings, the MGAA provides for the following: (i) that arbitration shall necessarily be administered by an institution,[9] thus excluding *ad hoc* proceedings; (ii) that the proceedings shall not be confidential; and (iii) that the merits of

---

[5] Brazilian Constitution, Article 37: "The direct or indirect public administration of any of the powers of the Union, the States, the Federal District and the municipalities, as well as their foundations, shall obey the principles of legality, impersonality, morality, publicity..." The principle is considered to limit the powers entrusted to the bodies of the public administration to act within the competences expressly delegated to them by statutes.

[6] *See* Lemes, Selma, "Arbitragem na Administração Pública," São Paulo: *Quartier Latin*, 2007, p. 115: "We conclude, therefore, that, as per the hermeneutical lesson above, it is evident that the Law 9,307 of 1996 is the governing law and contemplates the direct and indirect public entities. (...) Such Act [the BAA] grants full possibility to public entities to use arbitration clauses in public contracts."

[7] Salles, Carlos Alberto, "Arbitragem em Contratos Administrativos," São Paulo: *Forense*, 2011, p. 237: "The existence of a legal provision to the use of arbitration by the Administration is a requirement for arbitrability, which must be satisfied for the sake of the validity of the arbitration clause and the respective award."

[8] *See, e.g.,* the Public Concessions Law (Law 8,987 of 1995), the Telecommunications Law (Law 9,472 of 1997), the Oil Law (Law 9,478 of 1997), or the Public-Private Partnerships Law (Law 11,079 of 2004).

[9] MGAA, Article 4: "O juízo arbitral, para os fins desta Lei, instituir-se-á exclusivamente por meio de órgão arbitral institucional."

the case must be resolved in accordance with the law,[10] barring arbitration *ex aequo et bono*. The MGAA's controversial reception derives from the requirements laid out for prospective arbitrators and the eligibility of administering institutions. The MGAA sets forth that only arbitrators who are "Brazilian, of legal age and enjoying civil capacity" may function in such proceedings.[11] Likewise, the MGAA requires prospective arbitrators to integrate into the roster of an institution registered with the Minas Gerais' general list of service providers.[12]

B. CASES

B.1 Conflict of Competence between Arbitral Tribunals

In *Câmara Arbitral do Comércio Indústria e Serviços de São Paulo—CACI—SP v. Câmara de Mediação e Arbitragem de São Paulo—CMA*[13] the Superior Court of Justice ("STJ"), which is the highest court in Brazil for non-constitutional matters, ruled that the motion for the resolution of a "conflict of competence," an appeal provided for by the Brazilian Constitution to decide on the competent court,[14] is only available for conflicts between

---

[10] MGAA, Article 6: "Para os fins desta Lei, somente se admitirá a arbitragem de direito, instaurada mediante processo público."

[11] MGAA, Article 5: "São requisitos para o exercício da função de árbitro: I - ser brasileiro, maior e capaz."

[12] MGAA, Article 5: "São requisitos para o exercício da função de árbitro: (...) IV - ser membro de câmara arbitral inscrita no Cadastro Geral de Fornecedores de Serviços do Estado.'"

[13] STJ, CC 113.260-SP, Reporting Justice Nancy Andrighi, decided on 8 September 2010.

[14] According to Brazilian Law, a motion for the resolution of a conflict of jurisdiction may be brought by any of the parties involved, as well as by a judge or Public Prosecutor, in the event that (i) two or more judges or courts declare they have jurisdiction to hear and judge the same case; (ii) all the judges seized

state courts and may not be extended to decide conflicts of competence involving arbitration institutions.

The dispute arose between *Fazendas Reunidas Curuá Ltda. et al.*, as claimant, and *Pecuária Unit Santa Clara Ltda.*, as respondent, regarding an agreement providing for arbitration to be administered by the *Câmara de Mediação e Arbitragem da Federação da Indústrias do Estado de São Paulo—FIESP* ("CMA-SP").

Claimant filed for arbitration, but the proceeding was dismissed by CMA-SP due to the lack of payment of the arbitration costs. Claimant then filed a new request for arbitration, this time before the *Câmara Arbitral do Comércio, Indústria e Serviços de São Paulo* ("CACI–SP").

As a result, CMA-SP filed a motion before the STJ requesting that it resolve the jurisdictional conflict between the two institutions, arguing that the contract provided for the proceedings to be administered by the CMA-SP. The court ruled that the constitutional remedy to resolve jurisdictional conflicts between courts does not apply to arbitration institutions. The reporting judge stated that arbitration panels do not have a juridical nature, and thus fall outside the scope of the remedy. The dissenting opinion stated that arbitration has a juridical nature and should therefore be subject to the STJ's control of competence.

This was the first case on this matter and it is not binding, so the issue is still unsettled under Brazilian Law.

---

with the matter declare themselves incompetent; (iii) or in case any doubt arises about the jurisdiction between courts or judges. That proceeding is entrusted to the Superior Court of Justice by the Brazilian Constitution in its Article 105.

B. Cases

B.2 Nationality of Arbitration Awards

In *Nuovo Pignone SPA v. Petromec Inc.,*[15] respondent resisted enforcement of an arbitral award, contending that the award should first be recognized by the STJ, since it was a foreign award. Petromec's argument derived from the fact that the proceeding had been administered by a foreign arbitration institution (the ICC), even though the seat of arbitration was Rio de Janeiro.

The court confirmed the position of Brazilian scholars and the BAA[16] by reaffirming that, in Brazil, the distinction between foreign and domestic awards is "based solely on the place where the award is rendered." According to the court's unanimous ruling, whether the administrative institution is domestic or international is irrelevant for the nationality of the award.

B.3 Arbitration Clause and Public Bidding

In *Companhia Paranaense de Gás Natural—COMPAGAS v. Consórcio Carioca Passarelli,*[17] the STJ recognized the validity of an arbitration agreement included in a public contract, although this stipulation had not been previously included in the public bidding process. The full content of the court's opinion has not yet been published. However, the abstract of the decision summarized the matter as follows: "the fact that there is no stipulation for arbitration in the public bidding notice or the contract executed by the parties does not invalidate the arbitral

---

[15] STJ, REsp 1.231.554 – RJ, Reporting Justice Nancy Andrighi, decided on 24 May 2011.

[16] BAA, Art. 34, sole paragraph: "A foreign arbitral award is an award made outside of the national territory."

[17] STJ, REsp 904.813–PR, Reporting Justice Nancy Andrighi, decided on 20 October 2011.

agreement executed afterwards." The case represents another example of the pro-arbitration stance adopted by Brazilian courts as regards contracts with administrative law entities.

B.4 Arbitration of Employment Disputes

Brazilian labor courts have consistently held that individual employment rights cannot be subject to arbitration due to their mandatory and non-waivable character.

In *Norf Esportes e Bar e Restaurante Ltda. v. Joaquim Espínola*,[18] the Superior Labor Court ("TST") rendered a groundbreaking—albeit isolated—precedent on the arbitrability of individual labor claims, drawing a distinction as to the arbitrability of such disputes based on the moment in which reference to arbitration is made. In this decision, the TST ruled that reference to arbitration in employment contracts was admissible provided that reference to arbitration took place *ex post*, that is to say, through a submission agreement executed only once the dispute had actually arisen.

However, even if this question of timing appears operative, the distinction has only been drawn in this single isolated case. The predominant understanding holds that under the BAA, employment disputes fall outside the scope of objective arbitrability.

B.5 Writ of Mandamus against Decisions in Arbitrations

In *Rodrigo Garretano de Morares Rego v. Elisabete Aloia Amaro*,[19] the São Paulo Court of Appeals decided a motion for a

---

[18] Superior Labor Court, 4th Chamber. Appeal n° TST-RR-144300-80.2005.5.02.0040, decided on 10 December 2010. *Rapporteur*, Min. Barros Levenhagen.

[19] TJ/SP Appeal 0120145-96.2011.8.26.0100, Reporting Justice Pereira Calças, decided on 13 September 2011.

writ of mandamus filed against an act performed by an arbitrator. According to Brazilian law, the writ of mandamus is a legal remedy allowing courts to overrule illegal acts performed by public authorities.[20]

In the captioned case, claimant attempted to have the merits of an award—rendered by respondent as sole arbitrator—reviewed by the state courts through a writ of mandamus because the decision was allegedly illegal. Claimant contended that arbitrators, such as respondent, were tantamount to public authorities by analogy to state judges, and thus the arbitrator's decision could be challenged by a writ of mandamus. The São Paulo Court of Appeals ruled however that arbitrators are not equivalent to judges for the purposes of responding to writs of mandamus, and dismissed the motion.

This case goes in the opposite direction as last year's reported decision, *Consórcio Via Amarela v. Companhia do Metropolitano de São Paulo—Metrô*, in which the judge ruled that arbitrators are equivalent to judges for the purposes of writs of mandamus. Thus, it appears that the granting of writs of mandamus against decisions issued by arbitrators does not reflect a trend of Brazilian law.

---

[20] Federal Law 12.016/2009:

Art. 1º Writ of mandamus shall be granted in order to protect the liquid and certain right, not protected by *habeas corpus* or *habeas data* anytime that, illegally or with abuse of power, any individual or legal entity suffers from a violation or has a reasonable fear of suffering it by authority, independent of its category and whichever functions exercised.

§ 1º The representatives or political party bodies and the entities of the public administrators, as well as legal entity administrators or individuals exercising public functions with regards to said functions, should be construed as equivalent to authorities, for the purposes of this Law.

(Unofficial translation.)

B.6 Lack of Signature on the Arbitration Agreement

In *World Plus Travel Assurance S/C Ltda. v. Representações Guiwi Ltda.*,[21] the São Paulo Court of Appeals recognized as valid an arbitral clause that was not signed by the respondent.

The case concerns the sale of furniture through an order form. Claimant filed a lawsuit seeking a refund of amounts paid and moral damages incurred since the furniture purchased was not properly delivered. Respondent challenged the court's jurisdiction, arguing that the parties had entered into an arbitration agreement. The arbitration clause was inserted in the counterpart of an order form that was delivered by claimant to respondent, but which had never been signed.

The written form requirement for the validity of arbitration agreements is still debated in Brazilian courts. Even if there are decisions accepting tacit arbitration clauses,[22] another string of decisions adopt a very formalist position and reject the notion that an arbitration agreement can be entered into tacitly.[23] This decision differs from previous interpretations of Brazilian courts[24] and signals that the silence of the parties does not defeat recognition of the parties' agreement to arbitrate.

---

[21] TJ/SP, Appeal 9108611-84.2006.8.26.0000, Reporting Justice Jayme Queiroz Lopes, decided on 21 July 2011.

[22] *L'Aiglon v. Têxtil União*, STJ SEC 856/EX, Reporting Justice Carlos Alberto Menezes Direito, decided on 18 May 2005.

[23] *Oleaginosa Moreno v. Moinho Paulista Ltda*, STJ SEC 866/EX, Reporting Justice Felix Fischer, decided on 15 May 2005.

[24] *Indutech SPA v. Algocentro Armazéns Gerais Ltda.*, STJ SEC 978/GB, Reporting Justice Hamilton Carvalhido, decided on 17 December 2008 and *Ssangyong Corporation v. Eldorado Indústrias Plásticas Ltda.*, STJ SEC 826/KR, Reporting Justice Hamilton Carvalhido, decided on 15 September 2010.

C. PUBLIC POLICY IN INTERNATIONAL ARBITRATION

C.1 Sources of the Public Policy Exception

Several references to public policy are found within the Brazilian legal system. First and foremost, Article 17 of the Brazilian conflict of laws statute provides that foreign laws shall only be considered enforceable in Brazil to the extent that they do not violate "national sovereignty, public policy and public decency."[25] Many decisions wrongly associate this provision with mandatory rules.

In the BAA, the notion of public policy is found in three provisions. First, it is inserted as a barrier to party autonomy in the choice of the applicable law.[26] Second, public policy is referred to as a ground for refusing enforcement of a foreign arbitral award,[27] in language mirroring that of Article V(2)(b) of the New York Convention. Third, it tacitly pervades the grounds for setting aside an arbitral award rendered in Brazil, which are listed in Article 33 of the BAA.[28]

---

[25] Introductory Law to the Brazilian Civil Code, Law-Decree 4,707 of 1942: "the laws, acts and awards rendered in other countries, as well as any statements, will not be effective in Brazil, when offensive to *national sovereignty, public policy and public decency.*" (Emphasis added.)

[26] BAA, Article 2, first paragraph: "the parties may freely choose the rules of law applicable in the arbitration provided that their choice does not violate good morals and public policy."

[27] BAA, Article 39: "The request of homologation for the recognition or enforcement of a foreign arbitral award shall also be denied if the Federal Supreme Court ascertains that: (...) the decision is offensive to national public policy."

[28] For proceedings seated in Brazil, the BAA provides in Article 33 a list of grounds allowing for the annulment of the resulting arbitral award, making no express reference to the notion of public policy, neither domestic nor international.

However, despite the entry into force of the New York Convention in Brazil in 2002,[29] case law has not yet distinguished the elements of the notion of public policy that is applicable to international arbitration from the one that pertains to domestic agreements and court proceedings, notwithstanding the clear differentiation made by Brazilian doctrine. Nevertheless, a gradual disassociation of the notions of domestic and international public policy can be inferred from the recent cases decided by the STJ.

C.2   Application of International Public Policy in Brazil

The notion of international public policy is being consolidated by Brazilian courts, both as regards to procedural and substantive public policy.

C.2.1.   Case law on procedural public policy

For a long time, parties relied on the notion of public policy to object to enforcement of arbitral awards and court decisions on the grounds that no proper summons was served.[30] It is considered a matter of Brazilian public policy that a summons to appear before a foreign court be served exclusively through

---

Oftentimes, commentators assert that the precise grounds included in the law are mere corollaries of the notion of public policy, which should not be considered an exhaustive list. In fact, the doctrine considers that an arbitral award may be set aside due to a violation of public policy not expressly listed in Article 33 (Carmona, Carlos Alberto, "Arbitragem e Processo, um comentário à lei n° 9.307/96," São Paulo: *Atlas*, 2009, p. 416).

[29]   Decree 4,311 of 2002.

[30]   STJ, Special Formation, Contested Foreign Sentence 861 - PT, Reporting Justice Ari Pargendler, decided on 4 May 2005: "Homologation of Foreign Award. Service of Summons. The service of a summons to the respondent domiciled in Brazil must be carried out by letter rogatory, unless the communication, for this purpose, carried out by a consulate of a foreign country homologation is refused."

letters rogatory. As regards arbitration awards, that situation only changed in 1996 with the enactment of the BAA, in which Article 39 expressly allows for other means of communication.[31] Even though this hurdle has been removed in the context of arbitration, it still indicates the contents ascribed by Brazilian courts to the notion of public policy.

Another issue of procedural public policy in Brazil is the requirement for court decisions and arbitral awards to provide their *ratio decidendi*. That is referred to as the principle of motivation, which is included in the Constitution[32] and in the BAA.[33] Said principle integrates the notion of Brazilian public policy. However, this understanding is softened as regards to international arbitrations. In *L'Aiglon S/A v. Têxtil União S/A*,[34] respondent opposed enforcement of an award rendered in London under the auspices of the Liverpool Cotton Association, which consisted solely of the *dispositif* and did not include the grounds of the decision. The STJ held that the absence of reasons in the award was consistent with the arbitration rules agreed

---

[31] BAA, Article 39, sole paragraph: "The service of summons on a party resident or domiciled in Brazil, pursuant to the arbitration agreement or to the procedural law of the country in which the arbitration took place, including through mail with confirmation of receipt, shall not be considered as offensive to national public policy, provided the Brazilian party is granted sufficient time to exercise its right of defense."

[32] Brazilian Constitution, Article 93: "A supplementary law, proposed by the Supreme Federal Court, shall provide for the Statute of the Judicature, observing the following principles: (...) IX - all judgments of the bodies of the Judicial Power shall be public, and all decisions shall be justified, under penalty of nullity..."

[33] BAA, Article 26: "The mandatory requirements of the arbitral award are: (...) II - the grounds for the decision where questions of fact and law shall be analyzed..."

[34] *L'Aiglon v. Têxtil União* case, STJ SEC 856/EX, Reporting Justice Carlos Alberto Menezes Direito, decided on 18 May 2005.

upon by the parties, and did not amount to a violation of public policy for the purposes of enforcing foreign arbitration awards.

C.2.2.   Case law on substantive public policy

Brazilian courts often tend to associate Brazilian mandatory rules with the notion of public policy.[35] For example, agency agreements in Brazil are governed by a special statute that includes several mandatory rules.[36] Such mandatory rules include, namely, a requirement for a minimal indemnification of the agent in case of termination without cause, and a mandatory choice of forum provision establishing that the courts of the seat of the agent shall have exclusive jurisdiction over disputes arising out of the agreement. However, recent case law reveals that parties can waive the choice of forum clause and refer disputes arising therefrom to arbitration.[37] Moreover, in a clear distinction between mandatory rules and public policy, parties may derogate from the mandatory rules on agency through arbitration proceedings.[38]

Local mandatory rules were not applied in the *exequatur* proceedings for letter rogatory n° CR9970/EU, in which the interpretation of public policy advanced by the Supreme Federal

---

[35]   *See, e.g., Indústria Farmacêutica Basa Ltda. v. Dibasa Comércio e Representações Ltda.*, Rio Grande do Sul Court of Appeals, 16th Private Law Chamber, Appeal 70001634351, reporting Justice Ana Beatriz Iser, decided on 23 May 2001.

[36]   The "Agency Act," Law 4,885 of 1965, as amended by Law 8,420 of 1992.

[37]   *Total Energie S.N.C. v. Thorey Invest Negócios Ltda.*, Court of Appeals of São Paulo, 26th Civil Chamber, Appeal 1.111.650-0, Reporting Justice Waldir de Souza José, decided on 24 September 2002.

[38]   *Espal Representações e Conta Própria Ltda. v. Wilhelm Fette GmbH*, STJ, Third Chamber, Special Appeal 712.566 – RJ, Reporting Justice Nancy Andrighi, decided on 18 August 2005.

Court (Brazil's constitutional court) departed clearly from its latent association with mandatory rules. This proceeding concerned the service of a summons on a Brazilian citizen to appear before the U.S. District Court of New Jersey in a lawsuit for the collection of gambling debts, which are not enforceable under Brazilian law, and the question arose as to its admissibility. The court found that public policy should be construed as "the social, political and legal basis of a State, which is considered indispensable to its survival, which may exclude the application of foreign law."[39] In that case, the court took a detour on the notion of *comitas gentium*,[40] holding that respect for the foreign legal system should prevail for reasons of comity. The court's approach was consistent with the notion of international public policy as a more stringent standard than local mandatory rules.

More recently, in *Thales Geosolutions Inc. v. Fonseca Almeida Representações e Comércio Ltda.*,[41] respondent objected to enforcement of an award rendered by a panel seating in Houston, Texas, because the arbitration panel failed to give effect to a principle of Brazilian contract law.[42] After laying out several definitions of public policy, the STJ dismissed the objection and ruled that the arbitral panel's decision not to enforce this principle in the arbitral award did not amount to a violation of public policy

---

[39] STF. Letter rogatory n° CR 9.970/EU, Reporting Justice Marco Aurélio de Mello, decided on 18 March 2002.

[40] Araújo, Nádia de, "Direito Internacional Privado: Teoria e Prática Brasileira," Rio de Janeiro: *Renovar*, 2008, p. 131.

[41] STF. SEC 802 - EX (2005/0032132-9), *Thales Geosolutions Inc. v. Fonseca Almeida Representações e Comércio Ltda.*, decided on 15 August 2005.

[42] The *exception inadimpleti contractus* provides that in a bilateral contract, neither party may demand the performance of the other party's obligations before it has accomplished its own obligations. This rule is included in Article 476 of the Brazilian Civil Code.

that could justify refusal of enforcement. Commentators have suggested that the decision has been a tacit application of the concept of international public policy by the STJ.[43]

In summary, the determination of whether a given decision violates public policy under Brazilian Law is made on a case-by-case basis, and heavily depends on the circumstances in *concreto*. This is because, as pointed out by Professor Jacob Dolinger, public policy is a concept that is "relative, unstable and contemporaneous by essence."[44] Hopefully, the current trend is for Brazilian higher courts to better understand the distinction between domestic and international public policy. The main evidence thereof is that, since the competence to grant *exequaturs* of foreign awards shifted to the STJ in 2005, no such request concerning arbitral awards has been denied based on an alleged breach of domestic public policy.

---

[43] Wald, Arnoldo, "A Evolução da Arbitragem Internacional no Brasil," *Revista de Arbitragem e Mediação*, vol. 23, Oct. 2009, p. 19.

[44] Dolinger, Jacob, "A Evolução da ordem Pública no Direito Internacional Privado," Rio de Janeiro: *Renovar*, 1979.

CANADA

J. Brian Casey[1] and Christina I. Doria[2]

A. LEGISLATION, TRENDS AND TENDENCIES

A.1 Legislation

International arbitration in Canada is for the most part a matter of provincial jurisdiction. Each province and territory has enacted legislation adopting the UNCITRAL Model Law. The federal Parliament has also adopted a commercial arbitration code based on the Model Law, which is applicable when the federal government or one of its agencies is a party to an arbitration agreement, or where a matter involves an area of exclusive federal jurisdiction.

Each Canadian jurisdiction has also, either directly or indirectly, adopted the New York Convention.

A.2 Trends and Tendencies

In general, Canadian courts apply the Model Law and the general principles of arbitration in favor of enforcing arbitration agreements and referring parties to arbitration. Where an

---

[1]   J. Brian Casey is a Partner in Baker & McKenzie's Toronto office. Mr. Casey has served as arbitrator, chairman of the tribunal, and as counsel in numerous commercial arbitrations both *ad hoc* and institutional under the auspices of the LCIA, ICC, AAA/ICDR and ICSID. He is also a Fellow of the Chartered Institute of Arbitrators, has lectured and written extensively on various aspects of international disputes, and is the author of *Arbitration Law of Canada: Practice and Procedure.*

[2]   Christina I. Doria is an Associate in Baker & McKenzie's Toronto office, and a member of the International Arbitration Practice Group of the Firm's Global Dispute Resolution Practice Group.

arbitration agreement exists, and it is disputed whether the arbitration agreement is valid and covers the dispute, the courts will stay the judicial proceedings in favor of arbitration.

Courts may also be called upon to address the narrow issue of interim relief. Although arbitrators are given broad powers to grant interim relief, courts, consistent with the Model Law, may make interim orders for the detention, preservation and inspection of property, and for injunctions.

Unlike domestic arbitration awards in Canada, which may be appealed, with leave, on a question of law, international arbitral awards are final and cannot be appealed. The powers of the court are limited to a judicial review of whether the tribunal lacked jurisdiction or exceeded its jurisdiction in making an award, or where there was a lack of proper conduct and procedure during the arbitration, consistent with the New York Convention.

B. CASES

The jurisprudence relating to arbitration in the past year is highlighted by two cases: *Seidel v. TELUS Communications Inc.*,[3] where the Supreme Court of Canada dealt with whether consumer protection legislation in the province of British Columbia ("BC") can nullify an arbitration clause; and *United Mexican States v. Cargill, Inc.*,[4] where the Ontario Court of Appeal clarified the standard of review to set aside a foreign arbitral award on the basis of jurisdiction.

---

[3] *Seidel v. TELUS*, 2011 SCC 15.

[4] *Mexico v. Cargill*, 2011 ONCA 622.

B. Cases

B.1 *Seidel v. TELUS Communications Inc.*

The Supreme Court in *Seidel v. TELUS* addressed the issue of whether a provincial act can restrict the operation of an arbitration clause and the court's role in deciding the issue in the face of the *competence-competence* principle. In Canada, unlike the United States, the provinces have full constitutional power to legislate in the area of property and civil rights, to the exclusion of the federal government.

Michelle Seidel ("Seidel") entered into a contract with TELUS Communications Inc. ("TELUS"). The contract included an arbitration clause that purported to waive any rights of a consumer to commence or participate in any class action against TELUS related to any claim against it. A dispute arose with respect to how TELUS calculated its air time for billing purposes. Seidel filed a claim for false representation with the BC Supreme Court. TELUS, sought to stay the proceeding in favor of arbitration, arguing that based on the principle of *competence-competence*, the arbitral tribunal should determine whether it had jurisdiction over the matter. Seidel maintained that since she was seeking remedies under the BC Business Practices and Consumer Protection Act[5] ("BPCPA"), she had a right under the Act to go to court and to try to certify her action as a class.

At the trial level, TELUS' application was dismissed on the finding that it was premature to determine whether the action should be stayed prior to class certification being decided. TELUS appealed and was successful. The Court of Appeal stayed Seidel's action holding that it is for the arbitrator to determine which claims are subject to arbitration and which ought to go before a court.

---

[5]   SBC 2004, c 2.

The main issue before the Supreme Court of Canada was one of statutory interpretation, "whether the BPCPA manifests a legislative intent to intervene in the marketplace to relieve customers of the contractual commitment to 'private and confidential' mediation and arbitration."[6] In addition, the court had to determine whether the issues about the effect of the BPCPA ought to be decided by the court in first instance, or by the arbitral tribunal.

On the procedural issue, the court held that as a general rule, any challenge to an arbitrator's jurisdiction should first be determined by the arbitral tribunal, absent any legislated exceptions. However, a challenge can be dealt with by the court if it involves a pure question of law. Because the legal effect of Section 172 of the BPCPA is a question of law on undisputed facts, it was properly decided by the court of first instance.

On the substantive issue, the court held that Seidel had a statutory right under the BPCPA to bring an action to the court of first instance under Section 172, and once the action was brought under that section, the legislative protections in the BPCPA came into force, making the arbitration agreement void. Properly enacted provincial legislation will, if sufficiently broad, always trump a contractual arbitration agreement.

On the question of whether the claim may proceed as a class action, the court rejected TELUS' argument that the waiver of class action was severable from the arbitration agreement. As the class action waiver formed part of the arbitration clause, it too was found void pursuant to Section 3 of the BPCPA.

Of perhaps more significance, the majority of the court had no issue bifurcating those claims that fell within the BPCPA and those that could still be arbitrated. Those that fell within the

---

[6]   *Seidel v. TELUS* at ¶ 2.

consumer legislation were to proceed to court, but the other claims, dealing with simple breach of contract, if pressed would still have to go to arbitration. According to the court, such an outcome "is consistent with the legislative choice made by British Columbia in drawing the boundaries of s. 172 as narrowly as it did." This demonstrates the court's willingness to hold people to their agreements unless legislation clearly provides otherwise.

B.2 *United Mexican States v. Cargill, Inc.*

In *Mexico v. Cargill*, the Ontario Court of Appeal clarified the test for setting aside an international commercial arbitration award on jurisdictional grounds under the Model Law, holding that it is a standard of correctness. In other words, a court will set aside an award where the tribunal incorrectly determined its own jurisdiction.

Cargill, a US company that produces HFCS—a low-cost substitute for sugar cane used primarily in soft drinks—distributed its product in Mexico through its wholly-owned subsidiary in Mexico, CdM. Cargill manufactured its product in the US, and then had the product imported to Mexico through CdM. CdM then distributed the product in Mexico. Mexico enacted a number of trade barriers, which caused Cargill to shut down a number of its production plants. Cargill initiated arbitration proceedings in Toronto, claiming that Mexico breached NAFTA Chapter 11. Cargill was successful and was awarded damages for lost sales of its production in the US and lost sales of CdM in Mexico.

Mexico moved to set aside the award in the Ontario Superior Court on the basis that the tribunal exceeded its jurisdiction by awarding damages for Cargill's lost sales to CdM. Mexico's position was that Cargill was a producer and exporter, but not an investor in Mexico. The court of first instance held that Mexico's objection went to the merits of the dispute and not the tribunal's jurisdiction. Finding that an objection to the merits was beyond the scope of the Model Law, the court dismissed Mexico's application. It held that the standard of review when considering whether an arbitral tribunal exceeded its jurisdiction is one of reasonableness.

On appeal, Mexico was once again unsuccessful. However, the Court of Appeal reached a different conclusion, holding that the standard of review for questions on the tribunal's jurisdiction is one of correctness. It also warned courts to "limit themselves in the strictest terms to intervene only rarely in decisions made by consensual, expert, international arbitration tribunals."[7]

Two issues were before the Court of Appeal. First, what is the standard of review for reviewing a decision of an arbitral tribunal under Article 34(2)(a)(iii) of the Model Law? Second, did the lower court err in its application of the standard of review?

The court began its analysis by considering Article 34(2) and held that none of the grounds therein allows a court to review the merits of a tribunal's decision. Article 34(2)(a)(iii) of the Model Law gives the court the power to set aside a decision of an international arbitral tribunal if:

> The award deals with a dispute not contemplated by or not falling within the terms of the submission to arbitration, or contains decisions on matters beyond the scope of the submission to arbitration, provided that, if the decisions on matters submitted to arbitration can be separated from those not so submitted, only that part of the award which contains decisions on matters not submitted to arbitration may be set aside.

---

[7] *Cargill v. Mexico* at ¶ 46.

The court affirmed that reviewing courts in Canada repeatedly recognize that international arbitral tribunals should be afforded a high degree of deference and "should interfere only sparingly or in extraordinary cases."[8] The English Supreme Court decision of *Dallah Real Estate and Tourism Holding Co. v. Ministry of Religious Affairs of the Government of Pakistan*[9] ("Dallah") was considered, in that it dealt with the review of a tribunal's jurisdiction under Article V of the New York Convention. Citing the *Dallah* case, the Ontario Court of Appeal held that the tribunal's decision has *prima facie* credit, since the challenging party has the onus to set the award aside. The court then held that the tribunal could not act beyond its jurisdiction and stated as follows:

> The tribunal therefore had to be correct in the sense that the decision it made had to be within the scope of the submission and the NAFTA provisions. Its authority to make any decision is circumscribed by the submission and the provisions of the NAFTA as interpreted in accordance with the principles of international law. It has no authority to expand its jurisdiction by incorrectly interpreting the submission or the NAFTA, even if its interpretation could be viewed as a reasonable one.

It concluded that the standard of review to be applied is one of "correctness," in the sense that the tribunal had to be correct in its determination that it had the ability to make the decision it made. It is important, however, to remember that the fact that the standard of review on jurisdictional questions is correctness does

---

[8] *Cargill v. Mexico* at ¶ 33, citing *Quintette Coal Ltd. v. Nippon Steel Corp.* (1990), 50 B.C.L.R. (2d) 207 (C.A.), leave to appeal ref'd, [1990] S.C.C.A. No. 431; *United Mexican States v. Karpa* (2005), 74 O.R. (3d) 180 (C.A.); and *Canada (Attorney General) v. S.D. Myers, Inc.*[2004] 2 F.C.R. 368).

[9] [2011] 1 A.C. 763.

not give the courts a broad scope for intervention in the decisions of international arbitral tribunals. To the contrary, courts are expected to intervene only in rare circumstances where there is a true question of jurisdiction.[10]

On the issue of the application of the standard of review, the Court of Appeal noted that the inquiry under Article 34(2)(a)(iii) is restricted to the issue of whether the tribunal dealt with a matter beyond the submission to arbitration, rather than how the tribunal decided the issues within its jurisdiction. The court held that the tribunal acted within its jurisdiction by correctly indentifying its jurisdictional limits to award damages and considered Cargill's losses that arose from Mexico's breaches of NAFTA.

C. PUBLIC POLICY IN INTERNATIONAL ARBITRATION

C.1 Scenarios of Reliance on Public Policy

In Canada, there are typically three scenarios of reliance on public policy: before an arbitral tribunal as a defense to a claim; before a court in the provincial jurisdiction where the award was rendered to set aside an award; and before a court to respond to an application to recognize and enforce an award.

Under the Model Law there are two public policy grounds on which an award may be set aside[11] or recognition and enforcement of the award may be refused:[12]

---

[10] *Mexico v. Cargill* at ¶¶ 41, 42, and 44.

[11] Model Law, Article 32(2)(b).

[12] Model Law, Article 36(1)(b).

C. Public Policy in International Arbitration

- The subject matter of the dispute is not capable of settlement by arbitration under the laws of the enforcing province; or

- The award, or its recognition or enforcement, would be contrary to the public policy of the enforcing province.

Even if the parties' contract has a broad arbitration agreement that encompasses all types of disputes arising between the parties, the court has the power, on public policy grounds, to refuse to allow the matter to be arbitrated. Canada's Supreme Court has discussed the limits to the public policy exception in arbitration in *Desputeaux v. Editions Chouette Inc.*[13] In that case, it was argued that as the case required a decision about copyright issues, this implicated the civil law concept of "public order" and was therefore not arbitrable. Rejecting this conclusion, Justice LeBel held:

> The development and application of the concept of public order allows for a considerable amount of judicial discretion in defining the fundamental values and principles of a legal system. In interpreting and applying this concept in the realm of consensual arbitration, we must therefore have regard to the legislative policy that accepts this form of dispute resolution and even seeks to promote its expansion. For that reason, in order to preserve decision-making autonomy within the arbitration system, it is important that we avoid extensive application of the concept by the courts. Such wide reliance on public order in the realm of arbitration would jeopardize that autonomy, contrary to the clear legislative approach and the judicial policy based on it.

Turning to the second use of the public policy doctrine, the courts have the power to refuse to recognize and enforce an award where doing so would be contrary to the public policy in

---

[13]   2003 SCC 17.

the province. For example, in *Subway Franchise Systems of Canada Ltd. v. Laich*,[14] because enforcement of the arbitral award would amount to double recovery, the court refused to enforce it since double recovery would violate public policy.

C.2 Modes and Limitations of Reliance on Public Policy

Reliance on public policy in Canada can be invoked as a defense in arbitration, or before a court to either set aside an award rendered in the jurisdiction or to move to have recognition and enforcement refused. As a practical matter, the party moving to set aside an award on public policy grounds at the place the award was rendered will want to move quickly to preempt enforcement proceedings elsewhere. The party relying on public policy to refuse recognition and enforcement must raise its arguments on public policy in its response to an application for recognition and enforcement of the award.

A public policy argument can be raised at the enforcement stage, even if the defense was not argued before the tribunal. As a practical note, if there is any question of offending public policy under the proper law of the contract or the place of arbitration, it is best to raise the issue and have it dealt with by the arbitrator. If the matter has not been dealt with in the arbitration, it leaves the door open for the supervisory court or the court at the place of enforcement to make the enquiry with more vigor than might otherwise be the case if the arbitrator has fully dealt with it.

C.3 Rules that Constitute "Public Policy"

In Canada, there is no set of mandatory rules that are considered to be part of public policy. Litigants ought to examine relevant legislation and case law on a case-by-case basis to determine

---

[14] *Subway v. Laich*, 2011 SKQB 249.

whether a subject matter is arbitrable and/or whether the award's recognition or enforcement would be contrary to the public policy of the province in which the challenge or application is being heard.

Whether a subject matter is arbitrable typically turns on whether a statute removes the rights of parties to contract for a third party to resolve their dispute. The Supreme Court of Canada has made it clear that it is up to the legislature to determine what is not to be arbitrated.[15] Furthermore, if the legislature is to exclude arbitration in a particular field, it must do so clearly.[16] Courts have held that it is not against public policy for an arbitrator to assess a solicitor's account under the Solicitors Act,[17] or to have an arbitral tribunal hear and consider a Charter of Rights argument, including the power to declare a provision of the contract unconstitutional, in appropriate circumstances.[18]

With respect to enforcement, courts have refused to enforce an award on public policy grounds where the award would amount to double recovery,[19] and where enforcement would provide an unfair preference to a foreign creditor where the debtor is bankrupt. On the other hand, the Ontario Court of Appeal recently held that the existence of court proceedings in another jurisdiction did not amount to sufficient grounds to refuse enforcement.[20]

---

[15] *Seidel v. TELUS*, 2011 SCC 15.

[16] *Jean Estate v. Wires Jolley,* 2009 ONCA 339; *Desputeaux v. Editions Chouette,* 2001 SCC 17.

[17] *Jean Estate v. Wires Jolley*, 2009 ONCA 339.

[18] *Douglas/Kwantlen Faculty Association v. Douglas College* (1990), 52 B.C.L.R. (2d) 68 (S.C.C.).

[19] *Subway v. Laich*, 2011 SKQB 249.

[20] *Accentuate Ltd. v. Asigra Inc.*, 2011 ONCA 99.

There may be a distinction between domestic public policy and the public policy considerations of enforcing judgments and arbitral awards from other jurisdictions. For the enforcement of foreign awards, a party who wishes to raise a public policy argument must point to some provincial or Canadian law that is declarative of that public policy. Where parties intended a foreign law to apply, and the arbitration was legal under that law, the award should be enforced in the enforcing province unless the party resisting enforcement can demonstrate it would be against public policy to enforce the award.

For example, in *Boardwalk Regency Corp. v. Maalouf*,[21] the court dealt with whether a foreign judgment arising out of a gaming debt could be enforced in Ontario. The applicable law of the contract was that of New Jersey, where the indebtedness was legal. The court held that the Ontario Gaming Act and its restraints on gambling contracts did not necessarily amount to public policy. Justice Carthy stated "[i]t cannot be every statement or prohibition which raises this defence [of public policy] or little would be left of the principle of comity underlying conflict of laws jurisprudence."[22] Further, Justice Lacourciere stated "[w]here the foreign law is applicable, Canadian courts will generally apply that law even though the result may be contrary to domestic law."[23]

The *Boardwalk* decision dealt with the enforcement of a foreign judgment. The Ontario Court of Appeal has since dealt with

---

[21]   (1992), 6 O.R. (3d) 737 (C.A.).

[22]   *Subway v. Laich*, 2011 SKQB 249; *see also Auerbach v. Resorts International Hotel Inc.* (1992), 89 D.L.R. (4th) 688 (Que. C.A; and *Parsons & Wittmore Overseas Co. v. Societe Generale de l'Industrie de Papier (Rakta)*, 508 F.2d 969 (2nd Cir. 1974), which speaks in terms of "basic notions" of justice.

[23]   *Boardwalk Regency Corp. v. Maalouf*, [1992] O.J. No. 26 at ¶ 21.

imposing public policy considerations on foreign arbitral awards.[24] It did not adopt the reasoning in *Boardwalk*, it held:

> [T]he concept of imposing our public policy on foreign awards is to guard against enforcement of an award *which offends our local principles of justice and fairness in a fundamental way*, and in a way which the parties could attribute to the fact that the award was made in another jurisdiction where the procedural or substantive rules diverge markedly from our own, or where there was ignorance or corruption on the part of the tribunal which could not be seen to be tolerated or condoned by our courts.

[Emphasis in original.]

C.4 Review of Alleged Breaches of Public Policy

Except in certain fundamental matters, relating, for example, strictly to the status of persons,[25] an arbitrator may dispose of questions relating to rules of public policy, since they may be the subject matter of the arbitration agreement. The arbitrator is not compelled to stay his or her proceedings the moment a matter that might be characterized as a rule or principle of public policy arises in the course of the arbitration.[26] If a tribunal finds that there is no public policy defense, a court may nevertheless, based on public policy grounds, set aside the award if the place of arbitration is in Canada, or refuse to enforce the award if enforcement is sought there.

---

[24] *United Mexican States v. Feldman Karpa*, (2005) 74 O.R. (3d) 180 (C.A.).

[25] *Mousseau v. Société de gestion Paquin ltée*, [1994] R.J.Q. 2004.

[26] *Mousseau v. Société de gestion Paquin ltée*, at ¶¶ 52-53.

CHILE

Antonio Ortúzar, Sr.,[1] Rodrigo Díaz de Valdés[2] and Francisco Grob Duhalde[3]

A. LEGISLATION, TRENDS AND TENDENCIES

A.1 Legislative Framework

Arbitration in Chile is primarily governed by the Organic Code of Courts ("OCC"), the Code of Civil Procedure ("CCP") and Law 19.971 on International Commercial Arbitration (the "ICA Law").[4] Chile is also a signatory to the New York Convention, the Panama Convention and the ICSID Convention. Additionally, most of the free trade agreements as well as the BITs that Chile has entered into provide for specific arbitration mechanisms to settle disputes arising from their application.

---

[1] Antonio Ortúzar, Sr. is Of Counsel in Baker & McKenzie's Santiago office and the chairman of its Dispute Resolution Practice Group. His areas of expertise include litigation, domestic and international arbitration, antitrust, torts, product liability, bankruptcy and insolvency. He is a listed arbitrator with the Arbitration and Mediation Centre of the Santiago Chamber of Commerce.

[2] Rodrigo Díaz de Valdés is a Partner in Baker & McKenzie's Santiago office and a member of the Firm's Global Dispute Resolution and Antitrust Practice Groups. He is widely experienced in civil, commercial and constitutional litigation as well as in arbitration. He also serves as arbitrator at the Center of Arbitration and the Chamber of Commerce of Santiago.

[3] Francisco Grob Duhalde is an Associate in Baker & McKenzie's Santiago office and a member of the Firm's Global Dispute Resolution Practice Group. His areas of expertise include arbitration, litigation and international law.

[4] The ICA Law is entirely based on the UNCITRAL Model Law.

A.2 Enforcement of Foreign Arbitral Awards

For a foreign arbitral award to be recognized and enforced in Chile, it must be subject to an *exequatur* procedure as set forth in Article 246 of the CPP. This procedure is heard by the Supreme Court, which without re-examining the merits of the case, will generally grant the *exequatur,* provided that the arbitral award is "authentic" and "effective" and it complies with the requirements set forth in Articles 35 and 36 of the ICA Law, as well as the requirements set forth in the New York Convention (and, when applicable, the Panama Convention).

To this effect, once the foreign arbitral award has been duly legalized by the Chilean consulate abroad and translated into Spanish, it should be submitted to the Supreme Court along with a petition requesting that the *exequatur* be granted. If the Supreme Court concludes that the above legal requirements have been complied with, it will grant the *exequatur*, ordering the enforcement of the award in Chile.

A.3 Trends and Tendencies

There was no significant legislative change in arbitration law in Chile during 2011.

B. CASES

This year, two cases relating to the application of the ICA Law were reported. The first case concerns an *exequatur* proceeding of a foreign arbitral award, and the second one relates to a challenge against an arbitration agreement. Both cases are summarized below.

B. Cases

B.1 Enforcement of an Arbitral Award Annulled at the Place of Arbitration

In *EDF Internacional S.A. v. Endesa Latinoamericana S.A. and YPF S.A.*[5] the Supreme Court rejected the application for *exequatur* of an arbitral award rendered under the ICC Arbitration Rules in an arbitral proceeding conducted in Buenos Aires that was later annulled by the competent courts of Argentina.

In its decision, the Supreme Court confirmed its previous position according to which, in order to prove the authenticity of an arbitral award rendered under the auspices of an arbitral institution, the award does not require certification by a Chilean diplomatic or consular agent at the seat of the arbitration.[6] The award whose enforcement was sought was submitted to the ICC for verification, a situation that, according to the Supreme Court, allowed the Secretary General of the ICC International Court of Arbitration to appropriately certify the authenticity of this ruling.

As for the merits, the Supreme Court found, however, that in light of the provisions set forth in the New York Convention,[7] the Panama Convention[8] and the ICA Law,[9] an award that has been set aside by a court of the country in which that award was made cannot be considered "effective," as required by Article 246 of the CPP. The court, therefore, denied the request for recognition and enforcement of the arbitral award.[10] The court

---

[5]   Supreme Court, Docket No. 4390-2010 (September 8, 2011).

[6]   Under Article 246 of the CCP, for an arbitral award to be enforced in Chile, it must, among other things, be authentic.

[7]   *See* Article V(1)(b) of the New York Convention.

[8]   *See* Article 5(1)(b) of the Panama Convention.

[9]   *See* Article 36(1)(a)(v) of the ICA Law.

[10] Note, however, that none of the provisions quoted oblige the court to deny the enforcement of an arbitral award that has been set aside at the place of arbitration.

appears to have associated the concept of effectiveness with the enforceability of the award.

The court also held that it was inconsistent and contrary to the doctrine of estoppel for the applicant to request the annulment of the arbitral award in Argentina and then to request its recognition and enforcement in Chile through *exequatur* proceedings.[11]

B.2 Enforceability of the Arbitration Clause

In *Fastpack S.A. v. Bureau Veritas Chile S.A.*,[12] the plaintiff, Fastpack S.A., filed a claim before the 14th Civil Court of Santiago against the defendant, Bureau Veritas Chile S.A., for breach of contract and damages. Plaintiff requested the annulment of certain clauses included in the contract, specifically those concerning: (i) the limitation of liability of the defendant; (ii) dispute resolution through *ad hoc* arbitration in France; and, (iii) the choice of French law to govern the contract.

As a defense, the defendant challenged the court's jurisdiction under Article 8 of the ICA Law[13] on the ground that, according

---

[11] The applicant, EDF, filed a request before the correspondent Argentinean court to have the arbitral award partially set aside to the extent that it granted the counterclaims put forth by defendants. The defendant, in turn, requested the partial annulment of the arbitral award, inasmuch as it upheld EDF's claims. Ultimately, the Argentinean courts allowed both requests and annulled the arbitral award in its entirety.

[12] 14th Civil Court of Santiago, Docket No. C-36961-2009 (May 6, 2010) and, on appeal, Santiago Court of Appeals, Docket No. 2592 2010 (May 10, 2011).

[13] According to this provision "(1) A court before which an action is brought in a matter which is the subject of an arbitration agreement shall, if a party so requests not later than when submitting his first statement on the substance of the dispute, refer the parties to arbitration unless it finds that the agreement is null and void, inoperative or incapable of being performed." It further provides that "(2) Where an action referred to in paragraph (1) of this article has been brought, arbitral proceedings may nevertheless be commenced or continued, and an award may be made, while the issue is pending before the court."

to the arbitration clause, any dispute should be referred to arbitration in France.

The lower court partially sustained the challenge, upholding the claim for breach of contract and damages, but rejecting the alternative request for the annulment of contractual clauses. As a result, the first instance court ruled that court proceedings should be continued solely with respect to the request to nullify the limitation of liability, the arbitration and the choice of law clauses.

Plaintiff appealed the lower court decision, and the Court of Appeals of Santiago overruled the lack of jurisdiction defense raised by the defendant in its entirety. The court held that compelling plaintiff to arbitrate disputes arising out of the contract in France would severely impair its right to due process of law.[14] The court found that this conclusion was further supported by the fact that the contract was concluded in Chile by companies incorporated under the laws of Chile, and whose performance was to be carried out, at least partially, in Chile.[15]

In our opinion, this case strongly departs from the previous case law of the Court of Appeals of Santiago and even from the Supreme Court's previous decisions.[16]

---

[14] This is an uncommon argument since plaintiff can always contend that it is not able to resort to arbitration as agreed in the contract. Moreover, in the case at hand, there were no records showing that the plaintiff would actually be prevented from exercising its rights through arbitration in France.

[15] The problem with this reasoning is that contracts like the one under analysis—concluded in one country to be performed in another—have traditionally been regarded in Chile as truly international contracts that do allow the parties to choose the applicable law and to refer disputes arising therefrom to arbitration.

[16] *See, e.g., Marlex Ltda. v. European Industrial Engineering* (Sup. Ct. 2008) where, under similar circumstances, the first instance court accepted the lack of jurisdiction defense, dismissed the plaintiff's claim and referred the parties to arbitration in Italy. Both the Court of Appeals and the Supreme Court affirmed the decision.

C. PUBLIC POLICY IN INTERNATIONAL ARBITRATION

C.1 Concept of Public Policy under Chilean Law

The Supreme Court has defined public policy as "the set of rules established by the legislature to safeguard the best interests of the community or social morality."[17]

Modern commentators, however, promote a new definition according to which the notion of public policy that is applicable to international relations is not a set of rules but rather a set of fundamental principles underlying certain rules of particular importance. Likewise, modern commentators have distinguished domestic public policy from international public policy,[18] stressing that the latter is considerably less stringent than the former. Hence, enforcement of an arbitral award would only violate international public policy if it was contrary to the forum state's most basic notions of morality and justice.

C.2 Violation of Public Policy as a Ground for Refusing Recognition of an Arbitral Award

In Chile, violation of Chilean public policy is grounds for refusing recognition and enforcement of foreign arbitral awards under Article 36(1)(b)(ii) of the ICA Law,[19] Article 5(2)(b) of

---

[17]   Supreme Court, 29/05/1964 in R.t. 61, sec. 1°, p. 129.

[18]   The international public policy refers to a given state's public policy with respect to international relations.

[19]   According to this provision, "Recognition or enforcement of an arbitral award, irrespective of the country in which it was made, may be refused only … if the court finds that … the recognition or enforcement of the award would be contrary to the public policy of this State."

the Panama Convention[20] and Article V(2)(b) of the New York Convention.[21]

The public policy defense has been raised several times in *exequatur* proceedings;[22] however, the Chilean Supreme Court appears to have upheld this defense only once. In *Transpacific Steamship Limitada v. Euroamérica S.A.* (Sup. Ct. 1999), the Chilean Supreme Court refused to recognize an international arbitral award rendered by a sole arbitrator seated in England because the subject matter under arbitration was the subject of a court proceeding in Chile that had started before the commencement of the arbitration in the U.K., and was still pending when the award was rendered. Since the Chilean court had confirmed its jurisdiction to hear the case, the Chilean Supreme Court concluded that the international arbitral award ignored the *res judicata* effect of the ruling issued by the Chilean court, thereby violating Chilean public policy.

---

[20] According to this provision, "The recognition and execution of an arbitral decision may also be refused if the competent authority of the State in which the recognition and execution is requested finds (…)That the recognition or execution of the decision would be contrary to the public policy ('order public') of that State."

[21] According to this provision, "Recognition and enforcement of an arbitral award may also be refused if the competent authority in the country where recognition and enforcement is sought finds that (…) The recognition or enforcement of the award would be contrary to the public policy of that country."

[22] *See Kreditanstalt für Wiederaufbau v. Inversiones Errázuriz Limitada* (Sup. Ct. 2009) where the defendant opposed the enforcement of the arbitral award contending that such award was contrary to Chilean public policy because it allegedly impaired its right to a due process of law; and *Gold Nutrition Industria e Comercio v. Laboratorios Garden House S.A.* (Sup. Ct. 2008) where the defendant argued that the arbitral award granted interests that exceeded the maximum allowed by Chilean law.

CHINA

James Kwan,[1] Peng Shen[2] and Sarah Zhu[3,4]

China distinguishes between "domestic" and "foreign-related" arbitrations, with distinct legal regimes for each.

The PRC Arbitration Law, which is China's main legislation on arbitration, regulates both regimes but does not specifically define these terms. The Civil Procedure Law is likewise silent on the meaning of "domestic" and "foreign-related." The Arbitration Law, together with certain provisions in the Civil Procedure Law, other legislation, court decisions and rules issued by arbitration institutions, form the legal framework for arbitration in China.

An opinion of the Supreme People's Court ("the SPC")[5] provides some clarity by setting out the parameters for a "foreign-related" case. An arbitration will be considered "foreign-related" if one of the following conditions are met:

[1]   James Kwan is a Partner in the Dispute Resolution Group of Baker & McKenzie's office in Hong Kong. He leads the arbitration practice in Hong Kong. He specializes in infrastructure, engineering, and energy disputes. He has a range of international experience, having represented clients in arbitrations in Hong Kong, Asia, the Middle East, and Europe under the major institutional rules.

[2]   Peng Shen is a Consultant in the Dispute Resolution Group of Baker & McKenzie's office in Beijing. He represents international and domestic clients in domestic and international disputes in China. Prior to working in private practice, he was a judge of the Beijing People's Court.

[3]   Sarah Zhu is a Legal Assistant in the Dispute Resolution Group of Baker & McKenzie's office in Shanghai. Her practice focuses on arbitration and litigation for clients in the automobile, pharmaceutical and insurance sectors.

[4]   The authors would like to thank Victoria Yu of Baker & McKenzie's Hong Kong office for her assistance with this chapter.

[5]   *Supreme People's Court's Several Opinions Concerning the Implementation of the Civil Procedure Law,* dated 14 July 1992.

- One or both parties are foreign nationals or legal entities;
- The subject matter of the dispute is overseas; or
- The legal facts giving rise to the establishment, variation or termination of civil rights and obligations take place outside the PRC (i.e., an agreement completed in the PRC would be domestic).

A distinction should also be made between a "foreign" arbitral award and "foreign-related" arbitral award. A "foreign" arbitral award refers to an arbitral award issued by an arbitration body located outside China. A "foreign-related" arbitral award, refers to an award issued by a Chinese body inside mainland China (e.g., CIETAC) with respect to a foreign-related dispute.

Notably, the PRC-incorporated subsidiaries of foreign companies, e.g., foreign-invested entities ("FIEs") or wholly foreign-owned enterprises ("WFOEs") are considered to be domestic entities. Therefore, if two WFOEs are parties to a dispute, the dispute is considered domestic. That is, foreign investment is insufficient for the dispute to be considered foreign-related, even if the entity is wholly-owned by foreign investors or entities. On the other hand, Hong Kong-based companies are considered to be "foreign."

Whether an arbitral award is domestic or foreign-related makes a difference in setting aside and enforcement. There is no safeguard of review by the higher people's court or the SPC if the award in question is domestic; one would only have recourse to the basic people's court. On the other hand, only the higher people's court can refuse to enforce foreign-related or foreign arbitral awards. The opinion of the higher people's court must then be reported to the SPC, which is the ultimate arbiter of whether enforcement of the award may be refused. Effectively this means that basic people's courts and intermediate people's courts have no independent power to decide on questions of non-enforcement for foreign-related or foreign arbitral awards.[6]

A. LEGISLATION, TRENDS AND TENDENCIES

A.1 SPC Comments

In August of 2011, the SPC organized a seminar among the chief judges from various levels of the people's courts to discuss several issues relating to the trial of foreign-related civil and commercial disputes. At the end of the seminar, Judge Liu Guixiang from the SPC summarized the key points, which serve as guidelines for various levels of the courts. The SPC Comments cover, amongst others, two issues concerning judicial review of arbitral awards.

A.1.1. Law applicable to arbitral agreement

Article 18 of the Law of the People's Republic of China on Choice of Law for Foreign-related Civil Relationships, effective in 2011 ("Article 18"), provides that the parties concerned may choose the laws applicable to the arbitral agreement. If the parties do not choose, the laws at the locality of the arbitral authority or of the arbitration shall apply. These newly effective provisions are not consistent with the provisions under Article 16 of the Interpretation of the Supreme People's Court concerning Some Issues on Application of the Arbitration Law of the People's Republic of China ("Article 16"), which provide that the examination of the validity of a foreign-related arbitration agreement shall be governed by the applicable law agreed on by

---

[6] "Notice of the Supreme People's Court Concerning the Handling by People's Courts of Issues Relating to Foreign-related and Foreign Arbitration Matters," *Fa Fa* No. [1995] 18.

all parties. If the concerned parties do not agree on the applicable laws, but do agree on the place of arbitration, the law of the place of arbitration shall prevail. If the concerned parties do not agree on the applicable law or the place of arbitration, or the place of arbitration is ambiguous, the laws of the court shall prevail.

The inconsistency of the above provisions gives rise to two major issues: (i) the law applicable to the arbitration agreement, either the laws at the locality of the arbitral authority or of the arbitration, should be subject to the agreement of the parties or of the court; and (ii) the position of the application of the laws of the court.

As for the first issue, the SPC comments provide that the pre-condition for the application of the laws of the place of the arbitral authority or of the arbitration is the parties' inability to agree on the applicable law of the arbitration agreement. Therefore, it does not make sense to give the right to choose to the parties. Under those circumstances, the court obtains the right to decide the law applicable to the arbitration agreement.

As for the second issue, the SPC comments provides that Article 16 can be treated as a supplementary provision to Article 18, as Article 18 does not deal with the situation where the parties fail to agree on an arbitration commission or the venue of the arbitration. Accordingly, the laws of the court will apply to decide the arbitration agreement.

A.1.2. Property preservation in arbitration proceedings

Both the Civil Procedural Law and the Arbitration Law provide that the parties to the arbitration can apply for property preservation by submitting the application to the arbitration commission, which in turn transmits the application to the court of jurisdiction. However, there is no provision stating that an application for property preservation is permissible before the commencement of arbitration proceedings. The SPC Comments confirm that the court shall not accept any property preservation application before the commencement of arbitral proceedings.

A.2 New Proposed CIETAC Rules

The new CIETAC Arbitration Rules are subject to the final approval of the China Council for the Promotion of International Trade and China Chamber of International Commerce. A few noteworthy amendments to the proposed new CIETAC Arbitration Rules are set out below.

A.2.1. Service of documents

Due to difficulties in serving documents on the parties, the new CIETAC Arbitration Rules provide that correspondence to a party or its representative(s) shall be deemed to have been properly served on the party if delivered to the addressee or delivered at the addressee's place of business, registration, domicile, habitual residence or mailing address; otherwise, where, after reasonable inquiries by the other party, none of the aforesaid addresses can be found, the arbitration correspondence shall be sent by the Secretariat of CIETAC or its sub-commissions to the addressee's last known place of business, registration, domicile, habitual residence or mailing address by registered or express mail, or by any other means that can provide a record of the attempt at delivery.

A.2.2. Consolidation of arbitrations

The new CIETAC Arbitration Rules allows CIETAC to consolidate two or more pending arbitrations into a single arbitration at the request of a party and with the agreement of all the other parties.

A.2.3. Interim measures

In addition to the property preservation and evidence protection available under the current CIETAC Arbitration Rules, the new CIETAC Arbitration Rules allow the tribunal to grant any interim measure it deems necessary or proper, in the form of a procedural order or an interlocutory award.

A.2.4. Place of arbitration and language

The new CIETAC Arbitration Rules suggest that in the absence of such agreement, rather than China being the exclusive place of arbitration, CIETAC will have the discretion to decide the place of arbitration.

The new rules also provide that CIETAC has the discretion to decide the language used in the arbitration proceedings and that Chinese is not the default language.

A.2.5. Appointment of presiding arbitrator

The current rules provide that the parties may each recommend one to three arbitrators as candidates for the presiding arbitrator and shall submit the list of recommended candidates to CIETAC. The new rules include a mechanism that will enable the parties to have more power in the nomination of arbitrators, especially the presiding arbitrator.

A.2.6. Conciliation

The current rules provide that where both parties want to pursue conciliation or one party so desires and the other party agrees when approached by the arbitral tribunal, the arbitral tribunal may conciliate the case during the course of the arbitration proceedings. The new rules will also enable the parties to resort to conciliation prior to the arbitration proceedings.

A.2.7.   Expedited/summary procedure

The current rules provides that unless otherwise agreed by the parties, a summary procedure shall apply to any case where the amount in dispute does not exceed RMB 500,000, or to any case where the amount in dispute exceeds RMB 500,000, yet one party applies for arbitration under the summary procedure rules and the other party agrees in writing. The new rules will raise the threshold amount in order to improve efficiency and cut costs.

B.   CASES

In 2010, CIETAC accepted a total of 1,352 cases, and concluded 1,382 cases. Of the cases accepted, 418 were foreign-related and 934 were domestic. There were 51 different nationalities of disputants in 2010.[7]

Partly because the legal system does not rely on precedent to the same extent as common law jurisdictions, there are limited sources of reported case law in China. Consequently and with some exceptions, full and accurate reports of the decisions are not readily available.

B.1   *Subway International B.V. v. Beijing Sabowei Catering*

Subway International B.V. entered into a franchise agreement with Beijing Sabowei Catering that provided for arbitration under the ICSID Rules. Subway International B.V. obtained a favorable award against Beijing Sabowei Catering. However, as Beijing Sabowei Catering refused to carry out its obligations under the award, Subway International B.V. brought an enforcement application before the Beijing No. 2 Intermediate

---

[7]   Yu, Jianlong, Vice Chairman and Secretary General of CIETAC, Presentation on "CIETAC Arbitration," 5 July 2011.

People's Court. After the factual review of the case, the Beijing No. 2 Intermediate People's Court found that Beijing Sabowei Catering was not registered with the authorities of the Administration of Industry and Commerce, which meant that it was not an existing company under PRC laws. The court decided there was no legal basis to support the enforcement application under the New York Convention, as the Convention stipulates that an enforceable arbitral award should bind existing parties. However, Beijing Sabowei was not duly incorporated in China.

The Beijing No. 2 Intermediate People's Court reported the decision to the Beijing High Court, which elevated the case to the SPC. The SPC affirmed the decision of the Beijing No. 2 Intermediate People's Court.

B.2   *Liupanshui Hidili Industry Co., Ltd. v. Zhang Hongxing (2010) Min Er. Zhong Zi No. 86*

This Supreme People's Court case highlights that parties should not specify an arbitration venue outside of China (including Hong Kong) for Chinese domestic disputes. The parties agreed to arbitration administered by the HKIAC. There was no foreign element. In refusing to stay proceedings, the SPC stated that the "issue of resolution of civil and commercial disputes arising within a country's territory has a bearing on that country's judicial sovereignty. It also falls within the realm of that country's public policy. The parties may only reach an agreement only to the extent that current laws permit them to do so."

Thus, Hong Kong is close, but still too far away for "domestic" disputes to be referred there.

C. PUBLIC POLICY IN INTERNATIONAL ARBITRATION

C.1 Scenarios of Reliance on Public Policy

Under the New York Convention, recognition or enforcement of an arbitral award may be refused by a court on the basis that to do so would be contrary to the public policy of the country in which recognition and enforcement is sought.[8]

As a signatory to the New York Convention, China may likewise refuse to enforce foreign arbitral awards by invoking public policy. The provisions of the New York Convention are applied by the Chinese courts in proceedings concerning the recognition and enforcement of foreign arbitral awards.[9]

The term "public policy" does not appear in Chinese legislation relating to arbitration. Instead, Chinese law adopts the term "social and public interest." This term appears in the Arbitration Law, the Civil Procedure Law, and the Arrangements Concerning Mutual Enforcement of Arbitral Awards between the Mainland and Hong Kong and the Mainland and Macau ("the Hong Kong Arrangement" and "the Macau Arrangement").

Under the Civil Procedure Law, enforcement of an award may be resisted on the grounds of "public interest" for both domestic and foreign-related disputes.[10]

One may also apply to set aside a domestic arbitral award under the Arbitration Law if the award is contrary to the "social and

---

[8] Article V(2)(b) of the New York Convention.

[9] In accordance with the "Notice on Implementation of China's Accession to the Convention on the Recognition and Enforcement of Arbitral Awards," promulgated by the SPC on 10 April 1987.

[10] Article 213 (domestic) and Article 258 (foreign-related).

public interest."[11] A Chinese court may rule to either set aside or refuse enforcement of a foreign-related award on the basis that execution of the award would harm the "sovereignty, security or public interest" of the PRC.[12]

The Hong Kong Arrangement provides that the enforcement of an award may be refused if the court of the Mainland holds that enforcement would be contrary to the "public interest" of the Mainland, or if the Hong Kong court decides that enforcement would be contrary to the public policy of Hong Kong.[13] This supports the conclusion that "public interest" is a distinct concept from "public policy." An additional point to note is that the Macau Arrangement, on the other hand, does not refer to public policy in those terms. Under the Macau Arrangement, enforcement may be refused if the award conflicts with either the "basic principles of law" or the social public interests of the PRC, or the "basic principles of law" or the "public order" of Macau.[14]

C.2 Modes and Limitations of Reliance on Public Policy

Since 2008, the time limit for an enforcement application to be made is two years from the date of performance. This applies irrespective of whether a natural or legal person is making the application. Previously, the time limits were six months for legal persons and one year for natural persons (under the Civil Procedure Law). The extended time limit of two years for bringing an enforcement application is still one of the shortest

---

[11] Article 58 of the Arbitration Law.

[12] Article 70 (cancelling) and Article 71 (refusing enforcement) of the Arbitration Law.

[13] *See* Article 7(5) (Emphasis added).

[14] *See* Article 7(5) (Emphasis added).

among the New York Convention states. By way of contrast, the time limit is 30 years for Austria and Belgium.

Under the Arbitration Law, the time limit to apply for cancellation of an award is six months after the receipt of the award. The court shall, within two months after the receipt of the application, render its decision to either cancel the award or reject the application.

C.3 Rules that Constitute "Public Policy"

Unfortunately, both the Arbitration Law and the Civil Procedure Law do not contain a definition for "social and public interest." As a result, social and public interest has been invoked in a number of ways. However, it is a popular misconception that Chinese courts frequently invoke the ground to overturn arbitral awards. On the contrary, it is apparent from the body of cases that have developed that the SPC endorses a fairly restrictive interpretation of social and public interest.

Damage to the interests of state-owned enterprises[15] or state assets[16] has generally been held by the SPC to be insufficient to refuse enforcement on the basis of social and public interest. The SPC has also held that the fundamental interests of China falls under "social and public interest."[17] Mere unfairness or injustice in the arbitration procedure is not sufficient to invoke "social and public interest."[18] Moreover, violation of domestic

---

[15] *Kaifeng Dongfeng Garment Factory v. Henan Garment Import and Export Group*; *Hengjin (HK) Cereal & Oil Food Co., Ltd. v. Anhui Cereal & Oil Food Import & Export Co. (Group)*.

[16] *Shenzhen Baosheng Jinggao Environmental Development Co., Ltd. v. Hefei City Appearance Environmental Hygiene Bureau*, [2005] Min Si Ta Zi [Civil Court Ruling] No. 45, SPC reply, issued on 23 January 2006.

[17] *Ibid.*

[18] *Ibid.*

law does not necessarily lead to a violation of the social and public interest. [19]

Administrative regulations, such as State Administration on Foreign Exchange ("SAFE") regulations, do not generally appear to constitute public policy. Even a breach of a mandatory provision does not necessarily equate to a conflict with the social and public interest.[20]

The performance of heavy metal music without the requisite approval by the Ministry of Culture was held by the SPC to constitute a violation of social and public interest. It was held that the music was not suitable for and had a negative effect on Chinese society.[21]

Fraud is not necessarily sufficient to invoke the "social and public interest" ground. In the case in question, the contract in dispute was concluded based on fraud. Although the ruling to refuse enforcement of the Hong Kong award was affirmed by the SPC, it was held that the appropriate ground to use was Article 7(1) of the Hong Kong Arrangement. The SPC rejected the argument on social and public interest grounds.[22]

Fairness of outcome is not a relevant consideration when determining violation of social and public interest.[23]

---

[19] *ED&F Man (HK) v. China Sugar and Wine Company (Group)*, [2003] Min Si Ta Zi [Civil Court Ruling] No. 3, SPC reply, issued on 1 July 2003.

[20] *Mitsui Co. (Japan) v. Hainan Textile Industry General Co.*, [2001] Min Si Ta Zi [Civil Court Ruling] No. 12, SPC reply, issued on 13 July 2005.

[21] *American Production Co. and Tom Flight Co. v Chinese Women's Travel Agency*, Ta [1997] No. 35, SPC reply, issued on 26 December 1997.

[22] *Hengjin (HK) Cereal & Oil Food Co., Ltd. v. Anhui Cereal & Oil Food Import & Export Co. (Group)*.

[23] *Shanghai Feilun v. GRD Minproc, Ltd.*

A violation of public policy seems to require proof of an affront to the higher "social public interest" of China as a whole, whether it relates to the moral order of the country or the sovereignty of the Chinese courts.

The SPC issued a judicial interpretation on commercial and maritime cases that clarifies the scope of the term in 2004.[24] Article 43 provides that in foreign-related commercial cases, if foreign law is applicable, then PRC courts will examine whether the foreign law violates the social and public interest of China. If that law is in violation of the social and public interest, then it will be excluded. It further provides that, generally, where a law violates the fundamental principles of China's laws, national sovereignty, basic moral order, customs or traditions, then it violates the social and public interest of China.

C.4   Review of Alleged Breaches of Public Policy

As noted above, PRC courts have been very cautious in using the notion of social and public interest to annul a domestic arbitral award or to refuse to enforce an international arbitral award.

Prior to denying enforcement or refusing to recognize and enforce foreign-related or foreign arbitral awards, an intermediate people's court must first obtain approval from the higher people's court of the same jurisdiction. If the higher people's court agrees with the denial of enforcement and/or refusal of recognition, it has an obligation to report its opinion to the SPC. The ruling to deny enforcement or to refuse recognition may only be made after the SPC has made a reply.[25]

---

[24]   "Explanations on and Answers to Practical Questions in the Trial of Foreign-related Commercial and Maritime Cases," (No. 1), SPC, April 2004.

[25]   "Notice of the Supreme People's Court Concerning the Handling by People's Courts of Issues Relating to Foreign-Related and Foreign Arbitration," 28 August 1995.

In a speech to celebrate 50 years of the New York Convention, the President of the SPC, Mr. Wang Shenjun, stated that 12 international awards had been refused enforcement in the PRC.

The public policy ground under the New York Convention for refusal of enforcement was used in 2008 (for the first time by the Chinese courts, it was asserted) by the Jinan Intermediate People's Court in Shandong province in *Hemofarm DD v. Jinan Yongning Pharmaceutical Co. Ltd.* to refuse enforcement of an ICC arbitration award rendered in Paris under the New York Convention.

In *Hemofarm*, the Jinan Intermediate People's Court discovered that the tribunal had determined the tenancy agreement disputes between Jinan Yongning Pharmaceutical and a joint venture and rendered awards accordingly. However, these issues had already been tried and decided by the Chinese courts. The Jinan court held that the arbitral award should not be recognized or enforced as it violated the judicial sovereignty of China, as well as Chinese courts' jurisdiction over the dispute. The case was submitted to the Shandong High Court, which affirmed the Jinan court's judgment.

The case was then reported to the SPC for approval. The SPC upheld the lower courts' decisions and confirmed that the ICC award violated China's judicial sovereignty and the jurisdiction of the Chinese courts, which constituted a violation of the social and public interest. As a result, the SPC refused enforcement of the award under the public policy ground of the New York Convention.

Since then, the SPC has also reported a few cases where the local intermediate court or provincial high court used "social and public interest" as grounds to refuse enforcement of a foreign arbitral award. These cases were referred to the SPC, which then overruled the lower courts' decisions.

It seems that the requirement of "social and public interest" of China sets a fairly high bar for non-enforcement or cancellation of arbitral awards. The concept of "social and public interest" extends beyond domestic law and policy to the fundamental underpinning of Chinese law, sovereignty, and the wider societal moral order. Although the extent of application and overlap of the "public policy" ground under the New York Convention remains unclear at present, it seems that reliance on the "social and public interest" does not lead to many successful cases of non-enforcement of foreign-related and foreign awards.

COLOMBIA

Claudia Benavides[1,2]

A. LEGISLATION, TRENDS AND TENDENCIES

A.1 Overview of the Arbitral Legal Framework

International and domestic arbitration are both lawful practices for dispute resolution in Colombia. The Colombian Political Constitution provides that private individuals, vested with the power to act as arbitrators, can be temporarily brought in by parties to a controversy in order to resolve a dispute.[3] Likewise, the Statutory Law on the Administration of Justice provides that private individuals whom the disputing parties have empowered to act as arbitrators are entitled to exercise jurisdictional functions.[4]

---

[1] Claudia Benavides heads the Litigation and Arbitration practice in the Bogotá office of Baker & McKenzie. She has extensive experience in transnational litigation, acting for national and foreign corporations in disputes involving complex contractual and non-contractual claims. Claudia has represented clients before courts and arbitral tribunals in different types of commercial disputes, as well as in controversies involving distributorship agreements, unfair competition, insurance and real estate, amongst others. She is currently a listed, authorized secretary for the arbitral tribunals of the Center of Arbitration of the Chamber of Commerce of Bogotá.

[2] The author would like to thank Juan Guillermo Otero and Juan Pablo Caicedo of the Bogotá office for their assistance in preparing this chapter.

[3] Colombian Political Constitution, Article 116: "Private individuals may be temporarily vested with the function to administer justice as members of the jury in criminal matters, mediators or arbitrators empowered by the parties to issue awards either according to the law or *ex aequo et bono*, according to the terms provided for by the law."

[4] Law 270 of 1996 as amended by Law 1285 of 2009.

Both arbitration clauses and submission agreements are accepted in Colombia.[5]

Pursuant to Colombian law, only those disputes that can be the subject of a settlement agreement between the parties are arbitrable.[6] The parties may submit their differences to arbitration as long as the controversy refers to matters the rights to which the parties are entitled to freely dispose. In this respect, the Colombian Constitutional Court has established that arbitrators may not rule on disputes that involve public order, national sovereignty or constitutional order, as these are issues that, due to their nature, are to be addressed only by the state.[7]

As arbitrators in Colombia have the same powers as judges, they are entitled by applicable law to order certain provisional measures.[8] Similarly, arbitral awards are considered to be equivalent to judicial rulings[9] and, thus, arbitral awards issued in Colombia are as binding and enforceable as any other judicial decisions taken by a local court.

The decision of an arbitral tribunal on the merits of the case is not subject to appeal;[10] however, Colombian law sets forth two so-called extraordinary recourses against arbitral awards, both

---

[5] *See* Articles 117, 118 and 119 of Decree 1818 of 1998. Please note that Decree 1818 of 1998 contains most of the regulations on the matter. Nevertheless, a set of laws and decrees containing relevant rules that are still in force were not included in this Decree. Also, there are a few provisions included in Decree 1818 that are not currently in force.

[6] Article 115 of Decree 1818 of 1998.

[7] Ruling C-1436 of 2000 of the Colombian Constitutional Court.

[8] Rulings C-294 and C-431, both of 1995, of the Colombian Constitutional Court.

[9] Ruling C-242 of 1997 of the Colombian Constitutional Court.

[10] *See* ruling issued by the Supreme Court of Justice on July 21, 2005, case-file No. 2004-0034, Justice Edgardo Villamil Portilla.

aimed at protecting procedural due process: (i) an action to set aside the award;[11] and (ii) an action to review the arbitral award.[12] It is common practice for the losing party to file an action to set aside the award, but very rarely do the parties to arbitration file an action to review the award, as the grounds on which to file such recourse are very restrictive.

Actions to set aside and to review an award are decided by the higher court of the judicial district where the arbitral tribunal was seated.[13] However, actions to set aside awards in disputes arising out of contracts to which the state was a party are decided by the State Council (*Consejo de Estado*).[14]

Notwithstanding the above, it is worth mentioning that, according to a Colombian Constitutional Court decision in 2009,[15] parties to arbitration are entitled to bring a constitutional action for the protection of fundamental rights (*acción de tutela*) against an arbitral award. As a result of this decision, the Constitutional Court has opened the door to using constitutional actions to pursue the reconsideration of an arbitral award on its merits. This could be done on the basis of the protection of fundamental rights and, more specifically, the protection of the fundamental right to procedural due process.

The parties may agree to *ad hoc*,[16] institutional[17] or legal arbitration.[18] There is no doubt that legal arbitration has been the

---

[11] Article 161 of Decree 1818 of 1998.

[12] Article 166 of Decree 1818 of 1998.

[13] Articles 161 and 166 of Decree 1818 of 1998.

[14] Article 162 of Decree 1818 of 1998.

[15] We will comment on this case in further detail in Section B of this chapter.

[16] Pursuant to Article 116 of Decree 1818 of 1998, arbitration is *ad hoc* when the parties set forth and agree on the procedural rules that will be applied to the arbitral procedure.

modality most commonly used, but, nowadays, the parties have increasingly turned to institutional arbitration, particularly by referring arbitration to the rules of the Center of Arbitration of the Chamber of Commerce of Bogotá. *Ad hoc* arbitration is almost non-existent, as the Constitutional Court has ruled that the parties, when setting forth the rules, must respect the contents of the laws that regulate arbitral proceedings as well as comply with procedural due process.[19]

Furthermore, the decision on the merits of the case through arbitral awards can be made on the basis of applicable substantive law, *ex aequo et bono*[20] or on technical grounds.[21] In Colombia, awards are mostly based on substantive laws currently in force.

A.2 Specifics of International Arbitration

Colombian law makes a distinction between national and international arbitration. Law 315 of 1996 ("Law 315") sets forth the applicable criteria for determining whether arbitration can be regarded as international and introduces the most relevant regulations on the matter. Colombia has not yet implemented the UNCITRAL Model Law on international arbitration. However, a new statutory draft proposal is currently being considered by the Colombian Congress, which introduces substantive modifications

---

[17] According to Article 116 of Decree 1818 of 1998, arbitration is institutional when the parties refer arbitration to the rules set forth by an arbitral institution.

[18] Article 116 of Decree 1818 of 1998 establishes that arbitration is legal when arbitration is subject to the procedure set forth in applicable law.

[19] Ruling C-713 of 2008 of the Colombian Constitutional Court.

[20] An *ex aequo et bono* award implies that the decision has been taken according to common sense and equity.

[21] Article 115 of Decree 1818 of 1998.

to the Colombian arbitration regime, including the adoption of provisions based on the UNCITRAL Model Law.

Pursuant to Law 315, arbitration will be considered international as long as the parties so agree and provided that at least one of the following conditions is met:[22]

(a) At the time of entering into the arbitration agreement, the parties are domiciled in different states;

(b) The place where the substantial obligations that are the subject matter of the dispute should be performed is located outside the state in which the parties are domiciled;

(c) The seat of the arbitration is located outside the state in which the parties are domiciled, provided this situation has been agreed upon in the arbitration agreement;[23]

(d) The subject matter of arbitration clearly involves the interests of more than one state and the parties have expressly agreed to this; or

(e) The subject in dispute directly and unequivocally affects the interests of international trade.

According to Law 315, international arbitration shall also be governed by the treaties, conventions, protocols and any other acts of international law signed and ratified by Colombia, and shall prevail over the provisions set forth on the matter by the Code of Civil Procedure.[24]

---

[22] Article 1 of Law 315 of 1996.

[23] The Colombian Constitutional Court ruled on the constitutionality of such provision, provided that at least one of the parties to the arbitration is a foreigner. *See* ruling C-347 of 1997.

[24] Article 2 of Law 315 of 1996.

Furthermore, the parties are free to agree on applicable substantive law and on every aspect of the arbitration procedure,[25] including the request for arbitration, the constitution of the arbitral tribunal, the language, the appointment and nationality of the arbitrators, and the seat of the arbitral tribunal.[26]

Colombia is a signatory to the New York and Panama Conventions.[27] *Exequatur* before the Colombian Supreme Court of Justice is always required for the recognition and enforcement of foreign arbitral awards. In practice, the Supreme Court of Justice applies two sets of standards for the recognition and enforcement of foreign awards when such recognition is requested by nationals of a country signatory to the New York Convention: those established in the Code of Civil Procedure[28] and those established in the New York Convention. However, a recent decision of the Supreme Court of Justice[29] clearly ruled that only those standards established in the New York Convention shall apply in such situations. This position was later confirmed by the Supreme Court in an interesting ruling issued on December 19, 2011.[30]

---

[25] The parties may agree on the applicable arbitration procedure by directly establishing the rules or by reference to a specific set of arbitration rules.

[26] Law 315 of 1996 provides that the seat of arbitration can be in Colombia or in a foreign country.

[27] The Conventions were ratified by Law 39 of 1990 and Law 44 of 1986, respectively.

[28] Article 694 of the Colombian Code of Civil Procedure.

[29] Supreme Court of Justice, *Petrotesting Colombia S.A. and Southeast Investment Corporation*, Jul. 27, 2011, file 2007-01956.

[30] Supreme Court of Justice, *Drummond Ltd. – Ferrovías en Liquidación and FENOCO*, Dec. 19, 2011, file 2008-01760.

Law 315 specifically provides that an award issued by an arbitral tribunal seated outside of Colombia shall be deemed to be a "foreign" award.[31] In our opinion, that provision implies that if the venue of the international arbitral tribunal is in Colombia, the award shall not be considered a "foreign" award. Therefore, under the current state of affairs, arbitral awards issued by international arbitral tribunals seated outside of Colombia need to go through *exequatur* in order to be recognized and enforced within the country. However, when the venue of the international arbitration tribunal is in Colombia, the award, in principle, may not be regarded as a foreign award and therefore could be enforced without going through *exequatur*.

A.3 Trends and Tendencies

On October 27, 2010, the Colombian government created an experts' commission to work on the statutory draft proposal for a new law on domestic and international arbitration.[32] The government stated that, due to the high impact of arbitration as a method of dispute resolution in civil, commercial and contractual state-related issues, current regulation on the matter shall be updated so as to assure the development and strengthening of arbitration in Colombia. The Colombian government further considered that, given the significant number of rulings from various national courts related to arbitration, it was necessary to evaluate the convenience of making certain statutory modifications and adopting a unified, systematic, modern and inclusive law.

---

[31]   Article 3 of Law 315 of 1996.

[32]   The expert's commission was created through Decree 3992, issued on October 27 of 2010, which was thereafter modified by Decree 4146, issued on November 5 of 2010.

The commission was made up of two sub-commissions—one focused on domestic arbitration and the other on international arbitration. Each sub-commission had its own group of experts. The commission rendered its report on May 18, 2011 and delivered to the government two different sets of rules, governing national and international arbitration independently. The final version of the statutory draft proposal was submitted by the government to the Colombian Congress on July 26, 2011 and is currently under discussion.

The statutory draft proposal adjusts arbitration law in accordance with precedent set by the Constitutional Court, the Supreme Court, the State Council, the superior courts and the administrative tribunals. Regarding international arbitration, the draft seeks the modernization of the procedures and the improvement of procedural rules in order to have more agile and effective arbitral proceedings.

A.3.1. Trends in international arbitration

Law 315 regulates international arbitration in Colombia with a set of very few rules. The proposed statutory draft currently under debate in the Colombian Congress, provides more detailed regulation, by adopting many of the provisions of the UNCITRAL Model Law.

The proposed statute brings some interesting modifications to the regime currently in force in Colombia. It is worth mentioning, without entering into details, some of the changes that the proposed statute intends to introduce to international arbitration:

(a) A broad definition of the circumstances in which an international arbitration agreement will be considered a written agreement, reducing formal restrictions that have been traditionally used to challenge the existence and validity of such agreements.

(b) An express statement of the circumstances under which written communications should be considered effectively received by the addressee, expressly recognizing the validity of electronic communications within international arbitration.

(c) Stricter standards for challenges to arbitrators. Arbitrators are obliged to disclose any information that may affect their impartiality or that may result in a conflict of interests.

(d) A definition of the specific procedures that local judicial authorities may use to assist the arbitral tribunal, and an indication of the local authorities with competence to assist in each procedure.

(e) A change to the competent authority to decide actions to set aside arbitral awards when the arbitration involves private parties. Currently, the higher court of the district where the arbitration was seated is the competent authority to decide actions to set aside the award; the draft statute proposes the Supreme Court of Justice as the competent authority in such cases.

(f) The ability for the parties to request interim measures before Colombian courts, prior to or during the course of arbitration. This is not to be interpreted or understood as a waiver by the requesting party of its rights under the arbitration agreement.

(g) An express entitlement for arbitrators to order interim measures. The types of measures arbitrators may order are significantly broadened.

(h) Defined grounds on which the enforcement of an interim measure ordered by an international arbitral tribunal can be refused by local courts, reproducing the grounds on which the recognition and enforcement of a foreign award can be denied under the New York Convention.

(i) The establishment of the motion to set aside as the only remedy available against an arbitral award. Among others, this provision clearly intends to limit the possibility of challenging international arbitral awards through the *acción de tutela*, a constitutional remedy already referred to in this chapter.

(j) Changes to the grounds for the annulment of arbitral awards, leaving behind the provisions of Decree 1818 of 1998 and instead adopting the grounds provided by Article V of the New York Convention. A specific and short procedure for the annulment of arbitral awards is also established within the proposed statute.

(k) The ability, in arbitrations where none of the parties is domiciled or resides in Colombia, for parties to agree in writing to waive their right to file an action to set aside the award or to limit the grounds on which the award can be set aside.

(l) Changes to the grounds on which the enforcement and recognition of a foreign arbitral award may be refused. Consistent with the international provisions in force and with the modifications that have been listed above, the proposed statute reproduces the grounds set forth in Article V of the New York Convention, and explicitly provides that the grounds listed in the current Code of Civil Procedure do not apply.

If these new provisions are finally adopted by the Colombian Congress, Colombia is expected to become a more friendly and reliable seat for international arbitration.

B.   CASES

Colombian courts have played a significant role in determining the scope and implementation of arbitral procedures. For the purposes of this chapter, we have chosen a few recent court decisions that explicitly referred to public policy in the context of international arbitration and to the standards that should be applied by the Colombian Supreme Court of Justice when deciding whether or not to recognize a foreign award.

B.1   Rules that Constitute "Public Policy"

Public policy is an evolving concept. It limits individuals' freedoms, since public policy provisions cannot be validly waived or modified by the parties. For instance, in Colombia it has been traditionally understood that the civil status of an individual, procedural rules, criminal laws and property statutes are all public policy matters.

The Colombian Supreme Court recently analyzed the public policy defense within the context of international arbitration and the New York Convention.[33] In its ruling, the Supreme Court stated that recognition or enforcement of a foreign award could be denied pursuant to the public policy defense established in the New York Convention whenever the award is contrary to the basic or fundamental principles of the Colombian legal system. The court gave a few examples of such basic or fundamental principles that form part of Colombian public policy: the prohibition of abuse of one's rights, the duty of good faith, the impartiality of the arbitral tribunal and respect for procedural due process. Consequently, as the court ruled, the disregard of an

---

[33]   Supreme Court of Justice, *Petrotesting Colombia S.A. and Southeast Investment Corporation*, Jul. 27, 2011, file 2007-01956.

internal mandatory provision will not necessarily result in the denial of recognition of the award for violation of public policy, unless the disregard of such internal mandatory provisions also breaches fundamental and basic principles of Colombian law.

Thus, the Supreme Court of Justice acknowledges the distinction between domestic and international public policy. In the decision outlined above, the Supreme Court explicitly referred to this distinction, establishing that it is international public policy, and not domestic public policy, that must be considered when deciding on the recognition and enforcement of a foreign award.

On December 19, 2011, the Supreme Court of Justice issued another ruling in which the Court confirmed this position regarding the public policy implications of the recognition of foreign awards in Colombia.[34]

B.2 The Public Policy Defense Does Not Need to Be Invoked before the Arbitral Tribunal in Order to Be Relied upon at the Enforcement Stage

A recent decision of the Colombian Supreme Court of Justice analyzed several allegations made by a party against whom enforcement of a foreign award was sought. The party alleged, *inter alia*, that it was unable to present its case during the arbitral proceedings pursuant to Article V(1)(b) of the New York Convention, due to severe economic restrictions. The court ruled that this defense should have been raised within the arbitration proceedings to be considered and decided by the arbitral tribunal. Since that was not the case and because the defense was only raised for the first time by the losing party during its challenge to

---

[34] Supreme Court of Justice, *Drummond Ltd. – Ferrovías en Liquidación and FENOCO*, Dec. 19, 2011, file 2008-01760.

the recognition of the award, the court decided that the defense could not be considered to deny recognition of the award.[35]

The above analysis of the Court did not make express reference to the public policy defense. However, pursuant to the New York Convention, the recognition and enforcement of an award may be refused if the competent authority in the country where recognition and enforcement is sought finds that the recognition or enforcement of the award would be contrary to the public policy of such country. In our opinion, the fact that the local court may deny recognition of the award even if the party against whom enforcement is sought does not so request implies that the public policy defense does not need to be invoked before the arbitral tribunal in order to be relied upon later, at the enforcement stage.

B.3 Applicable Standards to Decide Whether a Foreign Award Shall Be Recognized in Colombia

Pursuant to the Colombian Code of Civil Procedure, in order to grant recognition to a foreign award, the award must be final according to the law of the country of origin. Therefore, a foreign award that was vacated in its country of origin will not be granted recognition and will not be enforceable in Colombia.

When it comes to recognition of awards issued in states that are parties to the New York Convention, the Colombian Supreme Court of Justice[36] recently ruled that only those standards established in the New York Convention shall apply for the recognition and enforcement of foreign awards. In other words, the Colombian Code of Civil Procedure is inapplicable.

---

[35] Supreme Court of Justice, *Petrotesting Colombia S.A. and Southeast Investment Corporation*, Jul. 27, 2011, file 2007-01956.

[36] *Id.*

Therefore, finality should be construed in accordance with Article V(1)(e) of the New York Convention, which is the standard to decide whether a foreign award may be recognized by the Supreme Court despite having been vacated in its country of origin.

In addition, the Supreme Court of Justice recently addressed the issue of recognition of so-called "partial awards."[37] In essence, the court ruled that partial awards shall be recognized in Colombia just like any other award, considering the nature and effects that partial awards have. In fact, said the court, a partial award has the same effects as a final ruling. An award is referred to as a partial award because it decides some of the claims contained in the proceedings, instead of deciding all of the issues at stake. Therefore, a partial award is final in terms of the controversies it decides, which means that partial awards can be subject to recognition and enforcement in Colombia.

B.4 Arbitrability of Contractual Controversies Where the State Is a Party to the Contract

The Supreme Court of Justice[38] recently adopted the position established by the Colombian Council of State, which had ruled that the New York Convention is applicable to foreign awards deciding contractual disputes involving the state as a party have been decided. The court further acknowledged as valid arbitral agreements that provide for foreign arbitrators to decide disputes arising out of such contracts. However, in line with the decisions of the Colombian Constitutional Court,[39] the Supreme Court also

---

[37] Supreme Court of Justice, *Drummond Ltd. – Ferrovías en Liquidación and FENOCO*, Dec. 19, 2011, file 2008-01760.

[38] *Id.*

[39] Constitutional Court. C-1436 of 2002.

pointed out that, in any event, arbitrators do not have jurisdiction to decide on the legality of administrative decisions taken by the state while exercising its exceptional powers within a contractual relationship.

C. PUBLIC POLICY IN INTERNATIONAL ARBITRATION

C.1 Scenarios of Reliance on Public Policy

In Colombia, a party may invoke public policy considerations as a defense against recognition and enforcement of a foreign award, pursuant to the Colombian Code of Civil Procedure and the New York Convention.[40]

The Colombian Code of Civil Procedure establishes that to be recognized by the Supreme Court of Justice, a foreign arbitral award must not be contrary to public policy laws or regulations. The Supreme Court of Justice has interpreted this provision narrowly. In fact, the Supreme Court has established that a foreign ruling contrary to mandatory domestic legal provisions does not *per se* entail the violation of Colombian public policy in a way capable of preventing recognition of a foreign arbitral award. According to the Supreme Court, a foreign award will be granted recognition if it respects the mandatory principles required for the protection of society and the protection of national interests considered to be essential to maintain the social, political, moral, religious and economical order.[41]

---

[40] Article 694 of the Code of Civil Procedure and Article V(2)(b) of the New York Convention.

[41] Supreme Court, Nov. 5, 1996.

Several court decisions have been consistent with this interpretation of the public policy defense. According to the court, hinging the enforcement of foreign awards to their consistency with domestic legal provisions would be tantamount to allowing Colombian courts to review the merits of the case, which is certainly not the role of the Supreme Court when deciding whether to recognize a foreign ruling. Instead, the public policy defense implies analyzing the effects of foreign rulings with respect to the internal fundamental principles of law. The breach of those principles may result in the refusal of the recognition of a foreign award.[42] This is consistent with the international interpretation of the public policy defense, which takes into account the needs of a global economy.

With respect to the grounds for challenging the validity of an arbitration agreement or for setting aside an award, Colombian law also takes into consideration public policy issues. For instance, arbitrability is a concept defined within the boundaries established by Colombian public policy. Pursuant to Colombian law, only those disputes that can be the subject of a settlement agreement between the parties are arbitrable.[43] The parties may submit their differences to arbitration as long as the controversy refers to matters the rights to which the parties are entitled to freely dispose. Therefore, if a party submits to arbitration controversies that are related to non-arbitrable matters, the other party may claim the nullity of the arbitration agreement before the arbitral tribunal. If the arbitral tribunal does not consider the arbitration agreement null, continues with arbitration proceedings and decides the merits of the case, the award could

---

[42] Supreme Court of Justice, *García Fernandes Internacional Importaçâo e Exportaçâo S.A*, Aug. 6, 2004, file 2001-0190.

[43] Article 115 of Decree 1818 of 1998.

later be set aside by the competent court, at the request of the interested party, on the same grounds.

C.2 Modes and Limitations of Reliance on Public Policy

As was previously indicated, public policy considerations can be invoked as a defense against recognition and enforcement of a foreign award pursuant to Colombian law.[44] In addition, public policy considerations also delineate the contents of several grounds on which the parties may challenge the validity of the arbitration agreement during the course of the proceedings or the grounds on which the parties may apply to set aside the award.

C.3 Review of Alleged Breaches of Public Policy

Alleged breaches of international public policy are reviewed by the Supreme Court of Justice when deciding on the recognition of a foreign award. However, as indicated above, there are certain public policy issues that can be raised by the parties during the course of arbitration and decided by the arbitral tribunals.

The Supreme Court of Justice, when deciding on the recognition of a foreign award, will essentially consider Colombia's principles of public policy. In other words, the Supreme Court will refuse recognition if the award is contrary to Colombia's main and most relevant principles and institutions, rather than taking into account foreign public policy considerations.

In any event, the Supreme Court may not carry out a *révision au fond* of the award during *exequatur* proceedings.

---

[44]   *See* Section C.1. above.

CZECH REPUBLIC

Martin Hrodek[1] and Jan Zrcek[2]

A. LEGISLATION, TRENDS AND TENDENCIES

A.1 Recent Developments in Legislation

Both international and domestic arbitration seated in the Czech Republic are governed by Act No. 216/1994 Coll., on Arbitration Proceedings and Enforcement of Arbitration Awards, as amended (the "Arbitration Act"). The Arbitration Act is based on the UNCITRAL Model Law and entered into force in 1995.

In the 2010-2011 *Yearbook*, we noted that the Arbitration Act was subject to three amendments. A fourth amendment, focusing on disputes arising from consumer contracts (the "Amendment"), had only recently been proposed. The Amendment was significantly modified before it was eventually adopted and published on 17 January 2012.[3] The Amendment will enter into force on 1 April 2012.[4]

Apart from stipulating special conditions for arbitrations arising from consumer contracts,[5] the Amendment introduced certain

---

[1] Martin Hrodek is a Partner in Baker & McKenzie's Prague office and head of its Dispute Resolution Practice Group. He specializes in litigation and arbitration matters, particularly those related to mergers and acquisitions. He also advises industry clients on a wide range of commercial matters, including private equity, divestitures and private competition claims.

[2] Jan Zrcek is an Associate in Baker & McKenzie's Prague office and a member of its Dispute Resolution Practice Group.

[3] Act No. 19/2012 Coll., amending the Arbitration Act.

[4] Article VI of Act No. 19/2012 Coll.

[5] In particular, these disputes can only be decided by specialized arbitrators who are qualified lawyers and are registered on a list maintained by the Ministry of

additional changes, which are applicable to any arbitration, including international arbitrations. In particular, as well as having legal capacity and being over 18 years of age, an individual can only become an arbitrator if he/she has not been convicted of a crime or after any conviction has been expunged. Consequently, the Amendment not only regulates arbitrations arising from consumer contracts, but it also prevents persons who have been convicted of a crime from becoming arbitrators.

A.2   Trends

Arbitration has become increasingly popular among Czech companies in matters without any international element. They now use arbitration not only for resolving international disputes, but also for purely domestic disputes. This has arisen because Czech courts are still deemed to be quite slow at handling commercial disputes, although they have improved substantially in recent times. For their domestic disputes, companies tend to use the Arbitration Court of the Czech Economic Chamber and the Czech Agrarian Chamber (which handles approximately 3,000 disputes annually), as well as arbitrations under the ICC Rules, mostly for more complex disputes.

Justice; entering into a consumer contract cannot be made conditional on entering into an arbitration agreement; the consumer should be advised of the consequences before entering into an arbitration agreement; rules on consumer protection cannot be waived in an arbitration; new grounds were introduced in the Arbitration Act for setting aside a domestic award due to, *inter alia*, non-compliance with the above-mentioned regulations.

B. CASES

B.1 Permanent Arbitration Courts versus Czech Private Companies Administering Arbitrations

In the Czech Republic, contrary to most other European countries, arbitration is also widely used for resolving purely domestic disputes, sometimes even domestic retail disputes. In recent times, some of these local arbitrations have been administered by private companies established by attorneys with no experience in arbitration, and this has resulted in controversial awards. In order to attract more disputes, these companies have sought to behave like arbitration courts, issuing their own rules and maintaining their own lists of arbitrators.

Even one of the three largest Czech banks has required its retail clients to agree to such arbitrations. This practice has resulted in contradictory court decisions on setting aside arbitral awards issued by arbitrators appointed by these companies – some arbitral awards were dismissed for circumventing Section 13 of the Arbitration Act, under which permanent arbitration courts may be established solely by law and must publish their statutes and rules in the official Commercial Bulletin used for the publication, for example, of notices of shareholders meetings of large public companies. However, some courts have upheld the arbitral awards issued in arbitrations managed by these private companies. Therefore, in order to make clear that these private companies cannot administer arbitrations, the large senate of the Supreme Court issued on 11 May 2011 Judgment No. 31 Cdo 1945/2010. It ruled that in arbitration agreements parties must either agree on concrete arbitrator(s) or on the method for their selection. The parties may also refer to the rules of the permanent arbitration court, which governs the appointment of arbitrators, but not to any rules of a limited company or other legal entity that is not a permanent arbitration court established by law. If they do so in an arbitration agreement, such agreement would be invalid. Since this judgment is binding on courts of lower instances when dealing with actions to set awards aside, it is now clear that Czech private companies cannot administer arbitrations in the Czech Republic.

While the reasons leading to this decision are understandable, its consequences are a bit unclear. This decision, although it focused solely on Czech companies, may motivate parties that lose an arbitration seated in the Czech Republic and administered by a traditional international arbitration institution to challenge the award based on the argument that the institution was not a permanent arbitration court established by law. However, since the Supreme Court judgment focused only on Czech companies administering arbitrations and not on international arbitration tribunals, we do not think that such challenges would succeed.

B.2   A Party's Opportunity to Present Its Case

There have recently been several Supreme Court decisions on how to interpret the expression "opportunity to present its case" contained in Section 19(2) of the Arbitration Act, which mirrors Article 18 of the UNCITRAL Model Law.

Supreme Court Judgment No. 32 Cdo 3299/2009 describes how proceedings should typically be conducted in order to provide parties with sufficient opportunity to present their case. Pursuant to the judgment, there should be an oral hearing which should be recorded in a protocol signed by the parties. At the hearing, the arbitrators should ask the parties whether they propose any new evidence. If the proceedings are conducted in line with these requirements, the parties will have sufficient opportunity to present their case in accordance with Section 19(2) of the Arbitration Act. From this case, it ensues that the protocol about the hearing should be prepared carefully, since it will serve as important evidence to prove whether the parties had sufficient opportunity to present their case.

Notwithstanding the above, the Supreme Court in its Decision No. 23 Cdo 1873/2010 admitted that the arbitration agreement may provide for resolving the dispute without a hearing and, if no hearing is held under those circumstances, the parties will still be deemed to have had sufficient opportunity to present their case.

Pursuant to Supreme Court Judgment No. 23 Cdo 3744/2009, it is usually necessary to provide a party with an opportunity to comment in writing on the arguments of the other party, i.e., the claimant should have an opportunity to file a reply to the respondent's answer and then the respondent should have an opportunity to file a rejoinder. The time limits for filing submissions must be sufficient in light of all the circumstances of the dispute. All evidence submitted or proposed should be taken into consideration unless it is *prima facie* clear that it is irrelevant and, if it is not taken for this reason, arbitrators must sufficiently explain why it is irrelevant. Also, parties should have an opportunity to file a final brief summarizing their arguments following the evidentiary phase.

B.3 Regulation No. 44/2001 and Court Proceedings Relating to Arbitration

It is beyond any doubt that Regulation 44/2001 (the "Regulation") is not applicable to arbitral proceedings as such, since its application is clearly excluded.[6] Whether the Regulation can be applied to court proceedings in which an arbitral award is to be set aside is not directly addressed in the Regulation. In this respect, the Supreme Court recently concluded that although the Regulation does not address this issue, the Regulation cannot also be applied to such proceedings.

---

[6]   Article 1(2)(d) of the Regulation.

C. PUBLIC POLICY IN INTERNATIONAL ARBITRATION

Public policy considerations under Czech law require that a distinction be drawn between domestic and foreign awards.

The Arbitration Act defines foreign awards as "[a]wards made in a foreign country."[7] This is in line with the definition of foreign awards under Article I(1) of the New York Convention. The New York Convention has been applicable in the Czech Republic since 1959.[8] As a matter of Czech Constitutional law, "[i]nternational treaties, which have been ratified by the Parliament and are binding on the Czech Republic, form part of Czech legal rules and, if there is a conflict between such a treaty and regular laws, the treaty shall be applied."[9] Consequently, to the extent that the New York Convention is applicable and it is in conflict with the Arbitration Act, The New York Convention should be applied. This may affect, *inter alia*, public policy considerations—as further explained below.

C.1 Scenarios of Reliance on Public Policy

Under Czech law, a party can invoke public policy grounds as a defense in a pending arbitration to challenge the validity of an underlying arbitration agreement,[10] it may also challenge the award before the court for such reason and, finally, it can also use these grounds as a defense against recognition and

---

[7]   Section 38 of the Arbitration Act.

[8]   Preamble of the Decree of the Ministry of Foreign Affairs No. 74/1959 Coll.

[9]   Article 10 of the Constitution of the Czech Republic.

[10]   Pursuant to Section 15 of the Arbitration Act, the arbitrators decide on their jurisdiction. This provision does not mention any reasons for challenging the arbitrators' jurisdiction. However, pursuant to Section 31(b) of the Arbitration Act, the arbitration agreement can be invalid also for "other reasons," one of them being public policy issues.

enforcement of a foreign award,[11] including those to which the New York Convention applies.[12]

Only public policy grounds for setting aside a domestic award under Czech law[13] can be relied upon in court proceedings to set aside a domestic award. Consequently, while a party may invoke certain public policy issues in a pending arbitration, they are no longer relevant in court proceedings to set aside an award unless they also fall within the permitted grounds for challenging a domestic award.

A party can invoke any public policy grounds as a defense against recognition and enforcement of a foreign award before Czech courts.

C.2   Modes and Limitations of Reliance on Public Policy

C.2.1 Public policy in the pending arbitration

A party may invoke public policy grounds in an arbitration having its legal place in the Czech Republic, if the following requirements are met:[14]

---

[11]   Section 39(c) of the Arbitration Act.

[12]   *Cf.* Article V(2)(b) of the New York Convention.

[13]   These grounds are enumerated in Section 31 of the Arbitration Act, as follows: (a) lack of arbitrability of the dispute in question, (b) an invalidity or prior termination of the arbitration agreement or arbitrators exceeding their powers, (c) an arbitrator participated in the proceedings without the capacity or standing to do so, (d) the award was not adopted by a majority of arbitrators, (e) a party was not granted a right to be heard and present its case (a breach of the principle of equality of arms), (f) the award provides for a relief that was not requested or for an impossible relief or for a relief that is not permitted under Czech law, (g) there are facts or evidence that could benefit one of the parties and were existing, but were impossible to present during the course of the arbitration without the fault of the party that stands to benefit from these facts or evidence.

[14]   Section 36 of Act No. 97/1963 Coll., on the Conflict of Laws and International Procedural Rules.

1. the relationships between the parties is governed by foreign (i.e., not Czech) law; and

2. the effects of applying foreign law to the respective relationships would violate the public policy of the Czech Republic.[15]

A party who invokes the invalidity of an arbitration agreement on public policy grounds in a pending arbitration must raise the objection in its first submission on the merits, at the latest,[16] or immediately upon becoming aware of the grounds for invalidity of the arbitration agreement for public policy reasons, provided, however, that it exercised due care. If such party does not do so and later challenges the arbitral award, the court cannot then set it aside.[17]

There is no time limit for raising public policy grounds that do not aim to invalidate an underlying arbitration agreement. Obviously, such grounds can be dealt with at any time during the course of the arbitration.

C.2.2. Public policy as a ground for setting aside a domestic award

As stated in Section C.2.1. above, Czech courts are prevented from setting aside a domestic award due to invalidity of an arbitration agreement (for any reason, including public policy issues) if a party, despite being able to do so, failed to raise the objection in time. A party has to raise the objection in its first submission on the merits, or at the latest, immediately upon becoming aware of the grounds for invalidity of the arbitration

---

[15]   *Cf.* Týč, V., Rozehnalová, N., "Law Shopping, Public Order Objections and International Mandatory Rules," *Lawyer* 2002, No. 6, p. 640.

[16]   Section 15(2) of the Arbitration Act.

[17]   Section 33 of the Arbitration Act.

agreement for the public policy reasons, provided, however, that it exercised due care.[18]

However, there are no time restrictions with respect to other grounds for setting aside a domestic award (which grounds can also incorporate public policy issues).[19]

C.2.3. Public policy as a defense against recognition and enforcement of a foreign award

The Arbitration Act and the New York Convention do not require that a party raise any public policy grounds in an arbitration in order to rely on such issues at the enforcement stage. In practice, it would be inappropriate to stipulate such a requirement unless the party could reasonably expect the award to be enforced in a particular country. Consequently, parties are generally free to raise any public policy grounds throughout the course of enforcement proceedings.

Regardless of any public policy considerations, a foreign award that does not fall within the scope of the New York Convention cannot be recognized and enforced if it was vacated in its country of origin.[20] In addition, the enforcement of foreign awards, regardless of their status under the New York Convention, is always subject to Czech procedural rules on enforcement,[21] according to which enforcement cannot proceed if the award was vacated after a decision on enforcement.[22] In theory, since the New York Convention, which does not contain

---

[18] Section 33 of the Arbitration Act.

[19] See the entire list of grounds in fn. 13.

[20] Section 39(a) of the Arbitration Act.

[21] Article III of the New York Convention.

[22] Section 268(1)(b) of Act No. 99/1963 Coll., the Rules of Civil Procedure, as amended.

any such rule, has priority over the Arbitration Act, Czech courts are free to recognize and enforce a foreign award that falls within the scope of the New York Convention regardless of whether it had been previously annulled in the courts of the seat of arbitration.[23] However, in practice we are not aware of any case where a previously vacated foreign award has been enforced by Czech courts.

C.3   Rules that Constitute "Public Policy"

C.3.1. Relevance of the definition of public policy rules

As ensues from Section C.1 above, the definition of rules that constitute public policy is only relevant to public policy grounds invoked as a defense in a pending arbitration and to the recognition and enforcement of foreign awards. Domestic awards cannot be affected by public policy grounds, if such issues cannot be subsumed under any of the grounds for setting aside a domestic award.[24]

C.3.2. Definition of public policy rules

There is no exhaustive or generally accepted definition of rules that constitute public policy under Czech law.

However, the following is a generally accepted starting point to identify public policy rules based on scholarly opinions and consistent decision making practices of Czech courts, including the Constitutional Court of the Czech Republic:

---

[23]   *Cf.* "enforcement of the award may be refused" in Article V of the New York Convention; similarly, for example, Bělohlávek, A. J. "Arbitration, Ordre Public and Criminal Law—Commentary," Part I, Edition 1, Prague: C. H. Beck, 2008, p. 507.

[24]   See the entire list of grounds in fn. 13.

[A] decision (an award) would violate public policy if the recognition of effects of such a decision violated fundamental principles of the constitutional and legal order, social system and, in particular, public order and the violation affected such a concern which has to be definitely upheld in any case (*cf.* Bělohlávek, A., *Arbitration, Ordre Public and Criminal Law—Commentary*. Part I. Edition 1. C. H. Beck: Prague. 2008. p. 415). The violation of public policy occurs in proceedings, in which the respective foreign decision was issued and fundamental rights of a party were breached; insisting on the protection of fundamental rights of a party clearly belongs to such fundamental principles of the Czech legal order (*cf.* decision Ref. No. I. ÚS 709/05, Collection of decisions and resolutions. Issue 41. p. 163). However, it should be noted that the term public policy must be construed restrictively; mere differences between procedural rules of a foreign arbitral tribunal and procedural rules of the country, where the recognition is sought, do not result in violating public policy; if the court in the country of origin followed its procedural rules, a violation of public policy could only occur in very exceptional cases (*cf.* Vaške, V. *Recognition and Enforcement of Foreign Decisions in the Czech Republic.* C. H. Beck: Prague 2007. s. 44).[25]

It is clear from the above that arbitral awards whose terms breach fundamental principles of the Czech constitutional and legal order, social system or public order, are not enforceable.

Czech courts apparently share an opinion that public policy rules, which can be invoked as a defense against recognition and

---

[25] Decision of the Czech Constitutional Court of 10 May 2010, Ref. No. IV. ÚS 189/10.

enforcement of foreign awards, are national (Czech) rules.[26] This approach is facilitated by the fact that international treaties ratified by the Parliament and binding on the Czech Republic form an integral part of Czech legal rules.[27]

Nevertheless, some scholars opine that only those public policy rules that protect fundamental principles of the international legal and public order (in contrast to rules protecting only principles of the Czech legal and public order) can be applied, if the relationship in question does not concern any Czech elements (no Czech parties, arbitrators, subject matter, etc.).[28] To the best of our knowledge, such opinions have not yet been applied in any court decisions.

C.4   Review of Alleged Breaches of Public Policy

C.4.1. Review by arbitral tribunals

Subject to limitations summarized in Section C.2.1. above, arbitrators in the Czech Republic are generally free to review any public policy grounds raised by a party in a pending arbitration (and regularly review these issues where invoked).

In contrast to the courts, arbitrators are also free to consider any foreign public policy issues. If arbitrators do not specialize in the law of the country concerned, they usually rely on opinions prepared by experts on the respective foreign law as submitted by the parties.

---

[26]   *Cf.*, for example, the above referred decision of the Czech Constitutional Court of 10 May 2010, Ref. No. IV. ÚS 189/10: ". . . fundamental principles of the *Czech* legal order . . ."

[27]   *Cf.* Article 10 of the Czech Constitution; *see also* Section C above.

[28]   *Cf.*, for example, Bělohlávek, A. J., "Arbitration, Ordre Public and Criminal Law," Commentary, Part I, Edition 1, Prague: C. H. Beck, 2008.

Arbitrators can also invoke any public policy issues *ex officio*, although this can only occur if a potential violation of public policy is ascertainable from the file.

C.4.2. Review by courts

As explained in Section C.1 above, courts can only deal with public policy issues directly when deciding on the recognition and enforcement of a foreign award. As also mentioned in Section C.3.2. above, only national public policy rules, including international rules incorporated into Czech rules through treaties, are relevant in this respect.

In annulment proceedings, courts only deal with the grounds for setting aside a domestic award and public policy considerations can only be relevant if they can be subsumed under these grounds.

Similarly to arbitral tribunals, courts can also invoke any public policy issues *ex officio*, if a public policy violation is ascertainable from the award whose recognition and enforcement is sought.

However, there is a strict rule established by consistent decision making practices of Czech courts and also supported by decisions of the Czech Supreme Court[29] and Constitutional Court[30] that a court cannot carry out *révision au fond* under any

---

[29] The Czech Supreme Court held in its decision of 29 March 2001, Ref. No. 21 Cdo 1511/2000, regarding an alleged violation of public policy by a foreign award: "When enforcing a decision, the court cannot review correctness of the decision as to the merits; the court is bound by the content of the decision, whose enforcement is sought, i.e., by its ruling and has to stand on it."

[30] When deciding on the compliance of Section 31 of the Arbitration Act (i.e., the list of grounds for setting aside a domestic award, which do not include a public policy violation) with the Czech constitutional order, the Constitutional Court held in its decision 8 March 2011, Ref. No. I. ÚS 3227/07: "The court review can

circumstances, including an alleged violation of public policy, regardless of whether it decides on setting aside a domestic award or on recognition and enforcement of a foreign award.

C.5 Conclusion

A party is generally free to invoke any public policy issues before arbitrators and arbitral tribunals in the Czech Republic, and these issues should be duly dealt with in an arbitration. However, given the strict prohibition against *révision au fond*, public policy issues invoked before Czech courts at the enforcement stage are limited to manifest procedural errors or irregularities. In addition, only those public policy grounds that can be subsumed under the statutory grounds for setting aside a domestic award can be relied on in annulment proceedings before Czech courts relating to a domestic award.

---

only focus on assessing fundamental procedural issues, such as the arbitrability, the equality of arms or on any defects of the award (such as the missing majority of arbitrators). . . In conclusion, the provision [of Section 31 of the Arbitration Act], under which courts cannot interfere with decision making powers of arbitrators, i.e., they cannot deal with the alleged violation of substantive law by the award, is not conflicting with the constitutional order."

FRANCE

Jean-Dominique Touraille[1] and Eric Borysewicz[2]

A.   LEGISLATION, TRENDS AND TENDENCIES

On 13 January 2011, France issued a new decree amending its arbitration law. By codifying well-established French case law, the new law has significantly enhanced the accessibility of French arbitration law for foreign users.[3]

Thirty years have passed since the decrees of 1981, which at the time were considered a modern framework for arbitration. These decrees contributed to making Paris one of the world's most favored seats for international arbitration. Nevertheless, the time had come for these laws to reflect the significant contribution of the French courts, which had maintained France's long-standing tradition of an innovative and arbitration-friendly approach under new and evolving circumstances.

---

[1]   Jean-Dominique Touraille is a Partner in Baker & McKenzie's Paris office and leads the office's Litigation & Arbitration Practice Group. He regularly delivers presentations on various subjects related to his area of practice, which includes distribution, product liability and post-acquisition disputes. He is actively involved in cases relating to ICC arbitration and in enforcement measures in the French legal system.

[2]   Eric Borysewicz is a Partner in Baker & McKenzie's Paris office and a member of the Litigation and Arbitration Practice Group in Paris. He represents clients in international arbitrations under ICC rules and other arbitration institutions. He focuses his practice on risk management issues, advising clients on major litigations involving industrial and infrastructure projects. He also assists clients in drafting and negotiating complex industrial and infrastructure project agreements, as well as in renegotiating existing agreements following an unforeseen change in circumstances.

[3]   Further comments could be found in Jean-Pierre Harb and Christophe Lobier, "New Arbitration Law in France: The Decree of January 13, 2011," *Mealey's International Arbitration Report*, Vol. 26, No. 3 March 2011.

First and foremost, the new decree maintained the clear distinction between domestic and international arbitration.

In domestic arbitration, the decree submits arbitration clauses and arbitration agreements[4] to mostly the same rules, thereby mitigating the often questionable distinction between the two. Under the new decree, a writing continues to be a requirement for the validity of an arbitration clause or an arbitration agreement, including through incorporation by reference. One significant improvement, however, is that the validity of an arbitration clause or agreement can result from a mere exchange of written correspondence. Furthermore, the decree follows the trend set by French courts of allowing the scope of an arbitration clause contained in one agreement to be extended to disputes arising out of other related agreements. In addition, the new law codifies the fundamental principle of the autonomy of the arbitration clause (or separability doctrine), according to which the arbitration clause is not affected by the nullity of the underlying contract.

The new decree also removed the unnecessary burden in domestic arbitration of requiring arbitration clauses or agreements to provide for the method of appointing the arbitrators, without which those clauses or agreements were considered void. Clauses or agreements without this provision are now valid, and where lacking, the parties may request the assistance of French courts to constitute the arbitral tribunal.

The decree also formally provides the parties with the ability, in case of urgency and provided the arbitral tribunal has not yet been constituted, to go before state courts in order to obtain provisional or conservatory measures or measures pertaining to evidence.

---

[4] An arbitration agreement, unlike an arbitration clause, is entered into after a dispute arises and reflects the wish of the parties to submit the dispute specifically identified in such agreement to arbitration.

Transparency during the arbitration process is also enhanced. Following the example of arbitration institutions regarding challenges to arbitrators, the new decree provides that, before accepting their assignment, arbitrators must disclose any and all facts that may affect their independence or impartiality, and must do so without delay if dictated by circumstances that appear after their acceptance. The rules regarding challenges to arbitrators have been simplified and confer jurisdiction on state courts or on the body in charge of administering the arbitration. In the interest of efficiency, unless justified by an impediment or by a legitimate cause, arbitrators are forbidden from terminating their mission before the end of the arbitral proceedings.

The chapter of the decree covering the proceedings themselves contains two significant improvements, which had already been established by case law. First, the law now specifically provides that arbitral proceedings are confidential. Second, the concept of procedural estoppel has been codified. A party who voluntarily refrains from raising any irregularities before the arbitral tribunal is considered to have waived its right to do so after the award is rendered.

The arbitral tribunal's authority is now reinforced by the ability to order parties, under the threat of penalty if necessary, to produce evidence that they may have in their possession. The arbitral tribunal may also order provisional or conservatory measures, except attachments of movable property or judiciary liens, both of which are under the exclusive jurisdiction of state courts. The arbitral tribunal may also authorize a party to request from state courts (from the President of the Tribunal de Grande Instance) an order against third parties to obtain evidence held by the latter.

The death, impediment, abstention, resignation, removal or challenge of an arbitrator can no longer lead to the termination of the arbitral proceeding, but merely to its stay. Thus, when such events occur, parties will no longer need to initiate new proceedings on the same facts and issues.

The new decree also broadens the jurisdiction of state courts to assist parties in the constitution of the arbitral tribunal. State courts already had jurisdiction to intervene under several circumstances, including (1) when the seat of the arbitration was in France, (2) when French procedural law was specifically chosen by the parties and (3) when the parties had specifically requested assistance from the French courts. The decree adds a fourth ground providing French state courts with jurisdiction to assist the parties if the intervention of the court is necessary to prevent a denial of justice. This is a direct consequence of the well-known case *NIOC v. Israel* of 2005.

The legislature took into account the special nature of arbitration and has allowed the parties to agree not to submit the notification of the arbitral award to the formal procedure for service of process. A mere notification of the arbitral award can be sufficient.

Furthermore, the new text imposes on the parties a three month time limit to request from the arbitral tribunal clarifications or amendments to the award. Among other provisions, this new time limit aims at avoiding unnecessary delays in the arbitration proceedings.

Although the principle is already well established, the decree formally provides that the procedure to have an award recognized in France is *ex parte*. The procedure for the recognition of an award has also been significantly improved. Parties no longer need to provide the court with an original of the award; a copy is now sufficient, provided it meets certain requirements to establish its authenticity.

A series of amendments will undoubtedly contribute to expediting the arbitration process. One of the major improvements of the decree concerns the right of parties to a domestic arbitration to appeal the award. Under the former rules, an appeal was allowed unless specifically waived by the parties. Under the new text, parties may no longer appeal an award unless they have specifically agreed to do so.

The procedure to have an award set aside has also been significantly improved. There is no longer any need to submit the award to a court for enforcement prior to requesting that it be set aside. This requirement was overly burdensome, especially in cases where the award was not to be executed in France but abroad. Furthermore, a request for revision of the award is no longer brought before state courts, but before the arbitral tribunal that rendered the award.

The provisions regarding international arbitration now take into account the international character of the proceedings. Hence, a request to have an award recognized and enforced no longer needs to contain a translation of the award by a certified translator. A free translation is now sufficient. The court may nevertheless subsequently request a certified translation if deemed necessary.

A major change introduced by the decree is the ability for the parties to international arbitration to waive their right to request that the award be set aside. Nevertheless, the parties would still have the ability to appeal an order enforcing the award on the same grounds as those on which an award may be set aside. Hence, this provision is truly useful only in cases where an award is rendered in France, but is to be enforced abroad.

Finally, in order to prevent delaying tactics, a request to have an international arbitration award set aside no longer automatically suspends its enforcement; however, if the enforcement of the award would cause significant harm to a party, the judge may adjust or prevent such enforcement.

The new decree will come into force on 1 May 2011. Transitional provisions will be included for arbitration agreements and clauses entered into before the decree comes into force, ongoing arbitration proceedings and recourse against awards rendered before that date.

B. CASES

B.1 A Non-Signatory to an Arbitration Agreement May Be Considered a Party to That Agreement If It Acts in a Manner Consistent with Being a Party

On 17 February 2011, the Paris Court of Appeal ruled that a party may be considered a signatory to an arbitration agreement if its behavior is consistent with that of a signatory to an arbitration agreement.[5]

In July 1995, a Saudi real estate company, Dallah, entered into a Memorandum of Understanding with the President of the Republic of Pakistan, under which Dallah was to purchase land near Mecca for the housing of Pakistani pilgrims (the "MoU"). In September 1996, Dallah and Awami Hajj Trust (the "Trust"), which had been specifically created by the President of Pakistan, entered into an agreement (the "Agreement"). The Agreement contained an arbitration clause providing for disputes to be brought before the ICC in Paris. The Trust, however, ceased to legally exist two months later.

Dallah launched arbitration proceedings against the Ministry of Religious Affairs of the Government of Pakistan pursuant to the

---

[5] Paris Court of Appeal, 17 February 2011, *Gouvernement du Pakistan – Ministère des Affaires Religieuses v. Société Dallah Real Estate and Tourism Holding Company*, no. 09/28533. The decision came in a case of such great notoriety that, before it was even brought on the court's docket, the case was known simply by the name of one of the parties, Dallah.

arbitration clause in the Agreement. The arbitral tribunal rendered three awards (on jurisdiction, applicable law and the merits) all in favor of Dallah. After French courts had recognized the awards, the Government of Pakistan sought to have the awards set aside on the ground that the arbitral tribunal did not have jurisdiction to hear the dispute.

The French Court of Appeal rejected the Government of Pakistan's request, ruling that the Government had acted consistently with the behavior of a proper party to the agreement throughout pre- and post-contractual dealings. In particular, the court pointed to the pre-contractual MoU between the President of Pakistan and Dallah, which stated that the Government had the authority to approve the terms and conditions of lease agreements and that it reserved the right to confide the management and upkeep of these buildings to a trust. However, even after the trust was established and had signed a contract with Dallah, members of the Government of Pakistan continued to play a role in the performance of the contract in their capacity as members of government, not as members of the trust. Furthermore, the court found that, given this behavior, as well as the fact that government members sat on the board of the trust and guaranteed its finances, the trust was a mere formality that could not shield the government from liability.

In deciding in this manner, the Court of Appeal chose an objective approach to determining who is a party to an arbitration agreement.

It should be noted, however, that the UK Supreme Court had also been asked to rule on the jurisdiction of the arbitral tribunal when the Government of Pakistan appealed the order to enforce the ICC award in England took a different approach. The UK Supreme Court, applying French law, refused enforcement on the grounds that the government was not a true party with regard to the "common intention" of the parties. Based on this standard, the court found that (1) the contract signed with the trust marked a clear change in the transaction, (2) that the structuring of the contract between Dallah and the trust was deliberate, meaning that lawyers on both sides were aware of the consequences of such a structure, and (3) that the trust, a corporate body capable of holding property, had commenced proceedings against Dallah in Pakistan. Although the French and English courts had to interpret the same set of facts and apparently applied the same law, they came to different conclusions as to the intent of the parties.

B.2 An Arbitral Award Does Not Violate Due Process or International Public Policy If, during Arbitral Proceedings, the Tribunal Has Been Shown Classified Documents, So Long As the Tribunal Does Not Base Its Decision on Such Documents

The Paris Court of Appeal added yet another judicial decision to the dispute between Thalès SA & Thalès Underwater ("Thales") and the Republic of China's Navy ("ROCN"), which has generated much judicial as well as media interest and activity.[6]

The dispute between Thales and ROCN involved a sales contract of frigates between the parties and the subsequent payments of funds by Thales to third parties that acted as intermediaries.[7]

The sales agreement provided that no commission was to be paid to third parties, failing which the price could be reduced

---

[6] Paris Court of Appeal, 9 June 2011, *S.A. Thales v. La Marine de la République de Chine*, no. 10/11853.

[7] As detailed in last year's *Baker & McKenzie International Arbitration Yearbook*, the Paris Court of Appeal had already ruled that the presence of classified documents only affected their admissibility, not the arbitrability of the dispute, and that arbitrators must determine when the amount of classified documents leads to a violation of international procedural public policy.

accordingly or the contract annulled. It appeared, however, that Thales had paid significant amounts to intermediaries pursuant to the sale. ROCN thus launched arbitration proceedings before the ICC requesting the reduction of the price as well as damages.

A first award was rendered in which the arbitral tribunal upheld its jurisdiction over the dispute. This was unsuccessfully challenged by Thales.

A second award was rendered in favor of ROCN ordering Thales to pay nearly USD 500 million.

Thales challenged the arbitral award on the grounds, *inter alia*, that it violated due process and international public policy because classified documents had been included in the arbitration file. Thales noted that, although certain documents were eventually withdrawn by the ROCN because information in these documents was retrospectively classified, the documents nevertheless remained on the file for two years, giving the arbitral tribunal ample time to obtain direct knowledge of their contents. Other documents remained in the case file despite Thales's belief that they were confidential and should consequently have been rejected by the arbitral tribunal.

The court concluded that the arbitral tribunal had based its decision on documents that were not deemed confidential or were obtained from the Swiss authorities. The court ruled that no violation of due process or international public policy could have occurred as the arbitrators did not rely on the classified information in making their decision.

B.3 A Domestic Arbitral Award Rendered Abroad and Set Aside May Still Be Enforced in France

On 24 November 2011, the Paris Court of Appeal ruled that an arbitral award that had been set aside in Egypt, the seat of arbitration, should be enforced and recognized in France.[8] The Paris Court of Appeal's decision emphasized the now well-established rule under French case law that an arbitral award is totally disconnected from any state legal system and may be enforced in France despite having been set aside in the country of origin.[9]

The Egyptian state-owned company Société Egyptian General Petroleum Corporation ("EGPC") entered into an agreement with the Egyptian company Société National Gas Company ("NATGAS"), governed by Egyptian law, which provided that any dispute arising out of the agreement should be settled by arbitration under the aegis of the Cairo Regional Centre for International Commercial Arbitration.

The dispute between NATGAS and EGPC involved a gas conveyance contract and the EGPC's refusal to pay damages requested by NATGAS as a result of a change in legislation on the currency exchange and its impact on NATGAS's finance.

On 2 February 2008, NATGAS launched arbitration proceedings against EGPC pursuant to the arbitration agreement. On 12 September 2009, the arbitral tribunal rendered an award in favor of NATGAS.

EGPC challenged the arbitral award in Egypt seeking its annulment. The award was finally set aside in Cairo by both the Court of Appeal and the administrative courts, which considered

---

[8]   Paris Court of Appeal, 24 November 2011, *Société Egyptian General Petroleum Corporation v. Société National Gas Company*, no. 10/16525.

[9]   *See* Cass. civ. 1ère, 23 March 1994, *Société Hilmarton v. Société Omnium de Traitement et De Valorisation*, no. 92/15137; Cass. civ. 1ère, 29 June 2007, *Société PT Putrabali Adyamulia v. Rena Holding*, no. 05/18053 and no. 06/13293; Paris Court of Appeal, 14 January 1997, *République Arab d'Egypte v. Société Chromalloy Aero Services.*

the arbitration clause to be invalid due to the Minister of Petroleum's failure to authorize EGPC to enter into an arbitration agreement.

In spite of the annulment of the arbitral award in Egypt, NATGAS sought to have the award recognized and enforced in France. The president of the Paris Tribunal de Grande Instance ordered that the award be enforced in France. EGPC appealed this order on a number of grounds.

EGPC argued, *inter alia*, that the arbitral award was purely domestic, part of the Egyptian legal order and set aside by the Egyptian domestic courts. Therefore, according to EGPC, the award did not exist and thus could not be enforced in France.

The Paris Court of Appeal denied the appeal on two grounds. The court first considered that Article 1498 of the French Code of Civil Procedure on the recognition in France of international and foreign awards applies to awards rendered abroad regardless of whether they are domestic or international.

Second, the Court of Appeal ruled that the "more favorable law provision" of Article VII(1) of the New York Convention allows French law to be more favorable than the provisions of the New York Convention and thus allows the recognition and enforcement of an award that has been set aside in its country of origin.

Hence, the Paris Court of Appeal extended the well-anchored *Hilmarton* rule, under which international awards rendered abroad may nevertheless be recognized and enforced in France, to an award of a domestic nature rendered abroad and annulled in its country of origin.

B.4 The Party Claiming Absence of Fair Deliberations Must Overcome a Presumption of Fair Deliberations between Arbitrators

In a ruling dated 29 June 2011, the Paris Court of Appeal found that the existence of a collegial meeting between arbitrators as well as the issuing of a dissenting opinion creates a presumption that the arbitral award has been fairly deliberated.[10]

In preparation for the 1987 Mediterranean Games, the President of the Arab Republic of Syria created an organizing committee, which in turn created a publicity committee placed under the aegis of the directorate of the Arab Organization for Publicity ("Golan"). Among other agreements, Golan entered into a framework contract with the Panamanian company Papillon Group Corporation ("PGC") that contained an arbitration clause.

The dispute involved the framework contract. PGC launched arbitration proceedings against Golan and also against the Arab Republic of Syria. The arbitral tribunal held that it lacked jurisdiction regarding the claims against the Arab Republic of Syria and dismissed the other claims on the ground that the statute of limitations had expired.

PGC moved unsuccessfully to have the award set aside by the Paris Court of Appeal. PGC then brought its claim before the French *Cour de Cassation* to have the award set aside. PGC argued, *inter alia*, that the principle of collegiality had been violated by the arbitral tribunal because the arbitrator appointed by PGC was excluded by the two other arbitrators from the deliberation meetings. PGC also argued that the chairman was biased in Syria's favor.

---

[10] Cass. civ. 1ère, 29 June 2011, *Arab Organization for Publicity v. Papillon Group Corporation*, no. 09/17346.

Both the Court of Appeal and the *Cour de Cassation* rejected PGC's claims. The courts noted that the arbitrator appointed by PGC had taken part in one collegial meeting and was given the opportunity to draft a dissenting opinion. This created a presumption of fair deliberations that must be overcome by the party claiming their unfairness, which PGC failed to do.

Finally, both courts rejected PGC's claims regarding the partiality of the chairman of the arbitral tribunal. PGC claimed that the chairman was biased in favor of the Arab Republic of Syria on the ground that he had authored articles criticizing the U.S. and Israel policies in the Middle East. PGC believed that the mere fact that it was based in the United States was detrimental and was sufficient for the chairman to rule in the favor of Syria. The courts rejected PGC's claim on the grounds that the chairman had not voiced in his articles any opinion in favor of Syria and that PGC had nothing to do with the conflict between Israel and Palestine.

B.5 **When a Party Delegates to a Third Party Its Rights and Duties under a Contract Containing an Arbitration Clause, the Third Party Will Be Bound If It Has Knowledge of the Arbitration Clause and Participated in the Performance of the Contract**

In a May 5 ruling, the Paris Court of Appeal added yet another view to the question of who is a true party to an arbitration clause.[11]

In 1974, Dupont de Nemours France and Usines Chimiques Rhône Poulenc entered into a partnership agreement for the purpose of creating a joint venture, Butachimie, for the

---

[11] Paris Court of Appeal, 5 May 2011, *S.A.R.L. Kosa France Holding v. S.A.R.L. Invista*, no. 10/04688.

production and development of the chemical adriponitrile, through the implementation of a technology called GEN I. The partnership agreement provided that the parties could not use or disclose to third parties any confidential information obtained through the joint venture for 15 years.

The partnership agreement contained an arbitration clause and attached numerous underlying agreements for the implementation of the technology, each of which contained an arbitration clause.

After a series of acquisitions, Rhodianyl, a wholly-owned subsidiary of Rhodia SA, succeeded Usines Chimiques Rhône Poulenc. Kova France Holsing, subsidiary of the Dutch company Investa B.V., which owned the Luxembourg company, Invista Sarl, succeeded Dupont de Nemours France.

In September 2007, Invista Sarl initiated legal proceedings against Rhodia SA before the courts of Texas, New York and Delaware, in order to prevent Rhodia SA from using the GEN I technology outside of Butachimie.

Rhodianyl, Rhodia Operations and subsequently Rhodia SA, launched arbitration proceedings before the ICC against Invista Sarl, Invista North America and Kosa France Holding, as per the arbitration clause found in the partnership agreement, in order to have an award assert that the GEN I technology was no longer protected by any law or agreement.

The tribunal found that it had jurisdiction over the claims pertaining to the partnership agreement, i.e., over the claims of Rhodianyl and Rhodia Operations against Kosa France Holding and Invista Sarl, thereby rejecting jurisdiction over the claims involving Rhodia SA and Invista North America. The arbitral tribunal held that the protection of confidential information under the contract was limited to a period of 15 years and, thus, Rhodia was entitled to use the information as it wished.

Invista Sarl and its holding company, Kosa, challenged the award in annulment proceedings on the ground, *inter alia*, that no valid arbitration clause existed between Rhodia Operations and Invista Sarl. Invista Sarl and Kosa argued that the arbitral tribunal should have assessed the intent of the parties to be bound by the arbitration clause and not merely their knowledge thereof and their involvement in the performance of the partnership agreement.

Invista Sarl and Rhodia Operations were not parties to the partnership agreement. They were, however, parties to several of the underlying agreements. The Court of Appeal first noted that Invista Sarl and Rhodia Operations necessarily had knowledge of the existence of the arbitration clause because the underlying contracts were attached to the partnership agreement. In addition, the court found that Invista Sarl's representatives played an active role in the execution of products, represented Invista at Butachimie's general assemblies at which they were systematically present, assumed power over certain financial matters, had full access to facilities, and had one representative on the partnership's IP Committee.

Representatives of Rhodia Operations also took an active role in the partnership, attending the general assemblies and replacing Rhodianyl in the performance of the latter's obligations.

The Paris Court of Appeal merely applied the now well-established principle that knowledge of the arbitration clause and an active part in the performance of the agreement are sufficient to extend the arbitration clause to non-signatories. The court rejected the argument that the intent of the parties to be bound by the arbitration clause was needed.

B.6 An Arbitrator Must Disclose Having Worked in the Same Firm as a Party's Counsel, but Being a "Facebook Friend" with Counsel Did Not Give Rise to a Reasonable Doubt as to the Arbitrator's Independence

In a 10 March 2011 ruling, the Paris Court of Appeal clarified the arbitrator's duties to disclose any link he/she may have with both parties and their counsels.[12]

This case had the distinction of being one, if not *the*, first arbitral dispute that involved an issue concerning the social networking website "Facebook."

An arbitral award had been rendered in a dispute between Tecso and Neoelectra. Tesco sought to have the award set aside on the ground that the chairman of the arbitral tribunal and the other party-appointed arbitrator had not disclosed links with Neoelectra's counsel.

The party-appointed arbitrator became "Facebook friends" with Neolectra's counsel after the award was rendered and this took place in connection with the election to the Paris Bar. The court held that this could not have caused the parties to have reasonable doubt as to the arbitrator's impartiality.

As for the chairman of the tribunal, he practiced in the same law firm as Neoelectra's counsel. Although he had left the firm before the counsel joined the firm, he remained a consultant with a functioning email address after his departure and had attended a conference in the firms' Paris office only four days before he was named chairman. Neoelectra responded that the conference took place in the context of an academic program and that he

---

[12] Paris Court of Appeal, 10 March 2011, *E.U.R.L. Tesco v. S.A.S. Neoelectra Group*, no. 09/28537.

represented Neoelectra in his own capacity and not as an associate of the firm.

Nevertheless, the court found that the arbitrator's relationship with the law firm should have been disclosed for it could have created doubts in the parties' minds as to his impartiality. The award was thus set aside.

B.7 Arbitrators Are Expected to Provide Parties with Statements of Independence When Requested

In this case, the arbitral panel refused to provide a party with statements of independence, despite several requests by one of the parties.

One party thus sought to have the award set aside on the ground that the arbitral tribunal was improperly constituted. After the arbitral panel refused to disclose any links to the claimants, respondent's counsel revealed that claimants' party-appointed arbitrator was taking part in several other arbitration proceedings involving the claimants.

The Paris Court of Appeal held that an arbitrator's refusal to provide a statement of independence, in and of itself, is sufficient to throw into doubt his/her impartiality and independence.[13]

B.8 The Allocation of Interest Is Considered an Issue Pertaining to the Performance of an Agreement

In a ruling dated 3 February 2011, the Paris Court of Appeal found that a tribunal that has already issued its award is not barred by the doctrine of *res judicata* from issuing a further

---

[13] Paris Court of Appeal, 10 March 2011, *Société NYKCOOL v. Société Dole France*, no. 09/21413.

award for interest on arrears when the first award neglected to mention this issue.[14]

The case involved a dispute between Sytrol, a Syrian petroleum company, and Babanapht, a Lebanese company, for the sale of petroleum. An arbitral award of 1982 applying Syrian law ordered Sytrol to pay Babanapht USD 5 million for failure to make deliveries stipulated under the contract, but did not mention any interest payments. However, when this sum was not paid by 1990, Babanapht started a second arbitration that ended in a 1998 award for payment of interest on overdue payments at the rate of 5% and USD 250,000 in arbitration costs.

Sytrol challenged this second award on the ground that Banadapht had not claimed interest in the first arbitration proceeding. Sytrol argued that the allocation of interest was not a breach of the agreement but an issue pertaining to the performance of the award which was in the exclusive jurisdiction of the French Judge of Execution. Sytrol argued therefore that the arbitral tribunal lacked jurisdiction to rule on the question of interests.

The court disagreed with Sytrol and held that the dispute regarding the payment of interest was a direct consequence of the performance of the agreement, thus falling within the jurisdiction of the arbitral tribunal.

B.9 Tort Actions against Arbitrators Are Not Covered by the Arbitration Clause under Which They Were Appointed

A series of rulings from the Paris Court of Appeal and the Tribunal de Grande Instance of Paris has raised some questions

---

[14] Paris Court of Appeal, 3 February 2011, *Département de Commercialisation du Pétrole Petroluem Marketing SYTROL v. S.A.R.L. Babanapht*, no. 08/20951.

about the infallibility and broad scope of the doctrine of "*compétence-compétence*." This dispute arose out of a contract between the Russian company Interneft and the French company Elf Neftgaz, owned by Elf Aquitaine, for the exploration of hydrocarbons in the Russian regions of Saratov and Volgograd. The contract included an arbitration clause providing for arbitration under the aegis of the SCC and with its seat in Stockholm.

Seeking to commence arbitration proceedings in accordance with the agreement after Neftgaz had been dissolved by a shareholder meeting, Interneft asked the Tribunal de Commerce of Nanterre to name an *ad hoc* trustee to represent Neftgaz. In a 28 July 2009 ruling, the Tribunal de Commerce named Mr. Carboni as *ad hoc* trustee. Carboni subsequently designated Mr. Mattei as an arbitrator. Interneft then named its own arbitrator, and the two arbitrators chose a president for the tribunal. However, on 18 September 2009, the Tribunal de Commerce retracted its earlier ruling on the grounds that there were inaccuracies in the claim presented to the tribunal. The Tribunal de Commerce appointed a new *ad hoc* trustee, Mr. Rouger.

Elf Neftgaz subsequently requested that French courts find that the arbitral tribunal was improperly constituted because Mr. Carboni did not have the power to appoint Mr. Mattei as arbitrator. The Court of Appeal confirmed the decision of the lower court and dismissed Elf Neftgaz's claim on the ground that it did not have jurisdiction to rule on the constitution of the arbitral tribunal before an award is rendered because the seat of the arbitration was not in France.[15]

On 21 March 21 the arbitral tribunal issued a provisional award noting that Elf Neftgaz had been validly represented as of 28

---

[15] Paris Court of Appeal, 6 January 2011, *Interneft v. Neftgaz*, no. 10/20243.

July 2009 and that the tribunal had been validly constituted upon the naming of the president. Thereafter, Elf asked the courts of Stockholm to declare that the three arbitrators did not have jurisdiction for reasons of public order and flaws in the constitution of the tribunal.

Additionally, Elf Neftgaz sued the three arbitrators in France, asking the Tribunal de Grande Instance to find that the arbitral process led by the three arbitrators was not only fraudulent, but an illicit act. The arbitrators argued that French courts had no jurisdiction to hear claims against the arbitral tribunal and its composition and that the French courts can only deal with an international arbitration once the award is rendered.

In a 29 June 2011 order, the Tribunal de Grande Instance held that the instant case did not constitute a situation covered by the arbitration agreement in the contract, as the arbitrators were sued in their individual capacities on the basis of their liability in tort, and thus the principle of *compétence-compétence* did not apply.[16] Furthermore, the court noted that it had both subject matter jurisdiction as well as territorial jurisdiction, due to the fact that two of the arbitrators resided in Paris.

B.10 A Party Is Estopped from Challenging a State Court's Jurisdiction If It Has Already Waived Its Rights under the Arbitration Clause

In a 26 October 2011 decision, the Cour de Cassation reaffirmed the principle that parties are subject to estoppel and thus a party may not challenge the jurisdiction of the state courts if it had already turned to the state courts for other claims against the

---

[16] Ordre of the Juge de la mise en état, 29 June 2011, *Elf Aquitaine and Total v. Mattei, Kamara and Reiner*, no. 10/13652.

same party and under the same agreement in disregard of the arbitration clause contained therein.[17]

Constructions Mécaniques de Normandie ("CMN"), which had been awarded a contract for the construction of two yachts (the contract included an arbitration clause), subcontracted the painting of the ship to the Swedish company Fagerdala Marine Systems ("FMS"), which subcontracted its work to the German company Patroun Korrosionsschutz Und Consuult Und Consulting ("PKC"). After CMN breached the contract, PKC sought payment of various sums from FMS and CMN in proceedings before a French judge. FMS in turn initiated arbitral proceedings against both CMN and PKC. CMN challenged the jurisdiction of the court over the claims brought by PKC.

Both the summary judge in first instance and the court of appeal held that the state court had jurisdiction and dismissed the jurisdictional challenges. CMN appealed the decision before the Cour de Cassation. Subsequently, CMN also initiated a suit against PKC before a state court for damages.

The court found that CMN was estopped from relying upon the arbitration clause. CMN could not waive the benefit of the arbitration clause when filing claims against PKC and FMW, while, at the same time, challenging the state courts' jurisdiction over the claims brought by PKC.

B.11 A Partner in a Company Can Be Deemed to Have Validly Agreed to an Arbitration Clause Found in the Company's Bylaws

The Court of Cassation ruled that a partner in a company is deemed to have implicitly and necessarily accepted the bylaws of

---

[17]   Court of Cassation, 26 October 2011, *Patroun Korrosionsschutz Und Consuult Und Consulting v. Constructions Mécaniques de Normandie*, no. 10/17708.

a company, including an arbitration clause found therein, if he or she chooses to participate in the company after being given the option of withdrawing.[18]

The subject of the dispute was a Saudi company created after the death of Mr. Mohammad Ben Awad X, the owner of a large construction corporation, to hold his assets for the purpose of his 58 heirs, all partners in the company. Mrs. Elham X, daughter of Mohammad X, sued Mr. Yeslam X, director of the company, in a Swiss court for damages. She also sued Mr. Issa X, a member of the company's board of directors, as well as the members of the company's supervisory board, and the company itself, before the Paris Tribunal de Grande Instance, asking that the defendants provide the accounts and balance sheets of the company for the years 1990 to 2001.

For their part, the defendants argued that the court did not have jurisdiction to rule on this matter in light of the company's bylaws, which includes an arbitration clause. Mrs. X argued that the arbitration clause was manifestly invalid because it provides for the King of Saudi Arabia to choose the arbitrators from the supervisory board (a party to the dispute), that she did not accept the arbitration clause as she did not personally sign the company's bylaws, and that the death of several members of the supervisory board made the arbitration clause manifestly inapplicable.

A ruling by the Tribunal de Grande Instance siding with the defendants on the subject of the court's jurisdiction was confirmed by the Court of Appeal. The Cour de Cassation upheld the lower court rulings, stating that the fact that the King would choose the arbitrators was sufficient to ensure the independence and impartiality of the tribunal. Furthermore, the

---

[18]   Court of Cassation, 26 October 2011, *Elham X... v. Issa X...,* no. 10/15968.

court ruled that Mrs. X had implicitly decided to adhere to the company's bylaws (and, thus, the arbitration clause) because she had been given the option to immediately receive her portion of the inheritance. Finally, the court ruled that the arbitration agreement was not manifestly inapplicable, noting that, under the agreement, the King had the power to replace deceased arbitrators.

B.12 Arbitrators Have a Duty to Disclose Factual Circumstances Involving Firms to Which They Belong and Parties May Still Seek to Set Aside the Award despite Not Having Challenged the Arbitrator during the Proceedings

The Reims Court of Appeal ruled that arbitrators must disclose factual circumstances involving firms to which they belong.[19]

The case concerned the chairman of the arbitral tribunal in a dispute between companies J&P Avax and Tecnimont. The chairman failed to disclose that he had been Of Counsel at a firm that had represented Tecnimont on six occasions. The award was set aside in 2009 by the Paris Court of Appeal on these grounds, but this ruling was overturned by the Cour de Cassation and remanded to the Reims Court of Appeal.

The Reims Court of Appeal came to the same conclusion as the Paris Court of Appeal and set aside the award on the ground that the chairman should have disclosed, during the entire length of the arbitration, any link between his firm and the parties.

One interesting aspect of the case involved the 30 day time limit prescribed by the ICC Rules to file a challenge to arbitrators (the new Article 1456 of the French Code of Civil Procedure, introduced earlier this year, also provides for a 30 day period to challenge an arbitrator) and its impact on parties' right to have an independent and impartial tribunal. The court found that Avax's

---

[19]   Reims CA, 2 November 2011, *Avax v. Tecnimont*, no. 10/02888.

failure to challenge the award within the 30 day period did not preclude it from applying to set aside the award on a similar ground (i.e., the defect on the constitution of the arbitral tribunal), noting that a challenge before an arbitral institution and a court's review on a request to set aside the award are separate proceedings that do not serve the same purpose and are not controlled by the same parties.

This particular ruling provoked some dismay among scholars who argue that ICC Rules cannot be bypassed because they contain contractual obligations that bind the arbitrators and the parties. This would also open the door to dilatory tactics. A party may decide not to challenge an arbitrator during the proceedings and nevertheless seek the annulment of an unfavorable award on those grounds.

The case has been appealed to the Cour de Cassation, which will weigh in on the Court of Appeal's ruling.

B.13 The Conseil Contitutionnel Does Not Have Jurisdiction to Rule on a Preliminary Question of Constitutionality From an Arbitral Tribunal

The Cour de Cassation recently held that an arbitral tribunal is not considered a "court" under Article 23-1 of the 1958 Ordinance establishing the Constitutional Court, which allows lower courts to request an opinion from the Conseil Constitutionnel, the highest court in charge of interpreting legislation and ruling on its constitutionality.[20]

In the instant case, an arbitrator named by the head of the Paris Bar Association to resolve a dispute between a lawyer and the law firm from which he resigned asked the Cour de Cassation to

---

[20]   Cass. com., 28 June 2011, *Mrs. A v. SCP Flichy Grangé Avocats*, no.11-40030.

allow him to request that the Conseil Constitutionnel rule on a constitutional challenge to Article 1843-4 of the Civil Code. The arbitrator asked whether the article, which provides for a final determination by an expert or arbitrator of the value of a departing partner's share in the organization, contravenes Article 16 of the Declaration of Rights of Men and the Citizen based on the final nature of the assessment.

The court ruled that the arbitral tribunal, the jurisdictional power of which results from the mutual intention of the parties, is not considered to be a "court" in the sense of Article 23-1 and, thus, may not refer a preliminary question of constitutionality. This decision is a direct consequence of the decision of the European Court of Justice in the *Nordsee* case, in which the ECJ held that arbitral tribunals cannot be considered as "courts" of a member state.[21]

C. PUBLIC POLICY IN INTERNATIONAL ARBITRATION

C.1 Scenarios of Reliance on Public Policy

Under French law, a party can invoke public policy considerations as a defense in pending proceedings to invalidate the arbitration agreement and as a ground to set aside an award or prevent its recognition and enforcement in France.

C.1.1. As a defense in pending proceedings to invalidate the arbitration agreement

While under French law, a violation of public policy can serve as a defense in pending proceedings to invalidate the arbitration agreement, in practice, French judges will most often not be in a

---

[21] ECJ, 23 March 1982, °102/81, *Rev. Arb.* 1982, 473.

position to invalidate the arbitration agreement at that stage based on a violation of public policy.

In effect, under the French Code of Civil Procedure, the arbitral tribunal has exclusive jurisdiction to decide any issue relating to its own jurisdictional powers.[22] The only exceptions are where the arbitral tribunal is not yet constituted and where the arbitration agreement is manifestly null or manifestly non-applicable.[23]

Similarly, where a party refuses to take part in the process provided for in the arbitration agreement for appointment of the arbitrator(s), a French judge shall appoint the arbitrator,[24] unless the judge finds the arbitration agreement manifestly null or manifestly inapplicable.

As a consequence, unless the judge is able to decide, on a *prima facie* review, that the arbitration clause is manifestly null, the judge must defer the issue of the validity of the arbitration clause to the arbitral tribunal.

Thus, as the judge is not entitled to carry out any analysis at that stage, only in very exceptional circumstances will a judge be in a position to decide that an arbitration agreement's violation of public policy is so obvious that the arbitration agreement is "manifestly null."

For instance, in circumstances such as the ones giving rise to the *Jivraj v. Hashwani* case,[25] French judges would most likely have

---

[22] Article 1465 of the French Code of Civil Procedure.

[23] Article 1488 of the French Code of Civil Procedure.

[24] See C.2. *infra.*

[25] In *Jivraj v. Hashwani* [2011] UKSC40, 27 July 2011, the arbitration clause provided as follows: "all arbitrators shall be respected members of the Ismaili community and holders of high office within the community." The issue was

considered that the alleged violation of the non-discrimination principle would not be so obvious as to render the arbitration agreement manifestly null. French judges would thus have appointed an arbitrator as per the arbitration agreement. It would then have been for the arbitrators to decide on their own jurisdiction including any issue regarding the alleged violation of the non-discrimination principle.

C.1.2. As a defense against recognition and enforcement of an award

Under French law, a party can invoke public policy both in an action to set aside an international award rendered in France and as a defense against recognition and enforcement in France of a foreign award.

Regarding actions to set aside an award, Article 1520(5) of the French Code of Civil Procedure provides that courts can vacate an international arbitral award rendered in France where the recognition or enforcement of the award would be contrary to international public policy.

Regarding recognition and enforcement of a foreign award, Article 1514 provides that arbitral awards shall be recognized or enforced in France if their existence is established and their recognition or enforcement would not be *manifestly* contrary to international public policy. Thus, in *ex parte* proceedings for recognition and enforcement of a foreign award, the review of compliance with international public policy is merely *prima facie*.

However, where the order granting recognition and enforcement of a foreign award is challenged, Article 1525 of the French

---

whether this constituted a valid arbitration clause in view of the UK equality (Religion and Belief) regulations 2003 prohibiting employment discrimination.

Code of Civil Procedure expressly provides that the *ex parte* order can be appealed on the same grounds as those provided for under Article 1520(5).

The standard of international public policy control is thus the same in an action to set aside an international award rendered in France and in an appeal against a recognition and enforcement order of a foreign award.

C.2 Modes and Limitations of Reliance on Public Policy

C.2.1. As a defense in pending proceedings

Public policy is invoked as a defense in pending proceedings at the stage of the constitution of the arbitral tribunal when one of the parties maintains that the arbitration agreement *per se*, or its enforcement under the circumstances, would be contrary to public policy.

Any refusal from any party to take part in the constitution of the arbitral tribunal, whether based on public policy or any other grounds, will be dealt with under the same principles and limitations.

Under French law, where the arbitration agreement does not provide for an arbitral institution, the President of the Paris Tribunal de Grande Instance, the civil court of first instance, acts as *juge d'appui*. This judge resolves procedural disputes regarding the constitution of the arbitral tribunal in international arbitration when proceedings take place in France, the parties have chosen French procedural law, the parties have expressly given French courts jurisdiction, or one of the parties is exposed to a risk of denial of justice.[26]

---

[26] Art. 1505, French Code of Civil Procedure.

As described above, the *juge d'appui*'s review is limited to ensuring that the arbitration agreement is not manifestly null or inapplicable. Only in limited circumstances will a violation of public policy be so patent that the *juge d'appui* would regard the arbitration agreement as manifestly null.

However, violation of public policy has been successfully raised in certain cases before the judge as a defense in pending proceedings to invalidate the arbitration agreement. For example, under French public policy, arbitration clauses in employment contracts, even of an international nature, cannot be enforced against the employee. French case law contains numerous examples of instances where arbitration clauses in international employment contracts have not been enforced by French judges based on that principle.[27]

C.2.2. As a defense against recognition and enforcement of an award

Proceedings to set aside awards rendered in France on international public policy grounds as well as on any other grounds must be made within a month from the notification of the arbitral award.[28]

An appeal against a recognition and enforcement order of a foreign award, whether on the grounds of violation of public policy or any other grounds must be brought within one month following service of the order.[29]

Under Article 1466 of the Code of Civil Procedure, a party that knowingly, and without a legitimate reason, failed to object to an

---

[27] Cass. Soc. 12 March 2008 no. 01-44.654, jurisdata: 2008-043200.

[28] Article 1519, French Code of Civil Procedure.

[29] *Id.* at Article 1525.

France

irregularity before the arbitral tribunal in a timely manner shall be deemed to have waived its right to avail itself of such irregularity. A party would thus be estopped from raising an international public policy objection at the stage of an action to set aside an award or challenging a recognition and enforcement order if it failed to do so in a timely manner before the arbitral tribunal. In this respect, the decision by the Reims Court of Appeal of 2 November 2011, discussed *supra* in section B.12[30] does not seem to be in line with this principle. This case has been appealed, but the Cour de Cassation has not rendered its decision yet.

Under French law, a foreign award can be enforced in France in spite of the fact that the award was vacated in its country of origin. In the *Hilmarton* case, the Court of Cassation ruled that an international arbitration award is international in nature and is not attached to any legal system, including that of the seat, meaning that the award continues to exist even if annulled at the seat.[31] This doctrine has since been confirmed in a number of instances, and is now regarded as well-established[32] (see, for instance, the decision by the Paris Court of Appeal of 24 November 2011 discussed *supra* at section B.3).[33] Therefore, even where a foreign award was vacated in its country of origin on the grounds of violation of international public policy, such an award can be recognized and enforced in France, unless the French judge rules that the award actually violates international public policy as understood in France.

---

[30] Reims CA, 2 November, 2011, *Avax v. Tecnimont*, no. 10/02888.

[31] Cass. Civ. 1ère 23 March 1994, no. 92/15.137.

[32] CA Paris, 14 January 2007, *Rev. Arb.* 1997 p. 395, and for a more recent example: CA Paris, 24 November 2011 see B.3 above.

[33] Paris Court of Appeal, 24 November 2011, *Société Egyptian General Petroleum Corporation v. Société National Gas Company*, no. 10/16525.

C.3 Rules that Constitute "Public Policy"

In this respect, French law distinguishes between international and domestic arbitral awards. For domestic awards, Article 1492(5) of the Code of Civil Procedure allows for vacating an award if it is contrary to public policy, whereas Article 1520(5) allows for courts to set aside only international awards whose enforcement or recognition are contrary to *international* public policy. The scope of public policy is thus more limited in international arbitration. While public policy in the context of domestic arbitration includes all French mandatory rules of public policy, international public policy in the context of international arbitration will be limited to French public policy of an international nature, i.e., the set of values a breach of which would not be tolerated by the French legal order, even in international cases.

International public policy has both procedural and substantive elements. The procedural element includes due process (also its own grounds for refusing enforcement or recognition), equality of the parties[34] and deception of arbitrators.[35] However, courts have ruled that an international award rendered without stating any reasons for the decision does not constitute a violation of international public policy.

Violations of international substantive public policy are rare. The result of an award must be contrary to the fundamental convictions of French law at the time the court is to decide to enforce or recognize the award. Examples of arbitral awards contrary to substantive international public policy would be awards upholding religious, racial, or ethnic discrimination.

---

[34] Cass. Civ. 1, 7 January 1992. *DUTCO*, no. 89-18708, 89-18726.

[35] CA Paris, 1 July 2010 – *THALES v. Marine de la République de Chine*, Rev. Arb. 2010, p. 863 *et seq.*

However, an award rendered by arbitrators appointed as per an arbitration clause similar to the one in the *Jivraj* case (see C.1.1 *supra*) would not be regarded as contrary to international public policy provided the result of the award itself is not discriminatory. French authors tend to think that arbitrators are not employees of the parties and the parties must be free to draft an arbitration clause that will provide for the appointment of arbitrators whom they believe will be the most suitable to decide their case. However, we are not aware of any French case law in circumstances similar to the *Jivraj* case.

Awards upholding a contract for an illegal purpose or a corrupt act, and violation of European competition law and some provisions of French bankruptcy law, are also contrary to international public policy.

In addition, French courts have introduced a severity threshold. Not every breach of international public policy can be invoked. The violation of international public policy must be "flagrant, effective, and concrete." Some decisions further state that the violation of international public policy must be "blatantly obvious."[36]

French courts have thus taken a "minimalist" and restrictive approach to the control of arbitral awards on the grounds of violation of international public policy.

C.4   Review of Alleged Breaches of Public Policy

While arbitral tribunals review all alleged breaches of public policy under the applicable law, the review of alleged breaches of international public policy by French courts at the stage of an action to set aside an award or a defense against enforcement of

---

[36]   CA Paris, 18 November 2004, *Thales v. Euromissile,* no. 2002/19606, which states in French that the violation must *"crever les yeux."*

an award are strictly limited to international public policy as seen above. In particular, French courts shall not consider foreign public policy rules and principles.

Furthermore, it is not the abstract rule of law that must be measured against international public policy, but the actual result that it produces. A recent example can be found in the Thales and ROCN decision (see B.2 *supra*) where it was alleged that the filing of classified documents constituted a violation of international public policy. The court ruled that no violation of due process or international public policy occurred, as the arbitrators did not rely on the classified information in making the award.

The Cour de Cassation is very cautious that no review of the merits of the award is carried out under cover of an alleged violation of international public policy.

GERMANY

Ragnar Harbst,[1] Heiko Plassmeier,[2] and Jürgen Mark[3]

A. LEGISLATION, TRENDS AND TENDENCIES

A.1 Duration and Cost of Arbitration Proceedings

Duration and cost of arbitration proceedings have been a concern of companies for quite a while, and the complaints are only getting louder. There is hardly an arbitration journal or conference where in-house counsel of multinationals do not voice their—justified—concerns about the downsides of the arbitral process. It seems that these concerns are gaining momentum in Germany.

From the user's perspective, the concerns are the length and the costs of arbitral proceedings. The sophistication of the arbitral process has reached a level that is becoming a problem. For businesses, a well-founded and "just" decision after four years of

---

[1] Ragnar Harbst is a Partner in Baker & McKenzie's Frankfurt office. He has acted in numerous international arbitration proceedings, both as party representative and as arbitrator. His practice focuses on construction and infrastructure related disputes. Mr. Harbst is also qualified as a solicitor in England and Wales.

[2] Heiko Plassmeier is a Counsel in Baker & McKenzie's Düsseldorf office. He advises and represents clients from various industries, including the energy and automotive sectors, in domestic and international litigation and arbitration cases and has served as an arbitrator in corporate and post-M&A cases. Mr. Plassmeier also handles insolvency matters.

[3] Jürgen Mark is a Partner in Baker & McKenzie's Düsseldorf office and a member of the Firm's European Dispute Resolution Practice Group Steering Committee. He practices in the areas of litigation and domestic and international arbitration. Mr. Mark has also acted as arbitrator in *ad hoc*, ICC and DIS arbitrations relating to corporate and post-M&A disputes, major construction projects, product distribution and products liability.

arbitration, hundreds of pages of submissions, thousands of exhibits, document disclosure, a two-week hearing and tremendous costs is often a cure worse than the disease. If offered a lesser degree of sophistication in the arbitral process in exchange for a guarantee that the dispute would be decided within a year and a half, quite a few businesses would take the deal. Planning is an important element of business, and businesses do not like the idea of being caught in arbitration for several years, with an unpredictable outcome at high costs. However one structures the process, the outcome will be hard to predict (otherwise there would not be a dispute). But such a risk is easier to accept for clients if the result is not four years away, and if the costs are manageable.

A.2   What is the Cause for the Complaints?

No. 1: Arbitration combines time- and money-consuming elements from both the civil law and the common law tradition

International arbitration proceedings are becoming more and more "transnational." That is to say that arbitrations in an international setting are no longer conducted either in "common law style" or "civil law style," rather, they are a combination of both. The written phase of the arbitration preceding the hearing resembles civil law proceedings in that it involves the exchange of not just skeleton arguments, but extensive and detailed written submissions. Already at this stage, however, there are elements of common law litigation added to the process, most importantly, the production of documents by one party at the request of the other. The oral phase predominantly follows the common law approach, in that there is an extensive evidentiary hearing with witnesses from both sides, on more or less relevant issues, and extensive questioning by attorneys. After the hearing, there will almost invariably be closing submissions, again often extensive, and occasionally including rebutting closing submissions. All elements may have their justification in the context of the legal tradition from which they derive. However, combining elements from both the civil and the common law world does not necessarily create the best of all possible worlds, but can make international arbitration a method of dispute resolution that is more complex than pure civil law or common law proceedings would be on their own.

No. 2: Tribunals are hesitant to manage cases actively

In international arbitration, there is a growing tendency for arbitrators to remain passive and not manage cases actively. Why is this so?

First, arbitrators are often afraid of procedural complaints. The notion that arbitration is more friendly and amicable than litigation has probably always been a myth, but it certainly is today. Arbitration is often fought with no holds barred. Tactically-motivated complaints about violations of natural justice or of the right to be heard or complaints about biased arbitrators occur more and more frequently. How do arbitrators respond to this development? They try to avoid situations that could make them a target for such complaints and are therefore reluctant to streamline proceedings in the sense that they, for example, restrict pleadings to issues which the arbitrators think are relevant and material. Arbitrators are also hesitant to turn down requests for leave to adduce additional evidence, pleadings, etc., because they want to avoid complaints that the right to be heard was violated.

Second, the international arbitral process leans to a large extent on the common law tradition, where the judge traditionally remained passive and decided the case on the basis of—more or less unrestricted—presentations by both sides ("The judge who opens his mouth closes his mind"). Or, as Lord Greene once put it, the judge who takes an active role "descends into the arena and is liable to have his vision clouded by the dust of conflict." Arbitrators from common law countries tend to give the parties and their lawyers a more active role in the proceedings. The result is a paradox; international arbitration nowadays tends to be more conservative than its role model, i.e., common law style litigation, as reforms in countries like England have made the role of the judge more active.

Third, an arbitral tribunal is not as homogenous as a chamber of judges. It is an open secret that party-appointed arbitrators tend to keep in mind, within the legal limits, which of the parties had appointed them. Accordingly, issuing procedural orders cutting off party statements on certain issues, or calling for additional statements on other issues, is not as easy for an arbitral tribunal as it would be for a chamber of state court judges.

Fourth, some arbitrators may prefer the passive approach because it makes their lives easier. Taking an active role requires a much better command of the facts of the case. For the arbitrators, the neutral and passive approach can lead to a welcome reduction in workload.

The passive role of the tribunal reinforces the problem. Faced with a silent tribunal, the arbitration counsel faces some tough decisions. He or she may believe that enough has been said on a certain issue, and that the submissions of the other party need not be commented upon. But what does the tribunal think? Does the tribunal share this view, or would it welcome further pleadings on certain aspects and if so, on which aspects? Faced with this situation, the lawyer will, and often must, under his or her professional liability rules, recommend the safest option to the client—to comment further.

A.3 Is There a Cure?

The pressure on the arbitral process to become more efficient is increasing. But what can be done? Some of the options will be discussed below.

Changing the Rules: Many arbitration institutions have changed their rules, or are in the process of doing so, in order to accommodate the user's need for more efficient proceedings. Recently, the ICC has promulgated its new rules that entered into force in January 2012. One of the objectives is to speed up the proceedings, i.e., by requesting the arbitrators to give a declaration on their availability before accepting the mandate, and by prescribing a case management conference at the beginning of the arbitration. It is doubtful, though, whether this will have a major effect on time and costs in arbitration, in particular if the scope of the arbitration is extended by the parties or the factual and legal issues are more complicated than expected.

Encourage Arbitrators to Take a More Active Role in Arbitration Proceedings: In our view, a lot of time and resources in international arbitration are spent, if not wasted, on elaborating on points that are not material and relevant to the outcome of the case. In the absence of an indication as to which points are material and relevant, the parties and their counsel are often stabbing in the dark and feel forced to "leave no stone unturned." It would help to streamline arbitral proceedings if the arbitrators were to actively manage the arbitration, and were to give an early indication as to which areas of the dispute they want the parties to focus on. Has enough been said on causation, delay, and liability quantum, or should the parties elaborate further? Would the tribunal welcome further pleadings on the legal aspects applying to the liability cap, repudiation or constructive delay? There is a tendency in international arbitration to hear all witnesses proffered by the parties. A lot of time and resources could be saved if witness hearings were restricted to testimony that is material and relevant to the outcome of the case.

The German civil court system incorporates such techniques which could also be used in international arbitration proceedings. Under German civil procedure rules, for example, judges have an obligation to ensure that parties make full statements about material facts, elaborate on insufficient statements and, to this end, discuss with the parties the case, issues, factual and legal aspects and to ask questions.[4]

A slightly similar provision is also found in Section 24.2 of the Rules of the German Institution of Arbitration, requiring the arbitral tribunal to obtain from the parties comprehensive statements regarding all relevant facts. German judges are also trained to analyze the parties' pleadings and to determine which of the pleaded facts are relevant and which of these relevant facts are disputed. A German court will only take evidence with respect to disputed relevant facts, and only if the party relying on such facts has provided evidence to support the allegation. Each party bears the burden of proof for the correctness of the factual allegations on which the party's case relies. Discovery/production of documents only exists in exceptional cases. The employment by arbitral tribunals of similar techniques could be a major asset for Germany as a seat for international arbitration.

Introducing such provisions in arbitration rules is often rejected on the basis that they would not be suitable for an international institution with customers from all parts of the world. Especially for users from common law countries, it is said that an obligation for the "judge" to participate actively and streamline the proceedings would be unacceptable. But is this correct? A user— that is a company—is not concerned about preserving the root

---

[4]   Section 139 of the German Code of Civil Procedure, ("ZPO").

ideas of the common law system, but about time and money. What is more, the English litigation system itself had to address very similar concerns and did so by implementing the Woolf Reforms. As a result, English judges are these days obligated to manage litigation actively in order to reduce expense and duration. In many respects, arbitration therefore runs the risk of becoming the hideaway of antiquated legal traditions. In addition, it is currently the civil law user who is forced to accept common law concepts, for example document production, as a standard process in international arbitration despite the fact that civil law parties are normally unfamiliar with and insufficiently prepared to face such proceedings. As a result, the expectations of parties from civil law countries as to the time and costs of international arbitration are often disappointed.

B.   CASES

B.1   No Preclusion of the Right to Resist Enforcement of an Award in Germany for Failure to Challenge at the Place of Arbitration

If the losing party in an international arbitration wants to resist the award, it is faced with the decision whether to challenge the award at the place of arbitration, or to defend itself in enforcement proceedings commenced by the other side. Whether to follow the "active approach," and commence challenge proceedings, or the "passive approach," and react in the enforcement proceedings, is determined by strategic considerations. More important, however, is whether and to what extent the law at the place of enforcement permits a defense in enforcement proceedings that the losing party could have argued if it had commenced challenge proceedings at the place of arbitration.

Different countries follow different regimes in this regard. The German Federal Supreme Court has recently changed its approach towards this question, at least in respect of objections to the jurisdiction of the arbitral tribunal.[5] The decision related to an arbitral award rendered by a tribunal under the auspices of the International Chamber of Arbitration for Fruit and Vegetables in Paris. The winning side sought a declaration of enforceability of the award before the Court of Appeal Munich. The Respondent resisted enforcement, arguing that no valid arbitration agreement existed. The same jurisdictional defense had already been submitted in the arbitral proceedings, but the arbitral tribunal had assumed jurisdiction in its final award. The losing party had not initiated proceedings to challenge the award before the competent Court of Appeal in Paris. Meanwhile, the time period for initiating such challenge proceedings in France had lapsed.

The Court of Appeal Munich, as later confirmed by the Federal Supreme Court, refused to declare the award enforceable due to the lack of a written arbitration agreement within the meaning of Article II(2) of New York Convention. It held that the respondent was not barred from raising the jurisdictional defense due to the fact that it had not initiated challenge proceedings at the place of the arbitration within the applicable statutory time period. The court further held that this would not constitute a violation of the principle of good faith. In this regard, the Federal Supreme Court notably held that the respondent had not waived its right to raise the jurisdictional objection in the enforcement proceedings.

---

[5] Federal Supreme Court, decision of 16 December 2010, file no. III ZB 100/09; *SchiedsVZ* 2011, 105. Most decisions cited in this chapter can be found in the database on the website of the German Institution of Arbitration ("DIS") – www.dis-arb.de – (often with an English summary). Where applicable, it is noted if a decision was also published in a law journal.

The decision is noteworthy, as it deviates from previous case law of the Federal Supreme Court. Under the former German arbitration law (in effect until 31 December 1997), the Federal Supreme Court had held that a party was barred from raising jurisdictional defenses that could have been argued in challenge proceedings at the place of arbitration if the time limit for such proceedings had expired.[6] According to Section 1044(2)(1) of the former German Code of Civil Procedure, the test for admissibility of jurisdictional objections in the enforcement proceedings was whether the arbitral award was "valid." Under the old arbitration law, the Federal Supreme Court had taken the view that the validity depended on whether the award could still be challenged at the place of arbitration. The court now held that the legal framework changed when Section 1061(1) of the new Code of Civil Procedure was enacted.

The resolution of this question has great practical importance. Both in decisions of various German courts of appeal and in academic writing, the question had previously been answered differently.[7] From the user's perspective, however, it is questionable whether the decision is a welcome one. Under the former arbitration law, the losing party was obligated to put its cards on the table, i.e., either to pursue its defense actively in

---

[6] Federal Supreme Court, decision of 26 June 1969, file no. VII ZR 32/67, BGHZ 52, 184, 188; BGH NJW 1984, 2763, 2764.

[7] The Courts of Appeal Stuttgart (decisions of 14 October 2003, files nos. 1 Sch 16/02 und 1 Sch 06/03, available in the database on the DIS website) and Karlsruhe (decision of 3 July 2006, file no. 9 Sch 1/06, *SchiedsVZ* 2006, 281) had held that the new legislation had not changed the position (to the same extent Münchener Kommentar-*Münch*, ZPO, 3rd ed. 2008, Sec. 1061, note 12), while the Bavarian Court of Appeal (decision of 16 March 2000, file no. 4Z Sch 50/99, NJW-RR 2001, 431), the Court of Appeal Schleswig (decision of 30 March 2000, file no. 16 SchH 5/99, RIW 2000, 706) and (e.g.) *Schwab/Walter*, Schiedsgerichtsbarkeit, 7th ed. 2005, Chapter 30, note 19 took the view that it had.

challenge proceedings or to surrender the defense for good. Under the new regime, the successful party must initiate costly proceedings for the recognition and enforcement of the award, not knowing whether the jurisdictional defense is still available. At the same time, however, it must be acknowledged that the losing party may have legitimate reasons for not initiating challenge proceedings at the place of arbitration. It may, for example, lack sufficient trust in the independence of the local courts, or such challenge proceedings may be overly burdensome for other reasons.

B.2   Termination of an Arbitrator's Mandate for Undue Delay of the Proceedings

On 17 December 2010, the Court of Appeal Munich decided on an application for termination of an arbitrator's mandate for undue delay of the proceedings in accordance with Section 1038(1) ZPO.[8] According to this provision, a court can terminate the mandate of an arbitrator if an arbitrator becomes *de jure* or *de facto* unable to perform his functions or if he for other reasons fails to act without undue delay.

The domestic decision concerned an arbitration about the dissolution of a partnership between two tax accountants. The arbitral proceedings had commenced in November 2002. In May 2003, the sole arbitrator tasked a tax accountant as an independent expert with the preparation of an expert opinion on the value of the due compensation payment. The expert opinion was only rendered in early 2008. The delay was partly due to the parties, partly due to the expert's failure to expedite his opinion, and partly due to a lack of attention by the arbitrator. The arbitrator then asked the parties to comment on the expert

---

[8]   Court of Appeal Munich, decision of 17 December 2010, file no. 34 SchH 06/10.

opinion, and after these comments were submitted, gave the expert an opportunity to comment on the parties' objections until July 2008. In June 2009, the arbitrator issued another procedural order, asking the expert to reply to further questions by the parties. In September 2009, the claimant requested to replace the expert. The arbitrator asked the respondent to comment on this request, the respondent explained in October 2009 that it did not deem such reply necessary and suggested to fix a date for a hearing in due course. Between November 2009 and July 2010, proceedings basically came to a standstill. In July 2010, the claimant filed an application with the Court of Appeal Munich to terminate the mandate of the arbitrator based on Section 1038(1) ZPO for undue delay of the proceedings.

The court determined that the arbitrator was *de jure* and *de facto* able to perform his functions, so that the only question was whether he had failed to act without undue delay. It determined that the relevant test was whether it would constitute an undue burden for the parties to wait for a longer period of time. Section 1038(1) ZPO was held to apply if arbitral proceedings are delayed in a way that causes the parties to suffer disadvantages that they would not suffer in state court proceedings. The court added that such undue burden could only be assumed in cases of evident misuse or in "one-off cases." The court also stated that parties would generally expect a more expeditious procedure from arbitration proceedings than from state court proceedings; in this regard, however, it had to be taken into account that— contrary to state court proceedings—an arbitral tribunal had to decide the matter in dispute in one instance only. The court further explained that Section 1038(1) ZPO was not intended as an opportunity for state courts to impose their own structure and timetables on arbitral tribunals. The termination of the mandate of an arbitrator in accordance with this provision could therefore only occur in exceptional cases. Further, the court explained that the overall duration of the proceedings and the difficulty of the case must be balanced against any delays that might occur during the proceedings.

Applying these guidelines to the facts of the case, the court held that the comparatively long period for preparation of the expert opinion was not within the responsibility of the arbitrator. The delays that occurred thereafter were held to have been comprehensibly explained by the arbitrator; they related to the restructuring of his own law firm. The court reasoned that one would have to compare the delays between 2008 and 2010 to the delays that had occurred before this date, i.e., between May 2003 and January 2008. In doing so, the court determined that no undue delay within the meaning of the Section 1038(1) ZPO had occurred.

B.3 Form Requirements for Arbitration Agreements with Consumers

In January 2011, the Federal Supreme Court held that an arbitration clause in a standard form contract between a foreign online broker and German consumers was invalid and that the German courts had jurisdiction to decide the complaints filed by the German consumers against the foreign broker.[9]

In that case, the plaintiffs sought compensation for losses suffered in connection with forward contract transactions executed by the defendant, a U.S. brokerage house with its seat in New Jersey. The contracts with the defendant had been arranged by German brokers who had cooperated with the defendant and who had introduced German customers to the defendant. The German brokers had presented the plaintiffs with

---

[9] Federal Supreme Court, decision of 25 January 2011, file no. XI ZR 350/08; *SchiedsVZ* 2011, 157.

the defendant's English language Option Agreement and Approval Form, which contained an arbitration clause providing for the application of New York law and for arbitration in New York. After the plaintiffs had basically lost all their investments, they initiated court proceedings against the U.S. defendant in Germany and argued that the defendant had participated in a scheme which intentionally inflicted damage on the plaintiffs in an unconscionable manner.

In response, the defendant argued that the German courts had no jurisdiction and that the claims were inadmissible due to the arbitration clause in the Option Agreement and Approval Form.

While the first instance courts had dismissed the claims, the Court of Appeal allowed the appeal. The defendant's appeal against the second instance judgment was dismissed by the Federal Supreme Court. The Federal Supreme Court considered the complaints to be admissible and confirmed the judgment of the Court of Appeal. The Federal Supreme Court held that the arbitration clause in the Option Agreement and Approval Form did not comply with the formal requirements of Section 1031(5) ZPO. According to this provision, arbitration agreements to which a consumer is a party must be contained in a document that has been personally signed by the parties and that contains no agreements other than those relating to the arbitral proceedings. The only exception is if the contract containing the arbitration agreement is certified by a notary.

Although the defendant had its seat in New Jersey and the forward contracts and option transactions had been executed in the United States, the Federal Supreme Court applied German law to the contracts, since they were between a foreign broker and German consumers and had been concluded in Germany after active solicitation by the German brokers who cooperated with the defendant. The fact that the plaintiffs were entrepreneurs did not affect their status as consumers in their contractual relationships with the defendant. The Federal Supreme Court held that bank and security transactions which an entrepreneur carries out in looking after his own assets do not alter the character of these transactions as private consumer transactions. As the Option Agreement and Approval Form did not only contain provisions relating to the arbitral proceedings, and since they were not personally signed by all parties, the arbitration agreement was considered to be invalid.

B.4 Consumers Cannot Decide to Treat Invalid Arbitration Clauses as Valid

Section 1031(5) ZPO—as discussed in Section B.3 above—is a provision that is intended to protect consumers. The Federal Supreme Court had to decide whether a consumer who is sued before a state court can waive the protection granted by Section 1031(5) ZPO and raise the objection that the dispute is subject to an arbitration clause.[10]

The case resulted from a lawsuit that an entrepreneur commenced against a consumer for payment of a student loan. The underlying contract had been drafted by the entrepreneur and contained an arbitration clause. The arbitration clause did not comply with the form requirements of Section 1031(5) ZPO. The entrepreneur thus initiated state court proceedings rather than arbitration proceedings. The consumer raised the objection under Section 1032(1) ZPO that, because of the arbitration clause, the state court had no jurisdiction to hear the dispute.

The court acknowledged that Section 1031(5) ZPO was intended to protect consumers. It held, however, that a consumer does not have the choice to treat an invalid arbitration agreement as valid.

---

[10] Federal Supreme Court, decision of 19 May 2011, file no. III ZR 16/11.

In this regard, the court referred to the *travaux préparatoires* of the arbitration law,[11] according to which an arbitration agreement that does not meet the form requirements of Section 1031(5) ZPO is "always invalid." Accordingly, the law was not intended to give the consumer a choice in this regard; the invalidity has to be considered *ex officio*. Only in exceptional circumstances can reliance on statutory form requirements be taken to violate the principle of good faith.[12] This was only held to be the case if the application of the form requirement would lead to unbearable results for the parties.

B.5 Effect of Administrator's Decision of Non-Performance in Insolvency on Arbitration Agreement

In the 2010–2011 edition of the *Baker & McKenzie International Arbitration Yearbook*,[13] we reported that if an administrator in insolvency opts for non-performance of a contract between the debtor and a third party that was concluded and not fully performed before the opening of the proceedings, this does not affect the validity of an arbitration agreement contained in that contract.[14] However, the Federal Supreme Court recently held otherwise.[15]

In October 2009, the administrator in insolvency of Qimonda AG ("Qimonda") had filed an application with the *Kammergericht* to determine the inadmissibility of an arbitration

---

[11] BT Drucks. 13/5274, p. 36.

[12] Section 242 of the German Civil Code.

[13] p. 259.

[14] Federal Supreme Court, decision of 20 November 2003, file no. III ZB 24/03, ZInsO 2004, 88; *Uhlenbruck*, Insolvenzordnung, 13th ed. 2010, Sec. 103, note 55.

[15] Decision of 30 June 2011, file no. III ZB 59/10; *SchiedsVZ* 2011, 281.

under Section 1032(2) ZPO.[16] The underlying arbitration clause was included in a cross patent licence agreement ("CPLA") concluded between the respondent and Qimonda's legal predecessor. After Qimonda filed for the opening of insolvency proceedings in April 2009, its administrator chose non-performance of the CPLA under Section 103 of the German Insolvency Code ("InsO"). The respondent brought arbitration proceedings for a declaration that its rights of use under the CPLA remained unaffected by the choice of non-performance.

At first instance, the *Kammergericht*, in a curious decision,[17] dismissed the application as belated and thus inadmissible, since it had been *filed* before the constitution of the arbitral tribunal (which was completed in February 2010), but had only been *served* upon the respondent abroad after the tribunal's constitution. Alternatively, in case the filing of the application was decisive, the *Kammergericht* held that the constitution of the tribunal had rendered the application inadmissible with retrospective effect. In an *obiter dictum* on the merits, the court declared that the application would in any event have failed, as it had been for the tribunal to conduct a comprehensive review of the parties' rights under the CPLA, including the question of whether the administrator's choice of non-performance affected the respondent's contractual rights.

The Federal Supreme Court reversed the decision on both counts and referred the matter back to the *Kammergericht* for further deliberation.[18] As to admissibility, it held that the decisive point

---

[16] This paragraph—which has no equivalent in the UNCITRAL Model Law—provides that "up until the constitution of the arbitral tribunal," an application can be brought before a state court "for determination of the admissibility or inadmissibility of an arbitration."

[17] Decision of 13 September 2010, file no. 20 Sch 3/09.

[18] The case is still pending.

in time was the filing of the application, not its service on the respondent, and that the subsequent constitution of the arbitral tribunal did not render the application inadmissible. On the merits, the Federal Supreme Court confirmed that an administrator is, in principle, bound by an arbitration agreement concluded by the insolvent party prior to filing for insolvency proceedings. However, it held that this binding effect only exists with respect to the insolvent party's contractual rights, but does not extend to rights of the administrator "that are not directly derived from the contract concluded by the debtor, but are based on the Insolvency Code and thus specific to insolvency," such as the administrator's right to rescind a transaction and "claw back" the proceeds[19] or his right to choose non-performance under Section 103 InsO. The rationale behind the distinction in the reasoning of the Federal Supreme Court is that contrary to rights derived from a contract, the insolvent debtor may not dispose of the rights conferred to the administrator by operation of the Insolvency Code or influence the exercise of these rights.

As a consequence, German state courts can now declare arbitration proceedings inadmissible to the extent that the subject matter of the proceedings—as a preliminary issue or otherwise—concerns the administrator's right to choose non-performance.

B.6 Setting Aside an Arbitral Award for Breach of Agreements between the Parties

In the first section of this chapter of the *Yearbook*, we dealt with the complaints of many users of arbitration about the time and costs spent in "modern" international arbitration. Although much of the criticism is justified, a case decided by the Court of

---

[19] As to this exception, cf. the *Baker & McKenzie International Arbitration Yearbook 2010 – 2011*, p. 265.

Appeal Frankfurt[20] in February 2011 shows that complex disputes create complex arbitration proceedings and that not only the arbitral tribunal, but also the parties and their representatives as well as experts involved in the arbitration, are responsible for the length and costs.

In this case, the applicant—a subsidiary of an automotive supplier—had asked the court to set aside an arbitral award which ordered it to pay to the respondent EUR 210 million in damages for breach of contract. The underlying dispute related to an M&A transaction. In 2004, the applicant had concluded a Sale and Purchase Agreement with the respondent, whereby it was to acquire the shares in respondent's subsidiary. The purchase price was agreed to be EUR 197,844,000. In addition, the applicant had to absorb certain debt obligations. The amount of these obligations was not yet fixed at the time of the conclusion of the Sale and Purchase Agreement, but had still to be determined at the time of closing in accordance with certain rules agreed between the parties. Until the closing, the respondent had to carry on the business of its subsidiary. Certain transactions outside the ordinary course of business were not allowed during this period. Finally, it was agreed that all disputes resulting from or in connection with the Sale and Purchase Agreement were to be settled by arbitration in accordance with the DIS Arbitration Rules.

Immediately after the signing of the Sale and Purchase Agreement, a number of disputes arose between the parties that finally led the applicant to terminate the agreement. According to the applicant, the respondent had breached the "ordinary course of business" clause in the Sale and Purchase Agreement and had manipulated the finance structure of the group to increase the amount of the applicant's debt. The applicant claimed that these

---

[20] Court of Appeal Frankfurt, decision of 17 February 2011, file no. 26 Sch 13/10.

actions caused the total financial burden resulting from the transaction to increase from EUR 253 million to at least EUR 352 million.

In October 2004, the respondent filed a request for arbitration and claimed damages from the applicant for breach of contract. The arbitration proceedings lasted until March 2010, when the arbitral tribunal rendered its award. During the course of the arbitration, at least 46 procedural orders were issued by the arbitral tribunal, several expert opinions were submitted, thousands of documents were reviewed, parallel proceedings were initiated by the parties in Canada and in the United States, and at its final stage, the applicant terminated the arbitration agreement for cause.

After the arbitral tribunal rendered its award, the applicant asked the Court of Appeal Frankfurt to set aside the award. It argued that, *inter alia*, the arbitral tribunal had breached the agreements between the parties, and that in any event, the arbitral tribunal was not allowed to render the award after the arbitration agreement had been terminated.

The court set aside the award, holding that the arbitral tribunal had not complied with the parties' agreement and that this non-compliance had presumably affected the award. The agreement to which the court referred was the tribunal's order requiring the parties to substantiate all submissions filed and to submit written witness statements and expert opinions as evidence for their factual allegations. It also required the experts to indicate and describe all documents and other information on which they had relied in preparing their opinions. Although both parties had expressly approved this order, the respondent, as claimant in the arbitration proceedings, failed to comply and facts relevant for the decision were apparently not sufficiently proven. The insufficiencies in the respondent's submissions to the tribunal did not prevent the tribunal from rendering the award in favor of the respondent, and the Court of Appeal Frankfurt considered this to be a breach of the agreed content of the procedural order.

The court did not follow the applicant's submissions with respect to the validity of the termination of the arbitration agreement. Although the court shared the applicant's view that the respondent's commencement of parallel litigation constituted a severe breach of the arbitration agreement, it did not consider this breach to be a sufficient basis to terminate for cause. The court held that this breach did not render it unbearable for the applicant to continue the arbitration proceedings. In addition, it considered that if the termination was allowed, the whole dispute would have to be repeated in litigation proceedings, which the court found to be unreasonable and not in the best interest of the applicant.

The case confirms the notion that arbitration is not necessarily a more amicable dispute resolution mechanism than litigation. The case also shows that it is in the best interest of the parties and the tribunal to reduce the complexity of the proceedings as much as possible so that the tribunal and the parties can keep track of the issues and of the procedural rules to be followed.

C. PUBLIC POLICY IN INTERNATIONAL ARBITRATION

C.1 Scenarios of Reliance on Public Policy

In an arbitration context, parties rely on alleged breaches of fundamental principles of German law primarily as a defense against an application to a state court to have an award recognized and declared enforceable. This applies equally to domestic and foreign awards. While the former can be set aside under Sections 1060(2) and 1059(2)(2)(b)[21] ZPO if "recognition or enforcement of the award would lead to a result that is contrary to public policy," the basis for vacating the latter is Article V(2)(b) of the New York Convention, which provides for the same requirements.[22]

Only in exceptional cases can recognition of an award be denied for breach of public policy. Under the general definition of the European Court of Justice,[23] a state court can deny recognition only where the infringement of public policy constitutes "a manifest breach of a rule of law regarded as essential in the legal order of the State in which enforcement is sought or of a right recognized as being fundamental within that legal order."

It is only on rare occasions that public policy principles are invoked in circumstances other than recognition and enforcement. A case like *Jivraj v. Hashwani*,[24] i.e., a challenge of an arbitration agreement based on equal treatment principles, is unlikely to occur in Germany.[25] Examples of cases where public policy was invoked before a German court or arbitral

---

[21] Equivalent to Articles 35 (1) and 36(1)(b)(ii) of the UNCITRAL Model Law.

[22] One difference in the wording—albeit not in substance—is that Sec. 1059(2)(2)(b) ZPO emphasizes that it must be the *result* of recognition or enforcement that violates public policy.

[23] Decision of 28 March 2000, Case C-7/98.

[24] [2011] UKSC 40, judgment of 27 July 2011 (on appeal from [2010] EWCA Civ 712), in which the English Supreme Court held that an arbitration clause that provided for disputes to be resolved by arbitration before three arbitrators, each of whom was required to be a respected member of the Ismaili community, was not avoided as an unlawful arrangement to discriminate on grounds of religion upon the Employment Equality (Religion or Belief) Regulations 2003 entering into force, since arbitrators are not "employees" as defined by the Regulations.

[25] *Cf. Wittinghofer/Neukirchner*, RIW 2011, p. 527.

tribunal to avoid an arbitration agreement[26] include the following:

- In a decision of 2006, the Court of Appeal Munich[27] was concerned with a forum selection and arbitration agreement in a terminated commercial agency contract between a California principal and a German agent. The court held that this agreement (which provided for arbitration under the AAA Rules and the competence of the state courts in California) was unenforceable, based on the assumption that neither an arbitral tribunal nor a state court in California would give due regard to the commercial agent's statutory claim for post-contractual compensation that is established in Section 89b of the German Commercial Code. The European Court of Justice had previously[28] declared this provision on post-contractual compensation mandatory so that the Court of Appeal Munich felt compelled not to give effect to a dispute resolution clause that in the court's view deprived the agent of this claim.

- An arbitration agreement may also fail for public policy reasons if it gives one party a prevailing influence on the constitution of the tribunal.[29]

---

[26] The "Subway" decision of the Court of Appeal Dresden of 7 December 2007 (File No. 11 Sch 0008/07, reported in the *Baker & McKenzie International Arbitration Yearbook 2007*, p. 44) is only an apparent example. In that case, the court had denied Subway's application for recognition of an award that a U.S. tribunal had rendered against a German subway franchisee. The court held that the underlying arbitration agreement was invalid not for public policy considerations, but under the law of Liechtenstein which was in any event the applicable law.

[27] File No. 7 U 1781/06, WM 2006, 1556; for a comprehensive review of the decision, *cf. Quinke, SchiedsVZ* 2007, 246.

[28] In the infamous *Ingmar* decision of 9 November 2000, Case C-381/98.

[29] Böckstiegel/Kröll/Nacimiento-*Kröll, Arbitration in Germany*, Sec. 1061, note 124 with further references.

C.2 Modes and Limitations of Reliance on Public Policy

A party who wishes to rely on public policy as a reason to deny the enforcement of an award can do so in one of two ways:

- In a domestic case,[30] a public policy objection can be pursued actively by way of an application to the competent state court to vacate the award. This application has to be brought within three months of service of the award (Section 1059(3) ZPO).[31]

- Alternatively, public policy may be raised as a defense against the opposing party's application for recognition and enforcement. While after expiration of the three-month period mentioned above, the other defenses listed in Section 1059 ZPO are time-barred, the public policy defense may still be used any time thereafter.[32] If the defense succeeds, the court dismisses the application for recognition and enforcement and vacates the award.

A party that could have raised an issue that potentially constitutes a breach of public policy in the arbitral proceedings, but failed to do so, is in principle precluded from relying on the same issue as a defense against recognition of the award.[33] This principle was recently confirmed in a decision of 30 May 2011 in which the Court of Appeal Saarbrücken[34]

---

[30] German courts are not empowered to vacate a foreign award absent an application for recognition.

[31] Equivalent to Article 34(3) of the UNCITRAL Model Law.

[32] BGHZ 145, 376 (380).

[33] Zöller-*Geimer*, ZPO, 28th ed., Sec. 1059, note 4; Böckstiegel/Kröll/Nacimiento-*Kröll/Kraft*, *Arbitration in Germany*, Sec. 1059, note 90; Court of Appeal Celle, decision of 24 July 2003, file no. 8 Sch 01/03 (available in the database on the DIS website).

[34] File No. 4 Sch 3/10; NJOZ 2011, 1363.

held that facts that render a contract unconscionable cannot be used in support of an application to set aside a foreign award if the party who seeks to rely on them was already aware of these facts during the arbitration proceedings and could have introduced them then.

A party that submits an arbitrator's bias as a reason not to recognize the award for breach of public policy is normally expected to have tried to challenge the arbitrator during the arbitral proceedings. It can only avail itself of the public policy defense where procedural remedies were not available or could not reasonably have been pursued in the originating state.[35]

C.3 Rules that Constitute "Public Policy"

Like the courts in most other countries, German courts normally only consider legal rules of the forum state, i.e., German law, under the umbrella of "public policy." It is only in exceptional cases that provisions of foreign law are taken into account.[36]

Public policy can be invoked for breaches of either substantive or procedural law.[37] Examples for breaches of substantive law that require an award to be vacated for breach of public policy include awards:

---

[35] Federal Supreme Court, decision of 1 February 2001, file no. III ZR 332/99 (available on the website of the Federal Supreme Court, http://juris. bundesgerichtshof.de/cgi-bin/rechtsprechung/list.py?Gericht=bgh&Art=en&Sort=3); Böckstiegel/Kröll/Nacimiento-*Kröll*, Sec. 1061, note 131.

[36] Stein/Jonas-*Schlosser*, ZPO, 22nd ed., Appendix to Sec. 1061, note 135.

[37] Many of these principles will also come under the headings of one of the other instances in which an award may be vacated under Sec. 1059 or the New York Convention.

- that order a party to render an impossible performance or a performance that would constitute a criminal offense;[38]

- that provide an obligation to carry out an act that could not be enforced under German law, such as an obligation to vote in a certain way in a shareholders' meeting;[39] or

- that are contradictory in terms.[40]

The most common examples for substantive law rules that are part of German public policy are provisions of competition or antitrust law,[41] export and import regulations or money laundering provisions.[42]

The purpose of procedural public policy is to ensure that the German minimum standards of fair trial have been observed.[43] The scope of procedural rules, the breach of which can amount to an infringement of public policy, comprises, *inter alia*, the right to be heard [44] (including proper service, sufficient time to file briefs, representation in the proceedings, consideration of

---

[38] *Schwab/Walter,* Chapter 24, note 41.

[39] RGZ 131, 179.

[40] Schwab/Walter, *ibid.*

[41] *See, e.g.,* European Court of Justice, judgment of 1 June 1999, Case C-126/97 ("Eco Swiss"); Federal Supreme Court, judgment of October 25, 1966, file no. K ZR 7/ 65. BGHZ 46, 365; judgment of October 25, 1983, file no. K ZR 27/8288, BGHZ 88, 314 (319)

[42] Böckstiegel/Kröll/Nacimiento-*Kröll/Kraft*, Sec. 1059, note 83; *Schwab/Walter,* Chapter 24, note 43.

[43] Court of Appeal Cologne, decision of 23 April 2004, file no. 9 Sch 01/03, *SchiedsVZ* 2005, 163; Zöller-*Geimer*, Sec. 1061, note 31.

[44] Court of Appeal Cologne, decision of 23 April 2004, file no. 9 Sch 01/03, *SchiedsVZ* 2005, 163 (165); Court of Appeal Munich, decision of 18 November 2004, file no. 34 Sch 19/04, *SchiedsVZ* 2006, 111 (112); Schwab/*Walter,* Chapter 24, note 50; Münchener Kommentar-*Münch*, Sec. 1059, note 45.

submissions and evidence provided), procedural neutrality of the tribunal,[45] and instances that would under domestic procedural law allow a *res judicata* case to be re-opened.[46]

However, German courts and academics emphasize that the threshold is high and that only grave breaches of procedural rules can give rise to a denial of recognition. In one illustrative decision of 23 February 2006,[47] the Federal Supreme Court considered a Belarusian award in a case in which the tribunal's jurisdiction had been at issue. In breach of Belarusian arbitration law, the tribunal had failed to issue an interim award as to its jurisdiction that would have been subject to appeal to the executive committee of the arbitral institution. Instead, it had issued a final award on the merits that, *inter alia*, comprised a positive decision on the tribunal's jurisdiction. The Federal Supreme Court held that this procedure did not amount to a breach of German public policy. In its reasoning, the court emphasized that under Article 16(3) of the UNCITRAL Model Law (and the corresponding German provision in Section 1040(3) ZPO), the tribunal "may rule on a plea" as to its jurisdiction "either as a preliminary question or in an award on the merits." The court thus concluded that there is an "international conviction" to grant arbitral tribunals greater leeway with respect to jurisdictional issues—not least because the final decision is one from a state court.

---

[45] Münchener Kommentar-*Münch, ibid.*

[46] Such as false testimonies under oath by either a party or a witness, the use of forged documents, conduct of a judge in the proceedings that amounts to a criminal offense to the detriment of one of the parties, blackmail of a judge, etc., *Schwab/Walter*, Chapter 24, note 51; Böckstiegel/Kröll/Nacimiento-*Kröll/Kraft*, Sec. 1059, note 87 *et seq.*; Zöller-*Geimer*, Sec. 1061, note 32; BGHZ 145, 376.

[47] File No. III ZB 50/05; *SchiedsVZ* 2006, 161.

The validity or scope of the underlying arbitration agreement may also become an issue under this heading: if the tribunal assumes jurisdiction in excess of the agreement to arbitrate, this constitutes an infringement of the parties' right to access a state court judge and thus is a breach of a fundamental constitutional right.[48]

German courts do make a distinction between "domestic" and "international" public policy, but this distinction hardly ever influences the outcome of the proceedings.[49] The distinction is one "of degree and not in kind."[50] The Federal Supreme Court mentioned it in one recent case,[51] holding that it amounts to a breach of German *ordre public interne*[52] to award a claim against an insolvent respondent if this claim had not previously been filed in the insolvency proceedings. However, the distinction between "domestic" and "international" public policy did not have a decisive bearing on the outcome of the case, so it remains uncertain whether the Federal Supreme Court would be inclined to treat foreign awards more generously than domestic ones.

The mere fact that an award violates a mandatory rule of German law is not *per se* sufficient to invoke public policy successfully.

---

[48] Böckstiegel/Kröll/Nacimiento-*Kröll/Kraft*, Sec. 1059, note 85, and Sec. 1061, note 121 *et seq.*

[49] Schwab/*Walter,* Chapter 30, note 21.

[50] Böckstiegel/Kröll/Nacimiento-*Kröll/Kraft*, Sec. 1059, note 79.

[51] Decision of 29 January 2009, file no. III ZB 88/07, *SchiedsVZ* 2009, 176; cf. *Baker & McKenzie International Arbitration Yearbook 2009*, pp. 161 and 162; 2010-2011, p. 262.

[52] The emphasis on the term "*ordre public interne*" in this decision is unusual. It may imply that the Federal Supreme Court is inclined to treat foreign awards more generously, even though a reason to distinguish between domestic and foreign awards is not readily apparent.

German law imposes a high severity threshold by only allowing an award to be set aside for breach of an "obvious" violation of its "fundamental principles."[53]

An example is an arbitral award that provides for payment of compound interest. German law does not recognize an entitlement to compound—as opposed to simple—interest. The mandatory rule in Section 248 BGB thus provides that interest may not be compounded. However, an award in which the respondent is ordered to pay compound interest would still be declared enforceable in Germany,[54] as the prohibition of compound interest is not considered a basic principle of German law.

An example to the contrary is an award that provides for punitive damages. It is one of the basic principles of German law that damages may only be compensatory. To the extent[55] an award grants a party punitive damages, the award would not be enforceable in Germany.[56]

C.4 Review of Alleged Breaches of Public Policy

German courts rightly emphasize that the public policy defense must not be abused to allow a party that is dissatisfied with an

---

[53] Böckstiegel/Kröll/Nacimiento-*Kröll/Kraft*, Sec. 1059, note 78.

[54] Court of Appeal Hamburg, judgment of 30 July 1998, file no. 6 Sch 3/98; Betriebsberater 1999, Supplement No. 11, 13; Böckstiegel/Kröll/Nacimiento-*Kröll*, Sec. 1061, note 118 m.w.N. in Fn. 295; Stein/Jonas-*Schlosser*, Appendix to Sec. 1061, note 142.

[55] Partial enforcement of the remaining contents of the award is possible, provided this remaining contents is severable.

[56] Federal Supreme Court, judgment of 4 June 1992, file no. IX ZR 149/91, BGHZ 118, 312 (concerning a judgment from a U.S. state court); Böckstiegel/Kröll/Nacimiento-*Kröll*, Sec. 1061, note 118; *Schwab/Walter,* Chapter 30, note 22.

award to re-open the case on the merits.[57] Thus, a *révision au fond* of an award is not permissible. The state court's review must be confined to verifying whether the effect of enforcing the particular award in question would be obviously contrary to the fundamental principles of German law. Within these boundaries, however, a state court is obliged to carry out a full review of whether an award violates German public policy without being in any way bound by the tribunal's findings.[58]

Even if an award is found to be obviously wrong, it may not amount to a breach of public policy, unless "the infringement of the law has reached a level that would seriously affect the principle of legal certainty and the confidence in arbitration."[59]

German courts have to consider possible violations of public policy *ex officio*,[60] i.e., the parties may not waive a breach of fundamental principles of German procedural law. However, a court may require a party that seeks to rely on a violation of public policy to specify the alleged violation and to explain how it would have argued its case in the absence of the violation. For instance, a respondent that raises a violation of its right to be heard will have to explain what it would have

---

[57] Böckstiegel/Kröll/Nacimiento-*Kröll/Kraft*, Sec. 1059, note 80, Court of Appeal Dresden, decision of 7 June 2006, file no. 11 Sch 02/06; Court of Appeal Cologne, decision of 26 November 2002, file No. 9 Sch 19/02 (both in the database on the DIS website); recently Court of Appeal Saarbrücken, decision of 30 May 2011, File No. 4 Sch 3/10; NJOZ 2011, 1363, 1365.

[58] *Schwab/Walter*, Chapter 24, note 46.

[59] Böckstiegel/Kröll/Nacimiento-*Kröll/Kraft*, Sec. 1059, note 82; Court of Appeal Dresden, decision of 20 April 2005, file no. 11 Sch 01/05, *SchiedsVZ* 2005, 210.

[60] BGHZ 145, 376 (380); 142, 204 (206); *Schwab/Walter*, Chapter 27, note 8; Münchener Kommentar-*Münch*, ZPO, 3rd ed. 2008, Sec. 1059, note 50.

submitted given the opportunity.[61] If this submission would not have altered the outcome of the case, the violation can be considered immaterial.

---

[61] Böckstiegel/Kröll/Nacimiento-*Kröll*, Sec. 1061, note 122; Court of Appeal Karlsruhe, decision of 29 November 2002, file no. 9 Sch 01/02 (available in the database on the DIS website).

HONG KONG

James Kwan[1] and Jasmine Chan[2,3]

A. LEGISLATION, TRENDS AND TENDENCIES

A.1 The New Hong Kong Arbitration Ordinance

The new Hong Kong Arbitration Ordinance (Cap. 609) came into force on 1 June 2011. It is based on the UNCITRAL Model Law, and incorporates elements of the 2006 amendments to the Model Law. The new Ordinance unifies domestic and international arbitrations. Arbitrations commenced on or after 1 June 2011 are governed by the new Ordinance.

The major changes under the new Ordinance are provided below.

A.1.1. One unifying regime

Previously in Hong Kong, the now repealed Arbitration Ordinance (Cap. 341) provided for distinct and separate regimes for domestic and international arbitrations. International arbitrations, including domestic arbitrations where parties agree to use the international regime, were governed by the UNCITRAL Model Law (as adopted in 1985, excluding the

---

[1] James Kwan is a Partner in the Dispute Resolution Group of Baker & McKenzie's office in Hong Kong and leads the arbitration practice in there. He specializes in infrastructure, engineering, and energy disputes. He has a range of international experience, having represented clients in arbitrations in Hong Kong, Asia, the Middle East, and Europe under the major institutional rules.

[2] Jasmine Chan is an Associate in the Dispute Resolution Group of Baker & McKenzie's Hong Kong office. Her practice focuses on international arbitration and commercial litigation.

[3] The authors would like to thank Shanti Foo, Peter Liang and Victoria Yu of the Hong Kong office for their assistance with this chapter.

2006 amendments). On the other hand, domestic arbitrations were governed by provisions in the old Ordinance which were based on the English Arbitration Act 1996.

This former distinction was regarded as unnecessary and problematic. It sometimes gave rise to disputes regarding the appropriate governing regime in particular cases. A significant difference between the two regimes was that the domestic regime provided the Hong Kong courts with additional powers to intervene in and assist with the arbitration process, which were not available under the international regime. This included appeals on questions of law with leave of the court, consolidation of proceedings, and determination of a preliminary point of law.

By contrast, the international regime as based on the UNCITRAL Model Law, followed the principle that the Hong Kong courts should support, but not interfere with, the arbitral process.

The new Ordinance, with an aim to simplify and streamline the administration and process of arbitration in Hong Kong, harmonizes both domestic and international arbitration proceedings under a single unified framework. The UNCITRAL Model Law (as amended in 2006) will now apply to all arbitrations commenced in Hong Kong. This new framework will increase efficiency as well as provide greater certainty and consistency for both domestic and foreign parties to arbitration.

The new Ordinance is also more user-friendly in that it is easily readable since it follows the order and chapter headings of the UNCITRAL Model Law. Amendments to the Model Law can also be easily identified.

A.1.2. Opt-in provisions

While the new Ordinance provides for a unified regime, there is an opt-in system which allows parties to agree to apply the provisions governing domestic arbitrations under the old Ordinance. These provisions are set out in Schedule 2 of the new Ordinance and include the following:

1. arbitration by a sole arbitrator in the absence of agreement;

2. appeal against an arbitral award on a question of law;

3. consolidation of arbitrations by the court;

4. determination of a preliminary question of law by the court; and

5. challenging an arbitral award on the grounds of serious irregularity.

The opt-in system was included mainly as a result of lobbying by the construction industry which was interested in preserving some features of the old domestic regime with which it was familiar. Therefore, parties from the construction sector and parties that prefer greater court intervention are most likely to utilize the opt-in provisions.

The provisions in Schedule 2 will also automatically apply to arbitration agreements that provide for "domestic" arbitration and were entered into before or within six years of the introduction of the new Ordinance. Arbitration clauses that involve construction projects in agreements involving the Hong Kong government provide for domestic arbitration. Developers and employers in construction projects also prefer to stipulate to domestic arbitration in their clauses.

A.1.3. Stricter confidentiality requirements

Previously, confidentiality in arbitration proceedings was governed by the common law duty; the old Arbitration Ordinance was silent on confidentiality. The new Ordinance imposes more stringent confidentiality requirements on parties to an arbitration

(Section 18). It aims to balance the demand for confidentiality in arbitration proceedings and the public interest relating to the need for a transparent, open and fair judicial process. By expressly codifying the common law duty of confidentiality, the new Ordinance provides greater certainty and assurance as to confidentiality in arbitrations seated in Hong Kong.

The provisions regarding confidentiality also extend to cover court proceedings relating to arbitration. Under Section 16 of the Ordinance, the starting point is that all arbitration related court proceedings are to be conducted *in camera*, unless the court in its discretion, on the application of any party or on its own initiative, orders proceedings to be heard in public. This marks a shift from the position under the previous Ordinance, under which the default position was that arbitration-related court proceedings would be heard in open court.

In conjunction with Section 16, Section 17 of the Ordinance imposes restrictions on the reporting of closed court proceedings in relation to arbitration, while at the same time recognizing that the publication of judgments of major legal interest provides an important foundation for the development of commercial arbitration law.

Hong Kong cases on the Model Law will increase as a result of court judgments interpreting the Model Law on issues such as the setting aside of awards. This will benefit other Model Law countries in Asia, particularly those with a less sophisticated arbitration judiciary. There is no reason why judges in other Model Law countries should not have recourse to Hong Kong judgments when ruling on provisions under the Model Law. It is hoped that courts in Asia will be influenced by arbitration-friendly Hong Kong case law.

The provisions on confidentiality are desirable from the parties' point of view as they reinforce the importance of the confidentiality of the arbitral process and related proceedings in court. It remains to be seen whether the provisions balance public interest considerations relating to transparency. It is hoped that the introduction of the provisions regarding confidentiality will not mean that the helpful statistics that are regularly published by the HKIAC on its website regarding the number of cases in which parties have sought to set aside or resist enforcement of arbitral awards before the Hong Kong courts will now become unavailable. These statistics show that Hong Kong is pro- arbitration and highlight the willingness of the Hong Kong courts to uphold and enforce arbitral awards.

A.1.4. Interim measures and relief granted by an arbitral tribunal and the courts

Under the old Ordinance, the term "interim measures of protection" was not specifically defined. The new Ordinance adopts the UNCITRAL Model Law amendments in 2006 in respect of interim measures. It expressly defines interim measures (which includes injunctions, *Mareva* injunctions, and *Anton Pillar* orders), and provides conditions for the granting of such measures. The arbitral tribunal may require security from the party requesting an interim measure (Sections 35 and 36).

Preliminary orders were not previously addressed. Under the new Ordinance, there is a specific and detailed regime. These include preliminary orders made on an *ex parte* basis (Sections 37 and 38).

A new regime for the enforcement of interim measures separate from the recognition and enforcement of awards has been created. This means that orders and directions for interim measures can be enforced by the court as a judgment, whether made within or outside of Hong Kong (Sections 43 and 61).

A.1.5. Greater efficiency in arbitration proceedings

The new Arbitration Ordinance enhances efficiency in the following ways:

- By providing that the arbitral tribunal give the parties a reasonable opportunity to present their case and to deal with the cases of their opponents[4] as opposed to a "full" opportunity[5] (as is provided in the Model Law).

- Judicial recourse to an arbitral award is only available in limited circumstances, i.e., setting aside an award.

- The default number of arbitrators is either one or three as decided by the HKIAC.[6] The Model Law provides that the default number of arbitrators shall be three.[7]

- Minimizing judicial intervention.

Under the domestic regime of the old Ordinance, parties could apply to seek a determination of a preliminary point of law, consolidation of proceedings, and appeal an arbitral award on a question of law. Parties now have limited scope to seek judicial interference (unless the parties agree to opt-in for Schedule 2 of the Ordinance).

Under the new Ordinance, the court should interfere only as expressly provided for under the Ordinance.[8] Moreover, certain supervisory functions of the court are assumed by the HKIAC, such as the default appointment of arbitrators and mediators,[9]

---

[4] Section 46(3)(b) of the Arbitration Ordinance.

[5] Article 18 of the Model Law.

[6] Section 23(3) of the Arbitration Ordinance.

[7] Article 10(2) of the Model Law.

[8] Section 12 of the Arbitration Ordinance.

[9] Sections 13(2), 24, and 32(1) of the Arbitration Ordinance.

and deciding on the number of arbitrators.[10] This will reduce costs and delays as it obviates making an application to the courts.

- The circumstances in which court intervention is allowed include:

  (a) challenging an arbitrator (Section 26);

  (b) terminating the mandate of an arbitrator (Sections 26 and 27);

  (c) setting aside an arbitral award (Section 81); and

  (d) assisting in taking evidence (Section 55).

A.2 Latest Developments in Hong Kong Arbitration

Number of HKIAC administered cases increasing

In 2011, the HKIAC handled 275 arbitrations, 178 of which were international in nature and 97 were domestic. There were 41 new administered cases in 2011 (rising from 16 in 2010). The total amount in dispute for administered cases rose from USD 1.4 billion to approximately USD 3.8 billion.

Trends observed for arbitration involving Chinese parties

We are starting to see arbitrations seated in Hong Kong involving PRC governed contracts held in both English and Chinese. We are seeing an increasing number of Chinese law firms representing clients in proceedings in Hong Kong.

Number of mediations increasing

We have seen a growing number of mediations. This is due to the Hong Kong court's support of mediation through the introduction of a Practice Direction on Mediation, which came

---

[10] Section 23(3) of the Arbitration Ordinance.

into effect in 2010. Pursuant to this Practice Direction, court litigants are under the duty to explore mediation. A party who unreasonably refuses to mediate may face costs consequences.

In the Lehman Brothers mini-bond saga, the HKIAC and the Hong Kong Monetary Authority developed a scheme for the resolution of disputes. There were over 280 cases. Eighty-six percent of the cases were resolved by mediation; none went to arbitration.

B. CASES

B.1 Enforcement against a Sovereign State in Hong Kong

Democratic Republic of Congo & Ors v. FG Hemisphere Associates LLC

The recent case of *Democratic Republic of Congo & Ors v. FG Hemisphere Associates LLC* (judgment of the Court of Final Appeal handed down on 8 June 2011)[11] regarding the non-enforcement of an award against a sovereign state does not affect the choice of Hong Kong as a place of arbitration.

FG Hemisphere concerned a distressed debt fund trying to enforce an arbitral award against the Democratic Republic of Congo ("DRC") in Hong Kong. The Court of First Instance granted *FG Hemisphere* leave to enforce the arbitral awards against the DRC. On appeal, the Court of Appeal held that the pre-1997 doctrine of restrictive immunity continued to apply in Hong Kong.

---

[11] [2011] 4 HKC 151.

B. Cases

Prior to the handover of Hong Kong to China in 1997, the common law and subsequently the U.K.'s State Immunity Act 1978 governed state immunity. Within this framework, states did not benefit from immunity from suit or enforcement when they were engaged in purely commercial transactions, and restrictive immunity applied.

However, the Court of Final Appeal overturned that. It ruled that as a constitutional imperative, the Central People's Government ("CPG") was responsible for policy on state immunity, so the Hong Kong courts or any other institution should not be responsible. The PRC's Standing Committee of the National People's Congress confirmed the Court of Final Appeal's provisional judgment in its interpretation (26 August 2011, as confirmed by the Court of Final Appeal's judgment of 8 September 2011).[12]

Hong Kong arbitral awards will still be enforceable in other jurisdictions under the New York Convention, and enforcement of awards against commercial entities is unaffected. This decision applies only to enforcement of arbitral awards in Hong Kong against foreign states. The situation is the same regardless of whether the place of arbitration is Hong Kong, Singapore or London.

It is clear that an arbitration clause, which is contractual in nature, will provide the arbitral tribunal with adjudicative jurisdiction over any dispute. There are also reasons to expect that an arbitration clause will amount to a waiver of immunity with respect to the supervisory jurisdiction of the Hong Kong courts in support of the arbitral process.

For example, there were *obiter* Court of Appeal remarks, endorsed by the Court of Final Appeal in *FG Hemisphere* that

---

[12]   [2011] 5 HKC 395.

the law of Hong Kong accords with customary international law on the issue of immunity from the supervisory jurisdiction of the courts of Hong Kong over the arbitration. Furthermore, court proceedings in support of arbitration are limited by the new Hong Kong Arbitration Ordinance. From the above, the new Arbitration Ordinance empowers the HKIAC to appoint arbitrators in default and to decide on the number of arbitrators, functions that have traditionally been part of the supervisory role of the courts.

There are two ways to waive immunity:

1. In the face of the court, i.e., by submission to the Hong Kong courts at the time when they exercise jurisdiction. For example, by filing a defense or taking a step in the proceedings.

   In practice, the waiver must be made at the time when the court exercises its jurisdiction. Accordingly, it will be insufficient for an effective waiver of immunity to be made by way of a pre-dispute contractual provision, such as an express waiver clause.

2. State-to-state treaty.

   DRC, the state counterparty which claimed immunity in *FG Hemisphere*, was not a party to the New York Convention. As the New York Convention contains a representation that each state party shall enforce arbitral awards against another state party where both are signatories, the Court of Appeal considered that the decision would have been different had the DRC been a party to the New York Convention. However, this still remains to be tested.

If an arbitration clause is adopted, it is only in relation to enforcement proceedings and execution in Hong Kong against assets that the combination of absolute immunity and the ineffectiveness of express waiver clauses will cause difficulties.

In many cases, the counterparty will have assets in other jurisdictions, many of which adopt a restrictive immunity regime or a more permissive approach to express contractual waivers, in which case enforcement in Hong Kong may be unnecessary.

B.2   Setting Aside Award for Procedural Irregularity

Pacific China Holdings Ltd. (In Liquidation) v. Grand Pacific Holdings Ltd.[13]

This case is a rare example of the Hong Kong courts setting aside an arbitral award. Pacific China Holdings Ltd. ("Applicant") applied to the Court of First Instance to set aside an ICC award in favor of Grand Pacific Holdings Ltd. ("Respondent") for serious procedural irregularity pursuant to Article 34(2) of the UNCITRAL Model Law. There were three discrete issues in this case:

Pre-hearing submissions on Taiwanese law

Both parties had agreed upon a procedural timetable whereby both were to file their pre-hearing submissions simultaneously. Due to the applicant amending its pleadings the day before the filing date, the tribunal allowed the respondent 10 days to file supplemental submissions dealing with the latest amendments. The applicant argued that this was unfair since it had already set down its "best case" in full and could not develop its case further. The proceedings were also no longer in accordance with the agreed timetable. The court accepted these arguments and found that there had been a breach of Article 34(2)(a)(ii) and (iv) of the UNCITRAL Model Law.

---

[13]   [2011] 4 HKLRD 188.

Additional legal authorities

The tribunal had indicated that both parties agreed that no new Taiwanese legal authorities could be adduced without leave, and such would not be granted unless the new authorities were "sensational." The applicant subsequently requested leave to rely on additional authorities, which the tribunal refused. As the tribunal had refused to receive or consider the additional authorities, it had no basis upon which it could say whether they came within the category of "sensational." The court found this had prevented the applicant from presenting its case and violated Article 34(2)(a)(ii) of the UNCITRAL Model Law.

Post-hearing submissions on Hong Kong law

The respondent had objected to the applicant raising issues relating to Hong Kong law, but nonetheless responded substantively to the applicant's submissions on the issue. The tribunal subsequently wrote to both parties in relation to the Hong Kong law issue, upon which the respondent made further substantive submissions, citing two new cases. The applicant sought leave to respond to the new material, but the tribunal refused, informing the parties that it had sufficient material to decide the issue. In deciding the Hong Kong law issue, the tribunal relied upon the new cases referred to by the respondent. The court found that the applicant had been denied the right to present its case and a violation of Article 34(2)(a)(ii) of the UNCITRAL Model Law had been established.

The court concluded that once a violation of Article 34(2) is found, it has discretion to set aside the arbitral award. If the court finds that the result of the arbitration may not have remained the same if the violation had not occurred, it must exercise its discretion to set aside the award. The court's residual discretion to refuse to set aside, despite the requisite grounds being established, is therefore narrowly construed.

The court found itself unable to say that even if the violations of Article 34(2) had not occurred, the result could not have been different. It was therefore ordered that the discretion be exercised in favor of setting aside the award.

B.3 Upholding Enforcement of Award

Shangdong Hongri Acron Chemical Joint Stock Co. Ltd. v. PetroChina International (Hong Kong) Co. Ltd.[14]

This case illustrates the mechanistic approach that Hong Kong courts adopt in enforcing awards. Hong Kong courts will refuse to go behind an award and look into the underlying dispute and the tribunal's reasoning.

Shandong Hongri Acron Chemical Joint Stock Co. Ltd. ("Shangdong Hongri") had obtained a CIETAC arbitral award in its favor, whereby Shandong Hongri was to return goods purchased from PetroChina International (Hong Kong) Co. Ltd. ("PetroChina") that it had found unsatisfactory, and PetroChina was to return the balance of the purchase price to Shandong Hongri. However, the arbitral award was silent on whether the return of goods was a condition precedent to the repayment of the purchase price, and the parties could not agree on the inspection and return of goods. PetroChina argued that its repayment obligations were conditional upon the return of rejected goods, and produced three letters from the CIETAC Secretariat suggesting that this was the correct understanding. The Court of First Instance accepted the letters as constituting a supplementary award and ruled in favor of PetroChina.

On appeal by Shandong Hongri, the Court of Appeal rejected PetroChina's arguments and held that the arbitral award imposed

---

[14] [2011] HKCU 1439.

no condition precedent. The task of a court asked to enforce an arbitral awards should be "as mechanistic as possible," and it is neither entitled nor bound to go behind the award in question and explore the reasoning of the arbitral tribunal or second-guess its intention. Since the award did not state that payment obligations were conditional or dependent on the return of goods, it could not impose a delivery condition and judgment was entered "in terms of the award."

As for the letters from the CIETAC Secretariat, PetroChina could not rely on those as a supplemental award as the case did not fall within Article 48 of the CIETAC Arbitration Rules, which permits a supplementary award to be issued where a claim put forward by a party was not dealt with in the award. The inter-relationship, if any, between the return of rejected goods and payment obligations was never raised as a claim or issue before the arbitral tribunal prior to the publication of the award. It was therefore not a case of a claim or counterclaim advanced in the proceedings but omitted from the award, which Article 48 covered.

The court reasoned that even assuming that Article 48 applied, the second and third letters were issued out of time and all three letters fell afoul of the formality requirements of Article 43 of the CIETAC Arbitration Rules. Article 43 stipulates that the CIETAC stamp shall be affixed to the award and the arbitral award shall be signed by a majority of arbitrators respectively. Furthermore, Shandong Hongri never had an opportunity to make submissions to the arbitral tribunal before the second and third letters were issued, resulting in a gross breach of the rules of natural justice. The court found that the letters did not constitute an additional or supplemental award.

C. PUBLIC POLICY IN INTERNATIONAL ARBITRATION

C.1 Reliance on Public Policy

In Hong Kong, there are two instances in which public policy can be invoked under the new Arbitration Ordinance (Cap. 609). First, public policy may be used to resist the enforcement of an arbitral award made in a New York Convention state,[15] in the People's Republic of China,[16] in a country which is not party to the New York Convention, or in Hong Kong.[17] Second, public policy may be relied upon as a ground to set aside an arbitral award.[18] However, an application to set aside an award may only be made within three months from the date of receipt of the award.

C.2 Rules that Constitute "Public Policy"

In Hong Kong, enforcement of an arbitral award may be refused if to do so would be "contrary to public policy." On the other hand, an arbitral award may only be set aside if it is in conflict with the public policy of Hong Kong.

In the case of *Hebei Import Export Corp v. Polytek Engineering Co. Ltd.*,[19] the Court of Final Appeal set out principles which form the starting point for cases concerning public policy:

---

[15] Section 89(3)(b) of the Arbitration Ordinance.

[16] Section 95(3)(b) of the Arbitration Ordinance.

[17] Section 86(2)(b) of the Arbitration Ordinance.

[18] Model Law Art 34(2)(b)(ii) read with Section 81(2)(b)(ii) of the Arbitration Ordinance.

[19] [1999] 2 HKC 205.

- Failure to raise a public policy ground before a court of supervisory jurisdiction cannot operate to preclude a party from resisting enforcement on that ground because each jurisdiction applies its own public policy.

- A party seeking to resist enforcement on public policy grounds is not obliged to elect between applying to the court of supervisory jurisdiction in the place where the award was made and applying to the enforcing court to refuse enforcement.

- However, where a party did not rely on public policy grounds in the first instance proceedings, a court, especially an appellate court, ought to view such a case with the utmost suspicion.

- It would be an unusual case where a competent authority ruled in favor of the validity of an arbitral award, yet the court in the enforcement jurisdiction concluded that enforcement should be denied for public policy reasons, as the practical result could be extremely unjust.

- The expression "public policy" is a multi-faceted concept. Woven into this concept is the principle that courts should recognize the validity of decisions of foreign arbitral tribunals as a matter of comity, and give effect to them, unless to do so would violate the most basic notions of morality and justice.

- There must be compelling reasons before enforcement of a Convention award can be refused on public policy grounds. The reasons must go beyond the minimum which would justify setting aside a domestic judgment or award.

- "International public policy" should be taken to mean only those elements of a state's own public policy that were so fundamental to its notions of justice that its courts felt obliged to apply the same not only to purely internal matters, but also to matters with a foreign element, that may affect other states.

Other key principles which have been set out by the Hong Kong courts include the following:

- "Public policy" covers not only basic notions of morality and justice, but also situations in which an award has been obtained by behavior that is criminal, fraudulent, corrupt, oppressive or otherwise immoral or unconscionable.[20]

- The New York Convention is clear that it is not for the enforcing court to rehear a case on its merits. It makes no difference if a party couches its submissions in terms of public policy.[21]

- There is a world of difference between a case that involved some issues of fraud and an arbitral award that was obtained by behavior that was fraudulent on the part of the successful party. In the case of the former, public policy is not engaged.[22]

- There are only limited technical grounds for resisting enforcement of Mainland awards. The Hong Kong court will give leave to enforce the award as a judgment unless there is a real ground for doubting the validity of the award. Given that the court is concerned only with the jurisdiction of the arbitration tribunal, it is no defense to an action on the award

---

[20] *Shandong Textiles Import and Export Corp v. Da Hua Non-Ferrous Metals Co. Ltd.* [2002] 2 HKC 122.

[21] *Qinhuangdao Tongda Enterprise Development Co. and Another v Million Basic Co. Ltd.* [1993] HKCU 0605.

[22] 昆明預應力制管廠 *v. True Stand Investments Ltd.* (全立投資有限公司) & *Anor* [2006] HKCU 2053.

that there is an error of fact or law on the part of the tribunal.[23]

- It may well be that it would not be contrary to public policy to enforce an award even if it could be shown that the arbitration tribunal applied the wrong law: "public policy" must not be extended to include every conceivable kind of error.[24]

- The court's role in an application for enforcement of a Mainland arbitral award is essentially that of an overseer. The court should not second-guess the award. The court should be as mechanistic as possible.[25]

- The court, when considering an application for enforcement of an arbitral award, must be vigilant against attempts to go behind the award and re-argue matters, in the guise of dealing with questions of public policy.[26]

C.3   Review of Alleged Breaches of Public Policy

Public policy as a ground raised to oppose enforcement of an arbitral award is generally construed quite narrowly by the Hong Kong courts. This approach is in line with their general pro-arbitration attitude. The recent Court of Appeal judgment in *Gao Haiyan & Anor v Keeneye Holdings Ltd. & Anor*[27] reinforces this attitude.

---

[23]   *Re Affluence Pictures Ltd.* (泰發影業有限公司) [2008] HKCU 1807.

[24]   *Werner A. Bock K.G. v. The N's Co. Ltd.* [1978] HKCU 36.

[25]   *Xiamen Xinjingdi Group Ltd. v. Eton Properties Ltd. & Anor* [2008] 6 HKC 287.

[26]   *Ibid.*

[27]   [2011] HKCU 2399.

In that case, arbitration was commenced at the Xian Arbitration Commission ("XAC") in a dispute concerning the validity of two share transfer agreements between the parties. At the end of the first arbitration hearing, the tribunal asked whether the parties were agreeable to mediation. The written record of the proceedings stated that the parties "agreed."

The tribunal appointed Pan, Secretary General of the XAC, and Zhou, an arbitrator, to contact the parties. Rather than contacting the respondents or their lawyers directly, they contacted a third-party ("Zeng"), who was regarded as friendly with the respondents. A mediation attended by Pan, Zhou and Zeng then took place over dinner at a hotel. Zeng was told to "work on" the respondents so that they would accept the proposal to settle the case by respondents paying RMB 250 million to the applicants.

Both parties later refused the proposal, and at the second arbitration hearing, no specific complaint was made against the conduct of Pan and Zhou. The tribunal dismissed the respondents' claim in its entirety and "recommended," on a non-binding basis, that the applicants pay RMB 50 million as compensation to the respondents. The respondents sought to set aside the award before the Xian Intermediate Court and contended that one of the arbitrators had manipulated the outcome of the arbitration and the tribunal had shown "favoritism and malpractice." The applicants obtained an *ex parte* order for enforcement of the award in Hong Kong. The respondents applied to set aside the order on the ground that it would be contrary to public policy to enforce the award as it was tainted by bias or apparent bias.

The Court of First Instance refused the enforcement of the award in Hong Kong on the basis that enforcement would be contrary to public policy in Hong Kong. The court held that the award was tainted by an appearance of bias. On appeal, the Court of

Appeal reversed the decision and allowed the enforcement of the award in Hong Kong. The Court of Appeal's judgment highlights several points:

- It is not for the court to express any opinion on the correctness or otherwise of the decision of the tribunal. The court is only concerned with whether enforcement of the award should be refused if it has been proved that "it would be contrary to public policy to enforce the award."

- The court's role in an application for enforcement of a Mainland arbitral award is essentially that of an overseer. The court should not second-guess the award. The court should be as mechanistic as possible.[28]

- The test for determining what is contrary to public policy is whether the act is contrary to "fundamental conceptions of morality and justice"[29] in Hong Kong.

- Even if the procedure adopted gives rise to an apprehension of bias if the same was adopted in Hong Kong, it would not necessarily amount to a breach of public policy. It is necessary to consider what is acceptable in the place of arbitration.

- It was emphasized that one should not too readily refuse enforcement of an award on the basis of one's notion of what may amount to apparent bias. It does not mean, for example, that if it is common for mediation to be conducted over dinner at a hotel in Xian, an award would not be enforced in Hong Kong because in Hong Kong, such conduct might give

---

[28]   *Xiamen Xinjingdi Group Ltd. v. Eton Properties Ltd. & Anor* [2008] 6 HKC 287.

[29]   *Quoting* from Sir Anthony Mason NPJ in Hebei (fn 19), which referred to *Parsons & Whittemore v. Societe General,* 508 F.2d 969 (1974).

rise to an appearance of apparent bias. A PRC court is better able to decide what is acceptable or unacceptable in the PRC.

- Greater weight should be accorded to the decision of the Xian court in refusing to set aside the award.

Overall, the Court of Appeal confirmed Hong Kong's pro-enforcement approach and the court's narrow construction of public policy. Hong Kong courts respect the finality of awards and will take into account what is acceptable in the place of arbitration, and accord weight to a decision by the supervisory court not to set aside an award.

HUNGARY

József Antal[1] and László Burger[2]

A. LEGISLATION, TRENDS AND TENDENCIES

A.1 Legislation

The Hungarian Arbitration Act[3] contains the fundamental rules of domestic and international arbitration procedures,[4] as well as related ordinary court procedures. The Hungarian Arbitration Act is based on the UNCITRAL Model Law as originally accepted in 1985. The amendments to the Model Law implemented in 2006 were not incorporated into the Hungarian Arbitration Act. The structure and content of the Hungarian regulations and the Model Law are mostly the same, with some

---

[1] József Antal is a Partner in Baker & McKenzie's Budapest office and heads the dispute resolution team of that office. His team is primarily responsible for handling litigation, alternative dispute resolution and public procurement matters. Mr. Antal has represented numerous multinational and local clients in civil lawsuits before ordinary courts, including the Supreme Court of the Republic of Hungary, as well as in arbitrations before the Permanent Court of Arbitration Affiliated with the Hungarian Chamber of Commerce and Industry and the Permanent Court of Arbitration of the Financial and Capital Markets.

[2] László Burger is an Attorney in Baker & McKenzie's Budapest office and specializes on drafting and negotiating a wide range of commercial contracts, both domestic and international, including distribution, supply, manufacturing, agency and outsourcing agreements. Mr. Burger has been involved in advising various global consumer products and manufacturing companies on their commercial agreements, cross border issues and related litigation and arbitration cases.

[3] Act LXXI of 1994 on Arbitration.

[4] Except for a few provisions, the Hungarian Arbitration Act applies only to those international arbitration procedures in which the place (registered seat) of the arbitration court concerned is in Hungary. *See* Section 1 of the Hungarian Arbitration Act.

minor differences which derive from the particularities of Hungarian law.

Recently, a new amendment to the Hungarian Arbitration Act has been proposed[5] according to which the entities of the public sector (e.g., the Hungarian state or the local governments) may not participate in arbitration proceedings if the amount in controversy exceeds HUF 400 million (approximately EUR 1.3 million). We emphasize that, as a general rule, the Hungarian Arbitration Act is applicable only if the arbitration court is seated in Hungary. Thus, the above-mentioned entities (at least in principle) would be allowed to participate in arbitration proceedings in foreign arbitration courts if the proposal is fully accepted in its current format. The Parliament has not voted on the proposal yet; thus, its provisions may be subject to change.

Another legislative change concerning arbitration is contained in Act No. CXCVI of 2011 on National Assets, which was adopted at the end of 2011, and most of its provisions have already entered into force. This Act provides, *inter alia*, that in a civil law contract concerning Hungarian national assets located in the territory of Hungary, only Hungarian may be stipulated as the governing language; only Hungarian substantive law may be stipulated as the governing law; and only the jurisdiction of the Hungarian state courts may be stipulated as the dispute resolution forum. Even Hungarian arbitration courts are expressly excluded. Therefore, while the proposal summarized in the preceding paragraph has not yet been adopted, an important legislative step to narrow the use of arbitration by state entities has already been made.

---

[5] No. T/4246 of 23 September 2011; for the full text of the proposal, see www.parlament.hu/irom39/04276/04276.pdf (only available in Hungarian language)

The four main permanent arbitration courts operating in Hungary are: (i) the Permanent Arbitration Court attached to the Hungarian Chamber of Commerce and Industry ("HCCI Arbitration Court"); (ii) the Energy Arbitration Court; (iii) the Arbitration Court of Financial and Capital Markets; and (iv) the Arbitration Court attached to the Hungarian Chamber of Agriculture.

The HCCI Arbitration Court, seated in Budapest,[6] continues to be the most frequently used and most well-known permanent arbitration court in Hungary.

The Energy Arbitration Court, which is also seated in Budapest, started to operate in 2009. The Energy Arbitration Court specializes in administering arbitrations relating to legal disputes arising from the articles of acts on gas supply and electricity and from contracts concluded between license holders under the scope of these acts, provided that the parties referred such matters to arbitration and they are not otherwise barred from having these matters decided through arbitration.[7] Targeted clients of the Energy Arbitration Court are traders, power stations and industrial customers. The list of arbitrators consists of industry experts and lawyers with considerable experience in the energy sector.

The Arbitration Court of Financial and Capital Markets has exclusive jurisdiction to handle domestic and international arbitrations arising in these industries.[8]

---

[6] For further information, visit www.mkik.hu (also in English).

[7] *See* Section 1.2 of the Memorandum of the Energy Arbitration Court. In our view, the jurisdiction of the Energy Arbitration Court may also be established on the basis of Section 3(1) of the Hungarian Arbitration Act, i.e., not only in energy-related disputes.

[8] *See* Section 376 of Act CXX of 2001 on the Capital Market.

The Arbitration Court attached to the Hungarian Chamber of Agriculture is designed to adjudicate arbitration cases involving companies in the agricultural sector.

A.2 Trends and Tendencies

Since the Hungarian Arbitration Act entered into force in 1994, there is a well-crystallized trend in Hungary towards valuing arbitration as an important method of dispute resolution. Arbitration has become a true alternative to civil litigation of commercial matters. Although *ad hoc* arbitration is also recognized, institutional arbitration is more accepted and used in practice. However, the number of arbitrations continues to be substantially below the number of cases filed in ordinary courts.

Below is a brief overview concerning the tendencies of arbitration practice in Hungary in recent years, which is based on the report of the HCCI Arbitration Court, published in 2011 ("Report"). [9]

According to the Report, the caseload of the HCCI Arbitration Court has been more or less stable in recent years, at roughly 300 cases per year. Approximately 15% of these cases are international.

Foreign parties involved in these cases include those from Germany, Austria, Italy, France, Romania, Switzerland, the USA, the Netherlands, Israel, Slovakia, Belgium, Bulgaria, Cyprus, Spain, Great Britain, Norway, Luxembourg, Poland, the Czech Republic, Lichtenstein, Ireland, Croatia, the Seychelles Islands, Canada, Finland, Egypt and the Isle of Man.

---

[9]   The full text of the report can be found in the journal "Gazdaság és Jog," 9/2011.

The number of arbitration proceedings has recently been decreasing while the amount in controversy relating to these arbitrations has been increasing.

According to the Report, the disputes are varied and they arise in connection with the following types of contracts: (i) sales and supply contracts; (ii) service contracts; (iii) lease contracts; (iv) loan contracts; (v) articles of association; (vi) license contracts; (vii) franchise contracts; and (viii) carriage contracts.

The average length of arbitration proceedings is 14 months. Proceedings in Hungarian courts, by contrast, can last as long as three to four years.

B. CASES

The vast majority of arbitrations in Hungary are confidential. In 2011, very few notable international arbitral awards were published. Below is the summary of a domestic case related to the question of the validity of an arbitration agreement under Hungarian law. In our view, the case may also be important for domestic and foreign companies operating in Hungary.

B.1 Arbitration Agreement Incapable of Being Performed— Lack of Accurate Determination of the Arbitration Court

Pursuant to the Hungarian Arbitration Act, a state court before which an action is brought in a matter that is the subject of an arbitration agreement shall refer the parties to arbitration unless it finds that the agreement is null and void, inoperative or incapable of being performed.

In a recent decision,[10] an ordinary court reviewed this provision of the Hungarian Arbitration Act. The parties concluded that an

---

[10]   *See* BDT2011. 2399.

agency agreement that contained the following arbitration clause: "any disputes concerning this agreement, shall be exclusively decided by arbitration court." The court found that an arbitration agreement or clause can be considered valid and capable of being performed only if it accurately determines whether the parties agreed to *ad hoc* arbitration or to arbitration before a permanent arbitration court. If the parties agreed to arbitrate before a permanent arbitration court, they must specify the arbitration court in their agreement.

Here, the court held that the arbitration agreement concluded by the parties was invalid because the parties failed to adequately specify an existing arbitration court.

C. PUBLIC POLICY IN INTERNATIONAL ARBITRATION

C.1 Scenarios of Reliance on Public Policy

When a Hungarian arbitration court issues an award, a party may petition the competent Hungarian state court to cancel the award on the basis of, among others things, an alleged violation of Hungarian public policy. In principle, if the arbitration agreement violates public policy, it might also be possible to raise the public policy argument to the arbitral tribunal's jurisdiction over the case. In the latter event, either party may request the competent state court to review the decision establishing jurisdiction.

Pursuant to the Hungarian Arbitration Act, Hungarian state courts are also entitled to deny enforcement of an arbitral award if a court finds that the award violates Hungarian public policy. This rule also applies to foreign arbitral awards subject to the New York Convention.

We are not aware of any Hungarian arbitration case in which the tribunal considered public policy issues in the context of the underlying arbitration agreement. (This does not mean that no such case exists. As discussed in part B, *supra*, publication of arbitration cases is quite limited in Hungary).

An interesting question is whether the public policy argument may be invoked before a state court in connection with a pending arbitration to invalidate the underlying arbitration agreement. Either before or during an arbitration, a party may initiate a lawsuit before Hungarian state courts on the same matter, and the state court will proceed if it finds that the arbitration agreement has not come into existence, is invalid, ineffective or impossible to comply with. The Hungarian Arbitration Act does not contain a reference to public policy in this context. However, it is conceivable that, in relation to determining the validity of an arbitration agreement, a violation of public policy could be relevant. At the same time, we are not aware of any case law on this issue.

C.2 Modes and Limitations of Reliance on Public Policy

Pursuant to the Hungarian Arbitration Act, a public policy argument may be raised after the award is issued, in which case the cancellation of the award may be requested from the competent state court within 60 days from the date of the receipt of the award. It is also possible to raise a public policy argument if it concerns the arbitration agreement itself. In the latter case, a party has 30 days from the delivery of the order establishing the tribunal's jurisdiction to turn to the competent state court for review of such order.

No time limit (statute of limitation) has been specified relating to the enforcement of a domestic or a foreign arbitral award. Therefore, the general statutory limitation period applies. (In cases in which Hungarian substantive laws apply, the statutory limitation period is generally five years.) In our view, raising the public policy argument in previous stages of the arbitration procedure (e.g., before or during the arbitration or in a cancellation case) is not a precondition to invoking this argument at the enforcement stage. At the same time, if a party believes that either the arbitration agreement or the Hungarian arbitral award violates public policy, it may be advisable to raise this argument earlier. Obviously, if a court issues a decision rejecting the public policy argument before the enforcement stage, this fact will considerably weaken the chances of succeeding on the violation of public policy argument during the enforcement stage.

Hungary is a party to the New York Convention. Therefore, considering Article V(1)(e) of the New York Convention, an award vacated in the country in which it was issued (country of origin) may not be recognized and enforced in Hungary.

C.3   Rules that Constitute "Public Policy"

Generally speaking, the term "public policy" has not been defined under Hungarian law. Based on the reasoning of several high-level state courts, however, it can be concluded that public policy is to be found in the general principles of law, especially in civil and constitutional law. For example, an award derogating from "the rules of the state with unconditional prevalence" may violate Hungarian public policy. Some references have also been made relating to public morality. Nevertheless, state courts have made it clear that "public policy" may not be used to argue that the arbitral tribunal interpreted the applicable law incorrectly, i.e., as a *quasi* appeal.

In addition, the courts have clarified several of the grounds for challenging an award that do *not* constitute a violation of public policy. For example, questions relating to the taking of evidence in arbitration proceedings do not fall within the scope of public policy. Also, controversies relating to an expert opinion or to the alleged lack of notice regarding a site inspection are not considered to be violations of public policy. Deficiencies in the reasoning of an award are also not against public policy. (There was a Metropolitan Court decision that found a violation of public policy due to severe deficiencies in the reasoning of the award. However, the Supreme Court overruled that decision.)

An interesting approach to raising the argument of a "public policy" violation can be found in a recent case, which held that if the decision in an award obviously undermines the principles of legal certainty and trust in arbitral tribunals, then the award containing such ruling is in violation of public policy.

The Model Law and the Hungarian Arbitration Act both refer to the public policy of the state in which the recognition, enforcement or challenge is sought. Therefore, in Hungary, there is no express right to challenge an award on international public policy grounds. At the same time, the fact that generally recognized principles of international law are accepted by the Hungarian legal system might open the door for litigants to make international public policy arguments in Hungarian court cases. However, this has yet to be tested.

Based on all of the above, there seems to be a high threshold in Hungarian jurisprudence when invoking a violation of public policy. Hungarian courts respect the autonomy of arbitral tribunals and have been refusing to act as an appellate court reviewing arbitral awards. Hungarian courts will cancel an arbitral award only in exceptional cases.

INDONESIA

Timur Sukirno,[1] Andi Yusuf Kadir[2] and Reno Hirdarisvita[3]

A.   LEGISLATION, TRENDS AND TENDENCIES

Arbitration in Indonesia is governed by Law No. 30 of 1999 on Arbitration and Alternative Dispute Resolution ("Arbitration Law"). Also, through Presidential Decree No. 34 of 1981, Indonesia has ratified the New York Convention.

Key features of the Arbitration Law include:

- The courts have no jurisdiction to hear disputes between parties bound by an arbitration agreement.

- Arbitration hearings must be completed within 180 days from the constitution of the arbitral tribunal unless otherwise agreed by both parties, or unless an extension is necessary for the arbitral tribunal to make a provisional award.

- The parties can seek a provisional award (such as an award to attach assets).

---

[1]   Timur Sukirno is a Partner in Baker & McKenzie's Jakarta office and has extensive experience in debt restructuring, bankruptcy, finance and projects, as well as commercial disputes and arbitration. He is a founding member and first chairman of the Indonesian Receivers and Administrators Association, and is a member of the Higher Education of Law Committee at the Department of Education and the sub-committee on the Development of Law in the Framework of Economic Recovery of the Indonesian government.

[2]   Andi Yusuf Kadir is a Senior Associate in Baker & McKenzie's Jakarta office and a member of the Firm's Global Dispute Resolution Practice Group.

[3]   Reno Hirdarisvita is an Associate in Baker & McKenzie's Jakarta office and a member of the Firm's Global Dispute Resolution Practice Group.

- A foreign arbitral award is enforceable in Indonesia once it obtains *exequatur*, and there are limited grounds for challenging foreign arbitral awards.

A party can only apply for an *exequatur* after a foreign arbitral award is registered with the Central Jakarta District Court. The Arbitration Law specifies that the arbitrator or his/her proxy registers the award.[4] In practice, however, the Central Jakarta District Court has deviated from this peculiar requirement and allowed the winning parties, or even the losing parties, to register the award.[5] In *Balmac International v. Firma Sinar Nusantara*, Balmac International Inc., the winning party, registered two awards rendered by the Cocoa Merchants' Association of America with the Central Jakarta District Court. In *Noble Americas Corp. v. PT Wahana Adhireksa Wiraswasta*, the Central Jakarta District Court also allowed Noble America Corp., the winning party, to register the award rendered by the Cocoa Merchants' Association of America. In *Karaha Bodas Co. v. Perusahaan Pertambangan Minyak dan Gas Bumi Negara*, the award rendered in Geneva was registered by Pertamina, the losing party.

Unlike the registration of domestic awards,[6] the Arbitration Law does not provide a statutory time limit for the registration of foreign arbitral awards. The Supreme Court recently affirmed this position in *PT Pertamina EP, PT Pertamina (Persero) v. PT Lirik Petroleum*.[7]

---

[4] Article 67(1) of the Arbitration Law.

[5] Tony Budidjaja, "Public Policy as Grounds for Refusal of Recognition and Enforcement of Foreign Arbitral Awards in Indonesia," *PT Tatanusa*, 2002, p. 28.

[6] Under Articles 59(1) and (4) of the Arbitration Law, failure to register domestic arbitral awards within this 30-day period shall render the award unenforceable.

[7] Supreme Court Judgment No. 904K/PDT.SUS/2009 dated 9 June 2010.

Under Article 66 of the Arbitration Law, the Indonesian court will grant the *exequatur* if:

(a) the award is rendered in a state that is bound by a bilateral or multilateral convention on recognition and enforcement of foreign arbitral awards by which Indonesia is also bound;

(b) the legal relationship on which the award is based can be considered as commercial under Indonesian law; and

(c) the award is not contrary to public policy in Indonesia.

In effect, Article 66(a) and (b) of the Arbitration Law exercise the "reciprocity and commercial reservations" provided for in Article I(3) of the New York Convention. Under the "reciprocity reservation," a foreign arbitral award can only be enforced in Indonesia if the award is made in a contracting state of the New York Convention, and under the "commercial reservation," Indonesia will only apply the New York Convention to awards adjudicating differences arising out of legal relationships, contractual or otherwise, that are considered as commercial under Indonesian law.

B.   CASES

B.1   Common Tactics to Defeat Arbitration Clauses

It is not uncommon for parties, despite the existence of a mutually agreed arbitration clause, to file claims in the courts. The justification commonly used is that the dispute is outside the realm of the contractual sphere, and instead falls under the category of an unlawful act pursuant to Article 1365 of the Indonesian Civil Code. In other words, the argument is that an unlawful act claim is not arbitrable.

Article 1365 of the Indonesian Civil Code provides that every unlawful act causing losses to another person shall oblige the person who is responsible for such losses to pay compensation. The Indonesian Civil Code does not provide any definition of the term "unlawful act." In practice, an unlawful act has been interpreted broadly to mean violations of statutory law as well as unwritten norms of law (such as good morals, customs and reasonableness). The concept of "unlawful act," therefore, can be said to be open-ended, leaving it to the courts to decide whether the particular conduct in question really constitutes an unlawful act. It is often the case that parties file this type of claim to exert pressure on or to frustrate their counterparts with the lengthy proceedings of Indonesian courts.

In 2005, the Supreme Court issued guidelines to district courts affirming that district courts do not have jurisdiction to hear disputes between parties bound by an arbitration agreement, even if the claims are based on an unlawful act as defined by Article 1365 of the Indonesian Civil Code. In spite of these guidelines, there remain a small number of cases in which parties bound by arbitration clauses file claims in court and attempt to re-characterize contractual disputes as unlawful acts.

In *Government of the Regency of Pasir, East Kalimantan (Regency of Pasir) v. Samtan Co. Ltd. and PT Kideco Jaya Agung and Samchully Pharmaceutical Co. Ltd.*, the district court, high court, and Supreme Court dismissed the Regency of Pasir's unlawful act lawsuit on the basis that Indonesian courts have no jurisdiction to hear a case where both parties are bound by an arbitration clause.[8]

---

[8] *See* Tanah Grogot District Court, Judgment No. 07/Pdt.G/2003/PN.TG dated 23 December 2003; Tanah Grogot High Court Judgment No. 47/PDT/2004/PT.KT.SMDA dated 18 May 2004; Supreme Court Judgment No. 790 K/Pdt/2006 dated 5 February 2007.

The case arose from a coal mining cooperation agreement between the Indonesian government and PT Kideco Jaya Agung, a joint venture company established by a consortium of Korean companies with Samtan Co. Ltd. as the leader. Under the agreement, PT Kideco Jaya Agung was granted the right to conduct coal mining as the government's contractor. The agreement also required the contractor to ensure that any shares owned by foreign investor(s) were offered for sale to the government, Indonesian nationals, or Indonesian companies controlled by Indonesians each year following the end of the fourth full calendar year after commencement of the operating period.

The operating period commenced in March 1993, which meant that by 1998, PT Kideco Jaya Agung had to implement the divestment clause. The regency government claimed that from 1999 to 2003, PT Kideco Jaya Agung had not offered its shares to the government. The regency government further claimed that by failing to implement the divestment clause, Samtan Co. Ltd., as the controlling shareholder of PT Kideco Jaya Agung, had committed an unlawful act that caused losses to the regency government. On this basis, the regency government filed an unlawful act claim with the Tanah Grogot District Court in East Kalimantan.

B.2   Indonesian Courts' Jurisdiction to Annul Foreign Arbitral Awards

Under the Arbitration Law, one of the possible recourses against arbitral awards is cancellation/annulment of the award. It is widely accepted that Indonesian courts have no jurisdiction to hear any application to cancel or annul foreign arbitral awards. The landmark precedent on this matter is the 2004 Supreme Court ruling in a case between Perusahaan Pertambangan Minyak dan Gas Bumi Negara (Pertamina) and Karaha Bodas

Company, in which Pertamina sought to annul an arbitral award rendered in Geneva in favor of Karaha Bodas. In its decision No. 01/Banding/Wasit-Int/2002, dated 8 March 2004, the Supreme Court declared that Indonesian courts do not have the authority to annul foreign arbitral awards.

This view was affirmed in subsequent cases. In *PT Bungo Raya Nusantara v. PT Jambi Resources*, Bungo filed an application to the Central Jakarta District Court to annul an award rendered under the SIAC rules in favor of Jambi. In its decision, the Supreme Court rejected Bungo's application and confirmed that applications for annulment of foreign arbitral awards can only be filed with the courts in the country where the award was issued.[9]

C. PUBLIC POLICY IN INTERNATIONAL ARBITRATION

As mentioned above, Article 66 of the Arbitration Law provides that a foreign arbitral award is not enforceable in Indonesia if it violates public policy. This provision appears to be mandatory. Thus, unlike Article V of the New York Convention, the text of Article 66 does not appear to give discretionary power to the state judicial body to recognize and enforce foreign awards if they violate public policy. The term "public policy" in Indonesia is defined by Article 4(2) of Regulation of the Supreme Court No. 1 of 1990 as "clearly in contradiction with the fundamental principles of the Indonesian legal system and social system in Indonesia." In practice, the notion of public policy has been interpreted broadly by Indonesian courts.

In *Bankers Trust v. Mayora Indah* and *Bankers Trust v. Jakarta International Hotels and Development* (the "Bankers Trust"

---

[9]   Supreme Court Judgment No. 64 K/Pdt.Sus/2010 dated 26 April 2010.

cases),[10] the Supreme Court held that enforcing awards when the validity of the arbitration clauses was still subject to a final and binding court judgment would violate public policy. The Bankers Trust cases seem to suggest that an award is not yet enforceable when a cancellation action against the arbitration clause is brought in Indonesian courts and a final decision on that issue has not yet been rendered.

These two cases involve International Swaps and Derivatives Association ("ISDA") master agreements between Bankers Trust and Mayora Indah, and between Bankers Trust and Jakarta International Hotels and Development ("Jakarta International").

In the Bankers Trust cases, Mayora Indah and Jakarta International commenced legal proceedings at the South Jakarta District Court seeking annulment of the ISDA agreements on the grounds that they were contrary to public policy, and alternatively, that it was *ultra vires* for Mayora Indah and Jakarta International to enter into such agreements. At the same time, the bank challenged the jurisdiction of the South Jakarta District Court and commenced arbitration proceedings against Mayora Indah and Jakarta International under the LCIA rules.

The LCIA tribunal rendered awards in favor of the bank, but the South Jakarta District Court rejected the bank's objection to the court's jurisdiction. Contrary to the findings of the LCIA awards, the South Jakarta District Court ruled that the arbitration clause was not part of the ISDA agreements and was therefore not binding upon Mayora Indah and Jakarta International Hotels. The court also annulled the ISDA agreements. The bank then

---

[10] Supreme Court Judgment No. 02K/Exr/Arb.Int/Pdt/2000 dated 5 September 2000 in *Bankers Trust Company and Bankers Trust International v. Mayora Indah*; Supreme Court Judgment No. 04K/Exr/Arb.Int/Pdt/2000 dated 5 September 2000 in *Bankers Trust Company and Bankers Trust International v. Jakarta International Hotels and Development*.

lodged an appeal against the court judgment and simultaneously filed an application for *exequatur* in the Central Jakarta District Court.

Another case regarding interpretation of public policy is *Astro Nusantara International B.V. (Astro) v. PT Ayunda Prima Mitra (Ayunda).*[11] This case concerned enforcement of an interim award for injunction rendered under the SIAC rules. The award ordered Ayunda to discontinue its litigation at the South Jakarta District Court against Astro, because the subject matter of the dispute fell under an arbitration clause agreed to by both parties.

Ayunda, however, refused to comply with the award, arguing that the South Jakarta District Court had asserted jurisdiction over Ayunda's case against Astro. Astro responded by lodging an application for *exequatur* with the Central Jakarta District Court, which was unsuccessful. The Central Jakarta District Court held that the award had violated the sovereignty of the Republic of Indonesia because it intervened with the state's judicial process, even though the award essentially only compelled Ayunda to adhere to the arbitration clause. The Central Jakarta District Court concluded that the award was contrary to public policy in Indonesia. The Supreme Court also accepted this reasoning.

In *Pertamina v. PT Lirik Petroleum (Lirik)*, Pertamina filed an application to annul an arbitral award (issued by an ICC tribunal) in favor of Lirik. One of Pertamina's arguments was that the award violated public policy because it disregarded Pertamina's authority as the government's only representative in the oil and gas sector. Pertamina claimed that as the authority on oil and gas mining in Indonesia, it had the right to regulate and control the policy for determining the commercialization of oil and gas

---

[11] Supreme Court Judgment No. 01K/Pdt.Sus/2010 dated 24 February 2010.

fields. As such, Pertamina viewed the ICC award sanctioning Pertamina for its failure to commercialize Lirik's oil and gas fields as a violation of Indonesian public policy. The Central Jakarta District Court rejected this argument and declared that the ICC award did not violate public policy, considering that the ICC tribunal, as the mutually agreed dispute settlement forum, had exclusive jurisdiction to examine and adjudicate the dispute between Pertamina and Lirik. The Supreme Court affirmed this finding in its decision No. 904 K/Pdt.Sus/2009, dated 9 June 2010. After the Supreme Court issued its decision, Pertamina tried to annul the ICC award by applying for a civil review with the Supreme Court. The Supreme Court dismissed this application as well on the grounds that the appeal decision previously issued by the Supreme Court was final and binding.[12]

---

[12]   Supreme Court Judgment No. 56 PK/Pdt.Sus/2011 dated 23 August 2011.

ITALY

Gianfranco Di Garbo[1]

A.   LEGISLATION, TRENDS AND TENDENCIES

As an implementation of the European Mediation Directive 2008/52/EC, effective as of 20 March 2011, Legislative Decree No. 28 of 4 March 2011 (the "Decree") has introduced a new mediation process that is mandatory for disputes involving:

- rights *in rem*,
- division of assets,
- inheritance,
- family agreements,
- lease of real estate or of ongoing businesses,
- loans,
- insurance and banking contracts and other financial contracts, and
- tort actions on defamatory statements in the media.

As of 20 March 2012, mediation will also become mandatory for disputes relating to damages arising out of automobile and nautical accidents and disputes concerning co-ownership of real estate.

The mediation procedure established under the Decree can only be brought before authorized mediation bodies that are included in a register maintained by the Ministry of Justice. Mediation is now a pre-condition for the commencement of court proceedings in all disputes covered by the Decree. Although the new law

---

[1]   Gianfranco Di Garbo is a Partner in Baker & McKenzie's Milan office and coordinator of the office's Dispute Resolution Practice Group. He is a member of the Firm's European and Global Dispute Resolution Practice Groups. His practice concentrates on litigation and arbitration.

does not apply to arbitration, Article 5 of the Decree provides that, when the contract or the bylaws of a company provide for a two-step settlement mechanism combining mediation and arbitration, and no attempt is made to mediate the dispute, the arbitrator, upon request of a party, should invite the parties to attempt to settle their dispute through mediation within 15 days, and shall not decide the case unless the parties have previously tried to resolve the dispute by mediation.[2]

B. CASES

B.1 Enforceability of an Arbitral Award against the Public Administration

In an important judgment, the Supreme Administrative Courtruled that after the reform of Law No. 80/2005 and Legislative Decree No.40/2006, an arbitration award has the same effect as an ordinary judgment and, therefore, the winning party may enforce it against the Public Administration using a special accelerated administrative procedure called *giudizio di ottemperanza*.[3]

---

[2]   The new legislation raised the forceful opposition of the bar associations on the grounds that it constituted a violation of the right to free access to justice and to defense. It was also alleged that this process for the selection of the mediators was inadequate. On 12 April 2011, the Regional Administrative Court of Lazio held that such criticism was not without foundation and challenged the constitutional legitimacy of the Law on two grounds based on two articles: (i) Article 5, concerning the mandatory effect of mediation as a precondition for a court order, and (ii) Article 16, regarding the lack of adequate criteria for the selection of mediators able to guarantee sufficient reliability and efficiency, in particular with respect to the mediator's legal expertise. The decision of the Constitutional Court is expected soon. In the meantime, the Law is in full force, particularly those aspects concerning mediation as a mandatory precondition for a civil action in matters covered by the Decree.

[3]   Judgment of the Consiglio di Stato, section VI, of 23 May 2011, no. 3047.

B.2 Arbitration and Insolvency Procedure

In a recent judgment, the Supreme Court[4] found that where a company is under extraordinary administration (an insolvency procedure for major companies in distress), an arbitration clause is not effective and any dispute against it has to be resolved by the insolvency courts.

B.3 Rules of Procedure in Arbitration Proceedings

Confirming the prevailing opinion of most commentators, the Supreme Courthas ruled that arbitrators are not bound by the procedural rules of the Code of Civil Procedure unless the parties expressly asked them to abide by them.[5] The arbitrators may therefore conduct the proceedings in the way they deem appropriate, with the caveat that the parties must be given ample opportunity to present their case.

B.4 Arbitration Clause in International Arbitration

The Supreme Court held that reference in an international contract to general terms and conditions that include an arbitration clause is sufficient to make such a clause valid and enforceable.[6] The Supreme Court based this decision on the interpretation of Article 2 of the New York Convention, which extends the meaning of the term "written agreement" to "an exchange of letters or telegrams." The court held that this also includes a reference to a standard form, even if this form is not signed by the parties.

---

[4] Judgment of the Court of Cassation of 17 February 2011, no. 3918.

[5] Judgment of the Court of Cassation of 17 February 2011, no. 3917.

[6] Judgment of the Court of Cassation of 16 June 2011, no. 13231.

C. PUBLIC POLICY IN INTERNATIONAL ARBITRATION

C.1 Relevance of Public Policy in the Enforcement of Arbitral Awards

Articles 829 and 839 of the Italian Code of Civil Procedure, as amended by the Legislative Decree No. 40/2006, address public policy and its relevance for arbitration:

- Domestic arbitration awards can only be set aside by reason of a violation of law (*regole di diritto*) if this is expressly provided for by the parties, by a special law or for public policy reasons.[7]

- For the enforcement of a foreign award in Italy, a motion must be filed under Article 839 of the Code of Civil Procedure, before the president of the court of appeal in the district in which the respondent is domiciled. If the respondent is not domiciled in Italy, the action has to be brought before the Rome Court of Appeal. After examining the regularity of the award, the court will declare the award enforceable (*exequatur*) unless the award violates Italian public policy[8] or the dispute cannot be resolved by arbitration under Italian law. Article 840 regarding an opposition to an

---

[7] Furthermore, under Article 829 of the Code of Civil Procedure, an arbitral award may be set aside because of a violation of law (i) when it relates to labor disputes (as defined by Article 409 of the Code of Civil Procedure) or (ii) the award deals with a question concerning a subject matter that cannot be the subject of an arbitration agreement.

[8] This is line with Article V(2)(b) of the New York Convention which expressly provides that the recognition or enforcement of a foreign award can be denied if it would be contrary to the public policy of the country where the recognition or enforcement is sought. For details see, *inter alia*, F. Consolo and F.P.Luiso, *Codice di Procedura Civile Commentato*, Milano 2007, 6138.

exequatur granted by the court of appeal uses the same language and allows such an opposition if the award contains provisions contrary to public policy.

C.2   The Meaning of "Public Policy" under Italian Law

Much has been written on the definition of public policy.[9] While the very broad definition of public policy as "the whole complex of general principles of justice of civilized countries" has been generally abandoned, most recent doctrine recognizes that the notion refers to Italian public international policy (*ordine pubblico interno internazionale*), consisting of the fundamental principles of the Italian juridical system and including fundamental principles of EU law. The notion is not identical with the merely mandatory rules of Italian law (*norme imperative*). There are statutory provisions that are mandatory in Italy but from which the parties can nevertheless derogate by choosing a foreign law as the law governing their contractual relationship.[10]

C.3   Examples of Breaches of Substantive Public Policy

Few cases about the notion of public policy are available. The leading case remains one that was tried before the Supreme Court in 2007. In that case, the Supreme Court had to decide whether a U.S. judgment granting punitive damages could be recognized and declared enforceable in Italy. The Supreme Court thoroughly considered the notion of public policy in its decision and held that a foreign judgment granting punitive damages is

---

[9]   On the subject see, for example, F. Ziccardi, "Il ruolo dell'ordine pubblico nel processo arbitrale, in Arbitrato ADR e Conciliazione," *Milano* 2009, 603 and M. Rubino Sammartano, "Il diritto dell'arbitrato," *Padova* 2006, 621.

[10]   On this point see A. De Pauli, "Comment to the judgment of the Court of Cassation no. 1183/2007," *Resp.Civ. e Prev.*, 2007, 10, 2100 and G. Ponzanelli, "Danni Punitivi? No grazie," Foro it. 2007, 5, 1461.

not enforceable in Italy because the fundamental principle of Italian law with respect to civil liability is that a wrongdoer may not be punished but has to compensate the injured party only for the actual damage suffered.[11]

The Supreme Court held that arbitrators have to observe public policy even when they are requested to issue an award based on equity.[12] Worth mentioning is also a judgment of the Court of Appeal Genoa ruling that a violation of public policy makes the award subject to being vacated, even if the arbitration agreement includes language to the effect that recourse to the ordinary courts of law is excluded.[13]

C.4 Examples of Breaches of Procedural Public Policy

Public policy also includes procedural public policy. A foreign award may be set aside not only if it contradicts a principle of Italian substantive public policy, but also if it breaches fundamental principles of the Italian procedural public policy. The procedural public policy includes for example the right to a fair defense (*contraddittorio*), which requires that each party has the opportunity to properly argue its case in the arbitration proceedings. It also includes the principle of impartiality of the arbitrators. Applying Italian procedural public policy, the Venice Court of Appeal and the Genoa Court of Appeal held that English arbitration awards rendered by the so-called "umpire" alone, in accordance with the former English Arbitration Act, were to be recognized and declared enforceable in Italy.[14]

---

[11]   Court of Cassation of 19 January 2007, no. 1183, concerning the judgment of a U.S. Court. The ruling may also apply in the case of a foreign award.

[12]   Court of Cassation of 8 November 1984, no. 1108

[13]   Court of Appeals of Genoa, 27 February 1995.

[14]   Court of Appeals of Venice, 22 May 1976 and Court of Appeals of Genoa, 5 May 1980.

C. Public Policy in International Arbitration

It has also been accepted that the time granted by an arbitral tribunal to the parties for submission of their arguments may be relatively short, provided, however, that the tribunal's deadline does not undermine the right of defense.[15] Finally, it has been established by the Genoa Court of Appeal[16] that a foreign award giving no written grounds for the decision is enforceable in Italy (and is therefore not in breach of public policy). This is because, although the basis for the decision must be established in any Italian judgment under Article 111 of the Italian Constitution, the Geneva Convention of 13 April 1961, applicable in Italy, allows for the enforceability of non-reasoned foreign awards if this is allowed in the country where the award was issued. Therefore, the principle that a decision has to include the grounds upon which it is based cannot be considered to be part of the Italian procedural public policy relating to international arbitration.

---

[15]   Court of Appeals of Rome, 23 May 1977.

[16]   Same judgment quoted under footnote no. 13.

JAPAN

Haig Oghigian,[1] Mami Ohara[2] and Hiroyuki Hamai[3]

A. LEGISLATION, TRENDS AND TENDENCIES

The new Arbitration Law of Japan (the "Arbitration Law") was promulgated on 1 August 2003 at the 156th session of the National Diet as Law No. 138 and came into force on 1 March 2004. Thus in 2004, Japan's arbitration system was completely overhauled. Japan modernized its outmoded arbitration law[4] and brought it in line with the UNCITRAL Model Law. At the same time, Japan's leading international commercial arbitral institution, the JCAA, revamped its commercial arbitration rules (the "Rules"), to bring them in line with the Arbitration Law, the UNCITRAL Arbitration Rules, and the rules of other leading international commercial dispute resolution organizations. This section will provide a brief summary of the historical background of the arbitration law in Japan as well as an introduction to the key reforms and unique features of the Arbitration Law and the Rules.

---

[1] Haig Oghigian is a Partner and co-chair of the Litigation and Dispute Resolution Group of Baker & McKenzie's Tokyo office. In addition to his work in dispute resolution, Mr. Oghigian advises clients on mergers and acquisitions, joint ventures, license agreements and distribution agreements, as well as construction and engineering contracts.

[2] Mami Ohara is an Associate in the Litigation and Dispute Resolution Group of Baker & McKenzie's Tokyo office.

[3] Hiroyuki Hamai is an Associate in the Litigation and Dispute Resolution Group of Baker & McKenzie's Tokyo office.

[4] English translation of the Arbitration Law can be found at http://www.kantei.go.jp/ foreign/policy/sihou/arbitrationlaw.pdf.

A.1 Historical Background

Before the enactment of the Arbitration Law, there was no stand-alone arbitration law in Japan. Rather, arbitration provisions were provided for under the 8th Book of the old Civil Procedure Law,[5] and they had not been amended for more than 110 years until the enactment of the Arbitration Law. Based on the German Civil Procedure Law of 1877, the old Civil Procedure Law contained provisions governing judgment, enforcement, provisional attachment and disposition, public notice and arbitration. When the current Civil Procedure Law was drafted and came into effect in 1997, provisions concerning arbitrations and public notices were not included in the Civil Procedure Law, and were renamed the Public Peremptory Notice and Arbitration Procedure Law. When the Arbitration Law was promulgated, provisions dealing with public notice procedures were then renamed as the Public Peremptory Notice Procedure Law.

In Japan, arbitration was and still is not utilized as much as it should be, and disputes are still normally resolved through negotiation and litigation. For a long time, therefore, it was not felt that there was a need for stand-alone arbitration legislation. Nevertheless, interest in arbitration increased and in 1979, an arbitration study group (*Chusai Kenkyukai*) was established.[6] The group undertook comparative studies of major or new arbitration laws in other countries in force at the time, and a draft for a new arbitration law was produced around 1989 (*Chusaiho Shian*). However, the draft was not adopted. A second draft was

---

[5]   Law No. 29 of 1890. The Civil Procedure Law itself was revamped in 1996.

[6]   Toshio Sawada, "The 2004 Japanese Arbitration Law in Relation to the UNCITRAL Model Law and the Japanese ADR and Attorneys Law," *Global Reflections on International Law, Commerce and Dispute Resolution: Liber Amicorum in Honor of Robert Briner*, 726 (ICC Publishing 2005).

produced in 2001, amidst calls for reform and the belief held by some scholars and promoters of arbitration that Japan needed to be promoted as a center for arbitration (*Chusaiho 2001 Shian*).[7] Nevertheless, this draft was also not adopted. Around the same time, as a part of the government's efforts to expand and facilitate the use of alternative dispute resolution ("ADR"), the Office for Promotion of Justice System Reform (*Shiho Seido Kaikaku Shingikai*) called for a new legal framework for arbitration that reflected worldwide developments and that used the Model Law as the basis for the new arbitration law. As a result, a draft of the Arbitration Law was created and passed by the Diet.

A.2   Main Features of the Arbitration Law

While the Arbitration Law in large part follows the provisions of the Model Law, it has made some modifications that are specific to Japanese contexts. Below are some of the special features of the Arbitration Law about which potential users should be aware before entering into an arbitration agreement specifying Japan as the place of arbitration:

- In Japan, in principle, only civil disputes that may be resolved by settlement between the parties may be submitted to arbitration.[8] Article 13(1) specifically lists divorce and separation as matters that are non-arbitrable.[9] In the

---

[7]   *Ibid.*

[8]   Article 13(1) of the Arbitration Law. This is in line with the Model Law, which leaves the issue of arbitrability to the laws of individual states (Model Law Article 1(5)). Following the practices in many civil law countries such as Germany, Switzerland, France, Italy and Sweden, Japan therefore prescribes to the possibility of settlement as a criteria for whether a dispute may be resolved by arbitration.

[9]   Divorce and separation matters relate to changes of personal status, the settlement by arbitration of which has traditionally been rejected and these disputes are normally determined by courts.

commercial fields, for example, applications for the invalidation of patents;[10] actions for declaratory judgment of absence of a new share issue; actions for declaratory judgment of absence or invalidation of a resolution of a shareholders meeting; or actions seeking revocation of a resolution of a shareholders meeting, are all deemed as matters that cannot be resolved through settlement,[11] and hence are not arbitrable.

- In line with litigation practices in Japan, where judges are expected to encourage amicable settlements, traditionally, many arbitration cases were settled through the active involvement of arbitrators. This has attracted criticism, especially from common law practitioners who do not like the idea of arbitrators acting as mediators. While recognizing the need to maintain its customary practice and recognizing the general trend in international commercial arbitration to separate arbitration and mediation proceedings, Article 38(4) of the Arbitration Law provides for the possibility of the involvement of an arbitrator in mediation; however, prior written consent from the parties is required.

- The Arbitration Law contains special provisions concerning consumers and employees. Under the Arbitration Law, consumers can unilaterally cancel an arbitration agreement even when they knowingly entered into it.[12] Further, an

---

[10]   As illustrated in Section B (Cases) below, while the issue of the validity of a patent is considered as non-arbitrable, claims for damages arising out of alleged patent infringement may be subjected to arbitration.

[11]   As these are matters that may greatly impact the interests of third parties when submitted to arbitration, they are therefore deemed non-arbitrable.

[12]   Article 3 of Supplementary Provisions of the Arbitration Law.

arbitration agreement contained in an individual's employment contract will be deemed invalid.[13]

- Perhaps one of the most significant features of the Arbitration Law is the continuance of significant involvement of the courts. The most obvious of these is the continuing notion espoused in Japan that arbitral tribunals should not involve themselves in interim measures. While other jurisdictions are embracing the idea that the tribunal has a role to play,[14] whether the arbitral tribunals should have the power to order interim measures was one of the most debated issues during the drafting process, and while the Arbitration Law contains supportive language,[15] uncertainties remain over whether interim measures issued by an arbitral tribunal would be enforceable.[16] The Arbitration Law also allows the court to "assist" a party in determining the place of arbitration if it is not clearly set out and where "there is a possibility" that the place of arbitration might be Japan.[17] Another provision allows the

---

[13] Article 4 of Supplementary Provisions of the Arbitration Law.

[14] For example, see Section 12 of the Singapore International Arbitration Act, and Section 19 of the Malaysian Arbitration Act of 2005.

[15] Article 24(1) of New Arbitration Law provides that "[u]nless otherwise agreed by the parties, the arbitral tribunal may, at the request of a party, order any party to take such interim measure of protection as the arbitral tribunal may consider necessary in respect of the subject matter of the dispute."

[16] The uncertainty over the enforceability of interim measures ordered by a tribunal is lessened somewhat by Article 24(2) of the Arbitration Law, which provides that the arbitral tribunal may order any party to provide appropriate security in connection with such measure. The JCAA also blunted the uncertainties regarding this issue by providing, under Rule 48, that the arbitral tribunal may issue interim measures of protection including the requirement to advance security.

[17] Article 8.

court to appear an arbitrator, particularly if "either party has a place of business in Japan."[18] Finally, Article 35 of the Arbitration Law allows the tribunal (on its own volition or through application by a party) to seek the assistance of the court in taking evidence.[19]

- In the past, arbitration proceedings in Japan were often criticized for being exceedingly lengthy and slow as arbitrators could be reluctant to limit the number of document exchanges. Further, hearings were often akin to court proceedings, where numerous short hearings were held weeks apart. This practice has been replaced with single hearings similar to those held in other arbitration centers.

- Article 45(1) of the Arbitration Law allows for enforcement of an arbitral award even if it is rendered in a jurisdiction not a party to the New York Convention. This is particularly relevant for a number of jurisdictions in Asia, such as Taiwan.

- Under the old law, no specific provisions dealing with the language of the arbitration existed. In the past, there were criticisms from non-Japanese parties that they were disadvantaged in arbitration proceedings in Japan due to huge expenses in connection with translation requirements. In an effort to make the law fairer, the Arbitration Law provides that the parties are free to agree on the language or languages to be used in the arbitral proceedings. In the absence of such an agreement, the arbitral tribunal may make such a determination.[20]

---

[18]   Article 17 read jointly with Article 8.

[19]   As described below in Section B, an application has indeed already been made to the court for assistance in taking evidence that raises some concerns.

[20]   Article 30.

As stated above, together with the reform of the Arbitration Law, the JCAA also completely revised its rules and a new set of rules came into effect in 2003.[21] The Rules have balanced and, in some contexts, clarified the provisions contained in the Arbitration Law.[22] Steps were taken to modernize, streamline and generally improve the Rules. Examples vary from allowing the tribunal to determine whether an agreement to arbitrate exists,[23] to allowing facsimiles and e-mail as evidence of a written arbitration agreement,[24] to allowing parties free choice of representation.[25]

While there are issues that may still be of concern to foreign parties, the Arbitration Law and the Rules allow for a flexible and modern arbitration system in Japan that is compatible with the laws and rules of other leading arbitration centers.

---

[21] The Rules were subsequently amended in 2006 (Rule 11, Language) and 2007 (Rule 28, Impartiality and Independence of Arbitrators). The current Rules are effective as of 1 January 2008.

[22] For example, Rule 28 sets forth both stricter guidelines for ensuring independence of arbitrators and a mechanism to remove an arbitrator for lack of impartiality. There is also greater flexibility to manage the case both by the JCAA and the tribunal, in order to prevent the process from grinding to a halt. For example, the JCAA can establish a tribunal even if one of the parties has raised a jurisdictional issue and the tribunal is then charged with ruling on its own jurisdictional power under Rule 16 (reflecting the thinking of *kompetenz/kompetenz*). Under Article 35, the tribunal is also permitted to proceed with the arbitral process even where one of the parties has refused to participate.

[23] Rule 16.

[24] *See* Rule 5.

[25] Rule 10; *but see* below for the implications of the Lawyers' Law on representation.

B. CASES

There have been a few interesting cases regarding the Arbitration Law since it came into force.

B.1 Court Assistance in Taking Evidence

This case was not a litigation case *per se*, but one involving Article 35(1) of the Arbitration Law. Article 35(1) allows an arbitral tribunal and a party to an arbitration proceeding[26] to apply to a court for assistance in taking evidence by any means that the arbitral tribunal considers necessary.[27] In this case, an examination of a witness in support of arbitration proceedings was conducted in the Tokyo District Court in accordance with Article 35(1).[28]

What is potentially troubling about this provision and this case is that, although the procedure was in support of arbitration proceedings, since it was conducted in court, it was considered a court proceeding rather than an "international arbitration case." It was therefore managed and administered by the court. In this situation, only a *bengoshi* (a licensed attorney of Japan) can represent an applicant or respondent in such proceeding. As a result, a *bengoshi* needs to be separately retained for such an application for court assistance and for conducting the witness examination. Even if a *bengoshi* is retained for the arbitration proceeding from the beginning, the *bengoshi* needs to be retained anew for such an application. This demonstrates the unfortunate

---

[26] The arbitral tribunal must consent to the application before it can be made.

[27] Such means include entrustment of investigation, examination of witnesses, expert testimony, and investigation of documentary evidence or inspection prescribed in the Code of Civil Procedure.

[28] Junya Naito, "Examination of Witnesses in Court for Arbitration Proceedings in Japan," *JCAA Newsletter,* March 2007, at 5.

effect of court intervention in international commercial arbitration. More significantly, it evidences the continuous obstacles created by the Lawyers' Law (*Bengoshi Ho*)[29] in relation to international commercial arbitration and, more specifically, in relation to the parties' rights to be represented by whomever they choose in international commercial arbitration proceedings. While this issue is partly dealt with by Article 58-2 of Special Measures Law Concerning the Handling of Legal Business by Foreign Lawyers (Law No. 66 of 1986), which allows a foreign lawyer to represent clients in procedures for an international arbitration case that he or she was requested to undertake or undertook in a foreign country, doubts remain as to the right to represent parties.[30]

B.2 Separability of Arbitration Agreement

The second case involving the Arbitration Law is more encouraging.[31] In this case, the plaintiff granted the defendant a non-exclusive license of its patents. The plaintiff alleged that the defendant had under reported the amount of sales of the licensed products, thus having underpaid the royalties owed to plaintiff.

---

[29] Law No. 205 of 1949. Article 72 of the Lawyers' Law provides that "[p]ersons who are not *bengoshi* or *bengoshi* juridical persons, as a business, may not for the purpose of receiving compensation, deal with legal advice, representation, arbitration or settlement or other legal work, or lend good offices, provided that the foregoing does not apply where there is a provision to the contrary in this or another law."

[30] This is so since Article 58(2) only deals with representation by a foreign lawyer practicing outside of Japan and specifically excludes a person who is employed and is providing services in Japan, based on his or her knowledge of foreign law. To eliminate doubts, Rule 10 explicitly states that a party may be represented by whomever it chooses and that the tribunal is not permitted to refuse a party's choice of representative except for good reason.

[31] Decision by the Tokyo District Court handed down on 21 October 2005, 1216 Hanrei Taimuzu 309; 1926 Hanrei Jiho 127.

The defendant asked the court to dismiss the plaintiff's action on the basis that there was an arbitration clause in the license agreement. The plaintiff argued that it had terminated the license agreement, which contained the arbitration agreement, and that the arbitration agreement therefore became invalid. The plaintiff further claimed that the defendant, in seeking an invalidation judgment of two of the patents licensed under the license agreement, had breached the arbitration agreement and rendered it invalid. The court held that even if a contract containing an arbitration agreement is null and void, the validity of the arbitration agreement was not necessarily affected. Furthermore, the patent invalidation judgment was held to be non-arbitrable, and therefore did not infringe the arbitration agreement. Even if it did infringe the arbitration agreement, it would only render the application unlawful, and thus did not necessarily invalidate the arbitration agreement.[32]

The plaintiff then made an appeal to the Intellectual Property High Court[33] based on two grounds:

1) Article 12(2) of the license agreement required a party seeking to contest a termination notice to initiate arbitration

---

[32] *See* "The First Case Applying the New Japanese Arbitration Law, Tokyo District Court, 21 October 2005," *JCAA Newsletter*, March 2007, at 9-10. The other interesting and encouraging aspect of this case is that although both parties to the license agreement were Japanese, they chose arbitration as the dispute resolution mechanism in their license agreement. Significantly, the parties chose ICC arbitration rather than JCAA, the leading arbitration institution in Japan, even though it concerned a domestic agreement.

[33] The Intellectual Property High Court was established on 1 April 2005, as a special branch within the Tokyo High Court in accordance with the Law for Establishing the IP High Court enacted in June 2004. The Intellectual Property High Court hears appeals from district courts in Japan on patent actions and suits against appeal/trial decisions made by the Japan Patent Office. It also hears any other cases before the Tokyo High Court, as far as the nature and contents of the case are related to intellectual property.

proceedings within 40 days from the date it received the termination notice. If the party receiving the termination notice did not initiate arbitration within 40 days from the date it received the notice, the arbitration clause expired together with the termination of the license agreement; and

2) even if the arbitration agreement continued to exist after the termination of the license agreement, the defendant continuously breached the license agreement through its unilateral actions stopping royalty payments rather than initiating arbitration proceedings in accordance with the parties' agreements; failing to initiate arbitration proceedings when there were questions concerning the validity of the termination of the license agreement; and deciding to seek the invalidation of relevant patents rather than initiate arbitration proceedings when there were concerns regarding the validity of the relevant patents. Based on the principles of fairness and equity, the defendant should therefore be barred from seeking a dismissal of the plaintiff's action.

The Intellectual Property High Court found that the 40-day period was a grace period for the correction of a breach under the license agreement, and Article 12(2) only clarified that the 40-day grace period would stop running once arbitration was initiated. It did not place any liabilities on a party to initiate arbitration proceedings. The Intellectual Property High Court also found that the arbitration agreement only required the parties to submit any differences and disputes to arbitration under the ICC Rules if the parties could not resolve their differences within a reasonable time, and it did not place an obligation on a party to pursue arbitration actively. The Intellectual Property High Court therefore dismissed the appeal.[34]

---

[34]   Case No. 10120 of 2005.

B.3 Public Policy

Another case relates to an application for provisional injunction against acts in breach of a contract. The applicant, a Japanese company selling semi-conductor related products trading between Japan and Korea, entered into an agency agreement with the respondent in 1994. The agreement specified that either party may refuse to renew the agreement upon expiration of the term, with 60 days' notice. The agreement also specified that all disputes arising out of the agreement shall be finally settled by arbitration in accordance with the rules of the Korean Commercial Arbitration Board and the governing law of the agreement was Korean law. On 22 January 2007, the respondent notified the applicant of its refusal to renew the agreement upon its expiration on 31 March 2007. The applicant filed an application for a provisional injunction in an attempt to preserve its contractual status. It claimed, *inter alia*, that the clauses concerning jurisdiction and governing law were invalid as they were in breach of Japan's public policy to protect continuous contractual relationships,[35] and that the jurisdiction and governing law clauses had been inserted into the agreement in order to avoid the protections Japanese laws gave to long-term contractual relationships.

Interestingly, the court found that the principle of party autonomy applied when determining the issue concerning governing law. Just because the application of the parties' chosen governing law may have a result that would be contrary to the public policy of Japan, did not mean that the choice of governing law (and jurisdiction) itself would necessarily be

---

[35] In Japan, irrespective of the written agreements of the parties, it is difficult to terminate a long-term contractual relationship, especially one with an automatic renewal provision that was contained in the contract in question, and where the relationship between the parties had continued for quite some time.

deemed as invalid. This case demonstrates Japanese courts' willingness to respect party autonomy and to enforce an agreement to arbitrate whenever possible.

B.4 Enforcement Order

The final case we review was not contested. It was nevertheless the first reported case of an enforcement order being granted under the Arbitration Law. In this case, due to the small monetary value of the claim, summary proceedings under the JCAA Commercial Arbitration Rules were carried out. After the award was handed down, the respondent was not willing to make the payment and a petition for an enforcement order was filed with the court of competent jurisdiction. In the end, the enforcement order was rendered and the respondent made the payment without the need for further compulsory enforcement measures.[36]

Under Article 45 of the Arbitration Law, an arbitral award shall have the same effect as a final and conclusive judgment unless any of the following grounds (for refusal of recognition) exist:

1) The arbitration agreement is not valid due to limits to a party's capacity;

2) The arbitration agreement is not valid for a reason other than limits to a party's capacity under the law to which the parties have agreed to subject it (or failing such agreement, the law of the country under which the place of arbitration falls);

3) A party was not given notice as required by the provisions of the country under which the place of arbitration falls;

---

[36] Masafumi Kodama, Jiri M. Mestecky, and Toshihiko Oinuma, "First Enforcement Order Granted Under Japan's Arbitration Act," *JCAA Newsletter*, Nov. 2008, at 7-9.

4) A party was unable to present its case in the arbitral proceedings;

5) The arbitral award contains decisions on matters beyond the scope of the arbitration agreement or the claims in the arbitral proceedings;

6) The composition of an arbitral tribunal or the arbitral proceedings were not in accordance with the provisions of the law of the country under which the place of arbitration falls;

7) The arbitral award has not yet become binding, or has been set aside or suspended by a court of the country under which the place of arbitration falls;

8) The claims in the arbitral proceedings relate to a dispute that is not arbitrable under the laws of Japan; and

9) The content of the arbitral award would be contrary to the public policy or good morals of Japan.

In order to enforce an arbitral award in Japan, an "enforcement order" from the court is necessary. Under the Arbitration Law, an enforcement order may be obtained through a court hearing called *Shinjin* in which the parties are given the opportunity to contest the enforcement, or when the case is more complicated, through a procedure called *Koutou Benron* in which public oral arguments along with witness examinations need to be carried out. In the current case, the respondent's attorney did not attend the hearing, asserting that "there is nothing specifically the respondent wishes to claim" and the enforcement order was rendered within 50 days from the filing of the enforcement petition. However, the lawyer in the case expressed the concern that had the respondent applied delay tactics by claiming the attorney's unavailability or fiercely contested the enforcement of the award, then substantial delays could have been foreseen.[37] He therefore believes this is one area where the court should monitor the practices of the parties and ensure effective progress of the case.[38]

C. PUBLIC POLICY IN INTERNATIONAL ARBITRATION

In this section, we will analyze issues involving the legal effects of arbitral awards that are in conflict with public policy in Japan.

C.1 Effect of Arbitral Awards Conflicting with Public Policy

The Arbitration Law provides two procedures through which an arbitral award may be processed if it violates Japanese public policy. First, a party may apply to a court to set aside the arbitral award.[39] Second, recognition and enforcement of an arbitral award (whether or not the place of arbitration is in the territory of Japan) may be denied if it is in conflict with Japanese public policy.[40]

---

[37] *Id.*

[38] We recently assisted a client in seeking recognition and enforcement of a foreign arbitral award that was initially contested. During the first hearing, the court explained clearly that it would not reopen the case based on substantive grounds. While the defendant attempted to contest the application for enforcement based on the ground that the arbitration agreement was invalid, after the hearing, the defendant immediately proposed settlement with our client. While no court decision was rendered in that case, the court's attitude in adhering strictly to the limited grounds for refusing recognition and enforcement is encouraging and is demonstrative of the courts' willingness to monitor the parties' practice to ensure effective and efficient enforcement.

[39] Arbitration Law, Article 44.

[40] Arbitration Law, Article 45.

C.2 Setting Aside Arbitral Awards

C.2.1. Relevant provisions of the Arbitration Law

The Arbitration Law specifically allows the parties to an arbitration to apply to a court to set aside an arbitral award if the award violates the public policy of Japan.[41] Although not explicitly stated in the relevant provisions of the Arbitration Law, it is generally accepted that the parties to an arbitration may rely on the same procedure as an appeal of a court judgment when the arbitral proceedings were handled in a manner that conflicts with the public policy of Japan.[42] Nevertheless, setting aside an arbitral award significantly differs from an appeal of a court decision in that the arbitrators' errors in their findings of facts and the application of the law are not subject to scrutiny. If a party applies to a court to set aside an arbitral award, the court renders its decision through a *kettei* procedure in which the court decides without hearing oral arguments (*koutou benron*). Further, as explained in Section C.3 below, arbitral awards that are in conflict with public policy may not be recognized or enforced.[43]

C.2.2. The burden of proof of the grounds for setting aside arbitral awards

In principle, the burden of proof for setting aside an arbitral award is on the claimant. However, as an exception, it is clearly stipulated in the Arbitration Law that an arbitral award may be set aside without the submission of proof by the claimant if it

---

[41] Arbitration Law, Articles 44(1) and (8).

[42] Masaaki Kondo, *et al.*, Arbitration Law Commentary, at 253 (2003), Takeshi Kojima and Akira Takakuwa Ed., *Chushaku to Ronten, Chusai Ho,* at 250 (2007).

[43] Arbitration Law, Articles 45(2) and (8).

conflicts with public policy.[44] The court may raise this issue *sua sponte*.[45]

C.2.3. Arbitral awards that may be set aside

Only arbitration awards rendered in Japan may be set aside under Article 44 of the Arbitration Law.[46] On the other hand, if an arbitration award issued in an arbitration with its seat outside of Japan had been set aside in that country, the Japanese court may refuse to recognize and enforce it.[47] This suggests that the Arbitration Law was drafted with the view that the primary jurisdiction for setting aside an arbitral award is the place of arbitration.[48] Accordingly, while the Japanese courts may deny recognition or enforcement of a foreign arbitral award pursuant to Article 45, they do not have the authority to set aside an arbitration award issued outside of Japan pursuant to Article 44.

C.3 Enforcement and Recognition of Arbitral Awards

An arbitral award (whether or not the place of arbitration is in Japan) has the same effect as a final and conclusive judgment.[49] However, the court may refuse to recognize and enforce an arbitral award that conflicts with public policy.[50] Although the Arbitration Law does not clearly specify the scope of public policy in this provision, the prevailing view in Japan is that, in light of the fact that public policy is aimed at protecting the

---

[44]   Arbitration Law, Article 44(6).

[45]   *Supra,* note 43.

[46]   Arbitration Law, Articles 3 and 4.

[47]   Arbitration Law, Articles 45(2) and (7).

[48]   *Supra,* note 43, at 252.

[49]   Arbitration Law, Article 45(1).

[50]   Arbitration Law, Articles 45(2) and (8).

existing legal system, whether an arbitration award is contrary to public policy in disputes involving cross-border matters should be decided based on the correlation between (i) the extent the recognition of the arbitral award may conflict with the legal order of Japan; and (ii) the degree of the matter's relevance to Japan.[51] An arbitration award might not necessarily be set aside if the degree of relevance of the matter to Japan is considered minimal. However, when the abnormality is significantly high, it is likely that the arbitral award will not be recognized regardless of the degree of relevance of the matter to Japan.

The Arbitration Law explicitly provides that the Japanese courts shall not recognize an arbitration award that has been set aside in the jurisdiction in which the arbitration award was rendered.[52] Article V(1)(e) of the New York Convention provides that the recognition and enforcement of an award may be refused, with proof that the award has been set aside or suspended by a competent authority of the country in which that award was made. However, the language in the Arbitration Law takes a step further and clarifies that such arbitral awards may not be recognized or enforced in Japan.

C.4 Invalidity of Arbitration Awards

Although not explicitly provided in the Arbitration Law, an arbitral award that contains a material error, including one that significantly conflicts with the public policy of Japan, may be considered invalid without having to go through the procedure of setting aside the arbitral award.[53] Similarly, foreign arbitral

---

[51] Yoshihisa Hayakawa, *Jittaiteki Kojyo* in *Kokusai Minji Soshohou*, at 359 (Masato Dogauchi and Akira Takakuwa eds., 2002).

[52] Arbitration Law, Articles 45(2) and (7).

[53] *Supra,* note 42, at 244.

awards that contain a material defect may not be recognized or enforced in Japan.

C.5 Pending Arbitration

Article 23 of the Arbitration Law provides that the arbitral tribunal may rule on assertions made with respect to the existence or validity of an arbitration agreement or the authority to conduct arbitral proceedings.

If the arbitral tribunal renders a preliminary ruling over the matters above, either party may request the court to decide on the arbitral tribunal's jurisdiction.[54] If the agreement to appoint an arbitrator in a particular case has been reached in a manner contrary to public policy, either party may theoretically raise that objection pursuant to Article 23.

---

[54] Arbitration Law, Article 23(5).

KAZAKHSTAN

Azamat Kuatbekov[1] and Alexander Korobeinikov[2]

A. LEGISLATION, TRENDS AND TENDENCIES

A.1 Domestic Legislation

Arbitration proceedings and the enforcement of foreign arbitration awards are regulated by a number of legislative acts, including the Arbitration Court Law[3] and the International Commercial Arbitration Law.[4] These laws, which were adopted in December 2004, were the first arbitration laws adopted by Kazakhstan following the collapse of the former USSR. One of the main objectives of the new legislation was to end the uncertainty and controversy concerning the right to arbitrate and enforce arbitration awards in Kazakhstan.

The Arbitration Court Law applies to disputes between residents of Kazakhstan and permits such disputes to be resolved by "arbitration courts." The law regulates every stage of the arbitration proceedings and provides a mechanism for enforcing awards made by such "arbitration courts" in the state courts. It

---

[1] Azamat Kuatbekov is a Partner in Baker & McKenzie's Almaty office. Mr. Kuatbekov represents large multinational clients in the natural resources sector, advising them on dispute resolution, acquisitions, and financing. He has also authored numerous articles on oil and gas, corporate law, bankruptcy and litigation in Kazakhstan.

[2] Alexander Korobeinikov is an Associate in Baker & McKenzie's Almaty office and a member of Baker & McKenzie's International Arbitration practice group.

[3] Law of the Republic of Kazakhstan on Domestic Arbitration, dated 28 December 2004 (as amended).

[4] Law of the Republic of Kazakhstan on International Commercial Arbitration, dated 28 December 2004 (as amended).

should be noted that the Arbitration Court Law prohibits the use of arbitration as a means of resolving disputes involving state interests, state enterprises or natural monopolies.

The International Commercial Arbitration Law largely mirrors the UNCITRAL Model Law. It applies to disputes where at least one party is not a resident of Kazakhstan; a wholly-owned Kazakhstani subsidiary of a foreign legal entity is considered to be a local resident for the purposes of this law. The International Commercial Arbitration Law regulates arbitration proceedings inside Kazakhstan and also sets out the procedures for the enforcement of foreign arbitration awards in Kazakhstani courts.

In addition to the specific legislation referred to above, international commercial arbitration matters are also governed by:

- the Code of Civil Procedure of the Republic of Kazakhstan, dated 13 July 1999, which deals with, *inter alia*, the recognition, enforcement and appeals of foreign arbitral awards; and

- the Law of the Republic of Kazakhstan On Commodity Exchange, dated 4 May 2009, which permits the arbitration of disputes arising out of commodity exchange transactions.

A.2 International Treaties

Kazakhstan is a party to the New York Convention and the European Convention.

Kazakhstan is also a party to a number of bilateral and multilateral agreements that grant investors of certain countries the right to arbitrate disputes relating to their investments in Kazakhstan. These treaties include:

1) the ICSID Convention;

2) the Treaty between the United States of America and the Republic of Kazakhstan Concerning the Reciprocal Encouragement and Protection of Investment dated 19 May 1992;

3) the Treaty between the Government of the Republic of Kazakhstan and the Government of the United Kingdom of Great Britain and Northern Ireland concerning the Reciprocal Encouragement and Protection of Investment dated 23 November 1995;

4) the Energy Charter Treaty dated 17 December 1994; and

5) a number of regional CIS treaties, including the Convention on Investor Rights Protection dated 28 March 1997.

A.3 Recent Amendments Concerning Mediation and the Arbitrability of Disputes Involving Consumers

New Mediation Law

In December 2010, Kazakhstan adopted a new law on Mediation ("Mediation Law"). The Mediation Law provides that the following disputes may be resolved through mediation: (i) civil disputes involving individuals and legal entities, and (ii) disputes concerning certain minor criminal offenses. Mediation is not available in the context of disputes involving state organizations or incapacitated persons.

Under the Mediation Law, parties have the right to execute a mediation agreement at any time prior to, or following, the initiation of legal proceedings. If the parties execute a mediation agreement once civil court proceedings have commenced, the court shall suspend the proceedings until the end of the mediation. Where the parties resolve the dispute through mediation, they must execute a settlement agreement and the court proceedings will be terminated.

Mediation procedures must generally be finished within 30 (or, at the parties' request, 60) calendar days. Where mediation results in a settlement, the parties must execute a settlement agreement identifying: (i) the parties to, and the subject matter of, the dispute; (ii) the mediator involved; and (iii) the agreed settlement terms, including the consequences for failing to comply with the settlement terms.

If one of the parties refuses to comply with the executed settlement agreement, the other party may seek to enforce the agreement in a state court.

Arbitrability of Consumer Disputes

Amendments have recently been made to Kazakhstani arbitration legislation relating to consumer disputes. Under the new 2010 Consumer Protection Law,[5] disputes involving the protection of consumer rights may be resolved through domestic or international arbitration.

A.4　Trends

In recent years, Kazakhstan has enacted various legislative amendments designed to confirm the right to arbitrate in Kazakhstan, and to facilitate the enforcement of foreign arbitration awards. Pursuant to the Conception of Development of Judicial Administration of Local Courts, which was adopted by the Committee of Judicial Administration of the Supreme Court in 2010, the Supreme Court intends to encourage the use of arbitration and mediation, as well as courts of *doyen*s (a traditional Kazakh means of resolving disputes).

---

[5]　Law of the Republic of Kazakhstan on Consumer Protection, dated 18 May 2010.

Nevertheless, for a variety of historical and cultural reasons, Kazakhstani courts are often perceived by foreign investors as being reluctant to fully enforce awards in favor of foreign parties against the government of Kazakhstan or influential Kazakhstani companies.

B.   CASES

B.1   Investment Disputes

The number of investment claims filed against the Kazakhstani government has significantly increased in recent years due to the government's attempts to regain control over various oil and gas assets.

Various investment-related claims against Kazakhstan have been determined by different arbitral tribunals (under the ICSID, SCC or UNCITRAL Rules) including: *Ascom S.A. (Moldova) v. Kazakhstan* (SCC), *AES Corporation and Tau Power B.V. v. Kazakhstan* (ICSID), *GEM Equity Management AG v. Republic of Kazakhstan* (UNCITRAL), *Türkiye Petrolleri Anonim Ortaklığı v. Republic of Kazakhstan* (ICSID), *Caratube International Oil Company LLP v. Republic of Kazakhstan* (ICSID) and *KT Asia Investment Group B.V. v. Republic of Kazakhstan* (ICSID).

According to information published by the United Nations Conference on Trade and Development, of the ten investment arbitration cases brought against Kazakhstan since 1996, only one was determined in Kazakhstan's favor.

B.2   Commercial Arbitration Disputes

In 2011, the Kazakh courts decided a number of complex cases concerning the enforcement of foreign arbitral awards and the application of arbitration clauses. While the outcomes of these cases generally reflect the Kazakhstani courts' growing tendency to support arbitration, some of the judgments were controversial. The significant cases are summarized below.

B.2.1. Recognition of ICC award appealed to the competent court of the place of arbitration

The Mangistau Regional Economic Court and the Court of Appeal of the Mangistau Regional Court granted Ciments Francais' request to recognize a declaratory ICC award issued in Turkey against the Russian Holding company Sibirskiy Cement. Sibirskiy Cement had assets in Kazakhstan in the form of shares in a Kazakhstani entity. Sibirskiy Cement relied on Articles V(1)(e) and V(2)(b) of the New York Convention to argue that the ICC award should not be recognized in Kazakhstan.

Specifically, Sibirskiy Cement claimed that recognition of the ICC award would violate Kazakstani public policy because, among other reasons, Ciments Francais had already applied to the Russian Kemerovo Oblast Arbitrazh Court for recognition of the award, yet the Russian court had denied recognition and invalidated the contract between Sibirskiy Cement and Ciments Francais, which was the subject of the arbitration. Sibirskiy argued as well that, because it was challenging the ICC award before the competent courts of Turkey (the country in which the award was made), recognition and enforcement of the award should be suspended pending the appeal before the Turkish courts.

The Kazakh courts rejected Sibirskiy Cement's arguments, holding that: (i) under the Kazakh Civil Procedure Code, only *enforcement* of a foreign arbitral award—but not recognition— can violate Kazakh public policy; and (ii) the fact that the ICC award had been appealed was not a reason for non-*exequatur* of the award, as Article IX(1) of the European Arbitration

Convention (which prevails in case of a conflict with the provisions of the New York Convention) provides that the courts can only refuse to recognize an award if it has been set aside by the competent court of the place of arbitration.[6]

B.2.2. Kazakhstani court confirms *kompetenz-kompetenz* and separability doctrines

A Danish company brought claims against a Kazakh company to enforce two Federation of Oils, Seeds and Fats Associations ("FOSFA") arbitral awards. The Kazakh company argued that the award should not be enforced because (i) the contracts that were the subject matter of the arbitration had not been signed by the claimant, and the arbitration clauses were therefore invalid, and (ii) the FOSFA arbitral tribunal did not have jurisdiction to determine whether the contracts containing the arbitration clauses were valid because the clauses did not provide for such a right.

The Kazakh courts (both the lower court and the court of appeal) rejected the Kazakh company's arguments, holding that the validity of the arbitration clause was not related to the validity of the main contract and the defendant and claimant had clearly agreed that disputes would be resolved under the FOSFA arbitration rules. The Kazakh court further held that, pursuant to Article V(3) of the European Arbitration Convention, the arbitral tribunal had the right to determine whether the contract containing the arbitration clause was valid, and that where, as here, the arbitral tribunal had already done so, the Kazakh courts could not reconsider those issues during enforcement proceedings. The Kazakh court also rejected the Kazakh

---

[6] Following the Mangistau Regional courts' ruling, the Turkish court set aside the ICC award. The Mangistau Regional Economic Court therefore annulled its previous decision and is reconsidering the case.

company's additional argument that enforcing the FOSFA awards would violate Kazakh public policy.

B.2.3. Kazakhstani court holds that arbitration clause does not cover disputes arising from pre-arbitration settlement agreements

The Kazakh joint venture IGS-Sichim (the "Contractor") filed a claim in the Atyrau Regional Economic Court against the Dutch company Bateman Kazakhstan Oil & Gas Company B.V. (the "Employer") concerning debts arising from construction contracts between the two companies.

Prior to commencing legal action, and in accordance with the contractual pre-arbitration provisions, the parties had tried to settle the dispute amicably. Following negotiations, they had executed several settlement agreements, which were annexed to the main contracts. The debts that the Contractor claimed in the Kazakh court proceedings arose as a result of the Employer's non-compliance with the settlement agreements.

The Employer argued that the Kazakh courts did not have jurisdiction on the grounds that the dispute resolution provisions in the construction contracts provided for all disputes between the parties to be determined by the LCIA under English law. However, the Kazakh court rejected this argument, interpreting the relevant contractual provisions as providing for arbitration only if the parties were unable to settle their disputes amicably through negotiation or mediation.[7] Since the alleged debts arose from non-compliance with the settlement agreements that the parties had freely negotiated, the court held that the arbitration clauses in the contracts did not extend to cover these disputes.

---

[7] While we do not know the exact wording of these arbitration clauses, it seems that they are similar to the dispute resolution provisions of FIDIC contracts.

The Kazakh court therefore refused to apply English law, holding that Kazakh law governed the matters under dispute.

Although the Kazakh court's judgment has been subject to criticism, it has been upheld by the regional court of appeal and the Supreme Court.

C. PUBLIC POLICY IN INTERNATIONAL ARBITRATION

C.1 Definition of Public Policy under Kazakh Law

Kazakh public policy is defined in both substantive and procedural Kazakh laws. The substantive element of the definition is contained in the Kazakhstani Civil Code,[8] while the procedural definition is set out in rules relating to challenging and enforcing domestic arbitral awards and to enforcing foreign judgments and arbitral awards.

Under the Kazakh Civil Code, the doctrine of public policy is used both to exclude the application of foreign law and to prescribe the application of Kazakh law. For example, Article 1090.1 of the Civil Code defines Kazakh public policy as "principles of law and order of the Republic of Kazakhstan" and provides that, where foreign laws contradict Kazakh public policy, they shall not apply and the law of the Republic of Kazakhstan shall apply. Furthermore, Article 1091.1 provides that the conflict of law rules shall not apply where imperative standards of legislation of the Republic of Kazakhstan (i.e., "supraimperative rules") apply. These supraimperative rules apply where the relevant applicable law itself so provides, or,

---

[8]   The Civil Code of the Republic of Kazakhstan (the Special Part) adopted by the Law No. 409 of 1 July 1999 (as amended).

where due to their importance in protecting the legal rights and interests of parties, their application is implied.

Pursuant to the above provisions of the Kazakh Civil Code, a party to an international commercial dispute technically has the right to rely on Kazakhstani public policy or supraimperative rules to challenge the validity of a contract or arbitration agreement under Kazakh law, even where conflict of law rules would otherwise provide for the application of foreign law.

The International Commercial Arbitration Law defines public policy slightly differently than the Kazakh Civil Code. Article 2(10) of this law defines public policy as "such fundamental principles of the state and social systems in the Republic of Kazakhstan as are institutionalized in its legislation." It is this more-detailed definition that the courts apply when deciding petitions to challenge or enforce an arbitral award in Kazakhstan. It should be noted that in such cases, courts apply the concept of public policy *ex officio*.

Because "public policy" was not defined under Kazakh law until 1999, there currently is no exhaustive list of supraimperative rules or rules that could be said to constitute Kazakh public policy.

C.2 Application of Public Policy

As far as we aware, the Kazakh courts have relied on the concept of public policy as a ground for refusing to enforce an award in just one case, *Byelocorp Scientific, Inc. and Supcodue S.K.L. v. Kulan Group LLP, Giprosviyaz LLP and Web.kz LLP* (2005). In this case, the court refused to enforce an award issued by the LCIA on the ground that simultaneous enforcement of the LCIA award against three Kazakh companies would be contrary to Kazakh public policy.

The court's decision has been criticized by Kazakhstani scholars and practitioners for being unreasonable and politically motivated. Consequently, the Kazakh courts have tended to reject public policy arguments since. As noted earlier in *Sibirskiy Cement*, the Kazakh courts have recently held that public policy cannot be relied upon as a ground for refusing to recognize an award granting declaratory relief.

Although the exact nature of Kazakh public policy remains unclear, Kazakhstani scholars have interpreted the doctrine as having very limited practical application and have argued that it may be relied upon only in extraordinary circumstances. It is generally accepted that the doctrine of public policy cannot be relied upon as a ground for *révision au fond* of arbitral awards, and that the incorrect application of legal rules by an arbitral tribunal does not contravene Kazakh public policy. The Kazakh courts have generally accepted this narrow approach and, while their practices may be somewhat controversial to some in Kazakhstan, the courts remain very reluctant to apply either the substantive or the procedural element of the doctrine of public policy.

MALAYSIA

Elaine Yap[1]

A. LEGISLATION, TRENDS AND TENDENCIES

A.1 Legislative Framework

The law and practice of arbitration in Malaysia is governed by the Arbitration Act 2005 ("AA"), which came into force on 15 March 2006. The AA repealed the outdated Arbitration Act 1952, which can be traced historically to the equivalent legislation in England in 1972. In a significant departure from this original framework, the AA is modeled closely on the UNCITRAL Model Law. The main body of the AA can be found in Part II, which follows Articles 3 to 36 of the Model Law almost word for word.

Malaysia has also been a signatory to the New York Convention since 1985. The New York Convention was passed into domestic law in Malaysia through the Convention on the Recognition and Enforcement of Foreign Arbitral Awards Act 1985. It should be noted, however, that this Act was repealed by the AA as of 15 March 2006. The AA now sets out a uniform procedure for the recognition and enforcement of both local and foreign arbitral awards within the same legislation.

---

[1] Elaine Yap is a Partner in the Dispute Resolution Practice Group of Baker & McKenzie's Kuala Lumpur office. She has more than 10 years of experience handling commercial litigation and arbitration. She represents clients in a wide variety of disputes, from breach of contract and negligence to fraud and economic torts. She also provides counsel on breach of directors' duties, shareholder disputes and insolvency litigation as well as construction, tax, intellectual property, employment and administrative law.

A.2   Trends and Tendencies

Consistent with the UNCITRAL Model Law, the AA distinguishes between domestic and international arbitrations and an "international arbitration" is defined in the same way it is defined in the Model Law. However, unlike Article 1(2) of the UNCITRAL Model Law, which sets out by reference to specific Articles, which part of the law also applies to arbitrations where the seat of arbitration is not the local territory, Section 3 of the AA only provides for the application of the Act to domestic and international arbitrations where the seat of arbitration is in Malaysia.

In 2008, the High Court in *Aras Jalinan Sdn Bhd v. Tipco Asphalt Public Company Ltd. & Ors,*[2] made a bold decision as concerns the jurisdiction of the courts in matters governed by the AA. The *Aras Jalinan* case involved an application by the plaintiff for an interim injunction pending determination of an arbitration between the parties in Singapore. In opposing this application, the defendants raised a preliminary objection against the jurisdiction of the court to grant the orders sought as the seat of arbitration was in Singapore, citing Sections 3 and 8 of the AA.[3]

The High Court agreed with the defendants and dismissed the plaintiff's application, holding that on a strict construction of Section 3 of the AA, read together with the provision on the restricted extent of court intervention in Section 8 of the AA, the High Court had no inherent or residual powers to intervene in arbitrations where the seat was outside Malaysia. It was also held that such jurisdiction could not be conferred by the agreement of the parties.

---

[2]   [2008] 5 CLJ 654.

[3]   Provision on the extent of court intervention in matters governed by the AA.

The effect of the *Aras Jalinan* decision, which was approved by the Court of Appeal in an unreported decision, left in serious doubt the ability of the High Court to exercise any powers in aid of arbitrations seated outside of Malaysia, including Malaysia's treaty obligation to enforce all valid arbitration agreements by, *inter alia*, ordering a mandatory stay of parallel court proceedings brought in breach of such agreements.

After much anticipation, the AA was finally amended[4] to address the implications of the *Aras Jalinan* case as well as other shortcomings of the AA. The significant changes made to the AA by the amendments, which came into force on 1 July 2011, can be summarized as follows:

(a) confirmation that all sources of jurisdiction of the courts other than the AA itself, including the inherent jurisdiction of the courts, are excluded, to clearly limit the ability of the courts to intervene in matters governed by the AA;

(b) express provisions were included in the AA on the application of the powers of the court to grant relief in aid of arbitration under Section 10 of the AA (stay of parallel court proceedings) and Section 11 of the AA (interim measures and other relief) to foreign-seated arbitrations;

(c) introduction of specific provisions under Sections 10 and 11 of the AA to govern admiralty disputes in arbitration, such as provisions on the arrest of vessels and the securing of the amount in dispute;

(d) removal of the ground that there is no dispute between the parties with regard to the matters to be referred to arbitration, as a reason for refusal to stay parallel court proceedings;

---

[4] Arbitration (Amendment) Act 2011.

(e) reinstatement of party autonomy in choice of governing law clauses for domestic arbitrations to enable parties to apply laws other than the laws of Malaysia; and

(f) additional requirement for the reference on questions of law arising out of an award that the question of law substantially affects the rights of one or more of the parties.

While these amendments have taken longer than expected to pass into law, they reflect a positive trend by the legislative arm of the government to respond to calls to harmonize Malaysian arbitration laws with that of the international arbitration community in order to promote Malaysia as another major regional centre for arbitration in Asia Pacific.

B. CASES

B.1 Construction of Arbitration Clauses

In *Lembaga Pelabuhan Kelang v. Kuala Dimensi Sdn Bhd & Anor*,[5] the Court of Appeal considered with approval the decision of the High Court in *Westbury Tubular (M) Sdn Bhd v. Ahmad Zaki Sdn Bhd & Ors*[6] on a point of construction of arbitration clauses. The issue arose in the context of an application filed for a stay of court proceedings commenced in apparent breach of an agreement to arbitrate.

The dispute resolution clause in *Westbury Tubular* provided, *inter alia,* that "[a]ny such dispute or difference which cannot be settled amicably may be referred to arbitration and final decision of a person to be agreed between the parties to act as arbitrator, or failing agreement, of a person nominated on the application of

---

[5]   [2010] 9 CLJ 532, COA.

[6]   [2001] 5 CLJ 67.

either party by [sic] the Director for the time being of the Regional Centre for Arbitration in Kuala Lumpur."

The High Court held that the usage of the word "may" in the clause suggested that it was not mandatory for the plaintiff to refer the disputes to arbitration. Since it was not a mandatory provision, the plaintiff could not be faulted for not referring the disputes to arbitration before filing the civil suit. The application for a stay of proceedings was accordingly dismissed.

The Court of Appeal in the *Kuala Dimensi* case construed a similar dispute resolution clause, also in the context of an application filed for a stay of court proceedings under Section 10 of the AA. The appellant argued that the *Westbury Tubular* case could not support the interpretation given by the High Court, since the application for stay of proceedings was filed pursuant to the corresponding provision in the Arbitration Act 1952,[7] under which the court always had an overriding discretion to refuse stay.

The Court of Appeal disagreed and confirmed that, unlike clauses where the peremptory word "shall" is used, the use of the permissive word "may" in the arbitration clause evidences a discretion to refer to arbitration, which is capable of being readily abandoned and opting for litigation instead. The mandatory requirement of the court to stay proceedings in breach of an arbitration clause under Section 10 of the AA, does not derogate from the importance of drafting the arbitration clause specifically to reflect the intention of the parties.

---

[7] Section 6 of the Arbitration Act 1952.

B.2 Setting Aside Arbitral Awards

In Malaysia, it is settled law that an arbitral award is final, binding and conclusive and can only be challenged in exceptional circumstances.[8] It is also widely accepted that the High Court exercises supervisory jurisdiction over arbitrations and not appellate jurisdiction.[9] These principles were re-affirmed by the High Court in *TPPT Sdn Bhd v. Asas Gabngan Sdn Bhd*[10] in respect of applications to, *inter alia,* set aside two interim arbitral awards under the provisions of the Arbitration Act 1952.

Essentially, the tribunal ruled in the two interim arbitral awards that it had no jurisdiction to determine the claim or the counterclaim because of the parties' failure to comply with certain conditions precedent to invoking the arbitration agreement. The conditions precedent required disputes of any kind that are connected with the contract to first be referred to the Employer's Representative for a decision.

On the facts, the arbitrator found that counterclaims were not pure defenses to the claim, and that the respondent could not have its counterclaim included in the arbitration due to failure to comply with the conditions precedent. Having lost on this score, the respondent raised a preliminary objection, and succeeded in persuading the arbitrator that he also had no jurisdiction to proceed with the main claim on the same ground, as there was in fact non-compliance with the condition precedent for arbitration, which rendered the claim premature.

---

[8] *Intelek Timur Sdn Bhd v. Future Heritage Sdn Bhd,* [2004] 1 CLJ 743 [Federal Court].

[9] *Pembinaan LGL Sdn Bhd v. SK Styrofoam (M) Sdn Bhd,* [2007] 3 CLJ 185 [Court of Appeal].

[10] [2011] 3 CLJ 228.

The awards were challenged before the High Court on the grounds that there was technical misconduct on the part of the arbitrator in deciding on a point that was not originally raised by either party. It was argued that there was an irregularity in the proceedings, and that a breach of the rules of natural justice had occurred. The High Court declined to intervene on the grounds that the conclusions reached by the tribunal fell within the area of findings of fact, or at any rate mixed fact and law, and applied the principles reiterated more recently by the Court of Appeal in *Cairn Energy India Pty Ltd & Anor v. The Government of India*[11]—that an arbitral award should not be upset unless there is a manifest error of law.

The Malaysian courts have now also applied a similarly restrictive approach in relation to the setting aside of arbitral awards under Section 37 of the AA, as recently exemplified by *Infineon Technologies (M) Sdn Bhd v. Orisoft Technology Sdn Bhd*,[12] and evident in the referral of questions of law under Section 42 of the AA. In *Majlis Amanah Rakyat v. Kausar Corporation Sdn Bhd*,[13] the High Court noted that due to the small body of case law in Malaysia and little guidance within the terms of Section 42 of the AA to delineate the guidelines or principles the court is to apply, the jurisprudence on manifest error established under the Arbitration Act 1952 will continue to apply.

The High Court in *Majlis Amanah Rakyat* also usefully observed that it is good policy and desirable commercial comity to ensure that Malaysian law does not depart significantly from international norms and practices, particularly in relation to common law jurisdictions.

---

[11] [2010] 2 CLJ 420.

[12] [2010] 1 LNS 889.

[13] [2009] 1 LNS 1766.

B.3 Recognition and Enforcement of Arbitral Awards

Open Type Joint Stock Company Efirnoye ("EFKO") v. Alfa Trading Limited[14] concerned an application under the AA to register and enforce an arbitral award issued from the Russian Federation after the defendant had failed to have the award cancelled before the Moscow Arbitration Court. The plaintiff, a Russian company, was the buyer of palm oil products from the defendant, a Malaysian company, the vendor of the palm products.

The defendant relied on two grounds under the AA to oppose the recognition and enforcement of the award, i.e., that the arbitral procedure was not in accordance with the agreements, and that the arbitral award was in conflict with the public policy of Malaysia.

Under the first limb of the defendant's challenge, the defendant argued that the plaintiff failed to adhere to the procedure stipulated in the contract when the plaintiff initiated arbitral proceedings in the International Commercial Arbitration Court ("ICAC") at the Chamber of Commerce and Industry ("CCI") in Russia, because prior to that, the defendant had filed a claim for arbitration before the ICAC CCI of Ukraine on a dispute arising from the same contract and the plaintiff had filed a counterclaim in those proceedings.

The court concluded that there was no failure to comply with the arbitral procedure because both the ICAC CCI in Russia and the Moscow Arbitration Court had considered the issue in detail and determined that the ICAC CCI in Russia, as an arbitral tribunal, had the jurisdiction to hear the plaintiff's claim notwithstanding the proceedings in Ukraine.

---

[14]   [2011] 1 LNS 1094.

Further, the claims and counterclaims between the parties before the Russian and Ukrainian arbitral tribunals were also different, albeit arising from the same contract. Significantly, there was already an express finding by the Russian arbitral tribunal that the defendant had submitted to its jurisdiction, which was upheld by the Moscow Arbitration Court when the defendant sought to have the award cancelled.

On the second limb of the challenge, the defendant asserted that it was contrary to the public policy of Malaysia to enforce an award that was contradictory to another existing award between the same parties in respect of the same subject matter and that this amounts to *res judicata*. The defendant also failed on this ground for the same reasons.

This decision follows a virtually unbroken line of cases where challenges to the recognition and enforcement of arbitral awards under the AA have failed, and confirms the attitude of the courts in Malaysia as enforcing courts that vigilantly guard against attempts made to go behind the award or re-open matters settled in the arbitration.

C. PUBLIC POLICY IN INTERNATIONAL ARBITRATION

C.1 Scenarios of Reliance on Public Policy

The question of public policy may be raised at every stage of a dispute where arbitration proceedings may be concerned. In Malaysia, it is most commonly invoked under Section 37 of the AA to set aside an arbitral award, and under the mirror provisions in Sections 38 and 39 of the AA to refuse recognition and enforcement of arbitral awards. These scenarios relate to the enforceability of arbitral awards. Equally, the public policy ground can be used to challenge the enforceability of the arbitration agreement at the outset of proceedings, whether before the arbitral tribunal or a state court or at any other stage of the proceedings.

Under the AA, the unenforceability of an arbitration agreement for public policy reasons is reflected in Section 4 of the AA, which provides that any dispute that parties have agreed to submit to arbitration under an arbitration agreement is arbitrable unless the arbitration agreement is contrary to public policy. Apart from the arbitrability of the subject matter in dispute, it is also a matter of contract law that agreements that are contrary to public policy are null and void, inoperative or incapable of being performed. These are objections that are commonly made under the following circumstances:

(a) when resisting an application to stay parallel court proceedings;[15]

(b) when challenging the jurisdiction of the arbitral tribunal;[16] and

(c) as separate and independent grounds to challenge an arbitral award.[17]

In domestic arbitrations or international arbitrations where the parties have opted to maintain a right to refer questions of law to the court,[18] the question of public policy may arise in the course of arbitration proceedings as part of the substantive dispute between the parties. The AA also does not remove the possibility of the question of public policy being raised in connection with other matters governed by the AA, such as the appointment and

---

[15] Section 10 of the AA.

[16] Section 18 of the AA.

[17] Sections 37, 38 and 39 of the AA.

[18] Section 41 and 42 of the AA.

removal of arbitrators and the grant of interim relief by the arbitral tribunal or the court.

C.2 Modes and Limitations of Reliance on Public Policy

The public policy ground may be invoked in any of the scenarios above according to the relevant provisions of the AA. There is no special mode or time limit for doing so, other than as provided in those provisions. Thus, as an example, any jurisdictional objection on grounds that the arbitration agreement is void for public policy reasons has to be raised no later than the filing of the defense in an arbitration governed by the AA,[19] and any application to set aside an arbitral award on public policy grounds must be filed within 90 days of receipt of the impugned award.[20]

Where no specific time limits are prescribed, there is a general requirement in Section 7 of the AA, which specifies that objections as to any non-compliance with the provisions of the arbitration agreement or the AA to be taken by a party promptly, at the risk of deemed waiver of the objections otherwise.

In addition, there is no requirement under the AA that the point of public policy must first be invoked and rejected before the tribunal in order to be relied upon. On the basis that the court will not lend its aid to enforce that which is against public policy, it is suggested that this may also be applied in the arbitration context, such that a party will not be precluded from raising breach of public policy at any stage. However, a foreign award that has been vacated in its country of origin on any

---

[19]   Section 18(3) of the AA.

[20]   Section 37(4) of the AA.

ground, including public policy grounds, would not be enforceable in Malaysia.[21]

C.3 Rules that Constitute "Public Policy"

There is no definition of "public policy" in the AA and there has been no attempt to ascribe to it any exhaustive definition, character or illustration. However, there are generally recognized categories of factors considered to be conflicting with public policy. For example, Section 37 of the AA provides, without limiting the generality of the term, that an award is in conflict with the public policy of Malaysia where:

(a) the making of the award was induced or affected by fraud or corruption; or

(b) a breach of the rules of natural justice occurred

(i) during the arbitral proceedings; or

(ii) in connection with the making of the award.

The extent of breach of natural justice in arbitration law was explained in *Taman Bandar Baru Masai Sdn Bhd v. Dindings Corporations Sdn Bhd.*[22] The High Court held there that there must be a breach of particular rules of natural justice that are incorporated in the Federal Constitution and other written law or rules of court, and that the prejudice that is thereby suffered must be something of substance. The rules of natural justice should not be allowed to be exploited as a purely technical weapon to undo a decision that does not in reality cause substantial injustice.

---

[21] Section 39(1)(a)(vii) of the AA.

[22] [2010] 5 CLJ 83.

In *Infineon Technologies (M) Sdn Bhd v. Orisoft Technology Sdn Bhd*,[23] the High Court noted that the concept of public policy as a ground to set aside an arbitral award is a thorny area in which the position of the law varies widely. In particular, it was noted that where it concerns an international arbitration award, the available comparative jurisprudence would appear to suggest a relatively narrow view being taken, whereas a somewhat wider approach would apply in relation to a domestic arbitration award.

In dealing with international arbitration awards, the High Court appears to take the view (referring to leading Hong Kong and Singapore cases where conflict of public policy requires the most basic notions of morality and justice to be offended) that a more restrictive approach to public policy would be applied in the interest of upholding international comity. Although the approaches have not been uniform in respect of domestic arbitration awards, the court held that a less rigid approach should in principle apply.

C.4 Review of Alleged Breaches of Public Policy

A review of alleged breaches of public policy can arise in relation to the enforceability of arbitral awards, and to challenge the enforceability of the arbitration agreement at the outset of proceedings, whether before the arbitral tribunal or a state court, or at any other stage of the proceedings. Reviews by state courts are restricted in the sense that the courts may not re-open or re-examine the merits of the case determined by the arbitral tribunal.

However, there is no defined limitation to the extent to which such reviews can occur before the arbitral tribunal. An example of where the arbitral tribunal ought to refrain from reviewing

---

[23]   [2010] 1 LNS 889.

public policy breaches is where neither party has raised it as an issue. A purely *ex officio* consideration of public policy by the arbitrator may result in an award being set aside or rendered unenforceable because the award may be found to have dealt with a dispute not contemplated by or not falling within the terms of the submission to arbitration, unless the issue originated from the underlying contract or was incidental to the dispute.

In the context of a challenge to the recognition and enforcement of a foreign arbitral award, only Malaysian public policy will be considered, as the relevant provision in the AA[24] makes specific reference to an award being refused recognition due to conflict with "the public policy of Malaysia." Foreign public policy may be considered collaterally in the sense that it is also a ground for refusal of recognition and enforcement of a foreign arbitral award if:

(a) the arbitration agreement is not valid under the law to which the parties have subjected it, or, failing any indication thereon, under the laws of the State where the award was made;[25] or

(b) the award has not yet become binding on the parties or has been set aside or suspended by a court of the country in which, or under the law of which, that award was made,[26]

which may be the prevailing circumstances caused by a breach of foreign public policies.

---

[24] Section 39(1)(b)(ii) of the AA.

[25] Section 39(1)(a)(ii) of the AA.

[26] Section 39(1)(a)(vii) of the AA.

MEXICO

Salvador Fonseca-González[1] and Javier L. Navarro-Treviño[2]

A. LEGISLATION TRENDS AND TENDENCIES

As mentioned in the *Baker & McKenzie International Arbitration Yearbook 2010-2011,* the Congress approved significant amendments to the federal Code of Commerce regarding commercial arbitration, specifically with respect to Mexican courts' intervention in arbitration-related matters. The amendments became effective on 28 January 2011.

The amendments, which are found in Articles 1464 to 1480 of the Code of Commerce, provide guidance concerning judicial intervention in aid of arbitration and are in line with the UNICITRAL Model Law (adopted by Mexico in 1993 and incorporated in Articles 1415 to 1463 of the Code of Commerce). Such amendments were made to Mexican legislation based on necessity and because of the support needed from the courts in aid of arbitration for the enforcement of interim relief orders and for the recognition and enforcement of awards.

Mexico has become the country with the most international arbitrations in Latin American after Brazil. This is not only due

---

[1] Salvador Fonseca-González is a Partner in Baker & McKenzie's office in Mexico City and a member of its Dispute Resolution Practice Group. He is widely experienced in domestic and international arbitration and litigation, with experience in both commercial and investment treaty cases. He has also served as sole arbitrator and chairman in several tribunals, and has been appointed to the list of arbitrators of diverse arbitral institutions. His practice extends to insolvency, restructurings and compliance work.

[2] Javier L. Navarro-Treviño is a Lawyer-Trainee in Baker & McKenzie's office in Mexico City.

to the size of the Mexican economy but it is also a consequence of the country's commitment to arbitration (as reflected in the adoption of the UNCITRAL's Model Law and the implementation of these recent additions to the Code of Commerce) and, in general, to a growing ADR culture that is reflected in a wider use of arbitration and other ADR methods to resolve business disputes in Mexico.

A.1 Constitutional Recognition

Since 2008, alternative dispute resolution methods are recognized in the Mexican Constitution as a means to resolve disputes. This put an end to an old debate on whether arbitration was constitutional and is a clear signal that the country is committed to arbitration and other ADR methods.

A.2 Mexico as a Seat for Arbitration

Mexico has become one of the most important seats for arbitration in Latin America due to its pro-arbitration legislation and the clear trend of judicial precedents favoring arbitration. Mexico is also known for having a roster of highly experienced and qualified international arbitrators and very good arbitration practitioners.

The Mediation and Arbitration Center of the Mexico City Chamber of Commerce ("CANACO") and the Arbitration Center of Mexico ("CAM"), the most recognized local arbitral institutions, have also consolidated their presence in the country and have seen a steady increase in the number of cases they handle.

It is also important to note that the ICC, through its Mexican national committee, and the ICDR, which has a collaboration agreement with CANACO, have been very active in Mexico and have successfully promoted the use of their arbitration rules in Mexico, particularly for international cases.

A.3 Recognition and Enforcement of Foreign Commercial Arbitral Awards in Mexico

Mexico is a party to the New York and Panama Conventions and its arbitration law follows, almost to the letter, the UNCITRAL Model Law. Moreover, as mentioned before, on 28 January 2011, a bill was passed by the Federal Congress adding Articles 1464 to 1480 to the Code of Commerce. These new Articles greatly improve the procedure for Mexican court intervention and support, when needed, in arbitration-related matters.

All of the above weigh in favor of considering Mexico not only as a strong seat for arbitration, but also as a reliable jurisdiction for enforcing a foreign arbitration award.

A.4 Interim Relief

As was stated in the *Baker & McKenzie International Arbitration Yearbook 2010-2011*, one of the most significant amendments is the adoption of a new regime to ensure the enforcement of interim relief measures related to arbitration in the country. In accordance with the 28 January 2011 amendments, judges have the authority to grant any form of interim relief that they deem appropriate. By the same token, a detailed procedure for the enforcement of interim relief orders issued by arbitral tribunals is provided for under the amendments.

Article 1480 of the Code of Commerce expressly provides that Mexican courts dealing with motions to enforce interim relief orders issued by arbitral tribunals may not review the merits of the action that is the subject matter of the order.

Despite being, in general, a favorable legislative reform for arbitration in Mexico, it is important to mention that the last paragraph of Article 1480 provides that the party requesting the interim relief order, as well as *the arbitral tribunal that issues it*, are responsible for the order and may be liable for damages resulting form its judicial enforcement.

A.5 Competence

The principle of *kompetenz-kompetenz* is included in Mexico's arbitration law.

In this regard, Article 1424 of the Commercial Code (following Article 8 of the UNCITRAL Model Law) establishes the following:

> 1. A court before which an action is brought in a matter which is the subject of an arbitration agreement shall, if a party so requests not later than when submitting his first statement on the substance of the dispute, refer the parties to arbitration unless it finds that the agreement is null and void, inoperative or incapable of being performed.

> 2. Where an action referred to in paragraph (1) of this article has been brought, arbitral proceedings may nevertheless be commenced or continued, and an award may be made, while the issue is pending before the court.

In turn, Article 1432 of the Code of Commerce (following Article 16 of the UNCITRAL Model Law) provides that:

> 1. The arbitral tribunal may rule on its own jurisdiction, including any objections with respect to the existence or validity of the arbitration agreement. For that purpose, an arbitration clause which forms part of a contract shall be treated as an agreement independent of the other terms of the contract. A decision by the arbitral tribunal that the contract

is null and void shall not entail *ipso jure* the invalidity of the arbitration clause. . .

In September 2006, the Supreme Court handed down a binding precedent (*Jurisprudencia 25/2006*) confirming the *kompetenz-kompetenz* principle but clarifying that there is one exception to the rule. Where a party files a lawsuit regarding a dispute over a contract and, at the same time, claims that the arbitral clause in that contract is null and void, inoperative or incapable of being performed, it will be the court, and not the arbitrator, who will have jurisdiction to rule on the validity of the arbitral clause. This put Mexico somewhat at odds with the current trend in most Model Law countries, which not only endorse the *kompetenz-kompetenz* principle, but also the right of the arbitrators to "shoot first"[3] in matters where the validity of the arbitral clause is questioned.

However, as part of the recent amendments of 28 January 2011 mentioned above, Article 1465 was added to the Code of Commerce. This article states that when ruling on the referral of the parties to arbitration under Article 1424 of the Code of Commerce (equivalent to Article 8 of the UNCITRAL Model Law), the judge shall deny the referral only if the nullity or invalidity of the arbitral clause are "evident" and shall observe a rigorous criteria (in favor of arbitration) when ruling on the matter. These amendments are a positive step towards bringing Mexico back to the mainstream regarding the interpretation of Article 8 of the Model Law.

---

[3] In other words, to have the opportunity to decide on the validity of the arbitral clause and on their own jurisdiction before a court of law finally decides on the validity of the clause.

B. CASES

To follow-up on a very important case mentioned in the previous edition of our *Yearbook*, a decision by the Superior Court of the State of Baja California declaring that Mexican courts lacked jurisdiction to hear and resolve an action to set aside an award rendered outside Mexico was challenged through a direct *amparo* action by the claimant and was referred for resolution to the Federal Circuit Courts of the XV Circuit with venue in Mexicali, Baja California.

On 19 January 2011, the First Chamber of the Mexican Supreme Court determined that the precedents to be established in the case were of considerable significance and decided to exercise its discretionary powers to accept the case and resolve the matter.

A decision by the Supreme Court on this important case was issued on 29 June 2011 (*Amparo directo* 9/2011 First Chamber of the National Supreme Court of Justice) with a positive result. The Supreme Court rejected the challenge, confirmed the decision of the Superior Court of the State of Baja California and determined that, based on the New York and Panama Conventions (to which Mexico is a party), as well as the Code of Commerce (which, as mentioned before, incorporates the UNCITRAL Model Law), an award rendered in an international arbitration seated in a foreign jurisdiction may not be challenged or annulled by Mexican courts, as jurisdiction to entertain such action is reserved to the courts of the seat of the arbitration.[4]

This is a clear example of Mexican courts applying the international treaties and conventions to which Mexico is a party,

---

[4] *Solicitud de Atracción* 153/2010, First Chamber of the National Supreme Court of Justice.

and demonstrating that awards are being honored without undue intervention of the Mexican courts.

C. PUBLIC POLICY IN INTERNATIONAL ARBITRATION

As previously indicated, Mexico's arbitration law follows the UNCITRAL Model Law and Mexico is a party to the New York and Panama Conventions. Therefore, an arbitration award may be vacated in Mexico if it goes against public policy.

Recognition and enforcement of an arbitral award may also be refused if such award is contrary to the public policy of the enforcement state.[5] It is understandable that a state may wish to have the right to refuse recognition of an arbitration award that offends that state's own notions of public policy, and in some jurisdictions the enforcing court is required to examine the possibility of a public policy violation *ex officio*.[6] However, the question has always been how to define "public policy."

The most recognized authorities in international arbitration tend to agree that public policy is an attempt to address a public issue by instituting laws, regulations, decisions, or actions pertinent to the problem at hand. However, judicial courts all over the world are not so unanimous as to the nature or definition of "public policy," and one can find many discrepancies and very parochial interpretations of this concept.

In this regard, it must be stated that things in Mexico are not as bad as one may think. Mexican courts have lately issued resolutions in cases related to arbitration where the issue of

---

[5] New York Convention, Article V(2)(b).

[6] *See* the decision of the Cour de Justice of Geneva dated 11 December 1997 (1998), *XXIII Yearbook Commercial Arbitration*, p. 764.

public policy was argued by the parties to deny the enforcement of an arbitral award or to have it set aside, and the judges have determined that not all violations of public interest laws are to be also understood as violations of public policy, and that the notion of public policy shall be interpreted having in mind the international nature of the New York Convention and the purpose and goals of the UNCITRAL Model Law from which Mexican arbitration law was derived.

THE NETHERLANDS

Frank Kroes[1] and Saskia Temme[2,3]

A. LEGISLATION, TRENDS AND TENDENCIES

A.1 Legislation

There have been no major legislative changes in Dutch arbitration law since the implementation of the Arbitration Act in the Dutch Code of Civil Procedure ("DCCP") on 1 December 1986.[4]

A.2 Proposed Changes to the Dutch Arbitration Act

As discussed in previous editions of *The Baker & McKenzie International Arbitration Yearbook,*[5] the Ministry of Justice indicated over a decade ago that Book 4 of the DCCP pertaining to arbitration would undergo major legislative changes.[6] A panel of arbitration specialists chaired by Professor A.J. van den Berg prepared a proposal for amending Dutch arbitration law ("Proposal") and submitted it to the Ministry of Justice on 21

---

[1] Frank Kroes is a Partner in Baker & McKenzie's Amsterdam office. His practice focuses on litigation and arbitration for financial institutions and other complex commercial disputes.

[2] Saskia Temme is a Senior Associate in Baker & McKenzie's Amsterdam office. Her practice focus is on commercial litigation and international arbitration.

[3] The authors would like to thank Esther Croonen of the Amsterdam office for her valuable assistance in preparing this chapter.

[4] Legislation of 2 July 1986, *Stb.* 1986, 372; amendments since 1986 include minor textual changes and—more fundamentally—the possibility to request preliminary witness examinations (Article 1022 DCCP).

[5] *See The Baker & McKenzie International Arbitration Yearbook 2009*, p. 207 and *The Baker & McKenzie International Arbitration Yearbook 2010-2011*, p. 297.

[6] Parliamentary papers II 1999/2000, 26 855, no. 5, p. 3.

December 2006.[7] The Proposal was based on the developments in national and international arbitration law, including the UNCITRAL Model Law, and recommended extensive changes to Dutch arbitration law.[8] In February 2007, the Minister of Justice indicated that the Proposal would be further developed in the course of 2007, but no visible action was taken.[9]

In November 2009, a member of Parliament asked why no action was taken for a legislative proposal,[10] but no concrete answer was given. On 15 June 2010, however, the Minister of Justice indicated that the Proposal is still on the Ministry's agenda.[11] The Minister promised that he would take the Proposal up himself and confirmed that he had already spoken with the relevant officials at the Ministry of Justice. It seems that the Proposal has indeed made it to the Ministry's agenda; the so-called Innovation Agenda of the Legal System of the Ministry of Safety and Justice dated 31 October 2011, states that legislation is being prepared in order to modernize arbitration.[12] The amendments are expected to be effective as of 1 January 2014. Although the Innovation Agenda does not explicitly mention the Proposal as a starting point for the announced legislation, the examples of the changes mentioned in the Innovation Agenda are

---

[7]   www.arbitragewet.nl/nieuws.xml.

[8]   *See* P. Sanders, *Herziening van onze arbitragewet* (Revision of our Arbitration Act), *TvA* 2008, 15.

[9]   Letter from the Minister of Justice, Parliamentary Papers II 2006/07, 30 951, no. 1, p. 31.

[10]   Proceedings II 2009/10, no. 20, p. 1589.

[11]   The speech was given at a conference on the occasion of Professor van den Berg resigning as the president of the Netherlands Arbitration Institute.

[12]   *Innovatieagenda rechtsbestel* (Innovation Agenda Legal System), Ministry of Safety and Justice, 31 October 2011, p. 11. The name of the Ministry was changed as of 14 October 2010.

all included in the Proposal. At a meeting hosted by the Netherlands Arbitration Institute ("NAI") on 19 December 2011, a representative of the Ministry of Safety and Justice confirmed that a legislative proposal will follow shortly. The internet consultation on the proposal will start in early 2012.

A.3 Trends and Tendencies

As part of the ongoing trend in Dutch arbitration practice – and also in the Dutch courts – to pay more attention to time and cost-efficiency, the "e-Court" initiative was launched in the Netherlands in early 2010. E-Court is an arbitration institute within the meaning of Article 1026 DCCP that provides a swift online arbitration.[13] E-Court advertises that an award is rendered in either eight weeks (for debt collection claims) or eighteen weeks (for other claims).[14] The most recent e-Court arbitration rules apply to e-Court arbitrations that commenced after 1 October 2011.[15]

Recent case law from the lower courts has revealed some flaws in e-Court arbitration, or at least the practice of e-Court arbitration. For example, the District Court of Zutphen refused to grant an *exequatur* (a court leave to enforce) for an arbitral award that was rendered by e-Court. The reason was that e-Court, which had requested the *exequatur* on behalf of the winning party, failed to submit the application for arbitration despite several requests from the court. The District Court of Zutphen therefore found that the procedure that led to the arbitral award was contrary to public policy, since it had to be assumed

---

[13] Besides online arbitration, e-Court also provides for binding third-party rulings (*bindend advies*) resulting in a notarial settlement agreement (*notariële vaststellingsovereenkomst*).

[14] *See* www.e-court.nl/procedures.

[15] Available in Dutch at www.e-court.nl/fileadmin/docs/Reglement.pdf.

that the respondent had not been given the opportunity to defend himself against the claims made in the arbitration, contrary to the principle that both parties must be heard.[16]

The District Court of Zutphen added some general observations as to e-Court arbitration. First, it pointed out that Article 26(1) of the e-Court arbitration rules indicates that the respondent cannot request an oral hearing, which is contrary to Article 1039(1), DCCP. A similar rule is included in the current e-Court arbitration rules (Part 1, Article 4(2)). It seems, however, that this objection is no longer valid, since Part 2, Article 3(6) of the current rules provides that e-Court, at the request of *either of the parties* (or on its own initiative), will give the parties the opportunity to give an oral explanation of their case. Second, the District Court of Zutphen found that the e-Court arbitration rules do not show how a respondent without an internet connection can defend himself against the claims made, which is also contrary to the principle that both sides must be heard. This final observation also seems to be superseded by the current set of rules, which provide in Part 1, Article 5(6) that a party without internet connection can file its defense by regular mail.

The District Court of Almelo rendered a similar judgment.[17] It also denied a request for an *exequatur* on the basis that no application for arbitration was submitted to the court. The court concluded that the procedure that led to the arbitral award was contrary to public policy, since it had to be assumed that the respondent had not been given an opportunity to defend himself against the claims made in the arbitration, contrary to the principle that both parties must be heard as the Zutphen District Court had observed.

---

[16] District Court of Zutphen, 7 October 2011, LJN: BT7213.

[17] District Court of Almelo, 7 October 2011, LJN: BT7088. *See also* District Court of Almelo, 7 October 2011, JLN: BT7606.

The District Court of Almelo[18] denied another request for an *exequatur* of an e-Court arbitration award. The award stated that it was a binding judgment (*gezag van gewijsde*), while Article 1059(2) DCCP provides that an arbitral award is not binding until after the period in which the award can be set aside. The e-Court arbitration rules provide that an arbitral award can be appealed within one month after the award is filed with a Dutch court.[19] That period had not yet lapsed when the award was rendered. The award therefore wrongfully stated that it was binding, which the District Court of Almelo considered to be contrary to public policy.

***

Separately, there seems to be a decrease in arbitrations held in the Netherlands or under Dutch arbitration rules. For instance, the NAI registered a total of 125 arbitrations in 2010 (32 international), as compared to a total of 145 in 2009 (44 international). In 2010, 53 arbitrations involved amounts of more than EUR 1,000,000. The final statistics for 2011 are not yet known.

B.   CASES

B.1   Court Proceedings: Recognition of Foreign Arbitral Awards in the Netherlands

The Supreme Court[20] decided a case concerning three arbitral awards rendered in an arbitration seated in Stockholm, Sweden between a Dutch party (Vastint) against foreign parties

---

[18]   District Court of Almelo, 28 October 2011, LJN: BU2930.

[19]   In the current e-Court arbitration rules: Part 2, Article 6(2).

[20]   Dutch Supreme Court, 24 December 2010, *NJ* 2011, 15.

(collectively, Svensson). Svensson applied to the president of the District Court of Amsterdam for recognition in the Netherlands of the third Swedish arbitral award. The president sustained that request and the Amsterdam Court of Appeal upheld the president's decision. Vastint appealed to the Supreme Court and, *inter alia*, complained that the Court of Appeal should have held —possibly even beyond the points raised by the parties—that the arbitral award could not be recognized because it was an interim award, and as such, was not binding on the parties. The Supreme Court found that whether an arbitral award is an interim award, and therefore not binding on the parties, does not affect public policy, but must be invoked by the party seeking dismissal of an application for recognition and enforcement.

B.2 Court Proceedings: Inclusion of Arbitration Clause in General Terms and Conditions Found to be an Unreasonable Burden for the Consumer

In a case decided by the Court of Appeal Leeuwarden, a Dutch construction company had made use of general terms and conditions in a contract with a consumer.[21] The general terms and conditions also included an arbitration clause, which provided that the parties gave up their right to litigate and instead agreed to arbitration in accordance with the statutes of the Arbitration Board for Construction companies in the Netherlands (*Raad van Arbitrage voor de Bouwbedrijven in Nederland*). A dispute arose and the consumer filed a claim before the Leeuwarden District Court (a state court). The construction company claimed that the court lacked jurisdiction. The court rejected the jurisdictional argument and decided that the arbitration clause was an unreasonable burden for the consumer.

---

[21]   Court of Appeal Leeuwarden, 5 July 2011, LJN: BR2500/*NJF* 2011, 382.

On the construction company's appeal, the Leeuwarden Court of Appeal also held that the arbitration clause was an unreasonable burden for the consumer within the meaning of Article 6:233(a) of the Dutch Civil Code ("DCC"). Specifically, the court of appeal found that the standard of an "unreasonable burden" must comply with EU Directive 93/13/EEG on unfair terms in consumer contracts. It held that it should take particular notice of the wording and the purpose of the relevant Directive in order to achieve the intended results of the Directive and comply with Article 288(3) of the Treaty on the Functioning of the European Union. The court of appeal therefore tested Article 6:233(a) DCC against the Directive.

With reference to Article 3 of the Directive, case law of the European Court of Justice and the annex to the Directive under question, the court of appeal found that the arbitration clause at hand was a clause within the meaning of the annex. The court added that arbitration may have disadvantages for consumers in that (i) the independence of an arbitrator is not guaranteed in the same manner as the independence of a state court, (ii) the arbitrator is not bound to apply the laws in the same manner as a state court, (iii) the consumer can be faced with higher costs than in state court proceedings and (iv) the distance between the consumer's place of residence and the offices of the Arbitration Board may prevent the consumer from bringing any claim or from appearing in the proceedings. Lastly, the court of appeal pointed out that the Proposal (for a new arbitration act)[22] provides that an arbitration clause in general terms and conditions can be nullified insofar as the consumer does not have a choice to bring his claim before an arbitral tribunal or a state court. Thus, the court of appeal held that the arbitration clause was unfair within the meaning of the Directive and

---

[22] *See* A.2 above.

unreasonably burdensome within the meaning of Article 6:233(a) DCC.[23]

B.3 Court Proceedings: Jurisdiction of Dutch Courts over Claim for Limited Discovery Where Arbitration is Outside the Netherlands

Article 843a DCCP provides that a party that is considered to have a justified interest can demand inspection of a copy of or an extract from identifiable documents relating to a legal relationship to which it is a party. A contract or a wrongful act gives rise to such a legal relationship. The request can, *inter alia,* be made before the president of the competent district court in summary proceedings. The party requesting the inspection (or copy or extract) may demand this information from any party that has these documents at its disposal or in its possession. However, circumstances such as professional or contractual confidentiality may lead to a denial by the court of a request pursuant to Article 843a DCCP.

In a case before the president of the Dordrecht District Court, a Singaporean company demanded copies of certain documents from its contractual counterparty, a Dutch company.[24] The Dutch company had argued that the president lacked jurisdiction because the parties had agreed upon arbitration in Singapore and were already involved in arbitral proceedings that included specific rules for disclosure. The president of the Dordrecht District Court held that an agreement providing for arbitration outside the Netherlands does not prevent a party from addressing the president of a Dutch court in summary

---

[23]   A few weeks later, the Leeuwarden District Court rendered a similar judgment with reference to the Leeuwarden Court of Appeal's judgment (Leeuwarden District Court, 3 August 2011, LJN: BR4256).

[24]   President of the Dordrecht District Court, 24 February 2011, LJN: BP5588.

proceedings (Article 1074(2) DCCP). He also considered that it had not been established that similar action was possible in the Singaporean arbitration, and found that whether or not this was the case was not decisive. The president of the Dordrecht District Court therefore decided that he had jurisdiction to decide on the Singaporean company's claim for copies of documents.

B.4 Arbitration Proceedings: Interpretation of a Contractual Clause on Dispute Resolution as a Valid Arbitration Agreement

In a recently published award of the NAI of 2008,[25] the arbitrators interpreted a clause on dispute resolution in a contract between a Dutch company and a foreign company.[26] The clause read: "All disputes and differences originating in connection with the present contract, non-authorized by negotiations, are subject to final settlement by arbitration of the Dutch Court." The parties agreed that Dutch law applied to the relevant clause. The claimant, the foreign company, argued that reference to "arbitration of the Dutch Court" was very clear: the parties intended to have their disputes settled by arbitration and not by a state court. Otherwise, the claimant argued, they would have used the term "trial of the Dutch court." Moreover, linguistically, arbitration means decision by recourse to an arbitration commission or an arbitration board. The claimant also argued that the arbitration clause led to application of the NAI Rules. The respondent, the Dutch company, argued that the parties did not agree upon NAI arbitration and that the NAI arbitral tribunal lacked jurisdiction on the ground that there was no valid

---

[25] Netherlands Arbitration Institute, 2 October 2008, *TvA* 2011, 58.

[26] The published award was redacted, so the nationality of the foreign company is unknown. The award merely mentions "A. Ltd." as the claimant.

arbitration agreement. According to the respondent, the dispute resolution clause was a selected forum or choice-of-court agreement giving jurisdiction to the Dutch courts. The word "arbitration" was to be interpreted in the meaning of "resolving a legal dispute by making an enforceable decision" or "settlement in case of controversy."

The arbitral tribunal decided that the clause could undoubtedly be referred to as a "pathological arbitration clause." Although this phrase usually refers to an arbitration clause that is unworkable and thus provides no basis for assuming jurisdiction, the arbitral tribunal in this case seems to have taken a different view of its meaning. The tribunal found that the parties had expressed their wish to go to arbitration and that the question therefore remained to be determined what the parties had in mind when they referred to "the Dutch Court." Since the parties had arbitration in mind, the tribunal considered they probably meant Dutch Court of Arbitration, which is the NAI. The tribunal added that such interpretation is consistent with "a basic principle of interpretation according to which one should give a provision a useful effect" and that such interpretation is also consistent with various other decisions of foreign (arbitration) courts.[27] The tribunal therefore decided that it had jurisdiction.

---

[27] The arbitral tribunal referred to the following cases: Italian Arbitration Association, Award in case no. 41/92 of 1993, *Manufacturer v. Distributor*, XXII Y.B. COM. ARB. 178 (1997); Court of Appeal Paris, 14 February, 1985, 1987 REV. ARB. 325; French Supreme Court, Cas. 1e Civ., 14 December, 1983, 1984 REV. ARB. 483.

C. PUBLIC POLICY IN INTERNATIONAL ARBITRATION

C.1 Reliance on Public Policy before Dutch State Courts

Under Dutch arbitration law, a distinction is made between arbitration *in* the Netherlands and arbitration *outside* the Netherlands. The sole determining factor is the place of arbitration, not the parties' nationality or any other factor. This distinction is relevant for the question of whether a party can rely on public policy considerations before the Dutch state courts.

Where the arbitration is seated in the Netherlands, public policy considerations are relevant in three situations before state courts.

First, a violation of public policy is a basis for a Dutch court to deny enforcement of an arbitral award in the Netherlands.[28] If the arbitral award is clearly contrary to public policy, the court must on its own initiative (*ex officio*) deny a request for enforcement of the award on the basis of Article 1063 DCCP. The other party does not have to invoke this reason for a court to deny the request.[29] The court will only review summarily whether the award is contrary to public policy; the violation must be apparent *prima facie*.[30] A violation of public policy can relate to both the contents of the award and the procedure that led to the award.

---

[28] A separate basis for denying an *exequatur*—that needs to be demonstrated by the party invoking this ground—is that the arbitral award was annulled by a competent authority in the country of origin (Article 1076, paragraph 1 under Ae, DCCP).

[29] There is no statutory basis for the other party to be heard, so there may not even be an opportunity to put forward any defense. *See also Tekst & Commentaar Burgerlijke Rechtsvordering* (Text & Comments to Code of Civil Procedure), comment 3 under c) to Article 1062 DCCP.

[30] Parliamentary papers II 1983/84, 18 464, no. 3, p. 27.

Second, a violation of public policy is a basis for annulment of an arbitral award by a Dutch state court. If the award or the procedure that led to the award is contrary to public policy, the award can be annulled by a Dutch court pursuant to Article 1065 DCCP. The party claiming annulment of an arbitral award on the basis that it is contrary to public policy, must invoke this ground for annulment itself on the basis of Article 1064(5) DCCP.[31] If a party seeks annulment of an arbitral award, a breach of public policy must be invoked in the writ of summons commencing the annulment action. The writ of summons must be issued either no later than three months after the arbitral award was filed with the court,[32] or, if the award including an *exequatur* is served upon a party, within three months after this service (Article 1064(3) DCCP). Contrary to the court's limited assessment under Article 1063 DCCP as mentioned above, the court will in this case fully test whether the award is contrary to public policy.[33]

Third, a violation of public policy can be relevant before the state courts under Article 1022(1) DCCP. This article provides that a state court must deny jurisdiction if a party invokes an arbitration agreement, unless the arbitration agreement is invalid. Under Dutch law, a breach of public policy can render an

---

[31] In addition, the Dutch Supreme Court has ruled that a request for annulment of an arbitral award on the basis that it is contrary to public policy because the arbitrators were not independent and impartial is not open to a party that had the right of challenging the arbitrators pursuant to Article 1035 DCCP, but chose not to exercise that right (*see* Dutch Supreme Court 18 February 1994, *NJ* 1994, 765).

[32] Filing the arbitral award with a district court is an obligation of the arbitral tribunal pursuant to Article 1058(1)(b) DCCP.

[33] *See also Tekst & Commentaar Burgerlijke Rechtsvordering* (Text & Comments to Code of Civil Procedure), comment 1 under a) to Article 1063 DCCP. It is important to note, however, that the annulment procedure may not lead to a *révision au fond*; *see Tekst & Commentaar Burgerlijke Rechtsvordering* (Text & Comments to Code of Civil Procedure), comment 1 under b) to Article 1065 DCCP.

arbitration agreement invalid.[34] In principle, the court does not review on its own initiative whether the arbitration agreement is valid, but if it is contrary to public policy, the court must declare the agreement invalid on its own initiative.[35] It seems that, thus far, a breach of public policy is the only reason for invalidity of an arbitration agreement that a court can review *ex officio*.

Where the arbitration is seated outside the Netherlands, public policy considerations are only relevant before the Dutch state courts under the following two circumstances.

First, they are relevant in relation to recognition and enforcement. The main relevant treaty on recognition and enforcement of foreign arbitral awards is the New York Convention, to which the Netherlands is a party. Where the New York Convention applies, recognition and enforcement of an arbitral award may be refused if the Dutch court finds that it would be contrary to Dutch public policy (Article V(2)(b) New York Convention).[36]

Where the New York Convention (or any other (future) treaty) does not apply or where an applicable treaty allows a party to invoke application of Dutch arbitration law, Article 1076 DCCP provides that a foreign arbitral award can be recognized and enforced in the Netherlands unless, *inter alia*, the court finds that

---

[34] *See, e.g.,* Arnhem District Court 14 June 2010, LJN: BN2002. Article 3:40(1) DCC explicitly provides that a legal act that because of its content or purpose is contrary to public policy, is null and void.

[35] *See also Tekst & Commentaar Burgerlijke Rechtsvordering* (Text & Comments to Code of Civil Procedure), comment 1 under b) to Article 1022 DCCP.

[36] The Netherlands is also a party to other treaties on recognition and enforcement of foreign arbitral awards. For an overview of those other treaties, see R van Delden, *Internationale Handelsarbitrage* (International Commercial Arbitration), Deventer: Kluwer 1996, no. 16 *et seq.*

recognition or enforcement is contrary to public policy. The court has to review this on its own initiative.[37]

Second, a violation of public policy can be relevant under Article 1074(1) DCCP. Parallel to Article 1022 DCCP for arbitration in the Netherlands, this article—which applies to arbitration outside the Netherlands—provides that the state court must deny jurisdiction if a party invokes an arbitration agreement, unless the arbitration agreement is found to be invalid under the law applicable to the arbitration agreement. As mentioned above, a reason under Dutch law for an arbitration agreement to be invalid is that the agreement is contrary to public policy. The court does not, in principle, review on its own initiative whether the arbitration agreement is valid, but it is likely that the court must review on its own initiative a potential violation of public policy that would render the arbitration agreement invalid, similar to the situation under Article 1022 DCCP.

C.2 Reliance on Public Policy in Arbitral Proceedings

Pursuant to Article 1052(1) DCCP, the tribunal is competent to decide on its own jurisdiction. The tribunal does not have jurisdiction if there is no valid arbitration agreement (see Article 1052(2)) or if the tribunal was not established in accordance with the applicable rules (see Article 1052(3)).[38] Article 1052(2) DCCP provides—in case of arbitration in the Netherlands only— that a party that has appeared in the arbitral proceedings must raise objections with respect to the tribunal's jurisdiction based on an invalidity of the arbitration agreement before entering any other defense. If a party fails to do so, that party can no longer

---

[37] *See also Tekst & Commentaar Burgerlijke Rechtsvordering* (Text & Comments to Code of Civil Procedure), comment 2 under a) to Article 1076 DCCP.

[38] *See* P. Sanders, *Het Nederlandse arbitragerecht* (Dutch arbitration law), Deventer: Kluwer 2001, p. 23.

claim that the arbitration agreement is invalid, either before the arbitral tribunal or before a state court.[39] As mentioned above, a reason under Dutch law for an arbitration agreement to be invalid is that the agreement is contrary to public policy. A violation of public policy can thus be used as a defense against jurisdiction of the arbitral tribunal for the reason that there is no valid arbitration agreement.

C.3 Rules that Constitute "Public Policy"

The Supreme Court has ruled that there is a violation of Dutch public policy within the meaning of Article 1065 DCCP if the contents of the arbitral award are contrary to an imperative law that is so fundamental that the observance of that law may not be precluded by limitations of a procedural nature,[40] such as the limitation of a legal dispute to the points that the parties themselves have put forward. This is, for instance, the case if the arbitral award is contrary to Article 101 of the Treaty on the Functioning of the European Union on Competition.[41]

The procedure that led to the arbitral award is contrary to Dutch public policy if the tribunal violates fundamental principles of procedural law. An example is the principle that both parties must be heard.[42] There is also a (sufficient) violation of public

---

[39] The NAI Rules provide for a similar rule and add that a party that participated in the appointment of the arbitrator(s) shall not be barred from raising the plea that the arbitral tribunal lacks jurisdiction on the ground that there is no valid arbitration agreement. This rule (Rule 9) will also apply to NAI arbitration outside the Netherlands, contrary to Article 1052 DCCP.

[40] Dutch Supreme Court 21 March 1997, *NJ* 1998, 207, under 4.2.

[41] ECJ 1 June 1999, *NJ* 2000, 339.

[42] Dutch Supreme Court 8 November 1963, *NJ* 1964, 139; Dutch Supreme Court 18 June 1993, *NJ* 1994, 449, under 3.3; Dutch Supreme Court 25 May 2007, *NJ* 2007, 294, under 3.5-3.7.

policy where facts and circumstances show that an arbitrator was not impartial or independent when rendering the award, or that his impartiality and independence was questionable to such an extent that it would be unreasonable for the losing party to be expected to accept the award.[43]

In the event that an arbitral award lacks any reasoning or if the decision in an award is so poorly explained that the award can be considered to be lacking any reasoning, the award may also be contrary to public policy.[44]

When applying Article 1076 DCCP to arbitral awards rendered outside the Netherlands, the court may also take international aspects of public policy into consideration (including, at the court's discretion, foreign rules and practice on public policy) and thus apply the so-called international public policy as a criterion. International public policy, from a Dutch perspective, is a more restricted concept than internal public policy. A violation of internal public policy does not necessarily mean a violation of international public policy.[45]

---

[43]   Dutch Supreme Court 18 February 1994, *NJ* 1994, 765, under 3.8.

[44]   Article 1065(1)(d) DCCP, however, also provides for a specific basis for annulment due to a lack of grounds in the award. *See also Tekst & Commentaar Burgerlijke Rechtsvordering* (Text & Comments to Code of Civil Procedure), comment 7 under b) to Article 1065 DCCP.

[45]   *See also Tekst & Commentaar Burgerlijke Rechtsvordering* (Text & Comments to Code of Civil Procedure), comment 2 under h) to Article 1076 DCCP and P. Sanders, *Het Nederlandse arbitragerecht* (Dutch arbitration law), Deventer: Kluwer 2001, p. 198.

PHILIPPINES

Emmanuel S. Buenaventura,[1] Lemuel D. Lopez and Jay Patrick R. Santiago[2,3]

A. LEGISLATION, TRENDS AND TENDENCIES

A.1 ADR Rules of Court

In 2004, to respond to the growing complexity of disputes in international commerce, the Philippine Congress enacted Republic Act 9285, otherwise known as the "Alternative Dispute Resolution Act of 2004" ("ADR Act"). Under the ADR Act, actively promoting party autonomy in the resolution of disputes was declared a policy of the state. In 2009, the Department of Justice promulgated its Implementing Rules and Regulations ("IRR of the ADR Act") to prescribe the procedures and guidelines for the implementation of the ADR Act.

In October 2009, the Supreme Court promulgated the Special Rules of Court on Alternative Dispute Resolution ("ADR Rules of Court"). The ADR Rules of Court are intended to limit court

---

[1] Emmanuel Buenaventura is a Partner in Baker & McKenzie's Manila office and its representative to the Firm's International Arbitration Practice Group. His practice includes general dispute resolution, tax and customs controversies, corporate rehabilitation and insolvency, labor appellate proceedings, maritime law, intellectual property litigation, administrative and regulatory disputes, mining, arbitration, alternative dispute resolution and sanctions proceedings before international organizations.

[2] Lemuel D. Lopez and Jay Patrick R. Santiago are Associates in Baker & McKenzie's Manila office. Their practice covers civil, criminal and commercial litigation, taxation, arbitration and alternative dispute resolution.

[3] The authors would like to thank Camille Aromas and Iris Ciela T. Villaluz-Garcia, Associates in Baker & McKenzie's Manila disputes resolution group, who provided valuable updates on the relevant laws and jurisprudence.

intervention in arbitration proceedings. In the limited instances in which they can intervene, courts are to assist and cooperate with arbitral tribunals. Thus, the rules require the courts—if a party so applies—to refer parties covered by an arbitration agreement to arbitration.[4] The ADR Rules of Court further provide that:

- The arbitral tribunal shall be accorded the first opportunity or competence to rule on the issue of whether it has the competence or jurisdiction to decide a dispute submitted to it for decision.

- When a court is asked to rule upon issue(s) affecting the competence or jurisdiction of an arbitral tribunal in a dispute brought before it, either before or after the arbitral tribunal is constituted, the court must exercise judicial restraint and defer to the competence or jurisdiction of the arbitral tribunal by allowing the arbitral tribunal the first opportunity to rule upon such issues.

- Where the court is asked to make a determination of whether the arbitration agreement is null and void, inoperative or incapable of being performed, under this policy of judicial restraint, the court must make no more than a *prima facie* determination of that issue.

- Where the place of arbitration is in the Philippines, the court must not enjoin the arbitration proceedings during the pendency of the petition involving the jurisdiction of the arbitral tribunal.

- Before or during arbitration proceedings, courts may, upon request of a party and when there is urgent need, and only to

---

[4]   Guerra, Gleo, "SC Promulgates Special ADR Rules" at http://sc.judiciary.gov.ph/publications/benchmark/2009/10/100903.php, 9 December 2011.

the extent that the arbitral tribunal has no power to act or is unable to act effectively, issue interim protection measures to: (i) preserve property; (ii) prevent the respondent from disposing of or concealing property; or (iii) prevent the desired relief from becoming illusory.

- Any court order granting or denying interim measures of protection is issued without prejudice to subsequent grant, modification, amendment, revision or revocation by the arbitral tribunal as may be warranted. An interim measure of protection issued by the arbitral tribunal shall, upon its issuance, be deemed to have *ipso jure* modified, amended, revised, or revoked an interim measure of protection previously issued by the court to the extent that it is inconsistent with the subsequent interim measure of protection issued by the arbitral tribunal. The court shall assist in the enforcement of an interim measure of protection issued by the arbitral tribunal that the tribunal is unable to enforce effectively.

- It is presumed that an arbitral award was made and released in due course and is subject to enforcement by the court, unless the adverse party is able to establish a ground for setting aside or not enforcing an arbitral award.

- A party to arbitration cannot file an appeal or a petition for certiorari questioning the merits of an arbitral award. A party may only appeal an order granting or denying recognition and enforcement to the court of appeals and then the Supreme Court.

A.2 IPO Arbitration Rules

Consistent with this public policy of promoting ADR, the Intellectual Property Office ("IPO") promulgated the IPO Arbitration Rules. The IPO Arbitration Rules apply to the arbitration of intellectual property disputes,[5] which under Philippine law,[6] shall be submitted to the IPO for determination where the parties have agreed to submit such disputes to arbitration.[7] The arbitral tribunal shall be the sole judge of the admissibility, relevance, materiality and weight of evidence.[8] A party is allowed to rely on experiments previously conducted, provided that the party relying on such experiment gives notice to the arbitration tribunal and to the other party and provides information on the purpose of the experiment, a summary of the experiment, the method employed, the results and the conclusion.[9] The arbitral tribunal may also rely on primers and models, where parties so agree. Aside from witnesses that parties may call to testify on their behalf, the arbitral tribunal may, after consultation with the parties, appoint one or more independent experts to report to it on specific issues designated by the arbitral tribunal.[10] Since there is strong interest in treating intellectual property itself or aspects thereof as confidential, the IPO Arbitration Rules provide for elaborate rules on the disclosure and treatment of confidential information.

---

[5] This includes, for example, disputes involving intellectual property that are already registered, or are in the process of registration or which are registrable under the IP Code, and all other disputes involving a breach of intellectual property rights that are actionable under the IP Code. IPO Arbitration Rules, Sec. 2 (b).

[6] The Intellectual Property Code of the Philippines ("IP Code").

[7] IPO Arbitration Rules, Sec. 2 (a).

[8] IPO Arbitration Rules, Sec. 48.

[9] IPO Arbitration Rules, Sec. 49.

[10] IPO Arbitration Rules, Sec. 55 (a).

A.3   Court-Annexed Mediation

In 2011, the Philippine Supreme Court further expanded the cases covered by court-annexed mediation to cover the following: (1) all civil cases and civil liability of criminal cases covered by the Rules on Summary Procedure, including civil liability for violation of the Bouncing Checks Law; (2) special proceedings for the settlement of estates; (3) all civil and criminal cases requiring a certificate to file an action under the Revised Katarungang Pambarangay Law; (4) the civil aspect of quasi-offenses under the Revised Penal Code; (5) the civil aspect of less grave felonies not exceeding six years of imprisonment where the offended party is a private person; (6) the civil aspect of estafa (swindling), theft and libel; (7) all civil cases and probate proceedings brought on appeal from the first level courts; (8) all cases of forcible entry and unlawful detainer brought on appeal from the first level courts; (9) all civil cases involving title or possession of real property or interest therein brought on appeal from first level courts; and (10) *habeas corpus* cases brought up on appeal from the first level courts.

A necessary adjunct of court-annexed mediation is Judicial Dispute Resolution ("JDR"), which enables judges during the pre-trial stage of a judicial action to attempt to settle disputes between party-litigants after the mediation proceedings have failed. The JDR judge becomes a mediator-conciliator-early neutral evaluator in a continuing effort to secure a settlement. As mediator and conciliator, the judge facilitates the settlement discussions between the parties and tries to reconcile their differences. As a neutral evaluator, the judge assesses the relative strengths and weaknesses of each party's case and makes a non-binding and impartial evaluation of the chances of each party's success in the case. On the basis of such neutral evaluation, the judge persuades the parties to agree to a fair and mutually acceptable settlement of their dispute. The JDR judge shall not preside over the trial of the case when the parties do not settle their dispute at JDR.

Any and all matters discussed or communications made, including requests for mediation and documents presented during the JDR proceedings before the trial judge, shall be privileged and confidential, and the same shall be inadmissible as evidence for any purpose in any other proceedings. Further, the JDR judge shall not pass any information obtained in the course of conciliation and early neutral evaluation to the trial judge or to any other person.

Notwithstanding the adoption of the ADR Rules of Court, IPO Arbitration Rules and expansion of cases covered by court-annexed mediation and JDR, alternative means of dispute resolution remain the exception rather than the general rule in the Philippines. The general tendency of parties is still to resort to litigation for the resolution of their disputes. This is perhaps attributable to the slow development of ADR laws and rules in the country. For instance, before the ADR Act passed in 2004, the Philippine Arbitration Law, which governed at the time, was significantly outdated. Parties are likewise discouraged because of the high costs associated with arbitration, especially with international arbitration.[11] Also, certain factors, like the fact that an arbitral award is subject to a process of judicial recognition and enforcement, tend to create a perception that arbitration may just prolong dispute resolution.

Nevertheless, though development may be slow, the future is bright for alternative modes of dispute resolution in the Philippines. As can be seen from the passage of the ADR Act and the recent adoption of its implementing rules, genuine efforts

---

[11] Raul Palabrica, "Risks of Arbitration" at http://business.inquirer.net/12177/risks-of-arbitration.

are being made to institutionalize alternative modes of dispute resolution, and to make Philippine arbitration laws more responsive to the changing times. Moreover, these developments are expected to aid in attracting more business in the country by improving the means by which parties can resolve their differences. After all, foreign investors include arbitration clauses in their contracts in order to be spared from the protracted delay involved in traditional litigation, but more importantly, to guarantee confidentiality in the proceedings and to safeguard impartiality.[12]

B. CASES

B.1 Jurisdiction of the Arbitral Tribunal *vis-à-vis* the Trial Court

In *Cargill Philippines, Inc. v. San Fernando Regala Trading, Inc.*,[13] the Supreme Court reiterated the "separability doctrine" (i.e., that the arbitration agreement shall be treated as a separate agreement independent of the main contract and the invalidity of the main contract does not affect the validity of the arbitration agreement), and ruled that it is for the arbitrator and not the courts to decide whether a contract between the parties exists or is valid.

In this case, the trial court issued an order denying petitioner's motion to dismiss or suspend the proceedings and to refer the controversy to voluntary arbitration. It found first that the Arbitration Law only directed a court to stay an action or proceeding arising out of an arbitration agreement, and did not impose the sanction of dismissal. Further, the trial court found

---

[12] Arthur P. Autea, "International Commercial Arbitration: The Philippine Experience," 77 *Phil. LJ* 143 (2002).

[13] G.R. No. 175404, 31 January 2011.

that suspension of the proceedings was not warranted. It reasoned that the Arbitration Law contemplates an arbitration proceeding that must be conducted in the Philippines under the jurisdiction and control of the trial court; before an arbitrator who resides in the country; that the arbitral award is subject to court approval, disapproval and modification; and that there must be an appeal from the judgment of the trial court. The trial court found that the arbitration clause in question contravened these procedures because it contemplated an arbitration proceeding in New York before a non-resident arbitrator (American Arbitration Association) and provided that the arbitral award shall be final and binding on both parties.

Petitioner then filed a petition with the Court of Appeals on the sole issue that the trial court erred in refusing to dismiss or at least suspend the proceedings *a quo*. In its decision, the Court of Appeals denied the petition and affirmed the trial court's orders. The Court of Appeals ruled that the case cannot be brought under the Arbitration Law for the purpose of suspending the proceedings before the trial court, since in its motion to dismiss or suspend proceedings, petitioner alleged that the contract between the parties did not exist or it was invalid and that the contract bearing the arbitration clause was never consummated by the parties. Thus, it was proper that such issue be first resolved by the court through an appropriate trial and the issue involved a question of fact that the trial court should first resolve. It held that arbitration is not proper when one of the parties repudiated the existence or validity of the contract.

Petitioner elevated the case to the Supreme Court which granted the petition and reversed the lower courts. The Supreme Court ruled that an arbitration agreement, which forms part of the main contract, shall not be regarded as invalid or non-existent just because the main contract is invalid or did not come into existence, since the arbitration agreement is treated as a separate agreement independent of the main contract. A contrary ruling would suggest that a party's mere repudiation of the main contract is sufficient to avoid arbitration—exactly the situation the separability doctrine seeks to avoid. Thus, even the party who has repudiated the main contract is not prevented from enforcing its arbitration clause.

Moreover, the Supreme Court found that in filing a complaint for rescission of contract and damages, respondent alleged that a contract existed between respondent and petitioner. It is that contract that included an arbitration clause stating that "any dispute which the buyer and seller may not be able to settle by mutual agreement shall be settled before the City of New York by the American Arbitration Association." The arbitration agreement thus clearly expressed the parties' intention that any dispute between them as buyer and seller should be referred to arbitration. It is for the arbitrator and not the courts to decide whether a contract between the parties exists or is valid.

B.2 Trial Court's Power to Issue Interim Relief

In *Department of Foreign Affairs and Bangko Sentral ng Pilipinas v. Hon. Franco Falcon, Presiding Judge of Regional Trial Court Branch 71 and BCA International Corporation*,[14] the Philippine Supreme Court discussed the availability of interim relief pending the constitution of an arbitration tribunal.

In this case, the Philippine government engaged BCA International Corporation ("BCA") to work on the Machine Readable Passport and Visa Project (the "MRP/V Project") of the Department of Foreign Affairs ("DFA"). To comply with the Build Operate Transfer ("BOT") Law, BCA incorporated a project company, the Philippine Passport Corporation ("PPC"),

---

[14]   G.R. No. 176657, 1 September 2010.

to undertake and implement the MRP/V Project. On 8 February 2001, the DFA and PPC signed a BOT Agreement. On 5 April 2002, the DFA and BCA, with the conformity of PPC, signed an amended BOT agreement that included an arbitration clause. During the implementation of the MRP/V Project, both the DFA and BCA imputed breaches against each other.

BCA filed a request for arbitration with the Philippine Dispute Resolution Center, Inc. ("PDRCI"). The DFA declined on the ground that the amended BOT agreement did not mention a specific institution to settle the dispute, and claimed that the arbitration should be had before an *ad hoc* arbitration body, not before the PDRCI.

Meanwhile, the DFA entered into a Memorandum of Agreement ("MOA") with the Central Bank of the Philippines for the latter to provide passports compliant with international standards (the "e-Passport Project"). BCA filed a petition for interim relief under the ADR Act with the Regional Trial Court of Pasig on the ground that the e-Passport Project would render BCA's remedies moot. After the hearing, the trial court issued a preliminary injunction to stop the e-Passport project.

On appeal, the Supreme Court ruled that the trial court had jurisdiction to issue a writ of preliminary injunction. The Supreme Court pointed out that the ADR Act allows the trial court to grant interim or provisional relief, including preliminary injunctive relief, to parties in an arbitration prior to the constitution of the arbitral tribunal. The Supreme Court held, however, that BCA could no longer be granted injunctive relief because during the pendency of the case, the PDRCI case was dismissed for lack of jurisdiction in view of the lack of agreement between the parties to arbitrate before the PDRCI.

B.3 Enforcement of Foreign Arbitral Award

In *Landoil Resources Corporation v. Al Rabiah Lighting Company*,[15] the Philippine Supreme Court affirmed the enforcement of an arbitral award in favor of a foreign corporation rendered by the Commercial Kully Court of Kuwait against two Philippine corporations who did not appear in the proceedings. Consistent with the Philippine policy in favor of arbitration, the case illustrates that foreign arbitral awards in favor of foreign entities will be recognized and enforced by local courts in the Philippines. Additionally, it shows that an objection by Philippine entities that the arbitral award is contrary to public policy or violates due process, generally cannot bar enforcement of the foreign arbitral award.

In the case, Al Rabiah Lighting Company ("Al Rabiah"), a foreign corporation existing under the laws of Kuwait, and Construction Consortium, Inc. ("CCI") entered into a sub-contract agreement for the electrical works of Kuwait Oil Company's New Industrial Training Centre project in Ahmadi, Kuwait. Al Rabiah started carrying out its works as agreed. Subsequently, the project owner withdrew the principal contract, leading to the termination of the services of CCI and Landoil Resources Corporation ("Landoil"), which were both domestic Philippine corporations. As a result, Al Rabiah's works were stopped before being completed.

On 9 June 1983, Landoil acknowledged its indebtedness to Al Rabiah in the amount of KD 91,580.059, plus general overtime pay of KD 8,126, and promised to pay the debt in installments. However, Landoil failed to pay Al Rabiah any part of the amount due. Thus, Al Rabiah referred the dispute to the Commercial Kully Court of Kuwait for arbitration as provided under the sub-

---

[15]   G.R. No. 174720, 7 September 2011.

contract agreement. Although the parties were duly notified of the scheduled arbitration sessions, only Al Rabiah and its counsel appeared. The arbitrator rendered its award in favor of Al Rabiah, finding "Landoil Resources Corporation and Construction Consortium" solely liable to pay KD 108,368.860.

Al Rabiah filed an action with the Regional Trial Court of Makati for the enforcement of the foreign judgment, plus damages, against CCI and Landoil. In its answer, Landoil claimed that the Commercial Kully Court of Kuwait did not acquire jurisdiction over it and the arbitral award was contrary to public policy, and hence, illegal. Meanwhile, in its answer, CCI claimed that it was not a party to the contract and that the Commercial Kully Court of Kuwait did not acquire jurisdiction over it and the arbitral award was contrary to public policy.

After trial, the court rendered its decision on 31 July, 1995 enforcing the foreign arbitral award against Landoil and CCI. The Court of Appeals affirmed the enforcement decision.

On appeal to the Supreme Court, Landoil argued that the lower courts erred in allegedly modifying the foreign arbitral award. Landoil contended that the foreign arbitral award adjudged only one defendant liable, Land Oil Resources Company (Construction Consortium Incorporation), which is a different entity as shown by the fact that its articles of incorporation do not indicate such appellation.

The Supreme Court ruled that Landoil was estopped from denying its participation and liability under the sub-contract agreement and resisting the enforcement of the foreign arbitral award against it. The court affirmed the finding of the Court of Appeals that Landoil could not deny its participation in the sub-contract because the agreement itself mentioned Landoil as one of the contracting parties. It was also a matter of record that Landoil, through its regional marketing director, wrote to Al Rabiah confirming that Landoil owes Al Rabiah the sum of KD 21,930.317.

The Supreme Court further noted that Landoil's argument that the party adjudged liable under the foreign arbitral award was a different entity was only raised for the first time in its motion for reconsideration filed with the Court of Appeals. Landoil never claimed in the trial court that it was not the party referred to in the foreign arbitral award.

C. PUBLIC POLICY IN INTERNATIONAL ARBITRATION

C.1 Scenarios of Reliance on Public Policy

As an arbitration agreement is a contract, its validity, like that of any contract, may be impugned on the ground of being against public policy. Under Philippines law, a contract violating public policy is defined as one whose cause, object or purpose is contrary to law, morals, good customs, public order or public policy.[16]

Based on the ADR Rules of Court, the court may set aside or refuse to enforce of a foreign arbitral award if the court finds that the recognition or enforcement of the award would be contrary to public policy.[17]

---

[16] Civil Code, Art. 1409. Notably, the following issues cannot be the subject of arbitration: (a) labor disputes covered by Presidential Decree No. 442, otherwise known as 'he Labor Code of the Philippines, as amended, and its Implementing Rules and Regulations; (b) the civil status of persons; (c) the validity of a marriage; (d) any ground for legal separation; (e) the jurisdiction of courts; (f) future legitime; (g) criminal liability; and (h) those which by law cannot be compromised. *See* Alternative Dispute Resolution Act of 2004, Sec. 6.

[17] Special ADR Rules, Rule 13.4.

C.2 Modes and Limitations of Reliance on Public Policy

Under the IRR of the ADR Act, a plea that the arbitral tribunal does not have jurisdiction must be raised not later than the submission of the statement of defense.[18] If the arbitral tribunal rules as a preliminary question that it has jurisdiction, any party may request, within 30 days after having received notice of that ruling, the regional trial court to decide the matter, which decision shall be immediately executory and not subject to motion for reconsideration or appeal. While such a request is pending, the arbitral tribunal may continue the arbitral proceedings and render an award.[19] If the arbitral tribunal renders a final arbitral award and the court has not rendered a decision on the petition from the arbitral tribunal's preliminary ruling affirming its jurisdiction, that petition shall become *ipso facto* moot and shall be dismissed by the regional trial court. The dismissal shall be without prejudice to the right of the aggrieved party to raise the same issue in a timely petition to vacate or set aside the award.[20]

Where the arbitral tribunal defers its ruling on the preliminary question on its jurisdiction until the final award, the aggrieved party cannot seek judicial relief to question the deferral and must await the final arbitral award before seeking appropriate judicial recourse,[21] i.e., a petition to vacate or set aside the award.

Under the ADR Rules of Court, a party in an international commercial arbitration in the Philippines may file a petition to set aside an arbitral award with the regional trial court within

---

[18]   ADR IRR, Art. 4.16 (b).

[19]   ADR IRR, Art. 4.16 (c).

[20]   Special ADR Rules, Rule 3.21.

[21]   Special ADR Rules, Rule 3.20.

three months from the time the petitioner receives a copy thereof. If a timely request is made with the arbitral tribunal for correction, interpretation or additional award, the three month period shall be counted from the time the petitioner receives the arbitral tribunal's resolution of that request. A petition to set aside can no longer be filed after the lapse of the three month period. However, the dismissal of a petition to set aside an arbitral award for being time-barred shall not automatically result in the approval of the petition filed therein and in opposition thereto for recognition and enforcement of the same award. Failure to file a petition to set aside shall preclude a party from raising grounds to resist enforcement of the award.[22]

Notably, violation of public policy is not one of the grounds a party can raise. Rather, the court may, upon its own determination that the enforcement or recognition of the arbitral award is against public policy, deny a petition for recognition and enforcement or grant a petition to set aside the arbitral award.[23]

In case a petition to recognize and enforce an award in an international commercial arbitration is filed with the regional trial court, the party opposing the petition may file its opposition within fifteen days from its receipt of the petition.[24]

In the case of a foreign arbitral award (i.e., one rendered outside the Philippines), the ADR Rules of Court do not grant a party the right to file a petition to set aside the award. Rather, only a petition for recognition and enforcement of the foreign arbitral award can be filed in the regional trial court at any time after its receipt. In such case, the court would grant the respondent 30

---

[22] Special ADR Rules, Rule 2.2 (b).

[23] Special ADR Rules, Rule 12.4.

[24] Special ADR Rules, Rule 12.8.

days from receipt of the notice and the petition within which to file an opposition.

As in the case of a petition for enforcement and recognition of an international commercial arbitral award, violation of public policy is not one of the grounds a party can raise to oppose the petition. The court may, upon its own determination that the enforcement or recognition of the arbitral award is against public policy, deny a petition for recognition and enforcement.[25]

It is not a requirement that an opposing party in an enforcement proceeding (of either an international commercial arbitral award or foreign arbitral award) in the regional trial court must have previously raised the issue of public policy before the arbitral tribunal. As discussed, it is for the court to determine whether the recognition and enforcement of the arbitral award is against public policy.

In the case of a foreign arbitral award, recognition and enforcement in the Philippines is barred if the opposing party furnishes proof that the arbitral award has been set aside or suspended by a court of the country in which the award was made.[26]

C.3 Rules that Constitute "Public Policy"

The Philippines does not have a clear and comprehensive category of legislation, rules and regulations, or case law which is deemed mandatory and considered to be part of the public policy of the Philippines. As succinctly described by the Supreme Court in *Gabriel v. Monte de Pieded y Caja de Aharros*,[27] "the term 'public policy' is vague and uncertain in

---

[25]   Special ADR Rules, Rule 13.4.

[26]   Special ADR Rules, Rule 13.4.

[27]   G.R. No. L-47806, 14 April 1941.

meaning, floating and changeable in connotation." Often in the Philippines, courts ask not what constitutes public policy, but rather what is contrary to public policy. Hence, the content of public policy in the Philippines becomes evident only when an act, omission or contractual stipulation is alleged to be something contrary to public policy.

In *Gabriel v. Monte de Pieded y Caja de Aharros*, the Supreme Court, in a non-arbitration case, provided a test for what is contrary to public policy:

> In the absence of express legislation or constitutional prohibition, a court, in order to declare a contract void as against public policy, must find that the contract as to the consideration or thing to be done, has a tendency to injure the public, is against the public good, or contravenes some established interests of society, or is inconsistent with sound policy and good morals, or tends clearly to undermine the security of individual rights, whether of personal liability or of private property.[28]

Arturo Tolentino, a noted civil law expert in the Philippines, observes that what is considered contrary to public policy usually depends on what has been previously condemned by public legislation, judicial decision or constitutional prohibition.[29]

The Philippines also does not clearly distinguish between domestic and international public policy. More often, what is termed as public policy is only the domestic public policy of the Philippines. Notably, the Philippine Constitution, in Article II, Section 2, "adopts the generally accepted principles of

---

[28] *Ibid.*

[29] Arturo Tolentino, "Commentaries and Jurisprudence on the Civil Code of the Philippines," 420.

international law as part of the law of the land." Thus, what could be traditionally deemed as "international" public policy is considered in the Philippines as part of its domestic public policy. Therefore, the distinction between domestic and international public policies is blurred from the point of view of Philippine courts. Remarkably, the term international public policy has not been used in cases decided by the Supreme Court. Nonetheless, Philippine courts have recognized public policy in the realm of international relations.[30]

Violations of public policy, without distinguishing between domestic or international, has been used as a defense against the enforcement of arbitration agreements or arbitral awards. A common argument prior to the passage of the Arbitration Law was that arbitration clauses are null and void for being contrary to public policy[31] since they oust courts of their jurisdiction and such effect was against public policy.[32] Arbitration clauses are also argued to be contrary to public policy because the issues that are subject thereto are not arbitrable.[33] Similarly, arbitral awards are opposed on the grounds that their enforcement in the Philippines is contrary to public policy.[34] Philippine courts do not adopt a severity threshold in appreciating these defenses against enforcement of arbitration agreements or arbitral awards.

---

[30] *See, e.g., AKBAYAN Citizens Party Action, et. al. v. Aquino*, G.R. No. 170516, 16 July 2006.

[31] *See, e.g., Wahl v. Donaldsons, Sims & Co.*, G.R. No. 1085, 16 May 1903; *Linte v. Law Union and Rock Insurance Co., Ltd.*, G.R. No. L-16398, 14 December 1921.

[32] *See Linte v. Law Union and Rock Insurance Co., Ltd., supra.*

[33] *See Philippine Economic Zone Authority v. Edison (Bataan) Cogeneration Corporation*, G.R. No. 179537, 23 October 2009; *Guevarra v. Guevarra*, G.R. No. L-48840, 29 December 1943.

[34] *See* Special Rules on Alternative Dispute Resolution, Rule12.4 (b)(ii); Rule13.4 (b)(ii); *Landoil Resources Corp. v. Al Rabiah Lighting Company*, G.R. No. 174720, 7 September 2011.

C.3 Review of Alleged Breaches of Public Policy

Breaches of public policy may be reviewed by arbitral tribunals. As earlier discussed, a breach of public policy may be considered by Philippine courts *moto propio ex officio* without the defendant expressly raising it as a ground.[35]

The ADR Act adopts the UNCITRAL Model Law,[36] which provides that an arbitral tribunal shall decide an international commercial arbitration[37] in accordance with the laws chosen by the parties as applicable to the substance of the dispute.[38] Since laws (statutory and case law) include the public policy of a state, an arbitral tribunal may also review alleged breaches of public policy of the state whose laws had been chosen by the parties. Under the ADR Rules of Court, a foreign arbitral award may be set aside by courts on the ground that its recognition or

---

[35] Special ADR Rules, Rule 12.4 (b); Rule 13.4 (b); *see also Dela Paz Vda. de Ongsiako v. Gamboa*, G.R. No. L-1867, 8 April 1950.

[36] Alternative Dispute Resolution Act of 2004, Sec. 19.

[37] UNCITRAL Model Law, Art. 1(3) defines international commercial arbitration:

3. An arbitration is international if:

(a) the parties to an arbitration agreement have, at the time of the conclusion of that agreement, their places of business in different States; or

(b) one of the following places is situated outside the State in which the parties have their places of business:

(i) the place of arbitration if determined in, or pursuant to, the arbitration agreement;

(ii) any place where a substantial part of the obligations of the commercial relationship is to be performed or the place with which the subject-matter of the dispute is most closely connected; or

(c) the parties have expressly agreed that the subject-matter of the arbitration agreement relates to more than one country.

[38] UNCITRAL Model Law, Art. 28 (1).

enforcement would be contrary to public policy of the Philippines.[39] The Philippine Supreme Court has not had an occasion to set aside an arbitration stipulation or arbitral award as contrary to the public policy of a foreign state.

---

[39] Special Rules on Alternative Dispute resolution, Rule 12.4 (b)(ii); Rule 13.4 (b)(ii).

POLAND

Marcin Aslanowicz[1] and Sylwia Piotrowska[2]

A. LEGISLATION, TRENDS AND TENDENCIES

A.1 Sources of Arbitration Law in Poland

The main source of arbitration law in Poland is the Code of Civil Procedure ("CPC"), which dates back to 1964 and applies to both domestic and international arbitration. The CPC underwent a significant amendment in 2005, and it now largely mirrors the UNCITRAL Model Law. Arbitration issues are regulated in Part V of the CPC (Articles 1154 to 1217).

International conventions, in particular the New York Convention and the 1961 European Convention on International Commercial Arbitration, are other sources of arbitration law in Poland. Poland is also bound by numerous agreements for the protection of investments, which provide for the settlement of disputes by arbitration.

A.2 Arbitrability

According to Article 1157 of the CPC, except for child maintenance claims, parties may agree to arbitrate any dispute regarding proprietary or non-proprietary rights that would otherwise be eligible for settlement in court. Upon the application

---

[1] Marcin Aslanowicz is a Partner in Baker & McKenzie's Warsaw office and heads the Litigation and Dispute Resolution Practice Group in Warsaw. Mr. Aslanowicz represents multinational and domestic clients in civil and commercial disputes before common courts as well as arbitral tribunals.

[2] Sylwia Piotrowska is an Associate in Baker & McKenzie's Warsaw office and a member of the Firm's Global Dispute Resolution Practice Group.

of a party, an arbitrator can determine whether a dispute is arbitrable or whether a legal relationship or right exists.

A.3 Arbitration Agreement

According to Article 1162(1) of the CPC, an arbitration agreement must be in writing and signed by both parties to be enforceable. Thus, an oral arbitration agreement is not enforceable. An exchange of correspondence or other documents indicating the intent to be bound by arbitration may be sufficient to establish the requirement of a written form. However, an agreement on arbitration cannot be inferred through the performance of acts or a course of dealing. Where an arbitration agreement is lost, evidence may be introduced through the testimony of witnesses and the examination of the parties to prove its existence.

In the arbitration agreement, the parties must specify precisely the object of the dispute or the legal relationship giving rise to (or which could give rise to) the dispute that is to be the subject of the arbitration. An inequitable arbitration clause, in particular an arbitration clause that gives only one party the right to pursue a claim in arbitration, is unenforceable.

An arbitration clause contained in a company's articles of association is binding on the company and its shareholders. This also applies to the statutes of cooperatives and associations. An arbitration clause applicable to a labor dispute, however, may only be entered into once the dispute has arisen (see Article 1164 of the CPC).

Unless otherwise provided for, a power of attorney granted by a commercial entity to perform legal acts includes the authorization to enter into an arbitration agreement with respect to disputes arising from those legal acts.

A.4   Arbitrators

Article 1170 of the CPC provides that any individual having full capacity to perform legal acts may be an arbitrator, regardless of citizenship. Polish law contains only one restriction regarding the capacity to fulfill the function of arbitrator: according to Article 1170(2) of the CPC, a state judge cannot be an arbitrator. This rule does not apply to retired judges.

The parties may set out specific requirements as to the selection of the arbitrators in their arbitration agreement. Provisions of the agreement that grant a party disproportionate rights in the appointment of an arbitral tribunal are unenforceable. Unless the parties agree otherwise, the procedure for appointing arbitrators is governed by Article 1171 and the provisions that follow it.

The parties may define the procedure for excluding an arbitrator and may make a joint statement in writing at any time to dismiss any of the arbitrators. A state court may dismiss an arbitrator on the motion of either party if it is obvious that the arbitrator is not fulfilling his or her duties within the appropriate deadline or if he or she delays the performance of those duties without cause.

Arbitrators are entitled to compensation for their activities, as well as to reimbursement of expenses incurred in connection with those activities (Article 1179(1) of the CPC). The parties are jointly and severally liable for these costs. If the parties do not reach an agreement on the compensation of the arbitrators, the rate of compensation will be set by a state court.

A.5   Jurisdiction of an Arbitral Tribunal

As with the UNCITRAL Model Law, under the CPC an arbitral tribunal may rule on its own jurisdiction, as well as on the existence, validity, or effectiveness of an arbitration clause (the so-called *kompetenz-kompetenz* principle). The invalidity or expiry of the underlying agreement containing the arbitration clause, however, will result in the invalidity or expiry of that clause.

In general, an objection to the jurisdiction of an arbitral tribunal must be made in the response to the statement of claim, and not later. An arbitral tribunal may rule on an objection to its own jurisdiction in a separate ruling, against which an appeal may be filed with a state court.

Under Articles 1181 and 1182, an arbitral tribunal can grant conservatory measures (such as injunctive relief or the provision of security). According to Article 1181(3), such a decision is implemented once a state court has ordered its enforcement.

A.6 Proceedings before an Arbitral Tribunal

The essence of arbitration proceedings is contractual freedom, and therefore the parties may agree on the procedure to be followed, subject to statutory requirements. Neither the parties nor the arbitral tribunal are bound by judicial civil procedure. If the parties have not agreed on the procedure to be followed, the arbitral tribunal may adopt whichever procedure it considers appropriate, subject to certain mandatory provisions of law. For example, the tribunal cannot exclude the right to petition a state court to set aside an arbitral award.

An arbitral tribunal may examine witnesses and experts and swear in witnesses, but may not use coercive measures (Article 1191(1) of the CPC). In proceedings before an arbitral tribunal, the parties should be granted equal rights. Each party has the right to present its case and to have its statements and related evidence considered (Article 1183).

A.7 Conclusion of Arbitral Proceedings

The arbitral tribunal issues an award after comprehensively examining the case. The award requires a majority, unless otherwise agreed by the parties (Article 1195(1) of the CPC). If the required majority cannot be reached, the arbitration clause will be deemed unenforceable. The award issued by the arbitral tribunal may be an award calling for a specific remedy or one that determines the existence or form of legal relationships or rights. An arbitral tribunal may issue interim, partial or final awards.

The award shall be issued in writing and signed by the arbitrators. When signing the award, the arbitrator who voted against the majority opinion may cast a *votum separatum*. A copy of the signed award shall be made available to the parties to the proceedings.

Proceedings before an arbitral tribunal are completed upon a final award being issued. After the award is served on the parties, an *ad hoc* arbitral tribunal must submit the case files to a state court together with the original award and other documents relating to the case (Article 1204(1) of the CPC). Only permanent arbitration courts are released from this obligation. Permanent arbitration courts keep the case files in their own archives and are required to provide them to the state courts upon demand. The state court to which such documents are sent is the court that would have had jurisdiction over the case had the parties not agreed to arbitrate.

A.8 Appeals against Arbitration Awards

Standard grounds for appeal are not available for arbitral awards. Instead, under Article 1206(1) of the CPC, a party may demand that the arbitral award be set aside on the following grounds:

(a) there was no arbitration clause or the arbitration clause was invalid or no longer enforceable;

(b) the party was not duly notified of the appointment of an arbitrator or of the proceedings before the arbitral tribunal, or was otherwise prevented from defending its rights;

(c) the award of the arbitral tribunal applies to a dispute not covered by the arbitration clause or extends beyond the scope of such clause;

(d) the requirements regarding the composition of the arbitral tribunal were not met or the general rules applicable to procedures before an arbitral tribunal were not respected;

(e) the award was obtained as a result of a criminal act or the award was issued on the basis of a counterfeit or modified document; or

(f) a final judgment of a state court has already been issued in the same matter between the same parties.

In addition to the grounds listed above, which may be raised by a party to the proceedings in an effort to invalidate an arbitral award, the state court considering a petition may *ex officio* set aside an arbitral award if it ascertains that:

(a) the dispute is not arbitrable under Polish law; or

(b) the award of the arbitral tribunal is in conflict with the basic rules of the legal order in Poland (public policy clause).

Petitions for setting aside an award must be filed with the state court within three months of the award being issued. However, if the petition is based on one of the grounds provided in (e) or (f) above, the three-month deadline runs from the time when the party learns of such grounds. In any event, a party cannot demand that the award be set aside after five years from the date on which it was issued. Unless otherwise agreed by the parties, setting aside an arbitral award will not result in the termination of the arbitration clause.

A.9 Recognition and Enforcement of an Arbitral Award

Arbitral awards have the same legal force as verdicts of state courts upon being recognized or enforced by the state court. Those arbitral awards that do not require any performance by a party but, for example, only determine the validity of a legal obligation, must be recognized or acknowledged (as opposed to "enforced") by the court. All other arbitral awards (such as those requiring the payment of damages) must be enforced by the state court. The court will recognize or enforce an arbitral award on the motion of a party. Motions for the recognition of awards are reviewed in closed hearings.

A state court can refuse to recognize or enforce an arbitral award *ex officio* or declare it (or the underlying agreement) unenforceable if it finds that:

(a) under Polish law, the dispute cannot be settled by an arbitral tribunal; or

(b) recognition or enforcement of the award conflicts with the basic rules of the legal order of Poland (public policy clause).

Article 1215(2) of the CPC provides the grounds on which the state court may refuse to recognize or enforce a foreign arbitral award. The grounds for refusal under the CPC are similar to those provided in the UNCITRAL Model Law and the New York Convention.

B. CASES

The Court of Appeal of the Polish Supreme Court and the Court of Arbitration at the Polish Chamber of Commerce passed several important rulings regarding arbitration.

In its ruling of 28 January 2011 (I CSK 231/10), the Supreme Court confirmed that it is only possible to assess any breaches of the procedural regulations made by the Court of Arbitration after establishing that an appeal may be filed with the state court against the award issued in the proceedings in which these breaches allegedly took place.

In the judgment of the Court of Appeal dated 10 November 2011 (I ACz 1608/11, I ACz 1687/11), the court confirmed that, in a case where it is clear from the wording of the settlement that the previous agreement (encompassed by the arbitration clause) had been terminated in whole and that the intention of the parties was to regulate all relationships arising from the earlier agreement, the arbitration clause does not remain effective. Since the parties did not introduce another arbitration clause in the settlement agreement, they implicitly agreed that any possible disputes would be settled by the state court.

In its award of 30 July 2009 (SA 128/08), the Court of Arbitration at the Polish Chamber of Commerce confirmed that the written form of the provision regarding the court should include the name of the permanent arbitration court (or a description enabling the identification and designation of the permanent arbitration court in question), and not just the elements specified in Article 1161(1) of the CPC. Therefore, Article 1161(1) of the CPC does not constitute a statutory definition of the obligatory (minimum) scope of the wording of every arbitration clause.

C. PUBLIC POLICY IN INTERNATIONAL ARBITRATION

Article 1206 of the CPC contains a broadly worded public policy clause, providing that an arbitral award may be set aside where it conflicts with the fundamental principles of the legal order of the Republic of Poland. Despite this open-ended wording, the Polish Supreme Court has clarified that the scope of the public policy clause should be construed quite narrowly, covering only fundamental constitutional rules and central principles of procedural and substantive Polish law.[3]

Several Supreme Court decisions in recent years have identified some of the rules and principles that fit under this rubric for public policy. In a decision on 30 September 2010, the court refused to enforce an arbitral award on the grounds that the award violated the principle of party autonomy provided in CPC Article 65(2), which it held was a central principle of Polish law. Article 65(2) states: "in contract construction, one should examine the common intention of the parties and the contract's purpose rather than relying on the contract's literal wording." Since the tribunal had based dismissal of the claim on the text and form of the contract, with little examination of the mutual intent of the parties, the court held that the award violated the principle of party autonomy and, therefore, Polish public policy as well. Other principles considered by the court to constitute substantive public policy grounds include the principle that compensation should correspond to damages inflicted;[4] the principle of

---

[3] *See* Decision of the Supreme Court, dated 9 March 2004, I CK 412/03, LEX No. 183721.

[4] Decision of the Supreme Court, dated 11 June 2008, V CSK 8/08, LEX No. 400965.

freedom of contract;[5] and the principle of freedom of business activity.[6]

Another recent case, dated 9 September 2010, addressed procedural public policy as a ground for setting aside an award. After the tribunal had rendered an award, the respondent discovered that one of the arbitrators had a professional and social connection to the claimant. In refusing to enforce the award, the court concluded that the constitutional right to be heard, contained in Article 45.1 of the Constitution, constituted a fundamental principle of the Polish legal order. The court found that the arbitrator's lack of impartiality violated Article 45.1's mandate that "everyone shall have the right to have their case heard by an independent court in fair proceedings."[7]

---

[5]   Decision of the Supreme Court, dated 27 November 2007, IV CSK 239/07, LEX No. 488974.

[6]   Decision of the Supreme Court, dated 11 July 2002, IV CKN 1211/00, OSNC 2003/9/125.

[7]   Decision of the Supreme Court, dated 9 September 2010, I CSK 535/09, LEX No. 602748.

RUSSIAN FEDERATION

Vladimir Khvalei[1] and Irina Varyushina[2]

A. LEGISLATION, TRENDS AND TENDENCIES

There have been no recent changes in the Russian legislation on arbitration.

However, in 2011, the Russian Constitutional Court rendered a decision of importance for arbitration which finally resolved the issue of the "arbitrability" of disputes concerning registered rights to immovable property.

The legislation of the Russian Federation does not contain a prohibition against referring civil law disputes concerning immovable property to courts of arbitration;[3] it in fact directly provides for such a possibility.[4] Nevertheless, over the course of

---

[1] Vladimir Khvalei is a Partner in Baker & McKenzie's Moscow office and heads its CIS Dispute Resolution Practice Group. He is also a steering committee member of the Firm's International Arbitration Practice Group. Mr. Khvalei serves as a Vice President of the ICC International Court of Arbitration and is included in the list of arbitrators of the arbitration institutions in Austria, Russia, Belarus and Kazakhstan.

[2] Irina Varyushina is a Professional Support Lawyer in Baker & McKenzie's Moscow office.

[3] As has been established in the legal doctrine, exceptions to the arbitrability of cases should be made only by federal law. *See* Makovsky A.L., Karabelnikov B.R. "Arbitrability of Disputes: the Russian Approach," // International Commercial Arbitration. 2004. N 3. p. 21.

[4] *See* part 1 Art. 25, Federal Law No. 102-FZ of 16 July 1998 "On Mortgage (Pledge of Property):" 1. Unless otherwise stipulated in the Federal Law or this Article, a registration entry on mortgage is expunged ... based on a declaration by the holder of a mortgage, a joint declaration of a pledgor and a pledgee, a declaration of a pledgor with presentation of ... a decision of a court, arbitrazh court or arbitration court to terminate the mortgage."

the last several years, the Supreme Arbitrazh Court and Supreme Court have quite consistently adhered to the point of view that such disputes are not subject to arbitration.

The Supreme Arbitrazh Court's logic boiled down to the following:[5]

- The decision of an arbitration court on the ownership rights to immovable property forms the basis for registering ownership rights to that property.

- Legal relations connected to registration of ownership rights (i.e., legal relations between the state registration authority registering rights to immovable property and the right holder) are of a matter of public law.

- The arbitration court is not entitled to take a decision compelling the state registration authority to register immovable property in the name of the party to the arbitration proceedings, since public law matters (such as the registration of real estate rights) cannot be submitted to arbitration.

The Supreme Arbitrazh Court stated that an arbitration court was also not entitled to levy execution on pledged immovable property, as those disputes likewise fall under the exclusive jurisdiction of state courts.[6]

In accordance with that logic, Arbitrazh courts in the Russian Federation declared that matters dealing with the termination or change of the term of long-term lease agreements for immovable property are also not subject to arbitration, since any lease of

---

[5] Clause 27, Information Letter of the Presidium of the Supreme Arbitrazh Court of the RF of 22 December 2005 No. 96 "Survey of the practice of arbitrazh courts' consideration of cases to recognize and enforce awards of foreign courts, to challenge awards of arbitration courts and to issue writs of execution for enforcement of awards from arbitration courts."

[6] *Ibid.* clause 28.

immovable property for longer than one year is subject to registration with state authorities.[7]

Without disputing the Supreme Arbitrazh Court's view that an arbitral tribunal cannot compel a state registration authority to register immovable property, one is hard-pressed not to notice an error in the logic of the highest judiciary. Indeed, legal relations between the parties to the sale of immovable property, and those between the state registration authority and the parties are different. And the fact that the arbitral tribunal is not entitled to resolve administrative disputes with a state registration authority related to a refusal to register rights to the property does not mean that it is not entitled to resolve disputes relating to ownership rights between the parties of a sale transaction.

It is interesting to note that the Supreme Court also excluded arbitrability of disputes related to immovable property, providing an even less persuasive justification. The Supreme Court stated that an arbitral award could not be grounds for registering rights to immovable property, since it did not possess that quality of decisions passed by courts of general jurisdiction, i.e., the "legal force of a court decision."[8]

Apparently realizing the weakness in the logic behind prohibiting the referral of immovable property disputes to arbitration, the Supreme Arbitrazh Court approached the Constitutional Court of the Russian Federation in 2010 for clarification as to whether arbitral tribunals could take a decision to levy execution on property under a mortgage agreement.

---

[7] Resolution of Moscow Region Federal Arbitrazh Court, 3 September 2007, No. KG-A40/8370-07.

[8] Reply to Question 2 on civil cases in Survey, appr. by Resolution of Presidium of RF Supreme Court of 7 November 2007. The text of the Survey was not officially published.

On 26 May 2011, the Constitutional Court handed down a Resolution, ruling that disputes over registered rights to immovable property could be subject to arbitration,[9] stating as follows: ". . . if the decision of a court of arbitration adopted upon the results of considering a dispute concerning immovable property establishes the rights to said property, the registering body must perform actions for their state registration . . ."

Accordingly, the Supreme Arbitrazh Court likewise stated:[10] "At present, federal legislation does not establish the exclusive jurisdiction of state courts to consider disputes concerning immovable property; courts of arbitration are entitled to resolve disputes on levy of execution on immovable property pledged under a mortgage agreement."

B. CASES

B.1 *Stena RoRo AB (Sweden) v. Baltiysky Zavod OJSC (RF)*

Under two shipbuilding contracts Baltiysky Zavod OJSC ("Baltiysky") was to design and build two ROPAKS-class vessels for Stena RoRo AB ("Stena".) On the same day the parties signed an option agreement for two additional vessels with the same characteristics, which option was to become

---

[9]   Resolution of the RF Constitutional Court of 26 May 2011, in a case to inspect the constitutionality of the provisions of Article 11.1 of the RF Civil Code, Art. 1.2 of the Federal Law "On Courts of Arbitration in the Russian Federation," Art. 28 of the Federal Law "On state registration of rights to and transactions involving immovable property," Art. 33.1 and 51 of the Federal Law "On mortgage (pledge of property)" in connection with a request by the RF Supreme Arbitrazh Court.

[10]   Resolution of the Presidium of the RF Supreme Arbitrazh Court of 27 September 2011 in case No. 530/10.

effective once the shipbuilding contracts came into force. All contracts were governed by Swedish law, and contained an SCC arbitration clause.

The shipbuilding contracts were made conditional on their approval by the board of directors of the Baltiysky and Stena. Stena considered the approval obtained, and the shipbuilding contracts entered into force. In 2005, Baltiysky changed owners, and a year later, the new owners of the factory, deeming the contracts a loss, refused to fulfill them.[11]

Citing the seller's improper performance of the contracts, as well as of the option agreement, Stena initiated arbitration under the SCC Rules against Baltiysky for recovery of EUR 145,563,862 in losses.

During the arbitration, Baltiysky mainly relied on a rather formal argument that the contracts had not entered into force because they had not been approved by the board of directors of the opposing party—Stena. Although Stena had produced a letter to Baltiysky confirming that its board of directors had approved those transactions, Baltiysky stated that this was not sufficient, because the decision should have been executed in the form of minutes, which was not presented to Baltiysky.[12]

The arbitral tribunal rejected that argument, stating that Baltiysky had accepted the letter about the Stena board decision without any criticisms, and failed to request a copy of minutes. What's more, additional agreements were signed and both sides acted as if the contracts were already in force. In particular, Baltiysky issued a press release on the conclusion of the contracts, took part in meetings and held negotiations on related

---

[11] http://pravo.ru/news/view/63281/

[12] Circumstances of the case are reconstructed in Resolution of the Presidium of the RF Supreme Arbitrazh Court in case no. 9899/09 of 13 September 2011.

contracts, proposed raising the price for the vessels, and only on 23 June 2006 did it inform Stena of its contention that there was no legal obligation to fulfill the contracts.

The arbitrators stated that formal approval was neither a requirement of the law nor of the contracts, and the lack of formal approval was significant only as a matter of proof regarding whether approval was in fact given.

In its final decision, on 24 September 2008, the arbitral tribunal awarded Stena EUR 20,000,000 in losses caused by the non-fulfillment of the contracts, arbitration costs, and expenses incurred in connection with the arbitration and interest.

It should be noted that this amount was in fact accepted by Baltiysky during the arbitration, which stated in its submission that "if the arbitral tribunal considers the shipbuilding contracts and option agreement as having come into force and being subject to fulfillment according to their conditions, the factory agrees to pay a fine of 20 million euro, i.e., in an amount equal to the 'estimated' losses in accordance with Article XI.B 2(b) of the shipbuilding contracts, including the option agreement."

Nonetheless, Baltiysky submitted an application to the Svea Court of Appeal to have the award set aside, citing the fact that there was no valid contract between the parties, and therefore also no arbitration agreement, since Stena's board of directors had not ratified the transaction within the stated deadline.

Meanwhile, Stena initiated enforcement proceedings in Russia.

On 20 February 2009, the Arbitrazh Court of St. Petersburg and the Leningrad Region refused enforcement of the SCC award, finding that it was against the public order of the Russian Federation, and "was made in a dispute not falling within the scope of the arbitration clause in the non-concluded contracts of which it is a component part." The court stated that the arbitration clause was contained in contracts that had not entered into force, as the decision of the Swedish company's board of directors to approve the transactions was not formalized by minutes. The fact that no official minutes were passed to Baltiysky constitutes a breach of a fundamental principle of Russian law, based on recognition of the equality of participants in civil law relations as laid down in Article 1 of the Civil Code.

In refusing to enforce the SCC award, the court also stated that enforcement of the award against Baltiysky—a strategic enterprise with a special management right on the part of the state—might cause it to go bankrupt. This would result in damage to the sovereignty and security of the state and would contravene the public order of the Russian Federation.[13]

On 24 April 2009, the Federal Arbitrazh Court of the North-Western Circuit upheld the decision of the trial court.[14] The cassation court, however, disagreed with the conclusions of the trial court that the arbitration agreement was not concluded and that the Factory's bankruptcy would result in damaging the state sovereignty and thus was contrary to the public order. The cassation court's reasoning was expressed as follows:[15]

> The public order of the Russian Federation . . . shall be understood to refer to the fundamentals of law and order in the Russian Federation.

> In turn, the fundamentals of law and order in the Russian Federation comprise, in addition to the foundations of morality, the major religious teachings, main economic and

---

[13] Ruling of the Arbitrazh Court of St. Petersburg and Leningrad Region in case no. A56-60007/2008.

[14] Resolution of FAS SZO [Federal Arbitrazh Court of the North-Western Circuit], 24 April 2009, in case no. A56-60007/2008.

[15] Resolution of FAS SZO, 24 April 2009, in case no. A56-60007/2008.

cultural traditions making up Russian civil society, and the basic principles of Russian law.

The basic principles of Russian law, in particular, include the principal fundamentals of civil law.

Likewise, the basic principles of Russian civil law include the main rules for assigning responsibility for non-performance of obligations, specifying in particular that responsibility for causing damage (tort liability) arises only in case of the guilt of the debtor (Article 1064 of the RF CC), and also that a party not performing (or improperly performing) an obligation when engaging in business activity bears liability if it does not prove that due performance was impossible as a result of force majeure (Article 401, RF CC))...

Due to the fact that there are no contractual obligations between [*Stena RoRo AB*] and [*Baltiysky Zavod OJSC*] to construct and deliver ROPAKS-class vessels, the latter may not be charged with liability in the form of compensation for losses due to their non-performance...

The supervisory proceedings initiated by *Stena RoRo AB* were stayed pending the appeal of *Baltiysky Zavod OJSC* in the Swedish state courts.[16]

On 20 May 2010, the Svea Court of Appeal upheld the SCC award, stating in its final judgment that *Stena RoRo AB* had presented sufficiently convincing proof to the effect that its board of directors had ratified the transaction within the stated deadline.

---

[16]   Judicial act not yet published. Information from the SAC RF's official site can be found at http://www.arbitr.ru/vas/presidium/nadzor/25447.html.

Thereafter, the Supreme Arbitrazh Court overturned the decision of the lower courts and passed a decision to enforce the foreign arbitral award.[17] The Supreme Arbitrazh Court did not agree with the conclusions of the Federal Arbitrazh Court of the North-Western Circuit that the absence of minutes of the company's board of directors on approval of the contracts ran contrary to the public order of the Russian Federation due to a breach in the principles of freedom of contract and equality of its parties. The Supreme Arbitrazh Court held that the question of whether the Swedish company's board of directors followed the procedure for approving the contracts had already been resolved by the arbitral tribunal, applying Swedish law as agreed by the parties, and the courts were not entitled to revisit this matter on its merits, and certainly not by applying Russian law. Furthermore, this same issue had been resolved already by the Svea Court of Appeal. The Supreme Arbitrazh Court stated:[18]

> Under the legislation of the Russian Federation, [*Baltiysky Zavod OJSC*] should have formalized, and actually did formalize in minutes, the consent of its board of directors to the conclusion of the contracts. However, it does not follow from this circumstance that the Swedish company, due to the factory's actions as conditioned by Russian law, and the necessity of observing in civil-law relations the principle of equality of the parties, acquires the counter-obligation to submit documents evidencing the similar consent of its own board of directors specifically in the form of minutes.
>
> The rules set forth by Russian legislation on documenting decisions by the management bodies of Russian legal entities

---

[17] Resolution of the Presidium of the RF Supreme Arbitrazh Court in case no. 9899/09 of 13 September 2011.

[18] Resolution of the Presidium of the RF Supreme Arbitrazh Court in case no. 9899/09 of 13 September 2011.

do not extend to Swedish companies. By entering into contracts with the terms of their being subordinate to Swedish substantive law, [*Baltiysky Zavod OJSC*] assumed risks connected with the fact that the relevant legal order might contain provisions differing from the norms of Russian law regulating analogous relations . . .

. . .

Determination of the losses was done by the arbitral tribunal based on Swedish law applicable to relations between the parties, taking into account the conditions of the contracts and option agreement specifying the possibility of recovering losses in a 'fixed,' previously agreed amount . . . the arbitrators awarded these losses as liquidated damages . . . By its legal nature, they are similar to the concept of a penalty used in Russian civil law . . .

Thus, both the penalty and the losses are specified by civil legislation and form part of the legal system of the Russian Federation. Therefore, *ipso facto*, application of these measures of liability cannot contravene the RF public order.

However, the story does not end here. The respondent also tried to employ certain "guerilla tactics" well known in Russia: a derivative action.

On 16 March 2010, the Arbitrazh Court of St. Petersburg and the Leningrad Region granted the claim of the minority shareholders in *Baltiysky Zavod OJSC* and rendered the shipbuilding contracts invalid. It also declared the option agreement invalid on the basis that it had "not been concluded."

The court of appeal agreed that under Russian law a claim seeking to declare a transaction null and void may be filed by any interested parties, including a company's shareholder.[19] The court of cassation affirmed.[20]

The courts found abuse of right on the part of Stena, in particular, because of the fact that it and the Swedish company knew that Baltiysky signed contracts that both were unfavorable for it. Baltiysky also signed a "consciously unperformable contract, "since it undertook to issue a guarantee from the Savings Bank of the RF which would be regulated by Swedish law (which is impossible under Russian law) and without indicating a specific term of its validity (which also contradicts mandatory requirements of Russian law regarding guarantee)."

On 13 September 2011, the Supreme Arbitrazh Court overturned the decisions of lower courts and issued a judgment on the merits of the case, rejecting the stated claims and saying:[21]

> . . . the courts' conclusion about the impossibility of a Russian bank to give a guarantee in accordance with Swedish law contravenes the norms of Russian law, specifically Articles 1186 and 1217 of the Civil Code, as well as the provisions of Article 27 of the ICC Uniform Rules on Demand Guarantees, according to which in a guarantee or counter-guarantee, only if otherwise is not set forth, the governing law is the law of the location of the guarantor or instructing party (depending on the case) or, if the guarantor or instructing party has several locations, then

---

[19] *See* Resolution of 13th Arbitrazh Court of Appeals, 7 July 2010, case no. A56-6656/2010.

[20] Resolution of Federal Arbitrazh Court of North-Western Circuit, 25 October 2010, case no. A56-6656/2010.

[21] Resolution of the Presidium of the RF Supreme Arbitrazh Court in case no. 1795/11 of 13 September 2011.

the law of the location of that branch office which issued the guarantee or counter-guarantee.

…

The other circumstances to which the courts referred as evidencing that [*Baltiysky Zavod OJSC*] performance of obligations under the contracts was knowingly impossible, in particular, the impossibility of the receiving by [*Baltiysky Zavod OJSC*] an advance payment in the absence of a bank guarantee, in and of themselves did not hinder the performance of obligations by [*Baltiysky Zavod OJSC*], as the works should have been done by using [*Baltiysky Zavod OJSC*] own funds.

Furthermore, the courts' conclusion about abuse of its rights by *Stena RoRo* when entering into the disputed transactions is not supported by Russian law . . .

…

Both cases were reviewed by the RF Supreme Arbitrazh Court on the same day, though the cases were not officially consolidated.

B.2   *Tabellion Limited* **(the Republic of Cyprus)** *v. A. G. Ischuk* **(Russian Federation)**

This case likewise furnishes an example of an attempt to use the guerilla tactics of "a derivative action," when a transaction which was the subject of international arbitration proceedings is declared invalid not upon the claim of a minority shareholder, but at the claim of a spouse of the individual. Here is the history of the case.

On 6 December 2007, the company Tabellion Limited ("Tabellion") and the company Federalevel Holdings Limited ("Federalevel") concluded a sale-purchase contract for shares and an option to sell. Performance of obligations by Federalevel was guaranteed by an RF citizen, A.G. Ischuk.[22]

Due to the failure of Federalevel and Ischuk to perform their obligations, Tabellion initiated proceedings under the LCIA Rules, which granted Tabellion's claims against Federalevel and Ischuk. In particular, Ischuk was obliged to pay (or ensure payment by Federalevel) of USD 43,426,229.51.

On 6 June 2011, the Samara Region Arbitrazh Court refused to enforce the LCIA award as being contrary to the Russian Federation public order. The trial court held that the fact that A.G. Ischuk's wife, I.A. Ischuk, was not a party to the LCIA arbitration was a breach of the public order. This was because enforcement of the award would involve the property belonging to her as Mr. Ischuk's wife in accordance with the provisions of Russian Federation Family Code (the "RF FC").

However, on 9 August 2011, the Federal Arbitrazh Court of the Povolzhsky Circuit overturned the trial court's decision, stating as follows:

> . . . under the provisions of Article 35.2 of the RF FC, when one spouse concludes a transaction to dispose of the spouses' common property, it is presumed that he or she is acting with the consent of the other spouse. A transaction completed by one of the spouses for disposal of the spouses' common property may be declared invalid by a court due to the absence of the other spouse's consent only at his or her demand and only in cases when it is proven that the other party to the transaction knew or should have known of the other spouse's lack of consent to the completion of that transaction.

---

[22] Case described in Resolution of Federal Arbitrazh Court of Povolzhsky Circuit, 9 August 2011, case no. A55-27265/2010.

The Supreme Arbitrazh Court shared the cassation court's view.[23]

B.3 Ciments Francais (France) v. Holding Company Sibirsky Cement OJSC (Russia) and İstanbul Çimento Yatırımları Anonim Şirketi (Turkey)

This case is an example of the successful application of guerilla tactics in international arbitration.

On 7 December 2010, an ICC arbitral tribunal with its seat in Istanbul, Turkey, issued a partial award in case No. 1624/GZ initiated by Ciments Francais against Holding Company Sibirsky Cement OJSC (hereinafter "Sibirsky Cement") and İstanbul Çimento Yatırımları Anonim Şirketi (hereinafter "İstanbul Çimento Yatırımları").

The arbitral tribunal in its partial award found that Ciments Francais duly exercised its right to terminate a share sale-purchase agreement concluded on 26 March 2008 between Sibirsky Cement, Ciments Francais and İstanbul Çimento Yatırımları (the "SPA"), and further, that it had the right to withhold the amount of the original payment of EUR 50 million paid by Sibirsky Cement. The arbitral tribunal also stated that the partial arbitral award was to be enforced immediately.

After the arbitral tribunal issued the partial award, it was set aside by a Turkish court of the first instance pursuant to an application by Sibirsky Cement.

The grounds for setting aside the award were the following:

(a) The Turkish court agreed with Sibirsky Cement's argument that the arbitral award was not issued within the set deadline.

---

[23] Ruling to refuse to refer a case to the Presidium of the RF Supreme Arbitrazh Court of 12 December 2011 in case no. SAC-15654/11.

This circumstance constitutes independent grounds for setting aside the arbitral award in accordance with Article 15.1.c of Law of Turkey No. 4686 "On International Arbitration" (hereinafter "Law No. 4686").[24]

(b) The Turkish court also concluded that the arbitral tribunal had exceeded its authority. This was based on the fact that the ICC arbitral tribunal did not consider the debtor's argument on the termination of the SPA in accordance with the principle of good faith. An arbitrator's (or tribunal's) exceeding of authority is a ground for setting aside an arbitral award under Law No. 4686.[25]

(c) The Turkish court found that the arbitral award contravened public order, as it provided for it to have immediate effect, and also due to the fact that the parties to the arbitration agreement waived the right to submit an application to set aside the award.

Further, in anticipation of the ICC partial arbitral award, FPS Sibconcorde LLC (a minority shareholder in Sibirsky Cement) submitted a claim to the Kemerovo Region Arbitrazh Court for invalidation of the SPA. The SPA, being a major transaction under the Russian Federation joint stock companies law, required the approval of the General Shareholders' Meeting of Sibirsky Cement. The decision of this meeting approving the SPA had been declared invalid in earlier court proceedings initiated by Sibconcorde LLC on the grounds that Sibconcorde LLC did not receive all information on that transaction, was not notified of the date of the general meeting, and did not take part

---

[24] This standard states "the award was not issued during the arbitration term."

[25] Art. 15.1.e of the Law says: "an arbitrator or arbitral tribunal handed down an award in a matter beyond the limits of the arbitration agreement, or did not hand down an award concerning all demands, or exceeded its authority."

in that meeting.[26] Ciments Francais was not a party to those proceedings.

On 13 August 2010, the Kemerovo Region Arbitrazh Court, disregarding the ICC arbitration clause in the SPA, granted the claim of the minority shareholder to declare the SPA invalid and ordered Ciments Francais to return EUR 50 million to Sibirsky Cement OJSC.[27] Ciments Francais argued that the courts should have stayed proceedings in this case due to the arbitration clause in the SPA. However, the court dismissed this argument on the basis that the claimant was not a party to the SPA and was thus not bound by it.

On 20 July 2011, the Kemerovo Region Arbitrazh Court,[28] which considered an application to recognize the foreign arbitral award, rejected the argument that it contravened public order because it was contrary to the Russian trial court's decision [the decision for invalidation of the SPA]. This was because this decision was disputed in a pending appellate procedure and as of the date of consideration had not entered into legal force (Arbitrazh Procedure Code provides that the trial court's decision does not enter into force while an appeal is pending).

The Kemerovo Region Arbitrazh Court, analyzing the provisions of the European Convention on International Commercial Arbitration, to which Russia is a party, concluded that setting aside the award in the country where it had been issued entailed a refusal to recognize and enforce the arbitral award only when it was set aside on one of the grounds indicated in subclauses (a)-

---

[26] Decision of Kemerovo Region Arbitrazh Court dd. 04 February 2009 in case no. A27-16841/2008-3.

[27] Decision of Kemerovo Region Arbitrazh Court dd. 13 August 2010, in case no. A27-4626/2009.

[28] Ruling of Kemerovo Region Arbitrazh Court, 20 July 2011, case no. A27-781/2011.

(d) of Article IX(1) of the European Convention.[29] As the grounds upon which the Turkish court set aside the award were not specified by the European Convention, the fact that it was set aside in Turkey did not entail refusal to recognize the arbitral award in the Russian Federation. Also, the Turkish court decision was being appealed in Turkey and thus was not final.

However, on 5 December 2011, a higher court overturned the lower court's ruling based on the violation of the Russian Federation public order. The court held that the law regarding the mandatory nature of the Russian state courts' decisions and their execution represent the elements of the Russian Federation public order. As the decision of the Kemerovo Region Arbitrazh Court whereby the SPA had been declared invalid, had entered into force the court concluded that: "Therefore, the recognition and enforcement of an arbitral award issued based on an invalid transaction will result in the existence on the territory of the Russian Federation of court acts of equal legal force with mutually exclusive conclusions, and will contradict the principles of the mandatory nature of Russian courts' decisions, which represent an inseparable part of the Russian Federation public order."[30]

Furthermore, the cassation court, referred to the fact that the arbitral award was set aside by a Turkish court, which in the cassation court's view was grounds for refusal to recognize the

---

[29] Article IX(1) of the European Convention states: "The setting aside in a Contracting State of an arbitral award covered by this Convention shall only constitute a ground for the refusal of recognition or enforcement in another Contracting State where such setting aside took place in a State in which, or under the law of which, the award has been made and for one of the following reasons …". That said, clause 2 of this Article IX states that clause 1 of Article IX takes priority over the respective provisions of the New York Convention.

[30] Resolution of the Federal Arbitrazh Court of West-Siberian Circuit dd. 05 December 2011 in case no. A27-781/2011.

foreign award based on Article V(1)(e) of the New York Convention as well as Subclause 1 of Article 36.1 of RF Law No. 5338-1 "On International Commercial Arbitration" dated 7 July 1993.

Thus, the cassation court in essence ignored the provisions of the European Convention, which take priority over the provisions of the New York Convention, as well as over the national legislation of the Russian Federation by virtue of the constitutional principle of the priority of international law over national law. It did so without explaining the reasoning for such a position.

C. PUBLIC POLICY IN INTERNATIONAL ARBITRATION

C.1 Scenarios of Reliance on Public Policy

In Russia public policy considerations can be invoked in any proceeding where the court considers, either on its own initiative or at the request of a party, that an arbitration agreement or arbitral award is contrary to a public policy of the Russian Federation.

In particular, these issues can be raised by a party or *ex officio* by court in proceedings where:

(a) one of the parties to the arbitration agreement, disregarding it, files a claim on a merit of the dispute covered by the arbitration agreement, before a Russian state court; or

(b) one of the parties files a claim to invalidate the arbitration agreement; or

(c) a party to arbitration files an application to set aside the arbitral award issued in Russia; or

(d) recognition and enforcement of a foreign arbitral award is sought.[31]

C.2 Modes and Limitations of Reliance on Public Policy

There are no time limits in Russian law for invoking the public policy defense.

From that perspective, it does not really matter whether the same issue was raised before the tribunal and how the tribunal dealt with this issue.

It is also worth noting that Russian law does not distinguish between international public policy and public policy of the Russian Federation, referring only to the latter. Similarly, Russian courts also mainly refer to the public policy of Russia in their decisions.

Russia is a party to the 1961 European Convention on International Commercial Arbitration ("the European Convention"). The European Convention limits the application of clause V(1)(e) of the New York Convention through its clause IX, which provides that the annulment of the award at the place of arbitration can lead to the refusal in recognition of the award only if the award has been annulled on the grounds specified in clause IX of the European Convention.

Violation of public policy is not listed among the grounds in clause IX of the European Convention, however, as was highlighted above in the summary of the *Ciments Francais v. Holding Company Sibirsky Cement OJSC (Russia) and İstanbul Çimento Yatırımları Anonim Şirketi (Turkey)* case, the Russian courts did not apply the European Convention according to its

---

[31] Sub-par. 2 Article 36(1) of the RF Law "On International Commercial Arbitration."

language and its spirit. It is therefore possible that Russian courts would adopt the same approach with regard to public policy issues.

C.3 Rules that Constitute "Public Policy"

Public order is referred to in Article 1193 of the Civil Code of the Russian Federation as "fundamentals of the legal order of the Russian Federation." However, there is no legal definition of public order in the Russian Federation Law "On International Commercial Arbitration" which leaves space for a broad interpretation of the concept by Russian state courts.

In its Ruling of 25 September 1998, the Supreme Court stated that when the court based its decision on Russian law the decision could not be reversed as being contrary to public order, as application of Russian law provisions could not be considered as breach of Russian public policy:

> RF public order is understood to mean the fundamentals of the social order of the Russian state. Invoking a public policy provision is only possible in those individual cases where the application of foreign law could bring about a result impermissible from the viewpoint of Russian legal conscience.[32]

This definition is still widely used by Russian courts.[33]

The Supreme Arbitrazh Court in one of its cases[34] stipulated that a foreign arbitral award violates the Russian Federation public order when its enforcement leads to actions that are:

---

[32] RF Supreme Court Ruling of 25 September 1998 in case no. 5-G98-60.

[33] Resolution of the Federal Arbitrazh Court of the North-Western Circuit of 28 December 2009 in case no. A21-802/2009.

[34] RF SAC Ruling No.13452/07 of 6 December 2007.

- expressly prohibited by the law;

- damaging the sovereignty or security of the state;

- affecting the interests of major social groups;

- incompatible with the principles of economic, political and legal system of the state;

- affecting the constitutional rights and freedoms of citizens; or

- contradicting the major civil law principles such as equality of the parties, inviolability of property, freedom of contract.

According to the Supreme Arbitrazh Court, the improper or unjustified assessment by the arbitral tribunal of the circumstances and facts of the case, as well as its failure to properly apply civil law rules regulating specific legal relations of the parties arising out of their contract, cannot be considered a breach of public policy.

In practice, there is no threshold for application of public policy arguments and in the past Russian courts usually applied it broadly. In recent years, however, the Supreme Arbitrazh Court, considering particular cases, employs a pretty narrow view as to what constitutes public policy. At the same time, lower courts often do not follow the same approach.

SINGAPORE

Chan Leng Sun, S.C.,[1] Celeste Ang,[2] Gerald Kuppusamy[3] and Shum Wai Keong[4]

A. LEGISLATION, TRENDS AND TENDENCIES

A.1 Proposed Amendments to the International Arbitration Act (Cap 143A, 2002 Rev Ed) ("IAA")

The IAA provides the legislative framework that governs the conduct of international arbitrations in Singapore. Public consultation has been sought on the following proposals to amend the IAA:

(a) to adopt Option 1 of Article 7 of the UNCITRAL Model Law on the definition of "arbitration agreement." Option 1 does not require that the arbitration agreement be signed. It is required to be in writing, although that term broadly includes any form of recording;

---

[1] Chan Leng Sun is a Partner and co-head of the Dispute Resolution Practice in Baker & McKenzie's Singapore office. He was appointed Senior Counsel by the Chief Justice of Singapore in January 2011. Apart from being counsel, he is an arbitrator and adjudicator on the panels of leading dispute resolution bodies in Singapore, Malaysia and China, such as SIAC, SCMA, KLRCA, CIETAC and CMAC. He also serves as arbitrator in ICC, LMAA as well as *ad hoc* arbitrations.

[2] Celeste Ang is a Partner in Baker & McKenzie's Singapore office. Her practice encompasses corporate litigation and arbitration, both domestic and international. Ms. Ang specializes in intellectual property, employment & labor law and oil and energy-related disputes.

[3] Gerald Kuppusamy is a Senior Associate in Baker & McKenzie's Singapore office. He advises clients on cross-border litigation and international arbitration in a wide variety of commercial disputes, and is a Fellow of both the Chartered Institute of Arbitrators and the Singapore Institute of Arbitrators.

[4] Shum Wai Keong is an Associate in Baker & McKenzie's Singapore office and a member of the Firm's Global Dispute Resolution Group.

(b) to expressly provide that arbitral tribunals have the power to award simple or compound interest on monies claimed as well as costs;

(c) to allow parties to seek judicial review of a tribunal's ruling that it does not have jurisdiction (a negative jurisdictional ruling); and

(d) to clarify that an "emergency arbitrator," appointed by the parties pursuant to the rules of arbitration agreed to or adopted by the parties, is considered an "arbitral tribunal" under the IAA.

Proposals (c) and (d) are the most notable. First, the proposal to allow judicial review of negative jurisdictional rulings follows criticism of the decision in *PT Asuransi Jasa Indonesia (Persero) v. Dexia Bank SA*[5] that such rulings are not awards and therefore cannot be reviewed by a court pursuant to Article 16(3) of the Model Law.

Second, the proposal to provide that orders of "emergency arbitrators" are enforceable follows the introduction of "emergency arbitrator" procedures in the 2010 edition of the SIAC Arbitration Rules. Similar emergency arbitrator procedures were also recently introduced in the ICC Arbitration Rules, which took effect on 1 January 2012.

A.2   Proposed Enactment of Foreign Limitations Periods Bill

This proposed legislation would provide that limitation periods, as a general rule subject to public policy, follow the governing law of the dispute. At common law, there was some uncertainty as to the applicable limitation period. The period might be determined by the law of the forum if it could be characterized as

---

[5]   *PT Asuransi Jasa Indonesia (Persero) v. Dexia Bank SA* [2006] 1 SLR 197.

procedural law, or the governing law if it could be characterized as substantive law. This proposal follows a trend in other common law jurisdictions to legislatively remove or reduce the uncertainty by providing a general rule that, subject to public policy, the limitation periods of the governing law shall apply.

B. CASES

We set out below an overview of noteworthy decisions of the Singapore courts in 2011.

B.1 Avoidance Claims in Insolvency Non-Arbitrable, but Pre-Insolvency Disputes Remain Arbitrable after the Commencement of Winding Up

In *Larsen Oil and Gas Pte Ltd. v. Petroprod Ltd.*[6] *("Larsen Oil")*, the Singapore Court of Appeal analyzed the concept of non-arbitrability and ruled that disputes arising from the operation of the statutory provisions of the insolvency regime are non-arbitrable, notwithstanding that such disputes fall within the scope of an arbitration agreement. However, disputes involving an insolvent company that stem from the company's pre-insolvency rights and obligations are arbitrable, and therefore an arbitration agreement in respect of such disputes should be enforced, unless the agreement affects the substantive rights of other creditors.

Petroprod, which was in liquidation, sought to avoid a number of transactions made with Larsen under a management agreement. One of the bases argued was that these payments amounted to unfair preferences or transactions at an undervalue within the

---

[6]   *Larsen Oil and Gas Pte Ltd. v. Petroprod Ltd (in official liquidation in the Cayman Islands and in compulsory liquidation in Singapore)* [2011] 3 SLR 414.

meaning of Sections 98 and 99 of the Bankruptcy Act,[7] read with Section 329(1) of the Companies Act[8] ("CA"). In turn, Larsen sought to stay the action in favor of arbitration on the basis that the management agreement contained an arbitration clause for arbitration in Singapore under the Arbitration Act[9] ("AA"). The Singapore High Court first heard and dismissed Larsen's stay application on the basis that the issues were non-arbitrable; and, further, on the ground that Petroprod's claim pertaining to Section 73B of the Conveyancing and Law of Property Act ("CLPA")[10] should be resolved in the same forum.

Larsen then appealed the High Court's decision. The issues on appeal were:

(a) whether Petroprod's claims against Larsen fell within the scope of the arbitration clause;

(b) whether the court's discretion to grant a stay of proceedings was dependent on the arbitrability of the dispute in question; and

(c) if the court's discretion was dependent on the arbitrability of the dispute, whether Petroprod's claims against Larsen were arbitrable.

B.1.1. Arbitration clauses to be construed generously, but do not ordinarily cover avoidance claims

In relation to the scope of the arbitration clause, the Court of Appeal considered the proper approach towards the construction of arbitration clauses and concluded that the preponderance of

---

[7] Bankruptcy Act (Cap 20, 2009 Rev Ed).

[8] Companies Act (Cap 50, 2006 Rev Ed).

[9] Arbitration Act (Cap 10, 2002 Rev Ed).

[10] Conveyancing and Law of Property Act (Cap 61, 1994 Rev Ed).

authority favors the view that arbitration clauses should be generously construed such that all manner of claims, whether common law or statutory, should fall within their scope unless there is good reason to conclude otherwise.

However, the Court of Appeal also drew a line between private remedial claims (either common law or statutory), which the company's pre-insolvency management had good reason to be concerned about, and claims that can only be made by a liquidator/judicial manager of an insolvent company (avoidance claims), towards which the pre-insolvency management of the company was completely indifferent.

The Court of Appeal held that arbitration clauses should not ordinarily be construed to cover avoidance claims in the absence of express language to the contrary (see below) and that in this case, the arbitration clause did not cover Petroprod's claims against Larsen.

B.1.2. Arbitrability as an important consideration in stay of proceedings

Although the holding on the scope of the arbitration clause was sufficient to dispose of the appeal, the Court of Appeal went on to consider the concept of arbitrability in Singapore. In this regard, the court opined that arbitrability is an important factor to consider when determining whether to grant a stay of court proceedings in favor of arbitration under the AA (and the IAA).

B.1.3. Insolvency claims *per se* non-arbitrable

In analyzing the arbitrability of the avoidance claims, the Court of Appeal drew a distinction between:

(a) disputes involving an insolvent company that arise only upon the onset of insolvency due to the operation of the insolvency regime; and

(b) disputes involving an insolvent company that stem from its pre-insolvency rights and obligations.

In relation to the former, the Court of Appeal observed that many of the statutory provisions in the insolvency regime are in place to recoup, for the benefit of the company's creditors, losses caused by the misfeasance and/or malfeasance of its former management. This objective could be compromised if a company's pre-insolvency management had the ability to restrict the avenues by which the company's creditors could enforce the very statutory remedies meant to protect them against the company's management.

Accordingly, the Court of Appeal was of the view that the insolvency regime's objective of facilitating claims by a company's creditors against the company and its pre-insolvency management overrides the freedom of the company's pre-insolvency management to choose the forum where such disputes are to be heard. The courts should therefore treat disputes arising from the operation of the statutory provisions of the insolvency regime as *per se* non-arbitrable, even if the parties expressly included them within the scope of the arbitration agreement.

B.1.4. Disputes that stem from insolvent company's pre-insolvency rights and obligations are arbitrable

On the other hand, different considerations apply in relation to disputes involving an insolvent company that stem from its pre-insolvency rights and obligations. Such disputes differ from those arising at the onset of insolvency because they do not involve public policy considerations, such as the protection of creditors.

In these cases, where the agreement is only to resolve the prior private *inter se* disputes between the company and another party and where the arbitration agreement does not affect the substantive rights of the other creditors, the terms of the arbitration agreement will usually be observed. Such claims are therefore *prima facie* arbitrable.

B.1.5. Appeal dismissed

In this case, the Court of Appeal held that Petroprod's claims based on Sections 98 and 99 of the BA, read with Section 329(1) of the CA, were only available to it at the commencement of its insolvency. These claims were derived from the insolvency regime and were therefore non-arbitrable.

As for Petroprod's claims under Section 73B of the CLPA, the Court of Appeal recognized that claims under this provision may straddle both a company's pre-insolvency state of affairs, as well as its descent into the insolvency regime. In this case, however, it was apparent from Petroprod's statement of claim that it based its CLPA claim on the insolvency of the four subsidiaries. Under these circumstances, the Court of Appeal held that Petroprod's Section 73B CLPA claim against Larsen was in fact a non-arbitrable insolvency claim. The appeal was therefore dismissed in its entirety.

B.2 Setting Aside Arbitration Awards for Exceeding the Scope of Submission to Arbitration

In *CRW Joint Operation v. PT Perusahaan Gas Negara (Persero) TBK*,[11] the Singapore Court of Appeal demonstrated that it would set aside an arbitration award in appropriate circumstances.

---

[11] *CRW Joint Operation v. PT Perusahaan Gas Negara (Persero) TBK* [2011] 4 SLR 305.

In that case, PT Perusahaan Gas Negara (Persero) TBK ("PGN") had engaged CRW Joint Operation ("CRW") to design, procure, install, test and pre-commission a pipeline and optical fiber cable in Indonesia. The contract was generally governed by the standard provisions of the Fédération Internationale des Ingenieurs Conseils' "Conditions of Contract for Constructions: For Building and Engineering Works Designed by the Employer (1st Ed, 1999)" (the "FIDIC Red Book").

Disputes arose and the parties submitted the same to the dispute adjudication board ("DAB") in accordance with the FIDIC Red Book. Subsequently, the DAB awarded more than USD 17.2 million to CRW. PGN then filed a notice of dissatisfaction ("NOD") against the DAB's decision. CRW, however, invoiced PGN for the sum awarded by the DAB. PGN refused to make payment on the basis that it had filed the NOD and, accordingly, the award by the DAB was not yet final and binding. As the parties remained unable to resolve their disputes, CRW filed a request for arbitration in accordance with the FIDIC Red Book for the sole purpose of "giving prompt effect to the [DAB's] decision."

The majority members of the arbitral tribunal issued what they described as a "final award" in favor of CRW, finding that PGN had an obligation to make immediate payment of the sum awarded by the DAB against it.

CRW subsequently applied and obtained a court order from the Singapore courts to enforce the award in Singapore.

Meanwhile, PGN filed separate applications to set aside the award. At first instance, the High Court set aside the award pursuant to Article 34(2)(a)(iii) of the Model Law, on the ground that the majority members of the tribunal had exceeded their jurisdiction under the arbitration provisions of the FIDIC Red Book.

In dismissing the appeal, the Court of Appeal held that the court's power to set aside an arbitral award is limited to the prescribed grounds provided under, *inter alia*, Article 34 of the Model Law. In particular, the Court of Appeal considered the applicability of Article 34(2)(a)(iii) of the Model Law.

The Court of Appeal set out three legal principles underlying the application of Article 34(2)(a)(iii). First, Article 34(2)(a)(iii) applies where the arbitral tribunal improperly decided matters that had not been submitted to it or failed to decide matters that had been submitted to it. Second, a failure by an arbitral tribunal to deal with every issue referred to it will not ordinarily allow a court to set aside the arbitral award, unless there has been real or actual prejudice to either or both parties. Third, it is well established that mere errors of law or even fact are not sufficient to warrant setting aside an arbitral award under Article 34(2)(a)(iii). Applying these rules to this case, the Court of Appeal found that (i) the majority members of the tribunal exceeded their jurisdiction, as they should have considered the merits of the DAB decision before issuing the award, and (ii) the award was not made in accordance with the provisions of the FIDIC Red Book. As such, the Court of Appeal held that PGN suffered real prejudice, as the award would require it to pay the sum awarded to CRW whilst being deprived of its contractual right to have the DAB decision reviewed.

B.3 Arbitrators May Only Decide within the Boundaries of the Parties' Pleadings

Shortly after the *CRW Joint Venture* decision, the High Court set aside another three arbitration awards (albeit arising from a single reference) on the grounds that those awards decided matters that were not pleaded, and therefore were beyond the scope of the submission to arbitration.

In *Kempinski Hotels SA v. PT Prima International Development*,[12] the applicant Kempinski, a Swiss company, entered into a contract to manage a hotel owned by respondent PT Prima. The Indonesian Ministry of Tourism subsequently issued three decisions that made it compulsory for the contract to be carried out by a company incorporated in Indonesia (the "Three Decisions"). Nonetheless, Kempinski remained the company managing the hotel pursuant to the contract. PT Prima terminated the contract. Kempinski commenced SIAC arbitration proceedings for alleged wrongful termination. In the course of the proceedings, PT Prima applied and was granted leave to amend its defense to include a plea of supervening illegality due to the Three Decisions.

The issues of illegality were heard in two tranches. The tribunal's first award found the contract valid but incapable of being performed except in a manner consistent with the Three Decisions. In a second award, the tribunal ruled out *force majeure* because the contract might still be performed through alternative methods consistent with the Three Decisions. Accordingly, Kempinski could claim damages.

Thereafter, Kempinski entered into a new contract for the management of another hotel with a third party in Indonesia (the "New Venture"), seemingly in contradiction with its submissions to the tribunal. PT Prima wrote to the tribunal to seek "clarification" on the first and second awards in light of this fact, prompting further discovery of documents and written submissions pertaining to this issue (the tribunal sought factual and expert evidence).

The tribunal then published its third award holding, *inter alia*, that the alternative methods to perform the contract consistently

---

[12] *Kempinski Hotels SA v. PT Prima International Development* [2011] 4 SLR 633.

with the Three Decisions were no longer possible in light of the New Venture.

Dissatisfied, Kempinski commenced proceedings in the Singapore High Court to set aside the third award on the basis that, amongst other grounds, the tribunal dealt with an issue that had not been formally pleaded.

The High Court agreed with Kempinski that the award should be set aside on the ground that failure to plead the New Venture resulted in the tribunal making a decision that was beyond the scope of the matters submitted to it. Article 34(2)(a)(iii) of the Model Law provides that a decision in an award on matters which were beyond the scope of the submission to arbitration may be set aside. The High Court reasoned that to determine whether matters in an award were within or outside the scope of the submission to arbitration, a reference to the pleadings would usually have to be made.

The High Court rejected the submission that jurisdiction in a particular reference was not limited to the pleadings, or that there was no rule of pleading in arbitration that requires all material facts to be stated and specifically pleaded, as would be required in litigation. The High Court noted that the tribunal, as well as the parties, had proceeded on the basis of the pleadings filed during the arbitration. This was reflected by the fact that PT Prima had earlier recognized that it had to plead the supervening illegality issue before that issue could be heard by the tribunal. Therefore, it was clear to the High Court that all persons engaged in the arbitration proceeded on the basis that the tribunal could only determine issues that had been pleaded.

The High Court commented that PT Prima should have applied to amend its pleading to include the allegation that the existence of the New Venture was a fact that made it impossible for Kempinski to perform the contract and therefore to claim damages from the date that the New Venture came into existence. The High Court also found that the tribunal could have ignored PT Prima's written request for the review of the first and second awards or pointed out that the same was erroneous.

The parties to the proceedings had demonstrated that they were aware of the need to plead an issue before the tribunal may decide on it. It may be argued that the party (PT Prima) that had earlier sought leave of the tribunal to amend its pleadings to include a new claim had acted inconsistently when it tried to introduce a new issue (pertaining to the New Venture) by way of a written request instead of seeking leave of the tribunal to amend its pleadings.

The case of *Kempinski Hotels* appears to stand for the proposition that an issue must be pleaded before the tribunal may decide on it. However, in arbitrations that have terms of reference or a memorandum of issues agreed to by parties (which often follow the pleadings), these should also be of relevance in defining the scope of the tribunal's jurisdiction.

B.4 Arbitral Award May Be Set Aside on Public Policy Grounds If It Enforces an Agreement with the Object of Breaching International Comity

In the previous edition of this yearbook we reported on the case of *AJU v. AJT*.[13] That case has since been appealed and the Singapore Court of Appeal's decision is discussed in Section C.3 below.

---

[13] *AJU v AJT* [2010] 4 SLR 649.

C.   PUBLIC POLICY IN INTERNATIONAL ARBITRATION

It is public policy in Singapore that courts minimize their involvement in matters that parties have agreed to submit to arbitration.[14]

C.1   Reliance on Public Policy

Apart from this overriding manifestation of public policy, parties may invoke public policy in two instances.

First, public policy may be used to resist the enforcement of an agreement to arbitrate by staying proceedings in court. Hence, Section 11 of the IAA provides that "any dispute which the parties have agreed to submit to arbitration under an arbitration agreement may be determined by arbitration unless it is contrary to public policy to do so." A clear example of this in operation is the non-arbitrability of avoidance claims in insolvency (see Section B.1 above).

Second, public policy may be invoked to set aside an award made in Singapore[15] or to refuse enforcement or recognition of a foreign arbitration award.[16]

C.2   Rules that Constitute Public Policy

First, there is no difference between the concept of public policy as a ground for setting aside an award made in Singapore and for refusing enforcement or recognition of a foreign award.[17]

---

[14]   *Tjong Very Sumito v. Antig Investments* [2009] 4 SLR 732, at [29].

[15]   Model Law Art 34(2)(b)(ii) read with Section 19B(4) of the IAA.

[16]   Section 31(4)(b) of the IAA.

[17]   *AJU v. AJT* [2011] SGCA 41, at [37].

Second, a public policy objection for resisting enforcement of an award must "involve either exceptional circumstances . . . which would justify the court in refusing to enforce the award . . . or a violation of the most basic notions of justice."[18]

Third, there are a few examples of the conditions that Singapore courts have accepted within this narrow scope:

(a) An award that enforces an agreement that undermines the administration of justice, such as an agreement to stifle the prosecution of a non-compoundable offense;[19]

(b) An award that enforces an agreement the object of which was a breach of international comity, in the sense that the object is to do something illegal under the law of the place of performance;[20] and

(c) Corruption, bribery or fraud.[21]

Fourth, the examples below illustrate what Singapore courts have rejected as being outside the narrow scope of public policy;

(a) Errors of law or fact, except an error of law as to what constitutes the public policy of Singapore;[22]

(b) Enforcement of an award that seeks to bind a non-signatory;[23]

---

[18] *Ibid.* at [38].

[19] *AJU v. AJT* [2010] 4 SLR 649, at [28], [32]-[33] reversed on other grounds in *AJU v. AJT* 4 SLR 749.

[20] *AJU v. AJT* [2011] 4 SLR 749 at [21].

[21] *PT Asuransi Jasa Indonesia (Persero) v. Dexia Bank SA* [2006] 1 SLR 197, at [59].

[22] *AJU v. AJT* [2011] 4 SLR 749 at [77].

[23] *Aloe Vera of America, Inc. v. Asianic Food (S) Pte Ltd. and another* [2006] 3 SLR(R) 174 [75]-[76].

(c) The tribunal failed to decide the matter in accordance with the facts and evidence presented by the parties;[24] and

(d) Any principle that costs incurred (and therefore awarded) should be proportional to the amount in dispute.[25]

C.3 Limitations on and Review of Alleged Breaches of Public Policy

A party seeking to challenge an award on public policy grounds must identify the public policy that the award allegedly breaches and show which part of the award conflicts with that public policy as demonstrated in *John Holland Pty Ltd. v. Toyo Engineering Corp. (Japan).*[26]

In *AJU v. AJT*,[27] the Singapore Court of Appeal held that Singapore courts will only review a tribunal's finding on illegality if the decision or the decision-making process is tainted by fraud, breach of natural justice or some other recognized vitiating factor, or if the tribunal makes an error of law as to what constitutes the public policy of Singapore.

AJU v. AJT concerned the legality of a settlement agreement— governed by Singapore law—according to which AJT was to terminate an arbitration in exchange for AJU providing evidence of the withdrawal, discontinuation or termination of all criminal proceedings against certain parties. Subsequent to this agreement, AJU withdrew the complaint it had made to the Thai

---

[24] *Galsworthy Ltd. of the Republic of Liberia v. Glory Wealth Shipping Pte Ltd.* [2011] 1 SLR 727, at [17].

[25] *VV v. VW* [2008] 2 SLR(R) 929 at [28]-[31].

[26] *John Holland Pty Ltd, v. Toyo Engineering Corp. (Japan)* [2001] 1 SLR(R) 443 at [25].

[27] [2011] 4 SLR 749.

prosecution authority and the prosecution authority then issued a non-prosecution order on the basis of lack of evidence. AJT then refused to terminate the arbitration. AJU therefore applied for and obtained from the tribunal, seated in Singapore, an award finding that the settlement agreement was legal and valid. The tribunal consequently terminated the arbitration. AJT applied to set aside the award.

The tribunal's award, made under the IAA, was initially set aside by the High Court on the grounds of public policy pursuant to Article 34(2)(b)(ii) of the Model Law, which has the force of law in Singapore through Section 3 of the IAA. The High Court agreed with AJT that the settlement agreement was illegal because it was a contract to stifle prosecution contrary to the law of Thailand (the law of the place of performance) and to the public policy of both Thailand and Singapore (the governing law).

However, the Singapore Court of Appeal reversed the High Court's judgment. It agreed with the arbitral tribunal that the underlying agreement was valid and upheld the arbitral award. The court found that the agreement was not contrary to public policy because the Thai prosecution authority had the ultimate discretion to decide whether or not to prosecute despite AJU's withdrawal of its complaint. This finding was not subject to review by the court.

The Singapore Court of Appeal preferred the more restrained approach set out by Colman J in *Westacre Investments Inc. v. Jugoimport-SPDR Holding Co. Ltd. and Others,*[28] as opposed to that of Waller LJ in another case, *Soleimany v. Soleimany,*[29]

---

[28] *Westacre Investments Inc. v. Jugoimport-SPDR Holding Co. Ltd. and Others* [1999] QB 740.

[29] *Soleimany v. Soleimany* [1999] QB 785.

which favored wider judicial discretion in the review of a tribunal's findings. Colman J set limits on the admission of new evidence to dispute an arbitral tribunal's findings on illegality. To be admissible, such new evidence must be of sufficient cogency and weight to be material and must not have been readily available at the arbitral hearing.

Consistent with its pro-arbitration approach, the Singapore court would not reopen an arbitral tribunal's findings of fact on the legality or otherwise of an agreement absent fraud, breach of natural justice or some other recognized vitiating factor (such factors being separate grounds for setting aside under the IAA). The power of the courts to set aside or refuse to enforce an award on the ground of public policy alone (i.e., Article 34(2)(b)(ii) of the Model Law) does not apply to errors of fact.

However, the Singapore Court of Appeal cautioned that where there is palpable or indisputable illegality (as in *Soleimany*), the court will decide for itself whether it is against public policy to enforce the arbitration agreement or any award under it. The court cannot abrogate to the arbitral tribunal its judicial power to determine the public policy of Singapore.

SPAIN

José Ramón Casado[1] and Víctor Mercedes[2]

A. LEGISLATION, TRENDS AND TENDENCIES

A.1 Amendment of the Spanish Arbitration Act

The Spanish Arbitration Act[3] (the "Arbitration Act") was recently amended.[4] The Arbitration Act was an important step in the regulation of arbitration, and established a new framework for domestic and international arbitration based on the UNCITRAL Model Law.[5] However, the Spanish legislature considered that given the current move towards modernization of the administration of justice, certain aspects of the Arbitration Act had to be amended in order to contribute to the promotion of alternative means of dispute resolution, especially arbitration. The amendment entered into force on 4 June 2011. This section provides a summary of those amendments that are likely to have the greatest impact on the practice of commercial arbitration or to be most controversial.

---

[1] José Ramón is a Partner is Baker & McKenzie's Madrid office. He has extensive experience in civil and commercial litigation and arbitration. He is mainly involved in unfair competition proceedings, intellectual property, corporate law, contracting, software, construction law and arbitration.

[2] Víctor Mercedes is a Partner in Baker McKenzie's Barcelona office and Co-Head of its Litigation Department. His experience includes domestic and international litigation and arbitration, insolvency and administrative law and white-collar criminal defense.

[3] Act 60/2003, dated 23 December 2003.

[4] Spanish Act 11/2011, dated 20 May 2011and published in the Spanish Official Gazette on 21 May 2011.

[5] 21 June 1985.

A.2 Procedural Aspects of the Amendment

The amendment has reallocated judicial functions in relation to arbitration. Functions relating to the appointment and removal of arbitrators, the annulment of awards and the competence to decide on the *exequatur* of foreign awards are now allocated to the civil and criminal chambers of the superior courts (*tribunales superiores de justicia*), while the enforcement of awards is dealt with by the courts of first instance (*juzgados de primera instancia*).

Certain procedural issues regarding actions for annulment have been amended (and improved, in our view). The distinction between final and enforceable awards has been eliminated, meaning that once an award is issued, it becomes *res judicata* and can be enforced, even if an action for annulment or review has been filed. With regard to the annulment of an award, the Arbitration Act[6] was expected to be amended so that an award could be annulled if it was "manifestly contrary to public policy." After further discussion, it was decided that the term "manifestly," should be eliminated since it was clear that if an award was contrary to public policy, given the strict interpretation and application of "public policy," it should be declared null and void in any case.

A.3 Arbitration in Equity

The bill to amend the Arbitration Act initially envisaged the elimination of equitable arbitration in domestic arbitration, in order to (i) place arbitration and litigation on the same level and (ii) reserve equity for mediation. This provision was extremely controversial and was eventually rejected.

---

6   Article 43.1.f.

A.4 Suitability of Arbitrators and Their Liability

In contrast to the previous position, arbitrators are no longer required to be practicing lawyers. Instead, at least one arbitrator must be a law graduate, unless the parties agree otherwise. If the dispute is to be resolved by three or more arbitrators, the others can be of other professions. Unless the parties agree otherwise, an arbitrator cannot also act as a mediator in the same dispute.

The amendment introduces an obligation for arbitrators, or arbitration institutions acting on their behalf, to obtain third party liability insurance or an equivalent guarantee.

Unless the parties expressly agree otherwise, the expiration of the relevant term for rendering a final award will not affect the validity of the arbitration agreement or any award issued; however, this does not absolve arbitrators of any liability that may arise from such delay.

A.5 Challenging Corporate Resolutions

Corporate disputes can now be subject to arbitration provided that at least two thirds of the shareholders representing the share capital vote for the introduction of a clause in the bylaws providing for arbitration. In addition, for challenges to corporate resolutions to be subject to arbitration, the arbitration proceedings and the appointment of arbitrators must be carried out by an arbitration institution.

An award deciding that a corporate resolution is null and void must be registered in the Commercial Register. If the challenged corporate resolution was itself registered in the Commercial Register, the award must also require the cancellation of such registration and any future registrations that are inconsistent with it.

A.6 Arbitration of Disputes between Public Administrations and Other Public Bodies

Under a new provision of the amended Arbitration Act, relevant legal controversies between public administrations and certain other public entities (*organismos autónomos, entidades públicas empresariales* and *empresas públicas*) will be submitted to a special kind of administrative arbitration, without recourse to administrative law courts (*tribunales contencioso-administrativos*). These special proceedings will also apply to disputes between public corporations and public sector foundations.

The concept of a "relevant" legal dispute is broadly defined to include claims that:

(a) regardless of their amount, generate or may generate a high number of claims;

(b) request at least EUR 300,000 in damages; or

(c) in the view of any of the parties, are of special relevance for the public order.

As to the procedure for this special administrative arbitration, the parties will submit the dispute to a specific executive committee for administrative dispute resolution, to be composed of members of the Ministry of Economy, Ministry of Justice and other ministries related to the entities concerned. This committee will request legal and technical reports before issuing a binding resolution establishing the measures to be taken to resolve the dispute. This resolution may not be challenged before the courts.

These special proceedings will not apply to criminal matters, certain excluded civil actions arising from them, so-called "jurisdictional capacity" conflicts between public administration bodies, which are subject to specific administrative procedures, or to matters related to the monitoring of public budgets, which are subject to a special accounting jurisdiction.

There is no doubt that disputes involving public companies and public bodies are arbitrable under Spanish legislation, but this does not exclude sovereign immunity issues from arising in the enforcement stage. The reform has been questioned due to the uncertainty in the scope of its application (e.g., the meaning of "special relevance for public order" is rather vague) and the specific exclusion of judicial recourse, which can be considered to be contrary to the nature of administrative law review in the public sector.

A.7 Insolvency Aspects of the Reform

The amendment to the Arbitration Act reforms certain aspects of the Spanish Insolvency Act in connection with arbitration cases. The main aim is that an arbitration not be halted if one of the parties becomes insolvent. Specifically, an insolvency declaration will not have any automatic effect on mediation or arbitration agreements signed by the debtor. However, the commercial court having jurisdiction in the insolvency proceedings may suspend the effects of such agreements if damage to the development of the insolvency case is identified, and it may do so without prejudice to international treaties and conventions. Before the amendment, such arbitration agreements immediately lost their effect, and disputes between the parties became non-arbitrable.

There is no change regarding ongoing arbitration proceedings, which will continue until the award is rendered, or regarding the enforcement of awards against the insolvent estate.

Enforcement of interim injunctions requested in an arbitration against a debtor involved in insolvency proceedings will be under the jurisdiction of the competent commercial courts.

B. CASES

B.1 Invalidity of an Arbitration Provision where Dispute Resolution Clauses are Contradictory

The Supreme Court (Section 1) issued a judgment in a case between a Dutch and a Spanish company involving contractual and non-contractual liability claims for defects. The parties had signed two contracts regulating their relationship: a purchase agreement containing a submission to the courts and a guarantee agreement containing an arbitration clause.

The Supreme Court concluded that relations between the parties were subject to different and incompatible dispute resolution provisions, which rendered the arbitration agreement under the guarantee agreement ineffective. According to Spanish arbitration law, the unequivocal consent of the parties is required for arbitration to be effective.

B.2 Annulment of an Award Rendered in an Arbitration Commenced after an Insolvency Filing

The Court of Appeal of Madrid (Section 8) annulled an award rendered after a defendant filed for insolvency and was adjudicated to be insolvent.[7] The judgment applied the former wording of Article 52 of the Spanish Insolvency Act, which provided for arbitration agreements to become ineffective where one of the parties is declared insolvent.[8] Under this provision, arbitrations initiated before the insolvency of one of the parties could be conducted until an award was rendered. However, arbitration proceedings initiated after the declaration of

---

[7] Judgment issued on 20 September 2010, published in 2011.

[8] For the position under the amended Arbitration Act, see Section A.7 of this chapter.

insolvency lost their effect, and jurisdiction over the dispute reverted to the commercial court managing the insolvency case.

The Court of Appeal concluded that in the case in question, the arbitration was initiated on the date on which the arbitrator communicated her acceptance of the appointment to the respondent. This took place after the insolvency declaration. The arbitration agreement's ineffectiveness constituted serious grounds for the annulment of the award.

B.3   Denial of Enforcement of an English Judgment on an Award

The Court of Appeal of Seville (Section 5) refused to enforce[9] an English decision by the Commercial Court. The English decision, a so-called "judgment on an award," opened the compulsory enforcement phase of a previous award rendered in a case between an English company and an individual arising from a charter agreement subject to English law. The English company requested the enforcement of the judgment on the award before the Spanish civil courts under Articles 32 and 33 of European Regulation 44/2001.

The Court of Appeal of Seville refused to enforce the judgment, stating that the Regulation did not include arbitration in its scope and did not allow the Spanish courts to enforce arbitral awards or judicial decisions related to arbitration cases. The court stated that the enforcement of judicial resolutions linked to arbitration awards is regulated by Article 955 *et seq.* of the Spanish Civil Procedure Act and not under European Regulation 44/2001:

> Not having been requested in the claim to recognize a foreign award according to the proceedings provided in the Spanish 1881 Civil Procedure Act applicable to this matter,

---

[9]   Judgment issued on 21 July 2011.

in the absence of any specific provisions under the Spanish 2000 Procedure Act, and since an English judgment which provides legal enforceability to an award is not directly applicable in Spain (as this matter is excluded from European Regulation 44/2001/CE), it must be concluded that no enforceable title has been submitted in Spain, and therefore a ruling should be issued refusing to enforce the judgment. It is thus appropriate to revoke the current ruling and to issue a new one refusing to enforce the judgment.

B.4   Special Matters Subject to Arbitration

The Court of Appeal of Madrid (Section 12) issued an interesting ruling[10] on the enforceability of an equitable award on an eviction claim arising from certain Spanish lease agreements. The court referred to the development of case law on the matter and to the nature of the regulation of lease agreements, and concluded that there were no public policy considerations or mandatory law that excluded the arbitrability of a dispute under a lease agreement, even if the dispute was focused strictly on the eviction process and claim for unpaid rent.

The Court of Appeal of Santa Cruz de Tenerife (Section 4) issued a ruling[11] on an appeal on the arbitrability of a corporate dispute. The ruling reviewed previous case law from the Supreme Court on the issue, focusing especially on a leading case dated 18 April 1998, under which claims to nullify corporate shareholders' resolutions or challenges to corporate decisions were not excluded from arbitration, without prejudice to the fact that arbitrators were not entitled to decide these questions in the award subject to the risk of partial or total

---

[10]   Ruling issued on 3 May 2011.

[11]   Ruling issued on 4 July 2011.

annulment of the award rendered in the case. The court referred to developments on this issue, mentioning certain precedent to the effect that, if it is necessary to resolve the dispute in order to apply mandatory law, the arbitrators are not entitled to avoid doing so. Therefore, it is possible to arbitrate disputes on corporate decisions based on the violation of corporate rights regulated by mandatory legislation.

B.5 Arbitration Clauses in Swap Agreements

The Court of Appeal of Castellon (Section 3) refused to determine the validity of an arbitration clause contained in a swap contract.[12] The court, after reiterating the exclusive capacity of the arbitrators to determine the scope of the arbitration (under the classic criteria of *kompetenz-kompetenz*), found that it was not entitled to discuss the existence or validity of an arbitration clause because the effective existence of a submission to arbitration is a matter reserved for the arbitrators under Spanish arbitration law.

B.6 Criminal *Lis Pendens* in an Arbitration Case

The Court of Appeal of Madrid (Section 14) ruled on an annulment case involving an award on a commercial dispute between Spanish and French companies arising from a service agreement for the use of automated dial-up systems. Under the terms of this agreement, the parties engaged in arbitration for breach of contract. A third party, the owner of the telephone lines, independently filed a criminal complaint for fraud committed by the final users of these lines.

The Court of Appeal rejected a request for annulment based on criminal *lis pendens* and violation of public policy. The court

---

[12] Ruling issued on 25 March 2011.

found that the facts investigated in the criminal case did not have a significant influence on the arbitration, and no evidence of responsible individuals was effectively obtained in the course of the investigation phase of the criminal proceedings.

B.7 Infringement of Procedural Public Policy Leads to the Annulment of an Award

The Court of Appeal of Madrid (Section 12) annulled an award due to the infringement of procedural public policy.[13] The claimant alleged that procedural public policy had been violated because of (i) a denial of the right to an impartial and independent arbitrator and (ii) an infringement of the right to evidence.

The Court of Appeal found that the arbitrator was not impartial and independent given his previous relationship with the defendant's lawyer. The following facts were indications of an unprofessional relationship that would qualify to prove the arbitrators' unsuitability: the arbitrator was friendly with several members of the law firm, as a result of which his son-in-law had been given a job there; the firm's managing partner had previously worked for the arbitrator; and the arbitrator's daughter had worked for the defendant. The court noted that, according to the Constitutional Court, it is possible to review the impartiality and independence of the arbitrator due to purely formal circumstances.

With regards to the infringement of the right to evidence, the court found that it had been infringed. The court noted that it was telling that the admitted evidence had not been produced. The court found that had the evidence been produced, the arbitrator's decision might have been different.

---

[13] Ruling issued on 30 June 2011.

As a result, the award was declared null and void due to the infringement of procedural public policy.

B.8 Dismissal of an Action for Annulment of an Award Based on an Infringement of Public Policy Unrelated to Basic Constitutional Rights

According to the Court of Appeal of Vizcaya,[14] it is not possible to declare an award null and void for infringing public policy if such infringement does not affect the core values of the Spanish Constitution.

The court stated that an action for annulment is not to be treated like a common appeal allowing one party to request the review of an arbitrator's decision, since such a review would defeat the purpose of the arbitration. In that case, the court concluded that the intention of the party was exclusively to review the arbitrator's decision. The court stated that: (i) the party did not allege (and prove) the specific right that had been violated in its view; and (ii) no constitutional right had been violated.

The decision was based on the restricted application of the concept of public policy. According to the court, public policy is only infringed "when the arbitrator issues an award in clear violation of fundamental rights ... being that the concept of public policy is limited to the values contained in article 53 of the Constitution."

B.9 Public Policy as a Pretext to Review an Arbitrator's Decision

The Court of Appeal of Madrid dismissed a complaint seeking the annulment of an award on the basis that: (i) the underlying arbitration agreement was invalid under consumer protection legislation; and (ii) public policy was infringed because of the

---

[14] Ruling issued on 16 June 2011.

arbitrator's lack of impartiality. The court reached its decision on the following grounds:[15]

(a) Consumer protection legislation did not apply to the case, since the claimant was a company that entered into an adhesion agreement with another firm; and

(b) the concept of public policy was very restricted, and should not be used as a means to review an arbitrator's decision. An arbitrator's lack of impartiality is not considered a public policy violation, and in this case, it had not been alleged during the arbitration.

B.10 It Is Not Possible to Use Arbitration in Equity to Obviate Mandatory Substantive Regulation

The Court of Appeal of Madrid dismissed a request for enforcement of an equity award that decided on the termination of a lease agreement for non-payment of rent with the subsequent eviction of the lessee.[16] The court issued this decision on the grounds that, despite the fact that it was possible to have an arbitration agreement within a lease agreement:

(a) it is a highly sensitive aspect of our system, in which regulation is mandatory to protect the rights of the lessee and the law considers invalid those provisions that modify the rules of law to the detriment of the lessee unless it is expressly authorized;

(b) the procedural system also contains mandatory rules that could be considered part of public policy when attempting to terminate a lease agreement and evict a lessee for non-payment of rent.

---

[15]   Ruling issued 22 February 2011.

[16]   Ruling issued 8 February 2011.

The court was essentially referring to the lessee's right (subject to certain conditions) to prevent the eviction by paying the sums due. However, the court did not state that all relationships subject to any kind of mandatory regulation are to be excluded from arbitration; what is relevant is that the envisaged relationship is subject to strong mandatory regulations intended for the protection of the rights of one party. In such cases, it is not permitted for the parties to set up an equitable arbitration to obviate the substantive mandatory regulation.

C. PUBLIC POLICY IN INTERNATIONAL ARBITRATION

C.1 Scenarios of Reliance on Public Policy

The Arbitration Act promotes the validity of the underlying arbitration agreement by stating that the arbitration agreement is valid if it meets the requirements of (i) the law chosen by the parties to govern the arbitration agreement, or (ii) the law applicable to the substance of the dispute, or (iii) Spanish law.[17]

Nonetheless, it is possible for public policy to be invoked to invalidate the arbitration agreement. An example would be an arbitration agreement within a business-to-consumer transaction, in which the consumer signs an adhesion agreement (*contrato de adhesión*) that includes general contract terms (*condiciones generales de la contratación*). Under the Spanish Consumer Act, the arbitration agreement could be declared null and void on the grounds that the consumer was not given any chance to negotiate the clause. The Court of Appeal of Barcelona (Section 15) concluded in its decision of 11 March 2010 that in the context of

---

[17] Article 9.6.

a domestic arbitration, such an arbitration agreement should not be considered valid.[18]

If an action for the annulment of an award has been submitted, the award may be withdrawn if the party alleges that the arbitration agreement does not exist or is not valid, or if the party, the court or the public prosecutor state that the award is contrary to public policy.[19]

The New York Convention,[20] enforceable in Spain since 1977, provides a system in favor of the extraterritorial validity of the award. However, it does not regulate the execution of the award, which according to Spanish case law,[21] is governed by domestic rules. Thus, in order to obtain the recognition of foreign civil and/or commercial awards in Spain, the Civil Chamber of the High Court of Justice must review whether certain conditions are met, including compatibility with Spanish public policy.[22]

C.2 Modes and Limitations of Reliance on Public Policy

Respect for Spanish public policy is one of the conditions for the recognition and enforcement of a foreign award. Spanish Supreme Court cases have held that public policy is breached when the judgment is irreconcilable with an earlier or pending judgment given in a dispute between the same parties in Spain.

---

[18] Decision of 11 March 2010, published in 2011.

[19] Article 41 of the Arbitration Act.

[20] The United Nations Convention on the Recognition and Enforcement of Foreign Arbitral Awards, New York, 10 June 1958.

[21] Supreme Court decision of 5 May 1998; Court of Appeal of Asturias decision of 31 March 2005.

[22] Article 955 of the Spanish Civil Procedure Act 1881 and 12.3 of the Spanish Civil Code.

C.3   Rules that Constitute "Public Policy"

The review of an award's compliance with public policy relates to international public policy, which is different from domestic public policy (although the international public policy in question is always that of the forum state, i.e., in the case of Spanish courts, international public policy as reflected in all legal instruments in force in Spain). The contravention of international public policy is subject to a restrictive interpretation. Spanish courts have indicated that recognition and enforcement should only be refused if (i) the award is manifestly against international public policy, (ii) there is a real link with Spanish society; and (iii) it entails a risk to the legal structure of Spanish society.

As stated by the Supreme Court, "the concept of public policy includes a substantive and procedural aspect and is a vague legal concept, which must consequently be applied in accordance with the entire legal system and socio-cultural experiences."[23]

The first Constitutional Court ruling on the question of the content of public policy (ruling 43/1986) was issued on 15 April 1986. The Constitutional Court commented on the content of public policy as the basis for rejecting the recognition of an international award, considering that public policy is a reservation or so-called "white clause" (*cláusula de reserva en blanco*) that allows for effective judicial control to verify that there is no breach of the Spanish constitutional restricted order (essentially the rights and freedoms recognized in Chapter II of Title I of the Spanish Constitution). Public policy is considered to be an indeterminate concept allowing judicial control of the content and effectiveness of fundamental rights, i.e., a "safety

---

[23]   Ruling of 19 October 2011; see also ruling of the Court of Appeal of Valladolid dated 20 February 1991, amongst others.

valve." The scope of public policy was partially clarified in a ruling dated 15 July 1985, in which it was identified with mandatory or prohibitive laws and with the general principles inspired by and deduced from the latter. According to the Supreme Court,[24] public policy has a "purely constitutional content."

However, there are a few examples where Spanish courts have confused internal and international public policy. This happened, for example, in a ruling of the Supreme Court in which the court denied *exequatur* of an international award because it did not comply with a purely formal internal requirement.[25]

C.4 Review of Alleged Breaches of Public Policy

An alleged breach of public policy can be considered *ex officio* or at the request of one of the parties or the public prosecutor. Theoretically, a foreign award will not be reviewed as to substance, since the basic principle of the prohibition of review of the substance is unassailable, according to Spanish case law.[26] Spanish case law also establishes that it is not possible to make a substantive examination of the law applied by the arbitrators.[27] This principle acts as an impenetrable shield when courts review domestic and international awards on an action for annulment or *exequatur*.

However, while courts claim respect for this principle of prohibition, they at the same time exercise real control over the substance of the award, as the Supreme Court did in

---

[24] Ruling dated 14 October 2003.

[25] Ruling dated 28 March 1994.

[26] Supreme Court decisions of 2 March 1989, 7 June 1990, 29 September 1998 and 24 November 1998; Constitutional Court decision of 16 March 1988; Court of Appeal of Asturias decision of 28 April 1994.

[27] Court of Appeal of Madrid decision of 12 June 1995.

Ets Sebtigrains v. Armengol Hermanos, S.A.[28] In that case, the Supreme Court stated that *exequatur* serves purely for standardization, "except for international public policy whose content should be controlled." It should also be noted that the Supreme Court, in a decision of 24 November 1998,[29] stated that it was "entering to decide on the substance..." thereby admitting that a review of the substance of an award is possible, provided that it is necessary to safeguard the essential principles of the Spanish legal system, and heavily grounded with the constitutional values that form the core of Spanish understandings of law and international order.

---

[28] 29 September 1988.

[29] *Sindicato Pesquero del Perú S.A. and Internacional de Productos Químicos S.A. v. Internacional de Productos Químicos S.A.*

SWEDEN

Anders Isgren,[1] Jonas Benedictsson,[2] Stefan Bessman,[3] Magnus Stålmarker[4] and Anders Nilsson[5]

A. LEGISLATION, TRENDS AND TENDENCIES

No significant legislative changes in relation to arbitration law have occurred in Sweden during 2011. The present Arbitration Act entered into force in 1999.

The present arbitration rules of the Arbitration Institute of the Stockholm Chamber of Commerce (the "SCC Institute") entered into force on 1 January 2010.

---

[1]   Anders Isgren is a Partner in Baker & McKenzie's Stockholm office. He practices arbitration and litigation, and has represented clients in arbitration proceedings before the SCC, the ICC and in *ad hoc* arbitrations involving general commercial and construction law disputes.

[2]   Jonas Benedictsson is a Partner in Baker & McKenzie's Stockholm office. His practice includes various aspects of arbitration, litigation, alternative dispute resolution and insolvency. He leads Baker & McKenzie's Dispute Resolution Practice Group in Stockholm and is a member of the Steering Committee of the Firm's International Arbitration Practice Group.

[3]   Stefan Bessman is a Partner in Baker & McKenzie's Stockholm office. He focuses on dispute resolution in banking, finance, and reinsurance. He has also been involved in several disputes relating to cross-border investment and joint venture projects.

[4]   Magnus Stålmarker is an Associate in Baker & McKenzie's Stockholm office. As a member of Stockholm's Arbitration & Litigation Group, he has acted as counsel and co-counsel in various domestic and cross-border matters.

[5]   Anders Nilsson is an Associate in Baker & McKenzie's Stockholm office and a member of Stockholm's Arbitration & Litigation Group.

B. CASES

In 2011, the courts of appeal rendered a number of decisions in arbitration matters. Some of these decisions are described below.

B.1 Arbitrator's Impartiality

A decision that has by far attracted the most attention in Sweden during 2011, both among lawyers dealing with arbitration and in the media, was rendered by the Svea Court of Appeal in a matter regarding impartiality of arbitrators due to conflicts of interest.[6]

In an arbitration between KPMG and Profilgruppen, KPMG appointed as arbitrator the well-reputed former chairman of the Swedish Bar Association, Mr. Axel Calissendorff, who is a senior partner at the Swedish/Finnish law firm Roschier. The arbitration began in the spring of 2008. The final hearing took place between 30 November and 3 December 2010. The award was subsequently rendered on 22 December 2010 and sent to the parties.

During the same time period, KPMG received a letter dated 20 December 2010 from two of Mr. Calissendorff's colleagues at Roschier representing HQ AB and HQ Bank in a matter against KPMG. In the letter, Mr. Calissendorff's colleagues at Roschier referred to a pending investigation concerning the bank and requested KPMG to produce certain documents and also notified KPMG of claims for compensation. KPMG had previously acted as the bank's auditor.

KPMG challenged the award at the Svea Court of Appeal (the appeals court for Stockholm). The ground for challenge was that Mr. Calissendorff was unauthorized to act as arbitrator due to

---

[6] Decision by The Svea Court of Appeal on 27 September 2011 in Case No. T 1085-11.

circumstances that might diminish confidence in his impartiality, i.e., his Roschier colleagues' concurrent assignment against KPMG.

KPMG further argued that information indicated that the assignment against KPMG had started at the end of October 2010. In October 2010, Roschier dispute resolution practice head, Mr. Claes Lundblad, was instructed by HQ AB and HQ Bank to represent them against a number of individuals, as well as against KPMG. Hence, Mr. Calissendorff's colleagues at Roschier had agreed to represent HQ and HQ Bank against KPMG at the same time as Mr. Calissendorff's appointment as arbitrator in the arbitration between KPMG and Profilgruppen. Consequently, KMPG argued, when Roschier accepted the assignment against KPMG, Mr. Calissendorff was no longer impartial and he was thus not in a position to act as arbitrator. Whether or not Mr. Calissendorff had any actual knowledge of his colleagues' concurrent assignment against KPMG was of no importance, KPMG argued, since the assessment is to be made objectively. KPMG, however, also argued that Mr. Calissendorff in fact had knowledge of his colleagues' concurrent assignment against KPMG. He had received information from Mr. Lundblad and discussed the assignment with him in October 2010. Nevertheless, Mr. Calissendorff did not resign as arbitrator. Neither did he disclose to the parties in the arbitration the circumstances of his colleagues' assignment against KPMG.

Profilgruppen disputed the challenge and argued that Mr. Calissendorff had no knowledge of any disqualifying circumstances and that KPMG was not an adverse party as regards Roschier's assignment until after the award had been rendered.

The Svea Court of Appeal concluded in its judgment that Roschier had accepted the assignment against KPMG on 19

October 2010, i.e., before the final hearing and more than two months before the award was rendered in the arbitration between Profilgruppen and KPMG where Mr. Calissendorff was one of the arbitrators.

Furthermore, the Svea Court of Appeal concluded that the fact that Roschier had accepted the assignment against KPMG concurrently with the pending arbitration with KPMG as party might diminish confidence in Mr. Calissendorff's impartiality as arbitrator. The assignment for HQ against KPMG was significant, with a substantial financial value for Roschier. According to the court, it was also of importance that Mr. Calissendorff had a very central position at Roschier as a partner responsible for the Stockholm office of the law firm.

The Svea Court of Appeal thus concluded that, irrespective of Mr. Calissendorff's knowledge thereof, the circumstances were such that they might diminish confidence in his impartiality. Consequently, the Svea Court of Appeal set aside the award against KPMG and ruled that Mr. Calissendorff was biased as arbitrator.

The Svea Court of Appeal granted leave to appeal and Profilgruppen has filed an appeal with the Supreme Court, which will hear the case. The outcome of this appeal might therefore be reported in an upcoming edition of this *Yearbook*.

B.2 Discovery of Trade Secrets in Arbitration Proceedings

In a dispute between Joint Stock Company Acron ("Acron") and Yara International ASA ("Yara") concerning a terminated shareholders' agreement between several parties, Yara alleged, *inter alia*, that it had assumed Norsk Hydro ASA's ("Norsk Hydro") remaining rights and obligations under the shareholders' agreement after the termination thereof. According to Yara, it inherited rights and obligations from the shareholders' agreement previously belonging to the Russian company, Nordic Rus Holding ("Nordic Rus"). Among other things, Yara claimed in the arbitration proceedings that Acron should participate in a liquidation of Nordic Rus and see to it that certain Nordic Rus contributed assets were "restituted" to Yara, and that Acron should indemnify Yara in the amount of USD 129,000,000 if such action were not taken.

Norsk Hydro, and subsequently Yara, held the shares in Nordic Rus indirectly through another company, Hydro Agri Russland AS ("Hydro Agri"). Acron alleged that it had emerged in the arbitration proceedings that Norsk Hydro had transferred its shares in Hydro Agri to another company – NAV Nordwest AG, and that these shares subsequently had been reacquired by Norsk Hydro or Yara. Therefore, Acron requested in the arbitration proceedings that Yara produce documents and information showing how the shareholders' agreement was considered and treated by the concerned parties in connection with certain disposals and acquisitions.

On 22 January 2010, the arbitral tribunal ordered Yara to produce the requested documentation. Since Yara did not comply with the order, the arbitral tribunal granted Acron permission to make an application to the competent district court for production of evidence substantiating how the shareholders' agreement was dealt with.

Both the district court and the Svea Court of Appeal[7] concluded that the requested documentation was sufficiently specific, since Acron's request only comprised agreements. The critical issues for the court were whether the documentation constituted trade secrets and if so, whether exceptional circumstances existed, which Swedish law requires, for production of trade secrets.

---

[7] Decision by The Svea Court of Appeal on 9 March 2011 in Case No. Ö 8181-10.

Yara stated that the requested documents contained sensitive information concerning cooperation, price indications and commercial considerations of substantial economic impact for Yara's business operations. Yara also stated that the documents were subject to confidentiality agreements with third parties.

Both the district court and the Svea Court of Appeal found that the requested documents constituted trade secrets, since the companies competed in the same market. The remaining question was, therefore, whether exceptional circumstances existed to compel their production. The Svea Court of Appeal took into account the following considerations in deciding the existence of exceptional circumstances. It weighed the trade secrets' importance as evidence and took into account their economic value. The court further took into account the probability that a production of the documents would cause substantial harm.

The Svea Court of Appeal noted that the arbitral tribunal had decided that there were valid grounds to take notice of the requested documentation and that it had importance as evidence in the arbitration proceeding and confirmed the view of the district court that there were strong reasons for allowing production of the documentation. The court found Yara's statement regarding the damage that production of the documents would impose to be too general. The documents were relatively old and Yara had not specified which information would lead to damage if produced and what damage the company would suffer in the event of the documents' production.

Therefore, the Svea Court of Appeal found that Acron's interest in having the documents admitted as evidence in the arbitration was stronger than Yara's interest in keeping the information secret. The documents therefore had to be produced to Acron.

C.   PUBLIC POLICY IN INTERNATIONAL ARBITRATION

C.1   Scenarios of Reliance on Public Policy

Arguments related to public policy and international arbitration may be invoked in various ways under Swedish law. Accordingly, public policy can be a defense (a) within an arbitration and (b) in the enforcement of an arbitration award.

First, even though foreign law is applicable to the arbitration agreement, the question of arbitrability is governed by Swedish law when it comes to arbitrations that take place in Sweden. The subject matter of the dispute in question has to be capable of settlement by arbitration under the laws of Sweden or the arbitration agreement is not valid. In this context, arguments related to public policy may be relevant. This might, for example, be the case where a party objects to the jurisdiction of an arbitral tribunal based on the assertion that the dispute in question is non-arbitrable under Swedish law. Another example might be if the arbitration agreement contains provisions that constitute a gross violation of basic principles of due process. Furthermore, should the arbitration agreement have been concluded in a way that clearly violates the basic principles of the Swedish legal system, it can be argued that the arbitration agreement is invalid.

Second, an award may be declared invalid by a state court due to public policy. Hence, according to Section 33 of the Swedish Arbitration Act (applying to domestic arbitration), an award is invalid if the award, or the manner in which the award arose, is clearly incompatible with the basic principles of the Swedish legal system. The invalidity may apply to a certain part of the award or the entire award, depending on the circumstances of the particular case.

Third, arguments related to public policy may also be used as a defense to prevent a foreign award, i.e., an award made abroad, from being recognized and enforced in Sweden. Hence, according to Section 55 of the Swedish Arbitration Act, recognition and enforcement of a foreign award shall be refused where a state court finds that to do so would be clearly incompatible with the basic principles of the Swedish legal system.[8]

However, it must be emphasized that, in general, the scope of applying arguments related to public policy, at least successfully, is very limited in Sweden.

C.2 Modes and Limitations of Reliance on Public Policy

Invalidity of an award due to violations of public policy may be asserted without any time limit. This means that the ordinary three-month time limit for challenging an award is not applicable to this specific type of action. However, the rules concerning invalidity of an award because of violation of public policy will be applied restrictively by the state court.

An action to have the award declared invalid due to violations of public policy has to be filed with the court of appeal within the jurisdiction where the arbitral proceedings were held. However, where the place of arbitration is not stated in the award, the action may be brought before the Svea Court of Appeal.

Foreign awards are generally recognized and enforced in Sweden. For this purpose, a party must lodge an application for the enforcement of a foreign award with the Svea Court of Appeal. When such an application has been lodged, the opposing

---

[8] This reflects Article V(2) of the New York Convention.

party must be afforded an opportunity to express its opinion upon the application.

In regards to public policy as a defense against recognition and enforcement of a foreign award, the starting point is that the Svea Court of Appeal shall of its own initiative consider whether enforcement should be refused because the award in question is contrary to public policy. However, should the opposing party be of the opinion that the award is contrary to public policy, it should not solely rely on the court's assessment in this respect, but should file a submission raising this defense. In general, the opposing party is afforded an opportunity to express its opinion upon the application within a certain time limit, which is normally two to three weeks. This means that the public policy defense should be raised within the time limit stated by the court (though it is, however, possible to request a reasonable extension of time). Even though it is possible to appeal against the decision on enforcement to the Supreme Court, execution of the decision on enforcement may be initiated immediately in cases where the court of appeal has granted the enforcement application. However, if the Supreme Court should subsequently reverse the decision, all collections by the enforcement agency must be returned.

If the foreign award had been vacated in its country of origin, this will affect the enforcement of the award in Sweden. A prerequisite in order to enforce a foreign award in Sweden is that the award is binding on the parties and that the award has not been set aside or suspended by a competent court or authority in the country in which the award was made.

C.3 Rules that Constitute "Public Policy"

The basic principles of the Swedish legal system constitute public policy. There is, however, no comprehensive definition of which sets of mandatory rules are considered to be part of public policy. The court has to decide on this matter in each specific case where a party refers to public policy. There are only a few court cases where the content of public policy has been discussed. Consequently, it is difficult to obtain any guidance from case law on this issue.

In doctrinal writings,[9] scholars have discussed the content of public policy and provided examples. For example, bribery and corruption as well as drug trafficking, slavery, racial, religious and sexual discrimination, violation of human rights, kidnapping, murder, piracy and terrorism would be considered to be incompatible with the basic principles of the Swedish legal system.

An award that orders someone to perform an act that is illegal would be incompatible with the basic principles of the Swedish legal system. The same would apply to an award that has been made under the influence of threat or criminal assault or bribery.

Furthermore, based on case law from the European Court of Justice,[10] certain fundamental principles of EU competition law constitute public policy.

C.4 Review of Alleged Breaches of Public Policy

Arbitrators have to determine whether an award would be invalid as contrary to public policy regardless of any motion by the parties. This means that the arbitrators have to consider an alleged breach of public policy *ex officio*, i.e., no express reliance by a party is required. Of course the arbitrators may

---

[9] *See, e.g.*, Hobér, *International Commercial Arbitration in Sweden*, 2011, p. 60.

[10] Case C-126/97, *Eco Swiss China Time Ltd. v. Benetton International NV*.

occasionally not understand that there is an alleged breach of public policy unless a party calls the arbitrators' attention to it.

In order to have an award declared invalid due to public policy, a party must file an application with the competent court. The court will then review whether the award is clearly incompatible with the basic principles of the Swedish legal system, i.e., public policy. The threshold is quite high.

Correspondingly, in order to avoid a foreign award being recognized and enforced in Sweden, the court has to come to the conclusion that it would be clearly incompatible with the basic principles of the Swedish legal system.

It is therefore quite unusual that arguments related to public policy are invoked at courts or arbitral tribunals in Sweden, because of the low chance of success.

SWITZERLAND

Urs Zenhäusern,[1] Joachim Frick,[2] Anne-Catherine Hahn[3] and Luca Beffa[4]

A. LEGISLATION, TRENDS AND TENDENCIES

We report below significant changes in 2011 that have affected and will continue to affect in 2012 the legal framework for arbitration in Switzerland. These revisions aim to maintain and even improve the Swiss legal system's traditionally pro-arbitration stance. Switzerland has repeatedly been ranked first in ICC statistical reports as a venue for arbitration, nationality of arbitrators and choice of law. Indeed, the upcoming revisions to the Swiss Rules of International Arbitration are almost certainly influenced by the revised ICC Arbitration Rules, which entered into force on 1 January 2012.[5]

---

[1] Urs Zenhäusern is a Partner in Baker & McKenzie's Zurich office. He regularly represents clients in arbitration proceedings as a party-counsel and also frequently serves as an arbitrator.

[2] Joachim Frick is a Partner in Baker & McKenzie's Zurich office. He often represents clients in mergers and acquisitions and related arbitration proceedings as a party-counsel. He has written various publications on Swiss and international commercial arbitration proceedings and teaches arbitration as honorary professor at Zurich University.

[3] Anne-Catherine Hahn is an Associate in Baker & McKenzie's Zurich office. She practices mainly in the area of international commercial arbitration and litigation and is also a lecturer at the University of Fribourg.

[4] Luca Beffa is an Associate in Baker & McKenzie's Geneva office. His practice focuses primarily on international and domestic arbitration as well as commercial litigation, sports and public law.

[5] All ICC arbitration proceedings filed after this date will be governed by the revised ICC rules. Since the revisions to the ICC rules are not specific to Switzerland, they shall not be summarized here.

A.1 New Swiss Federal Code of Civil Procedure

On 1 January 2011, the new Swiss Federal Code of Civil Procedure ("CCP") entered into force. It includes a full set of new rules concerning domestic arbitration, i.e., arbitration proceedings conducted by an arbitral tribunal with its seat in Switzerland between parties domiciled in Switzerland. While these new rules technically do not change the international arbitration rules in Switzerland as embodied in the Swiss Federal Private International Law Act ("IPRG"), the practice under the new domestic arbitration rules will likely have an effect on the practice of international arbitration. Accordingly, we summarize the most important changes resulting from the new rules on domestic arbitration as included in the revised CCP:

- An arbitral tribunal is entitled to order preliminary measures and decide on a claim for set-off; both of these features are new to Swiss domestic arbitration and will significantly enhance the powers of arbitral tribunals.

- An arbitration clause no longer must be signed by both parties. In line with IPRG Article 178(1), it is sufficient if the arbitral clause is in writing, even if it has not been signed by all parties.

- The parties are allowed to agree on non-statutory laws to apply (e.g., UNIDROIT principles, *lex mercatoria*, etc.). If the parties do not select the applicable law, a tribunal in domestic arbitration proceedings will apply Swiss law.

- There is only one procedure for setting aside domestic arbitral awards. This is in line with the rules of the IPRG. Likewise, a domestic arbitral award can only be set aside by the Swiss Federal Tribunal for limited reasons. These reasons comport with those stated in Article 190 of the IPRG. However, contrary to IPRG Article 190(2), a breach of *ordre public* is not a reason to set aside a domestic arbitral award. Instead, an arbitral award can be set aside based on "arbitrariness."

A.2 Revisions to the Swiss Rules of International Arbitration

Presumably during mid-2012, new revisions to the Swiss Rules of International Arbitration will enter into force and arbitrations initiated after that date will be subject to the new version of these rules.

The Swiss Rules of International Arbitration, adopted by the Swiss Chamber of Commerce on 1 January 2004, have been very successful. They are today probably the most frequently chosen rules of arbitration for international arbitration proceedings seated in Switzerland. The goal of the 2012 revision is to enhance efficiency in terms of time and cost and to give certain additional powers to the bodies administrating the proceedings.

The revisions can be summarized as follows:

- Article 1, concerning scope of application, is amended to state that the arbitral institution, i.e., the Chambers of Commerce and Industry in Switzerland (the "Chambers"), shall have full power to supervise the arbitral proceeding to the fullest extent permitted under the applicable law. It shall have a general fallback competence, particularly over any procedural issues that may arise.

- Articles 3.3(f) and 3.7(f) are amended to oblige the parties to nominate the arbitrators in the notice of arbitration or the answer thereto (provided the arbitral clause requires them to designate an arbitrator). This revision is a substantial change in the process for initiating arbitration under the Swiss rules and may significantly speed up the proceedings.

- Article 4 on consolidation of arbitral proceedings is revised to give the Chambers the power to consolidate a case with a pending proceeding after consultation with all parties as well as with all confirmed arbitrators to those proceedings (and if necessary, even by revoking the appointment of arbitrators).

- A new Article 4.3 provides for emergency relief before the arbitrators are confirmed and even before the notice of arbitration is submitted. A party to a (future) arbitration under the Swiss Rules may apply for urgent interim measures of protection to an emergency arbitrator who must render a decision within 15 days. The emergency arbitrator's decision has the same effect as a decision of an arbitral tribunal on interim measures under Article 26 and is binding until the arbitral tribunal renders its final award. In the event of special urgency, the emergency arbitrator can take an *ex parte* decision, provided that the other party is given an immediate opportunity to address the preliminary order.

- Article 10 on the challenge of arbitrators is revised to state that challenges must be raised within 15 days after the party becomes aware of the ground giving rise to the challenge. Furthermore, the Chambers may in some circumstances decide not to replace an arbitrator and authorize the remaining arbitrators to continue with the proceedings.

- A new Article 15.7 provides that all participants in the arbitral proceedings shall have an obligation to make every effort to contribute to efficient proceedings without unnecessary costs and delays; any breach may have an influence on the allocation of costs of the arbitration.

- A new Article 15.8 expressly provides that the arbitral tribunal may, if the parties agree, take steps toward facilitating the settlement of the dispute. The provision will ensure that arbitrators who made an effort to reach a settlement will not later be challenged for an alleged lack of impartiality.

- Articles 18.3 and 19.2 are revised to further speed up the proceedings: all documents and other evidence on which the parties rely shall already be attached to the statement of claim or the statement of defense, respectively.

We note that the revised version of the Swiss Rules of International Arbitration has not been approved or published yet, so changes may be forthcoming.

A.3 Proposals and Initiatives

Under Article 7 of the IPRG, Swiss courts must dismiss a case for lack of jurisdiction if an arbitral tribunal assumes jurisdiction, except, *inter alia*, if the court concludes that the arbitration clause is not effective. A motion is pending before the Swiss Parliament to add a second paragraph to this article to provide that Swiss courts must postpone their decision on jurisdiction until the arbitral tribunal has decided on its own jurisdiction, except when a summary (*prima facie*) examination reveals that the arbitration clause is invalid. The motion follows a decision of the Swiss Federal Tribunal[6] holding that, for an arbitration seated *in* Switzerland, a Swiss court has to make a decision based on a *prima facie* summary examination of the arbitration clause, so as not to preclude a decision of the arbitral tribunal on its own competence. However, if an arbitration clause provides for an arbitral tribunal with a seat *outside* Switzerland, the Swiss court has to fully examine the arbitration clause with respect to the objections raised by a party, in particular objections based on Article II(3) of the New York Convention. The Swiss court can then not limit its review to a *prima facie* examination.[7] The proposed revision would ensure equal treatment of both cases in the future. Similarly, Article II(3) of the New York Convention does not require a full examination of the arbitration clause by the court.

---

[6] BGE 122 III 139.

[7] BGE 121 III 38 E2b.

Some in Switzerland would like to use the introduction of the new CCP as an opportunity to revise Chapter 12 of the IPRG.[8] The goal would be to harmonize and improve access to Swiss best practice and case law for national and international arbitration proceedings. The revision could include, for example, the introduction of a new rule of disclosure (similar to Article 363 of the new CCP, a more comprehensive regulation on the challenge of an arbitrator (such as in CCP Article 369), a regulation of the problem of "truncated" tribunals (in line with CCP Article 382(2)), a review of decisions on costs (similar to CCP Article 393), and the filling of gaps in the IPRG (concerning revision of international arbitral awards and the power of an international tribunal to interpret or correct its own award).[9]

While the Swiss Rules on International Arbitration are up to date, it has been lamented that the Swiss chambers of commerce do not act as a full service provider in arbitration proceedings (by offering only rules and logistical services but not a convenient infrastructure, conference rooms, education and marketing services). Given the increasing competition between arbitration centers, the question has been raised whether a professional organization under one roof, consisting of an arbitration center with a full-time professional marketing staff and regular educational offerings, should be introduced – perhaps in Geneva, Zurich or Bern, or in all these cities.[10] The difficulty in agreeing on the location is probably the key reason why the initiative has not been further pursued thus far.

---

[8]   See for instance Berger, *SchiedsVZ* 2011, p. 305.

[9]   BGE 118 II 199 E2; 126 III 524 E2b.

[10] *See, e.g.,* Meyer, Pierre, "The Swiss Rules of International Arbitration – Five Years of Experience," publication of the Swiss Chambers Court of Arbitration and Mediation conference of 19 June 2009, p. 23.

B. CASES

The Swiss Federal Tribunal rendered more than 30 decisions in 2011 on international arbitration matters. The following is an overview of the most interesting cases.

B.1 "Truncated Arbitral Tribunals" and *Ne Bis In Idem*

In two decisions dated 3 January 2011,[11] the Swiss Federal Tribunal rejected two challenges brought by the Spanish cyclist Alejandro Valverde Belmonte against two decisions rendered by the Court of Arbitration for Sport ("CAS") in relation to doping. In the decisions, the Swiss Federal Tribunal clarified, *inter alia,* the issue of "truncated arbitral tribunals" and held for the first time that the principle of *ne bis in idem* is part of Swiss public policy.

In 2009, the National Anti-Doping Tribunal of the Italian National Olympic Committee ("CONI") banned Mr. Valverde from all competitions organized in Italy for two years.[12] Mr. Valverde appealed this decision to the CAS first, and then to the Swiss Federal Tribunal, both in vain.[13]

Prior to those decisions, in 2007, the Union Cycliste Internationale ("UCI") requested the Spanish Cycling

---

[11] Decisions 4A_386/2010 and 4A_420/2010.

[12] In 2004, a criminal investigation known as "Operation Puerto" was initiated in Spain for doping offenses and led to the arrest of Dr. Fuentes and other individuals. In 2006, the investigators seized a pack containing blood allegedly from Mr. Valverde from Dr. Fuentes' laboratory. In 2008, the CONI found that Mr. Valverde tested positive for banned substances. The analysis showed a correspondence between the blood samples given by Mr. Valverde in Italy and the ones seized in 2006 from Dr. Fuentes' laboratory.

[13] *See* decision 4A_234/2010 of 29 October 2010, summarized in the *Baker & McKenzie International Arbitration Yearbook 2010-2011*, p. 423 *et seq.*

Federation, the Real Federación Española de Ciclismo ("RFEC"), to initiate disciplinary proceedings against Mr. Valverde. The RFEC rejected the request and both the UCI and the World Anti-Doping Agency ("WADA") appealed the RFEC's decision to the CAS. In its final award, the CAS partially upheld the appeals, finding Mr. Valverde guilty of a violation of the UCI Anti-doping Rules and banning him from all competitions organized worldwide for two years.

Mr. Valverde challenged this award before the Swiss Federal Tribunal and filed a request for interpretation and correction of the award with the CAS. The CAS refused to address the merits of the request and Mr. Valverde filed an appeal with the Swiss Federal Tribunal against this decision as well. The Swiss Federal Tribunal did not enter into the merits of the appeal holding that Mr. Valverde had no legally protected interest in the annulment of the decision (decision 4A_420/2010). On the same day, the court rejected the challenge of the award (decision 4A_386/2010). In its decisions, the Federal Tribunal addressed a number of issues of interest. The most interesting concerns the constitution of the CAS tribunal and the principle of *ne bis in idem*.

Mr. Valverde had argued that his right to a correct constitution of the tribunal was violated when the arbitrator appointed by Mr. Valverde resigned before the award was rendered and without participating in the deliberations relating to the award. The Swiss Federal Tribunal admitted that this could have been a problem if the arbitrator had indeed formally resigned. In such a case, Swiss case law provides that, unless the parties agree otherwise, the proceedings cannot continue under a "truncated tribunal," even if the resignation of the arbitrator is unjustified. However, in the present case, the Swiss Federal Tribunal held that the arbitrator had not formally resigned, since his offer to resign was refused and he had not opposed that refusal. The

Swiss Federal Tribunal also held that there was no evidence that the arbitrator had not participated in the deliberations of the award, and that, in any event, the recalcitrant arbitrator who refuses to collaborate or obstructs the proceedings, in particular by abstaining, without valid reason (or formal resignation), from participation in the deliberations of the tribunal, cannot block the panel when a majority of its members decide to continue the proceedings and issue an award.

Mr. Valverde had claimed that the principle of *ne bis in idem* had been violated because he had been punished twice for the same offense, namely once by the CONI in the Italian proceedings and then again in the proceedings under discussion. Mr. Valverde therefore requested the Swiss Federal Tribunal to set aside the award on the basis of a violation of public policy. The Swiss Federal Tribunal held, for the first time, that not only the principle of *res judicata*, but also its corollary or negative aspect, namely the principle of *ne bis in idem*, are part of Swiss procedural public policy. However, the Federal Tribunal left open the questions whether the principle of *ne bis in idem* is part of procedural or substantive public policy, and whether sports disciplinary law should be subject to the principle of *ne bis in idem*. It simply noted that the CAS itself had found that the principle should apply in the present case, at least by analogy, in view of the severity of the disciplinary sanction imposed on Mr. Valverde. This gave the Swiss Federal Tribunal the power to decide how this principle had been applied *in concreto*.

In this respect, the Swiss Federal Tribunal held that the application of the principle *ne bis in idem* supposes that the protected interests are identical (identity of object). By contrast, according to the Swiss Federal Tribunal, the prohibition of double prosecution does not prevent trying the same person twice when the same behavior may have consequences that are not only criminal, but also civil, administrative or disciplinary. In

Mr. Valverde's case, the Swiss Federal Tribunal found that there was no identity of object. The suspension ordered in the Italian proceedings by CONI was essentially a preventive measure applicable to anyone (athlete or not, affiliated to the Italian Federation or not) aiming at ensuring that sport competitions on Italian territory are not distorted by the involvement of persons convicted of violating Anti-Doping Rules. By contrast, the suspension imposed on Mr. Valverde by the CAS award of 31 May 2010 had essentially a punitive character, to the extent that its purpose was to issue a worldwide sanction against a professional athlete.

B.2 Challenge against Refusal to Render an Additional Award and Power to Award Interest

In a decision dated 7 January 2011,[14] the Swiss Federal Tribunal confirmed, for the first time, that an arbitral tribunal's decision refusing to render an additional award can be challenged. It also clarified that, under certain conditions, an arbitral tribunal may award interest even if the parties do not raise this issue in their request for relief.

The decision concerns an arbitration administered by the WIPO. A sole arbitrator awarded interest on damages to a party although the latter had not claimed interest in its request for relief. The sole arbitrator thereafter rejected a party's request that the arbitrator render an additional award. Both the award and the refusal to render an additional award were challenged before the Swiss Federal Tribunal.

The Swiss Federal Tribunal held, first, that the rejection of a request for an additional award can be appealed, like a decision from an arbitral tribunal refusing rectification of an award. The

---

[14] ATF 137 III 85.

Federal Tribunal took the opportunity to confirm that proceedings seeking an additional award and appeal proceedings against a final award should not interfere with each other. The Federal Tribunal also confirmed that the filing of a request for an additional award shall not stay the time limit to challenge the initial award. Similarly, the right of appeal should not be subject to the prior submission of such a request. Conversely, a party is entitled to simultaneously challenge an award and seek an additional award that could render the appeal moot; in such a case, the appeal proceedings should be stayed until the arbitral tribunal's decision concerning the additional award has been rendered.

On the merits, the Swiss Federal Tribunal held that the sole arbitrator had not decided *ultra petita* by awarding interest to a party that had not made a specific request for relief in this respect. The Federal Tribunal explained that the party had manifested in its submission, albeit not expressly but at least in an easily recognizable implicit manner, that it intended to claim late payment interest from the opposing party on the amounts it would be awarded, if any. In addition, in its request for relief, the party had sought payment of royalties calculated "at a minimum" of EUR 1.4 million, without putting a cap on its claim. This justified that its case be treated differently from a case in which the payment of fixed amounts was sought and in which the issue of interest had not been raised. In these cases, the sole arbitrator could not order the creditor to pay interest *ex officio* without deciding *ultra petita*. Under the facts of this case, however, the principle *jura novit curia* allowed the arbitrators to apply the law *ex officio*, without being limited to the arguments advanced by the parties.

B.3 Legitimate Interest in Challenging an Award

In a decision of 11 April 2011,[15] the Swiss Federal Tribunal confirmed that a party may continue to have a legitimate interest in challenging an award even if it pays the amount ordered by the award.

The case involved a dispute between a French football coach, Luis Fernandez, and Fédération Internationale de Football Association ("FIFA"). Mr. Fernandez terminated his employment contract with a Qatari club by mutual consent in order to join an Israeli club. He undertook to pay the club the amount of EUR 400,000 in this respect. Upon instructions received by Mr. Fernandez from a Curacao company, the funds were transferred to a bank account in Geneva in the name of the Curacao company by a company incorporated in the Seychelles. The Qatari club claimed that it had not received the funds and sued Mr. Fernandez before FIFA, which found that the payment had not been proven and ordered Mr. Fernandez to pay the sums due. Mr. Fernandez appealed this decision before the CAS but the case was struck off the record because the advances on costs were not all paid.

Later on, the Qatari club requested FIFA to open disciplinary proceedings against Mr. Fernandez on the grounds that he still had not transferred the funds he had been ordered to pay. FIFA gave Mr. Fernandez a final 60-day time limit to settle his debt, under penalty of an automatic suspension from any football-related activity. Mr. Fernandez appealed this second decision before the CAS and filed a criminal complaint in Geneva against the owner of the Israeli club for embezzlement and/or fraud, but the CAS eventually rejected the appeal. Mr. Fernandez challenged the CAS award before the Swiss Federal Tribunal. In

---

[15]   Decision 4A_604/2010.

the meantime, he settled his alleged debt with the Qatari club in order to avoid being suspended from any football-related activity as FIFA threatened.

The Swiss Federal Tribunal held that, in principle, Mr. Fernandez no longer had an actual interest in the annulment of the award because he no longer risked a suspension and because he could not obtain the reimbursement of the funds paid to the Qatari club even if the award was annulled. However, it considered that it could not exclude any remaining interest of Mr. Fernandez in the annulment of the award: on the one hand, Mr. Fernandez could argue a violation of his rights, if not on the merits, at least as to the issue of costs; on the other hand, if Mr. Fernandez was successful, he could consider a claim against FIFA, either because FIFA's decision forced him to pay twice, or because the suspension from the date of the award to the date Mr. Fernandez settled the alleged debt resulted in financial or moral damages for him. For these reasons, the Swiss Federal Tribunal allowed the challenge but eventually dismissed it on its merits.

B.4 Extension of an Arbitration Clause to a Third Party Where a Contract is in Favor of That Third Party

In a decision of 19 April 2011,[16] the Swiss Federal Tribunal clarified the rules that govern the extension of an arbitration clause to a third party, in particular where a contract exists in favor of a third party.

The case concerned a long-lasting dispute between the members of a family active in private banking and asset management. Family members entered into two agreements aiming at separating the interests of the two elder brothers. The

---

[16]   Decision 4A_44/2011

contemplated plan was quite complex, and implied numerous steps, which were carried out in part, until one of the brother's sons was excluded from the bank and stopped collaborating in the implementation of the agreements by, *inter alia*, refusing to bring shares into a third company as contemplated.

The other members of the family and the above-mentioned company initiated arbitration proceedings with the Geneva Chamber of Commerce as provided for in the agreements, essentially seeking to compel the respondent to bring the contemplated shares into the company. In its final award, the arbitral tribunal found that it had jurisdiction as to the company and that the respondent was bound to the agreements and was not entitled to terminate them unilaterally. The tribunal hence ordered the respondent to bring the contemplated shares into the company.

The respondent challenged the award before the Swiss Federal Tribunal, arguing that the arbitral tribunal was wrong in assuming jurisdiction as to the company into which he had to bring the shares. After admitting that the respondent had a legally protected interest in the annulment of the award because the participation of the company in the arbitral proceedings had had serious consequences, the Swiss Federal Tribunal upheld the arbitral tribunal's jurisdiction as to the company even though the latter was not a party to the contract containing the arbitration clause.

According to the Swiss Federal Tribunal, even if an arbitration clause contained in a contract binds only the parties to the contract, in a number of situations the arbitration clause may exceptionally bind third parties that have not signed the contract and are not mentioned in it. This is the case, for instance, when a claim or the whole contract is assigned or when a third party is involved in the performance of the contract, but not when a third party merely guarantees a party's obligation.

The Swiss Federal Tribunal noted that there is a dispute among Swiss scholars about whether a third-party beneficiary of a contract is bound by an arbitration agreement to which she is not a party. Some scholars hold that the arbitration clause binds the third-party beneficiary *ipso iure*, at the very least when the latter accepts the rights stipulated in its favor; others consider that the beneficiary has to consent to the dispute being submitted to arbitration. Unfortunately, the Swiss Federal Tribunal did not clarify this issue and simply noted that, in the case at hand, the third-party beneficiary itself had taken the initiative to join the other claimants in the arbitration. The Federal Tribunal held that, under those circumstances, the beneficiary of a contract in favor of a third party normally acquires a claim against the debtor with all preference and accessory rights connected thereto, including the arbitration agreement; if it intends to use such rights in arbitral proceedings, the other parties cannot prevent it from doing so.

B.5 Multi-Tier Dispute Resolution Clauses

In a decision of 16 May 2011,[17] the Swiss Federal Tribunal annulled an award rendered by an *ad hoc* tribunal for violation of the parties' right to be heard. The Swiss Federal Tribunal seized this opportunity to confirm benchmarks on multi-tier dispute resolution clauses.

The dispute concerned the delivery of an industrial production line. The contract provided that, in case of a dispute concerning the conformity of supplies and services, the buyer and the supplier had to appoint a neutral expert before submitting the dispute to an arbitral tribunal. It also provided that, in case of a dispute concerning the interpretation or performance of the contract, the parties would first seek to find an amicable

---

[17] Decision 4A_46/2011.

settlement. If the conciliation attempt failed, the dispute would be submitted to an *ad hoc* arbitral tribunal.

The buyer initiated arbitration proceedings for alleged defects in the production line. The supplier objected and argued that the request could not be accepted because the buyer had not complied with the pre-arbitral requirements contained in the contract: no expert had been appointed and there had been no attempt to settle the dispute through conciliation. The arbitral tribunal rejected the supplier's objections at a hearing and confirmed this decision in the final award in which it partially upheld the buyer's claim.

The supplier challenged the award before the Swiss Federal Tribunal, claiming, *inter alia,* that the tribunal should have rejected its jurisdiction for non-compliance with the pre-arbitral requirements. The Swiss Federal Tribunal rejected this argument. It noted that the issue of sanctions resulting from non-compliance with mandatory pre-arbitral requirements is unsettled, but that the majority of Swiss scholars seem to favor staying the proceedings and setting a deadline to repair the omission, rather than rejecting jurisdiction. The Swiss Federal Tribunal refrained from deciding this controversial issue in the case, holding instead that (i) the preliminary appointment of an expert was not necessary because he would have had to decide technical rather than legal issues, (ii) the conciliatory attempt did not seem to be mandatory according to the text of the clause, and (iii) in any event, an unsuccessful meeting had actually taken place between the parties' representatives.

On the merits, the Swiss Federal Tribunal upheld the challenge because the arbitral tribunal had failed to address the statute of limitation objection raised by the supplier and had, thus, violated the supplier's right to be heard.

C. PUBLIC POLICY IN INTERNATIONAL ARBITRATION

C.1 Scenarios of Reliance on Public Policy

Under Swiss law, there are essentially two scenarios in which public policy violations can become relevant in international arbitration proceedings.

First, in arbitral proceedings governed by Swiss law, the violation of public policy constitutes a ground for appeal pursuant to Article 190(2)(e) IPRG. As such, it can lead to the annulment of an award rendered by a Swiss arbitral tribunal. The success rate for this particular ground for appeal is, however, very small; in fact, since the entry into force of the IPRG in 1989, it has been admitted in only a single case.[18]

Second, the violation of public policy may be raised as a defense against the recognition and enforcement of foreign arbitral awards in Switzerland. Pursuant to Article 194 IPRG, the recognition and enforcement of foreign awards in Switzerland is governed by the New York Convention, including in relation to non-contracting states.[19] At this level, the relevance of potential public policy violations is always analyzed in accordance with Article V(2)(b) of the New York Convention.[20]

---

[18] ATF 136 III 345, concerning a violation of the *res judicata* principle.

[19] That is, unless multilateral or bilateral agreements provide for more favorable conditions (*cf.* Article VII(1) New York Convention). In particular, ICSID awards must be enforced in the same ways as decisions by municipal courts, i.e., irrespective of any potential public policy violations, *cf.* Article 54 ICSID Convention.

[20] As Swiss case law rendered on the basis of Article 194 PILA is rather limited, reference is sometimes still made to older cases in which enforcement proceedings in relation to non-contracting states of the New York Convention

By contrast, the validity of arbitration agreements is generally not discussed as a matter of public policy under Swiss law. If the arbitration agreement has illegal content, it may be unenforceable pursuant to the contract law by which it is governed (*cf.* Article 178(1) IPRG). However, illegality of the main contract containing the arbitration clause does not automatically render the arbitration agreement unenforceable, since the doctrine of separability is recognized in Swiss law (Article 178(3) IPRG). For example, while contracts concerning illegal commission payments are likely to be invalid or voidable, depending on the applicable law, arbitration clauses contained in such contracts are generally enforceable.

C.2 Modes and Limitations of Reliance on Public Policy

In international arbitration proceedings governed by Swiss law, annulment requests against arbitral awards are handled solely by the Swiss Federal Tribunal, to the exclusion of any cantonal courts. To obtain the annulment of a Swiss arbitral award allegedly violating public policy, an appeal with the Federal Tribunal must be lodged within 30 days following the notification of the award (Article 191 IPRG; Article 77 of the Federal Supreme Court Act). The admissibility of the appeal does not, in principle, depend on whether the particular objection raised in the annulment proceeding was already discussed before the tribunal, but if a particular legal argument was not even mentioned before the tribunal, it is unlikely that the appellant will be able to present it as crucial in the annulment proceedings.

In enforcement proceedings, public policy violations must be considered *ex officio* pursuant to Article V(2)(b) of the New York Convention. However, under Swiss law, enforcement

---

were commenced based on other treaties, such as the Geneva Convention on the Execution of Foreign Arbitral Awards of 1927.

proceedings for the payment of money can be initiated simply by filing a debt enforcement request with an administrative office at the debtor's domicile. This office does not verify the substance of the claim, but simply notifies the debtor who can informally object to the enforcement proceedings simply by signing the debt enforcement form addressed to him. In a second step, the award creditor may commence summary court proceedings to obtain a court decision allowing him to proceed with the enforcement of the claim. These proceedings take place before the first instance court at the debtor's domicile, and it is in this context that legal obstacles to enforcement, including potential public policy violations pursuant to Article V(2)(b) of the New York Convention, are examined.

Generally Swiss courts do not recognize or enforce foreign awards vacated in the country of origin, regardless of the particular grounds that led to their annulment (Article V(1)(e) New York Convention).

C.3 Rules that Constitute "Public Policy"

There is no single concept of public policy under Swiss law. Apart from constituting a ground for the annulment of Swiss arbitral awards or for the non-enforcement of foreign awards, public policy considerations may lead courts (and arguably also arbitral tribunals) to exceptionally apply (Article 19 IPRG) or disregard (Article 17 IPRG) particular rules of foreign law in departure from the otherwise applicable conflict of law principles. In addition, public policy violations may also render foreign court decisions unenforceable pursuant to Article 27(1) IPRG and Article 34(1) of the Lugano Convention.

In the context of international arbitration proceedings, Swiss courts apply a very narrow concept of public policy. Annulment requests based on alleged violations of public policy are successful only if the result reached by the arbitral tribunal is evidently incompatible with those basic values and legal principles that should, from a Swiss perspective, enjoy universal recognition in jurisdictions following due process standards.[21] As explained by the Swiss Federal Tribunal, this notion of public policy is "Swiss" in terms of legal basis, but "transnational" in terms of content and function.[22]

In enforcement proceedings, the Swiss aspects tend to be emphasized somewhat more strongly, as the issue is not about exporting a Swiss award, but rather about allowing a Swiss or foreign award to be executed in Switzerland.[23] In practice, however, it is difficult to discern concrete differences in the standards applied under Article 190(2)(e) of the IPRG and under Article V(2)(b) of the New York Convention, if only because case law concerning Article V(2)(b) of the New York Convention is rather scarce.

As a matter of principle, public policy violations can relate both to the application of substantive legal rules and to those procedural guarantees that are not covered by specific grounds for annulment or non-enforcement, as is particularly the case for the right to be heard (*cf.* Article 190(2)(d) IPRG and Article V(1)(b) New York Convention).[24] Concretely, the concept of public policy is generally considered to comprise the following principles:

---

[21]   ATF 136 III 345, ¶ 2.1; ATF 132 389, ¶ 2.2.1; ATF 120 II 155, ¶ 6.

[22]   ATF 120 II 155, ¶ 6 a).

[23]   Swiss Federal Supreme Court, 8 December 2003, 4P_173/2003, ¶ 4.1.

[24]   *Cf.* ATF 93 I 49, ¶ 4 concerning the enforcement of an award rendered under the rules of a cotton trade association. The award was enforced in Switzerland, as there was no evidence that the arbitrators were lacking independence.

- the principle of *pacta sunt servanda*,

- the principle of good faith and the prohibition of abuse of right,

- the prohibition of discriminatory measures,

- the protection of minors and other individuals lacking capacity to act,

- the principle of *res judicata*,[25]

- basic fundamental rights, such as the prohibition of forced labor,[26]

- the principle of *ne bis in idem*,[27] and

- the principle of good faith pursuant to Article 2 of the Swiss Civil Code.[28]

Most, if not all, of the principles in this list are not directly applicable, but instead serve as the basis and justification for a number of legal rules and concepts in a broad range of situations. This is most evident with regard to the principle of good faith, from which concepts such as estoppel (*venire contra factum proprium*) or the prohibition of abuse of rights are derived. Likewise, neither the principle of *pacta sunt servanda* nor the prohibition of discriminatory measures provides definitive guidance as to how a particular fact scenario should be assessed. They require instead consideration of a number of case-specific factors, ranging, for example, from the question of the parties' actual obligations to the analysis of potential defenses. In

---

[25] ATF 136 III 345.

[26] Swiss Federal Supreme Court, 4A_320/2009; 4A_458/2009.

[27] Swiss Federal Supreme Court, 4A_386/2010.

[28] Swiss Federal Supreme Court, 4A_579/2010.

practice, it is very difficult to establish a public policy violation based on one of these broad principles. This is particularly so because their application typically leaves considerable room for discretion, making it less likely that the result reached by an arbitral tribunal will be deemed utterly unacceptable, as is required for the award to be annulled or to be denied enforcement.

Further, Swiss Federal Tribunal case law considers various core rules and principles to be crucial in domestic cases, but not part of public policy for purposes of international arbitration proceedings. This is the case, for example, in competition law rules: in a 2006 case involving an agreement allegedly made in breach of European competition law, the Swiss Federal Tribunal held that because of the differences in how the various jurisdictions approach the economics of this subject, competition law rules cannot be considered part of public policy for purposes of Article 190(2)(e) IPRG.[29] In so deciding, the court adopted a narrower understanding than the European Court of Justice in the "Eco Swiss" case, according to which the basic provisions of European competition law form part of public policy for arbitration proceedings taking place in EU Member States.[30] Importantly, the 2006 ruling of the Swiss Federal Tribunal does not prevent Swiss arbitral tribunals from applying domestic or foreign competition law rules to the extent they are relevant for resolving the dispute;[31] rather, the ruling only means that errors made in the application of such rules cannot be reviewed in annulment proceedings, just as the application of other legal rules is also not reviewed by the Swiss Federal Tribunal, unless they have a public policy character.

---

[29]   ATF 132 III 389, ¶ 3.2.

[30]   European Court of Justice, 1 June 1999, Case C-126/97.

[31]   *Cf.* ATF 118 II 193, ¶ 5, and *obiter* in ATF 132 III 393, ¶ 3.3.

Swiss courts have held that neither the failure to include reasons in an arbitral award, nor the existence of inherent contradictions in an award, is sufficient, in itself, to obtain annulment of the award, even though these grounds might suffice in an appeal against a domestic court decision.[32] The same applies to errors made in relation to the allocation of the burden of proof[33] or in the determination of the applicable law,[34] as well as in relation to the failure by a foreign tribunal to provide proper guidance regarding appeals.[35] Furthermore, an award cannot be annulled or denied enforcement for the sole reason that one party has been awarded punitive damages.[36]

C.4 Review of Alleged Breaches of Public Policy

In annulment proceedings pursuant to Article 190 IPRG, the appellant must expressly invoke the grounds for annulment on which he intends to rely and specifically explain how the tribunal violated public policy. In enforcement proceedings, public policy violations are in principle examined *ex officio* by the competent court pursuant to Article V(2)(b) of the New York Convention. Yet, this does not mean that the court will, of its own initiative, investigate whether the award is incompatible with public policy requirements, if this is not immediately evident.[37] Furthermore, if enforcement is granted, and the matter is appealed to the Swiss

---

[32] ATF 116 II 373, ¶ 7; Swiss Federal Supreme Court, 4A_464/2009, ¶ 5.1.

[33] Swiss Federal Supreme Court, 4A_524/2009, ¶ 5.2.3.

[34] Swiss Federal Supreme Court, 4A_444/2009, ¶ 5.1.

[35] *Cf.* ATF 101 Ia 154, ¶ 3.

[36] *Cf.* Berger/Kellerhals, Internationale und interne Schiedsgerichtsbarkeit in der Schweiz, Berne 2006, ¶ 1604, with further references; Swiss Federal Supreme Court, 4A_320/2009, ¶ 4.5.

[37] Cf. ATF 130 III 125, ¶ 2, noting that obstacles to enforcement must in principle be raised by the debtor.

Federal Tribunal, alleged public policy violations must be raised with the same degree of specificity as in annulment proceedings pursuant to Article 190(2)(e) IPRG.[38]

In reviewing alleged public policy violations, Swiss courts exercise great restraint. This is particularly evident in annulment proceedings, where the focus of the inquiry is on the result reached by the arbitral tribunal, rather than on the underlying legal reasoning. To obtain annulment of the award, the particular public policy violation criticized by one of the parties must be directly relevant to the outcome of the case, as reflected in the tribunal's orders.[39] In this regard, the public policy concept applied by the Swiss Federal Tribunal is clearly narrower than alternative concepts of "arbitrariness" or "manifest disregard of law," which purport to rectify evident mistakes in the application of the relevant legal rules. In line with this narrow approach, the Swiss Federal Tribunal generally pays deference to the arbitral tribunal's assessment of the facts of the case (no *révision au fond*). Thus, while an award ordering a party to pay illegal bribes is considered a violation of public policy, the Swiss Federal Tribunal will not review whether the evidence concerning potential bribes was properly assessed by the arbitral tribunal.[40] With regard to legal questions, a limited review of the legal analysis conducted by the arbitral tribunal is generally unavoidable in determining whether the result reached is acceptable. To conclude that the *res judicata* principle had been violated by an arbitral tribunal, for example, the Swiss Federal Tribunal had to analyze whether the earlier decision, which had been disregarded by the arbitral tribunal, was in fact susceptible of enjoying *res judicata* effects, and whether the two

---

[38]　*Cf.* Swiss Federal Supreme Court, 4P_173/2003, ¶ 1.2.

[39]　*Cf.* ATF 121 III 331, para. 3; 116 II 634, ¶ 4.

[40]　*Cf.* ATF 119 II 380, ¶ 4b.

proceedings dealt with the same subject matter.[41] However, where issues such as the interpretation of a particular contract are disputed, the Swiss Federal Tribunal will rarely interfere with the tribunal's assessment.

In enforcement proceedings, the standard of review tends to be somewhat broader, in particular if the public policy violation is derived from an alleged failure of the arbitral tribunal to observe fundamental procedural guarantees.[42] However, in this context, too, the focus is on the consequences associated with the enforcement of the particular award, and not on the underlying reasoning.[43]

---

[41]   ATF 136 III 345, ¶ 2.2.

[42]   *See, e.g.*, Superior Court of Basle, 3 June 1971, BJM 1973, 193, where objections were raised with regard to deadlines fixed by the arbitral tribunal and with regard to the independence of the arbitrators.

[43]   *See* Swiss Federal Supreme Court, 8 December 2003, 4P_173/2003, ¶ 4.1; Superior Court of Basle, 3 June 1971, BJM 1973, 193, 200.

TAIWAN

Tiffany Huang[1] and Amber Hsu[2,3]

A. LEGISLATION, TRENDS AND TENDENCIES

A.1 Overview

The Commercial Arbitration Act of Taiwan was promulgated on 20 January 1961, amended on 11 June 1982 and 26 December 1986, and subsequently renamed as the Arbitration Law on 24 June 1998. Thereafter, the Arbitration Law was further amended on 10 July 2002 and 30 December 2009. The Arbitration Law, which contains eight chapters (namely, Arbitration Agreement, Constitution of Arbitral Tribunal, Arbitral Proceedings, Enforcement of Arbitral Awards, Revocation of Arbitral Awards, Settlement and Mediation, Foreign Awards, and Additional Provisions), embodies the fundamental principles of international arbitration. Pursuant to Article 1 of the Arbitration Law, arbitrable matters are not limited to commercial disputes and parties may enter into an arbitration agreement to arbitrate any disputes that may be resolved by settlement.

There are existing laws that provide for compulsory arbitration mechanisms, under which a party may refer a dispute to arbitration even if it has not entered into an arbitration agreement with the counterparty. For example, Article 166(1) of the Securities and Exchange Act provides that any disputes arising

---

[1] Tiffany Huang is a Partner and head of the Insurance Practice and Energy & Environment & Infrastructure Groups of Baker & McKenzie's Taipei office.

[2] Amber Hsu is a Senior Associate of the Construction Group at Baker & McKenzie's Taipei office.

[3] The authors would like to thank Annie Huang (also of the Taipei office) for her assistance in preparing this report.

between the stock exchange and securities firms, or between securities firms themselves, shall be resolved by arbitration even in the absence of an executed arbitration agreement. If a party to a dispute files a legal action in violation of this provision, the other party may petition the court to dismiss the action as provided for under Article 167.

Article 85-1 of the Government Procurement Law, which took effect on 6 February 2002, also provides for arbitration as an alternative dispute resolution mechanism. This provision gives contractors under procurement of construction work from government agencies the right to arbitrate disputes when mediation fails if the relevant government agencies do not agree with the proposal or with the resolution for mediation proposed by the Complaint Review Board for Government Procurement. The construction industry, however, lobbied against this mechanism, finding it far from satisfactory. Accordingly, some legislators have proposed an amendment to Article 27 of the Construction Industry Act, providing that under certain circumstances, contractors are entitled to arbitrate disputes against government agencies. The bill was not passed because there was concern that such a compulsory arbitration system would deprive the government agencies of their right to refer to litigation, which is protected under Article 16 of the Constitution of the Republic of China (Taiwan).

A.2 Arbitration Associations

There are four arbitration associations registered with the Ministry of the Interior of Taiwan: (1) the Arbitration Association of the Republic of China[4] (the "CAA"), (2) the Taiwan Construction Arbitration Association (the "TCAA"), (3) the Chinese Construction Industry Arbitration Association (the

---

[4] "Republic of China" is the formal country name of Taiwan.

"CCIAA"), and (4) the Labor Dispute Arbitration Association of the Republic of China (the "CLDAA").

The CAA is the oldest and the most active arbitration association in Taiwan. It administers different disputes, ranging from construction, maritime, securities, international trade, intellectual property rights, insurance, cross-strait disputes, information technology, and the like. Disputes involving construction and infrastructure projects represent a substantial percentage of the total cases administered under the auspices of the CAA. The CAA currently does not administer arbitration proceedings under the rules of foreign arbitration institutions.

The TCAA and the CCIAA focus primarily on the administration of arbitrations of disputes concerning various construction projects. Compared to the CAA, these two associations are relatively small in terms of the number of arbitration cases administered.

A.3   Recent Developments across the Taiwan Strait

Due to political sensitivity between Taiwan and the People's Republic of China (the "PRC"), the Act Governing Relations Between the People of Taiwan Area and the Mainland Area (the "Relations Act") came into effect in 1992. The PRC is referred to in the Relations Act as the Mainland Area, and PRC arbitral awards may be recognized and enforceable in Taiwan, provided that: (a) the PRC arbitral award is not contrary to the public order or good morals of Taiwan, and (b) an arbitral award made in Taiwan will be recognized and enforceable in the PRC on a reciprocal basis.[5]

The Act Governing Relations with Hong Kong and Macau, promulgated in 1997, stipulates that the Arbitration Law shall

---

[5]   Article 74 of the Relations Act.

apply, *mutatis mutandis*, to the validity, petition for court recognition, and suspension of compulsory execution proceedings for arbitral awards made in Hong Kong or Macau.[6] Since the promulgation of this Act, Taiwan courts have recognized a number of arbitral awards made in Hong Kong,[7] but there were also cases where Taiwan courts dismissed the petition to recognize arbitral awards because of a defect in service of notice.[8]

After the Relations Act was enacted, the PRC issued a rule in 1998, stipulating to the recognition and enforcement of Taiwan arbitral awards in the PRC. According to relevant court cases, an arbitral award made by CIETAC – South China Sub-Commission was recognized in Taiwan.[9] Nevertheless, a Taiwan court refused to recognize one arbitral award made by CIETAC Shanghai Commission on the basis of inadequate service of notice.[10]

On 29 June 2010, Taiwan and the PRC concluded the Economic Cooperation Framework Agreement (the "ECFA"). Under the ECFA framework, Taiwan and the PRC agreed, among other things, to commence comprehensive negotiations on several critical issues, including dispute resolution procedures, within six months after the ECFA became effective. However, so far, Taiwan and PRC have not reached a consensus on the dispute resolution mechanism. It has been reported that Taiwan prefers using international arbitration to resolve investment disputes with the government, while the PRC favors compulsory mediation.

---

[6] Article 42(2) of the Act Governing Relations with Hong Kong and Macau.

[7] *See, e.g.*, Taiwan Taipei District Court, Ruling 87-Chung-Sheng-Tze No. 4 (30 November 1998).

[8] *See, e.g.*, Taiwan High Court, Kaohsiung Branch Court, Ruling 89-Zai-Tze No. 76 (30 January 2001).

[9] Taiwan Taoyuan District Court, Ruling 97-Chung-Jen-Tze No. 1 (31 July 2009).

[10] Taiwan Taipei District Court, Rulings 95-Kung-Tze No. 71 (28 July 2006) and 93-Chung-Sheng-Tze No. 15 (6 December 2005).

B.   CASES

B.1   Definition of a Valid and Effective Arbitration Agreement

Under the Arbitration Law, an arbitration agreement must be in writing.[11] An oral agreement between the parties will not suffice. An agreement to arbitrate reached by way of an exchange of fax messages, telegrams, letters or any other similar means can be treated as an arbitration agreement in writing.[12]

The parties may determine the rules governing the arbitral proceedings, the place of arbitration and the language of arbitration. The Arbitration Law empowers the arbitral tribunal to rule on its own jurisdiction and competence, on the existence or validity of the arbitration agreement, and on irregularities in the proceedings.[13]

The Arbitration Law expressly stipulates that the validity of an arbitration clause that forms part of a principal contract may be determined separately from the rest of the contract. An arbitration clause continues in force and effect after the contract is rendered null, void, revoked, rescinded or terminated, in accordance with the principle of severability.[14]

If one of the parties to an arbitration agreement commences a legal action in contravention of the arbitration agreement, the court shall, upon application by the adverse party, stay the legal proceedings and order the plaintiff to submit the dispute to arbitration within a specified time period, unless the defendant

---

[11]   Article 1(3) of the Arbitration Law.

[12]   Article 1(4) of the Arbitration Law.

[13]   Articles 22 and 30 of the Arbitration Law.

[14]   Article 3 of the Arbitration Law.

proceeds to respond to the legal action.[15] The civil section of the Taiwan Supreme Court passed a resolution on 13 May 2003, ruling that even if an arbitration clause requires the arbitration venue to be outside the territory of Taiwan, the defendant will be entitled to raise this procedural objection.

An arbitral award can be annulled if there is no effective arbitration agreement between the parties. In some countries, if an arbitration clause provides an option to arbitrate or litigate, such clause is ineffective, meaning an effective clause must refer to arbitration as the sole dispute resolution method of first recourse.

The Taiwan Supreme Court, however, opined that where the parties had agreed that the dispute be resolved by either arbitration or litigation, the agreement would grant an option to the parties to choose between the two methods.[16] In addition, as soon as one party chooses one method over the other, the other party must be bound by this choice. Consequently, after a party initiates litigation, the respondent may not raise a procedural objection that the dispute must be resolved by arbitration,[17] and vice versa.

Taiwan courts have ruled that where an arbitration clause is silent on matters such as the arbitral institution, the governing substantive law or the place of arbitration, it is still an effective and enforceable arbitration agreement.[18] Where an arbitration

---

[15]   Article 4 of the Arbitration Law.

[16]   Taiwan Supreme Court, Judgment 96-Tai-Shang-Tze No. 1491 (5 July 2007) and Ruling 96-Tai-Shang-Tze No. 2246 (11 June 2007).

[17]   Article 4 of the Arbitration Law.

[18]   Taiwan Supreme Court, Judgment 93-Tai-Shang-Tze No. 2008 (30 September 2004) and Ruling 87-Tai-Kang-Tze No. 324 (12 June 1998), Taiwan High Court, Rulings 86-Kang-Tze No. 1183 (26 May 1997) and 73-Kang-Tze No. 1798.

clause provides that the dispute shall be determined by arbitration administered by an international arbitral institution that in fact does not exist, such clause is still effective on the basis that the parties only failed to reach agreement on arbitration rules and procedures.[19] After one party has referred the dispute to arbitration, it may then invoke the Arbitration Law to fill in the missing parts of the clause.

B.2 *Ad hoc* Arbitration

Another issue is whether an *ad hoc* arbitration award has the same legal force and effect as an institutional award. Some Taiwan courts appear to question the effect and enforceability of the non-administered award.[20] In its decision, 99-Fei-Kang-Tze No. 122 (15 September 2010), the Taiwan High Court approved the Taipei District Court's Ruling 99-Kang-Tze No.63 (2 July 2010), which held that the *ad hoc* arbitral award was not enforceable, and opined that the *ad hoc* arbitral tribunal was not an arbitration institution established under Article 54 of the Arbitration Law, so an *ad hoc* arbitral award did not have the same effect as that of a final court judgment, and was therefore not enforceable. However, after the respondent filed a complaint to revoke the *ad hoc* arbitral award, the Taiwan courts were silent on whether the *ad hoc* nature of the award constituted grounds for revocation.[21]

---

[19] *See, e.g.*, Taiwan Taipei District Court, Judgment 88-Chung-Sue-Tze No. 8 (9 May 2000).

[20] Taiwan Supreme Court, Judgment 94-Tai-Shang-Tze No. 433 (10 March 2005), and Ruling 90-Tai-Kang-Tze No. 213 (27 April 2001).

[21] Taiwan Taipei District Court, Judgment 98-Chung-Sue-Tze No. 7 (5 March 2010), Taiwan High Court, Judgment 99-Chung-Shang-Tze No. 700 (26 April 2011) and Taiwan Supreme Court, Judgment 100-Tai-Shang-Tze No. 1875 (27 October 2011).

On the other hand, some opinions hold that the Arbitration Law allows for both institutional arbitration and *ad hoc* arbitration. This was the case, for instance, in the ruling of the Ministry of Justice, Executive Yuan, dated 9 October 2007 with Reference No. Fa-Lu-Tze 0960038134. Also, the Executive Yuan and the Judicial Yuan jointly promulgated the Rules on Arbitration Institution, Mediation Procedures and Fees, under which Article 38 provides that the fees of an arbitration, which are not handled by an arbitration institution, may be collected, *mutatis mutandis*, in accordance with those rules. This suggests that an *ad hoc* arbitration shall be acceptable under the Arbitration Law.

B.3 Appointment of Arbitrators by the Court or Arbitration Association

Parties to a dispute may appoint a single arbitrator or an odd number of arbitrators to constitute an arbitral tribunal.[22] If the parties do not have an agreement on who shall be appointed and the method of such appointment, the tribunal will be composed of three arbitrators, with one arbitrator appointed by each party and the appointed arbitrators jointly designating a third arbitrator as chairman of the arbitral tribunal. The arbitral tribunal shall notify the parties, in writing, of the final appointment.[23]

If the arbitrators appointed by the parties fail to agree on a chair within thirty (30) days of their appointment, the final appointment shall be made by a court upon application by either party; however, if the parties have agreed that the arbitration shall be administered by an arbitration institution, the third arbitrator shall be appointed by that arbitration institution.[24]

---

[22] Article 1(1) of the Arbitration Law.

[23] Article 9(1) of the Arbitration Law.

[24] Paragraphs 2 and 4 of Article 9 of the Arbitration Law.

Despite this rule, there is one reported case where the court held that if the parties merely agreed to refer a dispute to an arbitration institution without expressly empowering that arbitration institution to appoint the third arbitrator, only the court could make the appointment.[25]

B.4 Challenge and Withdrawal of Arbitrators

According to Article 16(1) of the Arbitration Law, a party may challenge an arbitrator if:

(a) there is a cause requiring a judge to withdraw from a judicial proceeding in accordance with Article 32 of the Code of Civil Procedure;

(b) there is or was an employment or agency relationship between the arbitrator and a party;

(c) there is or was an employment or agency relationship between the arbitrator and an agent of a party or between the arbitrator and a key witness;

(d) there are other circumstances that raise justifiable doubts as to the impartiality or independence of the arbitrator; and

(e) the arbitrator does not meet the parties' qualifications.

If a challenge of an arbitrator is accepted, such arbitrator shall withdraw. The arbitral tribunal shall decide on the admissibility and the merits of a challenge, but there have been many cases where the Taiwan courts held that the arbitrator being challenged should not be involved, and a new arbitrator should be appointed so that he/she together with the arbitrators who are not challenged would form another tribunal to decide on the

---

[25] Taiwan Shihlin District Court, Ruling 90-Chung-Sheng-Tze No. 1 (29 March 2002).

challenge.[26] A party may apply to the court for a judicial ruling within fourteen days of receiving the tribunal's decision, but a party shall not challenge the ruling of the court. In a case where the tribunal is constituted by a sole arbitrator, the court will decide on the challenge.

If an arbitrator breaches the provisions of the Code of Ethics for Arbitrators of the CAA, the Ethics Committee of the CAA may:

(a) advise the arbitrator to make corrections;

(b) suspend the arbitrator from acting as an arbitrator of the CAA for six months to three years;

(c) prohibit the arbitrator from acting as an arbitrator of the CAA and cancel his/her registration; or

(d) demand that the arbitrator withdraw from the case if a party files a complaint on the arbitrator's breach of the Code.[27]

B.5 Notification of an Intervention in the Arbitration

In civil proceedings, a third person who is legally interested in an action between the parties may, for the purpose of supporting a specific party, intervene in the action. Alternatively, either party may notify a third party to intervene in the proceeding. After intervening in the proceedings or being duly notified of the litigation, the third party shall not dispute the correctness of the decisions made in the action against the party who notified the third party of the litigation, except where the third party has been denied a means of attack or defense, either due to the progress of the litigation at the time of the intervention, or by an act of the

---

[26] Taiwan Supreme Court, Judgment 96-Tai-Shang-Tze No. 1845 (23 August 2007) and Taiwan Taipei District Court, Ruling 100-Chung-Shen-Tze No. 7 (19 July 2011).

[27] Article 26 of the Code of Ethics for Arbitrators of the CAA.

notifying party, or where the party who gives notification of the litigation has willfully, or through gross negligence, failed to employ certain means of attack or defense unknown to the third party.[28]

With respect to arbitration, the arbitral tribunal has the discretion to allow or disallow a third party to intervene or to be notified.[29] The Taiwan Supreme Court in Judgment 95-Tai-Shang-Tze No. 2277 (13 October 2006), held that where a third party voluntarily applied for intervention in an arbitration and was permitted by the arbitral tribunal to intervene, relevant articles of the Code of Civil Procedure should apply, *mutatis mutandis*, so that the third party would not be allowed to dispute the correctness of the arbitral award rendered against the assisted party.

Nevertheless, if the third party did not voluntarily apply for intervention, but was passively notified to intervene in the arbitration, it remains disputed whether that party would be obliged to intervene and whether it would will be barred from disputing the correctness of the arbitral award against the party who made the notification.

B.6 Time Limit for Rendering Arbitral Awards

According to Article 21 of the Arbitration Law, the arbitral tribunal shall render an arbitral award within six months of commencing the arbitration; provided that if the circumstances so require, the arbitral tribunal may extend the decision period for another three months. Such time limit shall start from the

---

[28] Articles 58, 63, 65 and 67 of the Code of Civil Procedure.

[29] Taiwan High Court, Judgment 97-Chung-Shang-Tze No. 497 (28 April 2009) and Taiwan High Court, Kaohsiung Branch Court, Judgment 95-Chung-Shang-Tze No. 64 (23 January 2008), approved by Supreme Court, Judgment 97-Tai-Shang-Tze No. 2094.

date the last arbitrator is notified of the appointment.[30] The arbitral tribunal shall still meet the time limit even where the respondent makes a counterclaim.[31]

If the arbitral tribunal fails to render and serve the arbitral award to the parties[32] within this time period, either party may refer the dispute to the court, unless this matter is also are required to be resolved by arbitration. In such case, the arbitral proceedings shall thereafter be deemed terminated.[33] Nevertheless, if neither party brings the dispute to the court, the arbitration agreement is still binding and effective, and the arbitral award shall not be revoked solely because the arbitral tribunal failed to meet the time limit.[34]

Any time period during which the arbitration cannot proceed (because the arbitrator has died, has resigned or is unable to perform his or her duty for some reason, or the parties agree to stay the procedure, or because of a *force majeure* or other unavoidable events preventing the arbitral tribunal from performing its duties) shall, however, be excluded from the calculation of the time limit.[35]

B.7 Enforceability of Arbitral Awards

Under Article 37 of the Arbitration Law, an arbitral award is binding on the parties and has the same force as a final judgment

---

[30] The ruling of the Ministry of Justice, Executive Yuan dated 6 May 2004 with reference No. Fa-Lu-Chueh-Tze 0930017621.

[31] *Ibid.*

[32] Taiwan Supreme Court, Ruling 93-Tai-Kung-Tze No. 798.

[33] Article 21(3) of the Arbitration Law.

[34] Taiwan Supreme Court, Judgments 81-Tai-Shang-Tze No. 2578 (6 November 1992) and 89-Tai-Shang-Tze No. 2677 (24 November 2000).

[35] Taiwan Supreme Court, Ruling 95-Tai-Kung-Tze No. 449 (20 July 2006).

of a court. However, an award may not be enforceable unless a competent court has, on application of a concerned party, granted an enforcement order. The court will only reject an application for enforcement under certain conditions, as set forth in Article 38 of the Arbitration Law. However, the court does not render a new judgment in respect of the matter in dispute. Whether the opinion of the arbitrators is proper and whether the award is proper in terms of substance are matters to be determined by the arbitrators at their sole discretion. The court will not review the substantive aspects of the arbitral award.

In principle, the court's enforcement order is required to enforce an arbitral award. By virtue of Article 38 of the Arbitration Law, however, a court shall not grant an enforcement order if:

(a) the arbitral award concerns a dispute not contemplated by the terms of the arbitration agreement, or exceeds the scope of the arbitration agreement, unless the inconsistent portion of the award may be severed and the severance will not affect the remainder of the award;

(b) no reasons are stated in the arbitral award (unless subsequently amended by the arbitral tribunal); or

(c) the arbitral award commands a party to do an act prohibited by law.

Either before or after the court grants an enforcement order,[36] a party who has petitioned the court for revocation of an arbitral award may apply to stay the enforcement of the arbitral award once the applicant has paid the court a suitable and certain security.[37]

---

[36]   Taiwan Supreme Court, Ruling 93-Tai-Kung-Tze No. 821 (28 October 2004).

[37]   Article 42(1) of the Arbitration Law.

In addition, after the compulsory execution proceedings commence and in case a party files an appeal against the enforcement order, the court may stay the compulsory execution if the court deems it necessary, or upon application with adequate security.[38]

B.8 Revocation of Arbitral Awards

A party may bring a lawsuit in the court for revocation of an arbitral award on the following grounds:[39]

(a) The circumstances stipulated in Article 38 of the Arbitration Law (see above) exist.

(b) The agreement to arbitrate is null and void, has been invalidated or has not taken effect before the arbitration proceedings are closed.

(c) The arbitral tribunal failed to direct either or both of the parties to present its or their contentions, or if either or both of the parties were not lawfully represented in the arbitration proceeding.

(d) The composition of the arbitral tribunal or the arbitration proceedings was in violation of the stipulations of the arbitration agreement or law.

(e) One or more of the arbitrators lacked independence thereby violating the obligation of disclosure stipulated in Article 15(2) of the Arbitration Law or were challenged by the parties but still participated in the arbitration proceedings, unless the challenge had been rejected according to the Arbitration Law.

---

[38] Article 18(2) of the Compulsory Execution Law.

[39] Article 40 of the Arbitration Law.

(f) Any participating arbitrator violated his or her duty in the arbitration, and such violation amounts to criminal liability.

(g) Either of the parties or its agent committed a criminal offense in respect of the arbitration.

(h) Any of the evidence upon which the arbitration was based was found to be forged or fraudulently altered.

(i) The criminal or civil judgment, court order, or administrative decision upon which the arbitration was based had been rescinded or modified by a subsequent judgment, duly affirmed by an appellate court, or by a subsequent administrative decision.

Paragraphs (f) to (h) are applicable only where a conviction has been confirmed, or where criminal proceedings have not been started or have been discontinued owing to insufficient evidence. Paragraphs (d) and (e) to (i) are applicable only when the arbitration result can be adversely affected.

Once an arbitral award is revoked by a final judgment of a court, a party may bring the dispute to the court unless the parties agree to arbitrate, as provided by Article 43 of the Arbitration Law. An issue arises as to whether a party may refer the dispute to arbitration based on the arbitration agreement upon which the revoked arbitral award relies. The Taiwan High Court, Tainan Branch Court in its Judgment 98-Shang-Yi-Tze No. 203 (30 March 2010) has ruled that a party was not allowed to arbitrate the dispute after the arbitral award had been revoked by a final court judgment. This suggests that if the parties do not reach another arbitration agreement after the arbitral award is revoked, neither party may arbitrate on the same dispute.

B.9   Enforcement of Foreign Arbitral Awards

Taiwan is not a signatory to the New York Convention, but it still follows the spirit thereof. Enforcement of foreign arbitral awards in Taiwan is governed by the Arbitration Law and involves application to a Taiwan court for recognition. As the recognition is non-litigious, open hearings and oral arguments are normally required, unless there are exceptional circumstances.

The Arbitration Law defines foreign arbitral awards as an arbitral award that is rendered outside the territory of Taiwan, or that is rendered within the territory of Taiwan but pursuant to the "foreign laws," which include: (a) foreign arbitration laws, (b) rules of a foreign arbitral institution (such as the ICC Rules), and (c) rules of an international organization (such as the UNCITRAL Arbitration Rules).[40]

Article 49(1) of the Arbitration Law provides that a court shall dismiss the plea for recognition of a foreign arbitral award if:

(a) the recognition or enforcement of the arbitral award will run counter to public order or the good morals of Taiwan; or

(b) the dispute is not arbitrable under the laws of Taiwan.

In addition, a court may dismiss a plea for recognizing a foreign arbitral award if the place or state where the arbitral award was made does not recognize Taiwan arbitral awards on a reciprocal basis.

The reciprocity requirement arises under Article 49 of the Arbitration Law. As Taiwan is not a signatory of the New York Convention, the reciprocity requirement can be an impediment to the recognition of foreign awards. However, Article 49 does not

---

[40]   Taiwan Taipei District Court, Judgment 88-Chung-Sue-Tze No. 8 (9 May 2000).

make such a clause compulsory. The courts have given a liberal interpretation to the term "reciprocity" in some cases.[41]

The Supreme Court has held that even though the foreign jurisdiction where the arbitral award was made does not recognize and enforce arbitral awards made in Taiwan, the court, rather than dismissing the plea, may still decide to recognize and enforce the foreign arbitral award at its discretion for the purpose of enhancing international judicial cooperation.[42]

If a party applies to the court for recognition of a foreign arbitral award concerning any of the following circumstances, the respondent may request the court to dismiss the application within twenty days from the date of receipt of the notice of the application:

(a) The arbitration agreement is invalid as a result of the incapacity of a party according to the law chosen by the parties to govern the arbitration agreement.

(b) The arbitration agreement is null and void according to the law chosen to govern said agreement or, in the absence of choice of law, the law of the country where the arbitral award was made.

(c) A party is not given proper notice either of the appointment of an arbitrator or of any other matter required in the arbitral proceedings, or any other situations which give rise to lack of due process.

(d) The arbitral award is not relevant to the subject matter of the dispute covered by the arbitral agreement or exceeds the

---

[41] *See, e.g.*, Taiwan High Court, Ruling 94-Kung-Tze No. 433 (30 March 1995) and Taiwan Taipei District Court, Ruling 80-Chung-Chih-Geng-Tze No. 39 (28 April 1992).

[42] Taiwan Supreme Court, Ruling 75-Tai-Kung-Tze No. 335 (7 August 1986).

scope of the arbitration agreement, unless the inconsistent portion can be severed from and cannot affect the remainder of the arbitral award.

(e) The composition of the arbitral tribunal or the arbitration procedure contravenes the arbitration agreement or, in the absence of an arbitration agreement, the law of the place of the arbitration.

(f) The arbitral award is not yet binding upon the parties or has been suspended or revoked by a competent court.[43]

The Taiwan courts have recognized and enforced some foreign arbitral awards made in a number of US states, and in a number of countries such as the UK, France, Switzerland, South Korea, Japan, Finland, Russian Federation, South Africa and Vietnam, as well as some awards made in accordance with the arbitration regulations of the London Metal Exchange, the arbitration rules of the Liverpool Cotton Association Limited,[44] the arbitration rules of the Singapore Commodity Exchange Limited, the AAA Rules, the ICC Rules and the UNCITRAL Arbitration Rules, etc. However, there is no court precedent recognizing arbitral awards rendered in countries that have substantial commercial and cultural interests with Taiwan, such as Germany and Canada. This uncertainty is one of the reasons that contracting parties may be reluctant to choose a foreign country as their venue for arbitration.

---

[43] Article 50 of the Arbitration Law.

[44] On 9 December 2004, the Association was renamed "The International Cotton Association."

C. PUBLIC POLICY IN INTERNATIONAL ARBITRATION

C.1 Scenarios of Reliance on Public Policy

Under Article 49(1) of the Arbitration Law, if the recognition or enforcement of a foreign arbitral award will run counter to public order or the good morals of Taiwan, a court shall dismiss the plea.

According to Articles 38 and 40 of the Arbitration Law, if a domestic arbitral award directs a party to act contrary to the law (that is, the decision violates an imperative or prohibitive provision of the law or is against the public order or the good morals of Taiwan[45]), the court shall reject an application for enforcement of such arbitral award and shall revoke it.

It is not a requirement for reliance on public policy at the enforcement stage that the defense was invoked – but rejected – before the tribunal. Regardless of whether the defense had been invoked in the arbitration proceedings, the court will consider it.

C.2 Modes and Limitations of Reliance on Public Policy

Article 51 of the Arbitration Law provides that where a party to an arbitration applies for a judicial revocation of a foreign arbitral award or for suspension of enforceability thereof, the court at the request of the respondent may order the applicant to pay a suitable and certain security to suspend the recognition or enforcement proceedings prior to issuing any order for recognition or enforcement of the foreign arbitral award. And, if the foreign arbitral award in question has been revoked

---

[45] *See, e.g.*, Taiwan Supreme Court, Judgments 94-Tai-Shang-Tze No. 492 (18 March 2005) and 92-Tai-Shang-Tze No. 234 (29 January 2003).

according to its country of origin, the court shall dismiss any application for recognition or upon request, revoke any recognition of such foreign arbitral award.

C.3 Rules that Constitute "Public Policy"

The Supreme Court has construed "public order and the good morals of Taiwan" as the general concept of interests and morals that are fundamental principles governing the society of Taiwan.[46] There have not been cases reported where the Taiwan courts refused to recognize a foreign arbitral award because such award was in breach of Taiwan's public policy.

C.4 Review of Alleged Breaches of Public Policy

As dictated by Articles 40(1) and 49(1) of the Arbitration Law, when reviewing a petition to recognize a foreign arbitral award or to enforce a domestic award, the Taiwan courts would not invoke foreign public policy considerations but only consider Taiwan's principles of public policy. The party who intends to allege breach of public policy should expressly delineate the violation in its pleadings.

---

[46] Taiwan Supreme Court, Precedent 69-Tai-Shang-Tze No. 2603 (21 August 1980).

TURKEY

Ismail G. Esin[1] and Ali Yesilirmak[2]

A. LEGISLATION, TRENDS AND TENDENCIES

A.1 General

The history of legislation on arbitration in Turkey dates back to the 1850s. The Code of Civil Procedure of 1927 included a chapter on arbitration.[3] With the aim of promoting international arbitration and foreign investment, the International Arbitration Law ("the IAL") was ratified, and came into effect on 5 July 2001 after its publication in the Official Gazette.[4] The IAL mainly adopts the UNCITRAL Model Law. However, some

---

[1] İsmail G. Esin, is the Managing Partner of Esin Attorney Partnership now associated with Baker & McKenzie. He has advised various international companies on their dispute resolution matters in Turkey and abroad, and is the author of seven books published in English, German, and Turkish on mergers and acquisitions and international arbitration. He is a member of the ICC Turkish National Committee, the LCIA, the International Bar Association, the Swiss Arbitration Association, the German Arbitration Institute (DIS), the German-Turkish Chamber of Industry and Commerce and the American Business Forum in Turkey.

[2] Ali Yesilirmak is a member of the Istanbul Bar Association and of the Faculty, Istanbul Sehir University and a visiting lecturer at Queen Mary College, CCLS. He has published numerous books and articles on international commercial and investment law as well as dispute resolution. He has served as arbitrator and counsel in over 20 institutional and *ad hoc* arbitrations. He was a member of the drafting committee for the Turkish Code of Civil Procedure (2011), the draft Mediation Law on Civil Law Disputes and the draft Law on Istanbul Arbitration Center.

[3] Law No. 1086, published in the Official Gazette No. 622-624 of 2-4 July 1927.

[4] Law No. 4686, published in the Official Gazette No. 24453 on 5 July 2011. *See* Article 18 of the IAL.

provisions reflect those of the ICC Rules and Chapter 12 of the Swiss Federal Act on International Private Law of 1987.[5] The IAL is applicable to international arbitration. The Code of Civil Procedure containing a chapter on arbitration was recently adopted to address domestic arbitration.[6]

Turkey is a member of several arbitration treaties. Turkey has ratified the New York Convention,[7] the European Convention on International Commercial Arbitration of 1961[8] and the ICSID Convention.[9] It is noteworthy that Turkey is a party to several bilateral investment treaties and to several judicial cooperation treaties containing provisions regarding arbitration.[10]

In respect of recognition and enforcement of foreign arbitral awards, it should be noted, however, that pursuant to Article 2 of Law No. 3731, a party will be able to have an arbitral award recognized under the New York Convention only when the award was rendered in a state that is also a signatory to the New York Convention. Furthermore, the same provision dictates that this only covers commercial contractual disputes between the parties; the element of commerciality is to be determined

---

5   *See* Kalpsüz, T., "The Provisions of the International Arbitration Law Inspired by the ICC Rules of Arbitration and the IPL," International Arbitration Seminar (2003), pp. 17-18 (Kalpsüz, T., "Milletlerarası Tahkim Kanununda ICC Tahkim Kuralları ile IPL'den Esinlenen Hükümler," Milletarası Tahkim Semineri (2003), pp.17-18).

6   Law No. 6100, published in the Official Gazette No. 27836 of 4 February 2011.

7   Law No. 3731, published in the Official Gazzette No. 20877 on 21 May 1991.

8   Law No. 3730, published in the Official Gazzette No. 20877 on 21 May 1991.

9   Law No. 3460, published in the Official Gazzette No. 19830 on 2 June 1988.

10 *See, e.g.*, Yesilirmak, A., "Negotiation, Mediation, Expert-Determination and Arbitration: Problems and Solutions" (Doğrudan Görüşme, Arabuluculuk, Hakem-Bilirkişilik ve Tahkim: Sorunlar ve Çözüm Önerileri) (XII Levha Publishing: Istanbul, 2011), at pp. 69-70.

pursuant to the laws of the Republic of Turkey. The recognition and enforcement procedure is also set forth in the International Private and Procedural Law of 2000.

The IAL is comprised of seven chapters. A short summary of each chapter is provided below, with an emphasis on some of the important provisions of the law.

A.2 Part I—General Provisions of the IAL

Article 1(2) stipulates that the IAL[11] is only applicable to disputes where the place of arbitration is Turkey or where the parties or the arbitral tribunal determine that the provisions of the IAL should apply, provided that the dispute has a foreign element. The term "foreign element" is defined in Article 2.

The existence of any one of the following conditions will satisfy the foreign element required: (a) where the domicile, habitual residence or place of business of the parties to the arbitration is in different states; (b) where the domicile, habitual residence or place of business of the parties and the place of arbitration as stated in the arbitration agreement, or determined pursuant to the arbitration agreement, is in different states; (c) where the domicile, habitual residence or place of business of the parties and the place where a substantial part of the obligations arising from the underlying agreement is to be performed or the place where the dispute is most closely connected is in different states; (d) where at least one of the shareholders of the company that is a party to the underlying agreement constituting the basis for the arbitration agreement has brought in foreign capital pursuant to the laws relating to the encouragement of foreign capital, or where a loan or guarantee agreement needs to be entered into for

---

[11] All references to provisions below are, unless otherwise stated, references to provisions of the IAL.

the execution of the underlying agreement; and (e) where the underlying agreement constituting the basis for the arbitration agreement relates to the transfer of capital or goods from one state to another.

The competence of a court to hear matters relating to the arbitration agreement is to be determined pursuant to Article 3. Article 3(1) provides that where a court is to take steps foreseen under the IAL, the competent court is the civil court of first instance (*asliye hukuk mahkemesi*) where the respondent has its domicile, habitual residence or place of business. If the respondent does not have its domicile, habitual residence or place of business in Turkey, the competent court is the Istanbul Civil Court of First Instance (*İstanbul Asliye Hukuk Mahkemesi*).

Article 3(2) specifically provides that the courts are only permitted to interfere in disputes arising from international arbitration within the boundaries of the IAL and the circumstances specified therein, thereby giving effect to the wishes of the parties to resolve their disputes by way of arbitration with minimal judicial interference.

It should be noted that the IAL does not apply to disputes relating to real property rights concerning immovables and to disputes that are not at the free disposal of the parties (Article 1(3)).

A.3 Part II—The Arbitration Agreement

Article 4(1) defines an arbitration agreement and provides that an arbitration agreement can be entered into by the inclusion of an arbitration clause in the underlying agreement or by a separate agreement. An arbitration agreement will be found to exist where an arbitration clause contained in another document is incorporated by reference in the underlying agreement (Article 4(2)).

An arbitration agreement must be in writing (Article 4(2)). This condition is satisfied when it is in a document signed by the parties or in an exchange of letters, telegrams, telex, fax or other similar means of telecommunication that provide a record of the agreement, or where the statement of claim alleges the existence of an arbitration agreement and the respondent fails to object in its reply to such an allegation.

Article 5 provides the mechanism for a party to raise objections to the arbitration before the court where the proceedings commenced in breach of an agreement to arbitrate. If the objection is upheld, the claim will be dismissed on procedural grounds (Article 5(1)).

The final section of Part II, Article 6, concerns interim measures of protection. Article 6(1) provides that the fact that a party applies to the court, before or during the arbitral proceedings, requesting an interim injunction or attachment, and the court granted such injunction or attachment, will not constitute a breach of the arbitration agreement. Article 6(2) gives the same power to the arbitral tribunal, albeit with a restriction that interim measures must not be ordered against official bodies or third parties. A party may apply to the court to obtain an order compelling the other party to comply with the arbitral tribunal's decision (Article 6(3)).

Where a preliminary injunction or attachment was ordered by the court before the arbitral proceedings were commenced, the party who obtained the order must commence arbitration within 30 days. Otherwise, the preliminary injunction or attachment will automatically cease to have effect (Article 10(1)). The preliminary injunction or attachment automatically ceases to have effect from the moment the award becomes enforceable or the claimant's claim is dismissed (Article 6(5)).

A.4 Part III—The Appointment, Challenge, Liability, Jurisdiction and Termination of Office of the Arbitrator(s)

Unless otherwise agreed, the number of arbitrators has been set as three (Article 7A (2)). Otherwise, the number must be an odd number (Article 7A (1)). Unless otherwise agreed, the following rules apply in relation to the selection of arbitrators: (a) only natural persons can be appointed as arbitrators; (b) where a sole arbitrator is to be appointed, the civil court of first instance is to appoint that arbitrator if the parties are unable to agree; (c) where three arbitrators are to be appointed, each party will appoint an arbitrator and the appointed arbitrators will appoint the third arbitrator who will serve as the chairman. The civil court of first instance will make the appointment where one party fails to appoint its arbitrator within 30 days of being notified of the other party's appointment or where the arbitrators appointed cannot agree on the appointment of the chairman; (d) the same rules apply for the appointment of the last arbitrator where more than three arbitrators have been agreed upon (Article 7B (1)). Any dispute as to the procedure relating to the appointment of arbitrators is to be determined by the relevant civil court of first instance and such decisions are final (Article 7B (2) and (3)).

An arbitrator can be challenged where it is determined that he does not possess the qualifications agreed upon by the parties, where the parties have agreed upon a reason for challenging him/her and that reason exists or where circumstances exist that give rises to justifiable doubts as to his/her impartiality (Article 7C(2)). The challenge must be made within 30 days after the challenging party becomes aware of the circumstance that gives rise to its entitlement to a challenge (Article 7D(1)). The challenge will be heard by the arbitral tribunal and, if rejected, the challenging party must apply to the civil court of first instance within 30 days to quash the decision and for an order for the removal of the arbitrator(s) (Article 7D(2)). The challenge must be made to the civil court of first instance if it relates to a majority of the arbitrators or the entire tribunal (Article 7D (3)).

If the challenge is accepted, the arbitral proceedings will come to an end if the challenge related to a sole arbitrator, the majority of arbitrators or the entire arbitral tribunal. Unless the names of arbitrators were specified, the process of appointing arbitrators will have to start from the beginning (Article 7D (4)).

In relation to the liability of arbitrators, the IAL provides that, unless the parties agree otherwise, an arbitrator who accepts office will be obliged to compensate the losses suffered by the parties as a result of the arbitrator's failure to perform his/her duties without a justifiable reason (Article 7E).

The universally known and well-established principle of "*kompetenz/kompetenz*" is incorporated in Article 7H. It stipulates that the arbitral tribunal may rule on its own jurisdiction, including objections relating to the existence or validity of the arbitration agreement (Article 7H(1)). Article 7H also provides that the invalidity of the underlying agreement will not necessarily mean the invalidity, ineffectiveness or non-existence of the arbitration agreement (Article 7H(1)). This provision therefore gives effect to the principle of separability. If it is alleged that the arbitral tribunal does not have jurisdiction, that objection must be raised early in the proceedings or with the reply, unless a valid reason is provided justifying the delay in raising this objection (Article 7H(2) and (4)).

A.5 Part IV—The Arbitral Proceedings

The parties are entitled to select the rules to be applied by the arbitral tribunal during the proceedings or to incorporate the rules contained in legislation, international or institutional rules of arbitration by reference, subject to the mandatory rules contained in the IAL. If the parties have not made such an agreement, the procedural rules of the IAL will be applied in the arbitral proceedings (Article 8A).

Unless determined by the parties or by the arbitral institution selected by the parties, the place of arbitration will be determined by the arbitral tribunal having regard to the circumstances of the case (Article 9(1)). Pursuant to Article 10B(1), the arbitral award must be rendered within one year from the appointment of the sole arbitrator or the first meeting of the arbitral tribunal. The one-year period can be extended by agreement or by order of the court (Article 10B(2)).

In relation to the law to be applied in the arbitral proceedings, Article 12C(1) provides that the arbitral tribunal is to determine the dispute in accordance with the terms of the parties' agreement and the applicable law chosen by the parties. The selection of the laws of a state as the applicable law does not, unless otherwise agreed, mean that the laws relating to the conflict of laws apply but, rather, that the substantive laws of that state apply to the contract (Article 12C(1)). If the parties have not determined the applicable law, the substantive law of the state with which the dispute is most closely connected will be applied (Article 12C(2)). The arbitral tribunal can determine the issues in the case pursuant to just and equitable principles only if the parties expressly authorized them to do so.

Articles 13 and 14 deal with, in short, the procedure that will be adopted by the arbitral tribunal in rendering its award, the termination of the arbitral proceedings, the form, content, correction and interpretation of the award, additional awards and the rules as to written notifications.

A.6 Part V—Challenging Arbitral Awards

Under Article 15A(1) of the IAL, an action can only be brought against an arbitral award to set it aside; the IAL contains no provisions as to appeals of arbitral awards. The application to set aside an arbitral award must be commenced in the relevant civil court of first instance and is to be afforded priority. Arbitral awards may be set aside where the party making the application demonstrates that: a party to the arbitration was under an incapacity; the arbitration was invalid under the chosen applicable law or, if no such choice has been made, under Turkish law; the procedure agreed upon by the parties or contained in the IAL relating to the appointment of the arbitral tribunal was not adhered to; the award was not rendered within the time specified; the arbitral tribunal determined that it had or lacked jurisdiction contrary to the law; the arbitral tribunal determined upon an issue that fell outside the scope of the arbitration agreement, failed to decide all of the issues brought to its attention or exceeded its authority; the arbitral proceedings were not conducted in accordance with the rules agreed upon by the parties or, if no such agreement exists, pursuant to the IAL, and this failure influenced the outcome of the case; or the equal treatment principle was not adhered to (Article 15A(2)).

Furthermore, the award may be set aside where the court determines that the subject matter of the dispute is not arbitrable under Turkish law or that the award is contrary to public policy (Article 15A(2)).

The application to set aside an award must be made within 30 days and the making of the application will automatically stop the enforcement of the award (Article 15A(4)). It should be noted that the parties are free to waive their right to make an application to set aside an award (Article 15A(5)). The right to appeal the judgment of the civil court of first instance exists but is limited to the grounds enumerated in Article 15 (Article 15A(7)).

Once the application to set aside the award is dismissed, the civil court of first instance will issue a certificate of enforceability upon request (Article 15B).

A.7 Part VI—Costs of Arbitration

Unless otherwise agreed, the costs of arbitration will be borne by the unsuccessful party. If both parties are successful in part, the costs will be apportioned in the manner proportionate to the success of each party's claims (Article 16D(1)). The costs of arbitration include: the arbitrators' fees,[12] travel and other expenses of the arbitrator(s), fees paid to experts and other persons appointed or whose assistance was sought by the arbitrator, travel and other expenses of the witnesses to the extent authorized by the arbitrator, fees of the legal representative of the successful party deemed appropriate by the arbitrators, fees paid for applications made to the court and expenses incurred in the making of notifications related to the arbitral proceedings (Article 16B).

B. CASES

B.1 Jurisdiction of the Courts to Determine Whether the Arbitration Agreement is Valid

In its decision dated 27 June 2007,[13] the Court of Appeal decided that where the parties agreed to submit disputes that

---

[12] For the Arbitrator's Fee Tariff, see Communique published in the Official Gazette No. 28070 of 30 September 2011.

[13] Court of Appeal, 15th Civil Chamber, File No. 2007/2145, Decision No.2007/4389, Decision Date: 27 June 2007 (excerpts published in *Kazancı Case Database* (Kazancı İçtihat Bilgi Bankası).

may arise or have arisen to arbitration for resolution, the courts do not have jurisdiction to hear applications requesting that the arbitration agreement be declared null and void, thereby bringing the dispute within the jurisdiction of the national courts.

The dispute in question arose from an agreement with an arbitration clause stipulating for the resolution of disputes pursuant to the IAL provided that the conditions in Article 1(1)(1) were satisfied. A dispute arose between the parties and the claimant commenced arbitration proceedings. The respondent applied to the court requesting that the court stay the arbitral proceedings and declare the arbitration clause invalid for being unclear and ambiguous. The civil court of first instance decided in favor of the claimant but, upon appeal, the Court of Appeal overturned the lower court's decision. The court held that, "pursuant to paragraph H of Article 7, arbitrators have been granted the power to decide on matters relating to their jurisdiction, including objections relating to the existence or validity of the arbitration agreement."[14] The court therefore noted that a party must wait until the award is rendered and then seek to challenge the award on one of the grounds enumerated in Article 15.

What this case demonstrates is that not only has the principle of "*kompetenz/kompetenz*" been adopted into Turkish law under the IAL, it has also been respected and enforced by the Turkish courts.

---

[14] *Id.*

B.2 An Arbitration Agreement Can Be Incorporated into Another Agreement by Reference

The Court of Appeal has held[15] that an arbitration agreement is "in writing" for the purposes of Article II(1) and (2) of the New York Convention where the agreement signed between the parties incorporates an arbitration clause included in another document by way of reference.

The dispute arose between Sarılar Uluslararası Nak. Lth. Lhr. Şti. ("Sarılar") and Batinak Shipping Trading Co. Ltd. ("Batinak") in relation to a voyage charterparty for the carriage of two cranes from Dubai to Turkey onboard a nominated vessel. The charter agreement contained the following clause: "Other terms are like those contained in GENCON 76 Charter Party." GENCON 76 contained a clause referring disputes to arbitration in London. The vessel was not ready to load on the contractually agreed date, which resulted in the charterer chartering two other vessels for the carriage of the cranes. Sarılar commenced legal proceedings seeking damages caused as a result of the carrier's breach of contract. Batinak, however, disputed the court's jurisdiction, contending that the dispute was to be resolved by arbitration. Sarılar counter-argued that the court had jurisdiction because the arbitration agreement had not been signed, thereby falling afoul of the requirement imposed by Article II(1) and (2) of the New York Convention.

The court of first instance decided in favor of Batinak, holding that the arbitration agreement between the parties was valid under the terms of the New York Convention and therefore binding. The Court of Appeal, taking into account the circumstances of the case, the reasons relied upon in the

---

[15] Court of Appeal, 11th Civil Chamber, File No. 2005/104, Decision No. 2006/316, Decision Date: 19 January 2006 (unpublished).

decision of the lower court and the unambiguous arbitration agreement, upheld the lower court's decision. This decision brings the rules relating to the New York Convention in line with the provisions of the IAL, which provides that an arbitration agreement can be incorporated into an agreement by reference (Article 4(2)).

B.3   The Principle of Severability

The principle of severability dictates that the validity or invalidity of an arbitration agreement cannot be determined according to the invalidity of the underlying agreement. As was mentioned in Part A above, this rule is expressly incorporated into the IAL by virtue of Article 7H(1).

The Court of Appeal was provided with the opportunity to examine this principle within the context of the then in force Code of Civil Procedure of 1927.[16] A dispute arose from an agreement between the parties relating to the transfer of real property rights to an immovable. Pursuant to Turkish law, such agreements must be executed in writing before a notary public to be valid. The property in question was owned by more than one individual and not all of the owners had signed the agreement, contrary to Turkish law. It therefore meant that the underlying contract had not been validly executed and was therefore invalid. The issue before the Court of Appeal was whether the arbitration agreement had been rendered null and void as a result of the invalidity of the underlying agreement. The court answered in the negative and held that the arbitration agreement survived the

---

[16]   Court of Appeal, 15th Civil Chamber, File No. 2007/193,   Decision No. 2007/3494, Decision Date: 24 May 2007 (excerpts published in Ekşi, N., Court of Appeal Decisions relating to the International Arbitration Law No. 4686 (4686 Sayılı Milletlerarası Tahkim Kanunu'na ilişkin Yargıtay Kararları) (Istanbul, XII LevhaYayıncılık, 2009), pp. 48-53).

invalidity of the underlying agreement. In doing so, the court specifically referred to Article 4(4) of the IAL to support its conclusion. What this decision demonstrates is that the Turkish courts are now more pro-arbitration and tend to adhere to the generally recognized principles in arbitration, unless a legislative provision or public policy provides otherwise.

C. PUBLIC POLICY IN INTERNATIONAL ARBITRATION

Article 15A(3)(2)(b) of the IAL provides that an arbitral award may be challenged if the court, on its own initiative, determines that the award is contrary to public policy. The scope and content of what constitutes public policy has not been expressly defined. The determination of the scope and content of the concept of public policy is left to the court's discretion. The general view adopted is that public policy encompasses the fundamental principles on which the domestic law is based, as well as the cultural and moral principles and rules aimed to protect the fundamental benefits of the community.[17]

Since the concept of public policy varies from time to time and from individual to individual, it is not possible for one to simply list the circumstances that contravene public policy requirements. A judge therefore has discretion to determine whether or not an objection based on public policy justifies setting aside an award. An example of a public policy ground being considered by the Court of Appeal is a decision dated

---

[17] *See, e.g.,* Tanrıver, S., "The Role of Public Policy in the Enforcement of Foreign Arbitral Awards in Turkey" (Yabancı Hakem Kararlarının Türkiye'de Tenfizinde Kamu Düzeninin Rolü), *International Law and International Private Law Bulletin* (Milletlerarası Hukuk ve Millerlerarası Özel Hukuk Bülteni), Vol. 17-18, pp. 1-2.

2 July 1997.[18] Pursuant to Article 529 of the then Code of Civil Procedure (now Article 427(1)),[19] an arbitral award had to be rendered within six months from the date the arbitral tribunal had its first meeting. In that case, the 15th Civil Chamber of the Turkish Court of Appeal held that where that requirement is not complied with, the award will not be enforced, as it contravenes public policy. The court reasoned that the legislative provision that the award must be rendered within six months concerns public policy because if not followed, a party would be unable to seek redress in a court of law. Although this decision and the provision it considered concerned domestic arbitration, the principle should be equally applicable to Article 10B(1) of the IAL which, as mentioned above, foresees a one-year time period for rendering an award.

C.1   Scenarios of Reliance on Public Policy

A party is entitled to rely upon public policy grounds where the matter has come before the court and the other party has advanced its objection as to the matter being dealt with in the arbitral proceedings as opposed to the courts. In such a case, the court will be required to conduct a *prima facie* review of the arbitration agreement and determine whether the arbitration agreement is in breach of public policy. If the agreement is held to constitute a breach of public policy, the court must rule that the matter is non-arbitrable. A party is also permitted to invoke public policy as a defense when resisting the recognition and enforcement of an arbitral award in line with Article V(2)(b) of the New York Convention. In addition, it should be noted that

---

[18]   Court of Appeal, 15th Civil Chamber, File No. 1997/2567, Decision No. 1997/3420, Decision Date: 2 July 1997.

[19]   The time limit for the rendering of the award under the New Code of Civil Procedure is one year.

issues such as those that were the subject matter of the English Supreme Court's decision in *Jivraj v. Hashwani*[20] will not arise in Turkey. Parties are entitled to freely determine the characteristics of an arbitrator in their arbitration agreement.

C.2 Modes and Limitations of Reliance on Public Policy

A public policy objection could be invoked at any time in an arbitration proceeding and also in pending enforcement proceedings under the New York Convention. The court may also *ipso facto* take into account the breach of public policy at any time. It is not required under Turkish law that the public policy defense was initially invoked and rejected in the arbitration proceedings. Whether or not it was raised in the arbitration, a public policy defense can also always be asserted in the enforcement proceedings.

If the award is vacated in the country of origin, its enforcement could not be refused under the public policy ground in accordance with Article V(2)(b) of the New York Convention. In such a case, however, enforcement could be refused in accordance with Article V(1)(e) of the New York Convention.

C.3 Rules that Constitute Public Policy

One must note that under Turkish law, the most essential legal, ethical or economic mandatory rules of law constitute public policy. The Turkish Court of Appeal does not make a distinction between "domestic" and "international" public policy. Some scholars argue that such a distinction should be made.[21] There is

---

[20]   [2011] UKSC 40.

[21]   *See, e.g.,* Nomer, E. *International Private Law (Devletler Hususi Hukuku)*, 16th Eds (Istanbul: Beta Publishing, 2008), p.173.

no severity threshold yet accepted by the Turkish Court of Appeal regarding the breach of (international) public policy.

C.4 Review of Alleged Breaches of Public Policy

In June 1999, the Court of Appeal was provided with the opportunity to consider whether a clause providing claimant with a choice of one of two institutions to administer the arbitral proceedings was contrary to Turkish public policy.[22] It should be kept in mind that, if the answer to that issue was in the affirmative, the court would be entitled to refuse recognition of the arbitral award pursuant to Article V(2)(b), as explained above. The court, however, answered in the negative, deciding that the award was not contrary to public policy and therefore had to be recognized under the New York Convention.

---

[22] Court of Appeal, General Assembly, File No. 1999/19-467, Decision No. 1999/489, Decision Date: 9 June 1999.

UKRAINE

Svitlana Romanova,[1] Olga Shenk,[2] and Kseniia Pogruzhalska[3]

A. LEGISLATION, TRENDS AND TENDENCIES

A.1 Introduction

Ukraine is a civil law country, and issues of international arbitration are governed primarily by international conventions and treaties (which, upon their ratification by the *Verkhovna Rada,* Ukrainian Parliament, have priority over national legislation) and by applicable national legislation. Court precedent is not considered to be a source of binding law in Ukraine, except for decisions of the Supreme Court of Ukraine made in cases regarding the different application by cassation courts of the same material law provision.

Ukraine is a party to the New York Convention and the European Convention. Ukraine is also a party to a number of bilateral investment treaties, many of which provide for arbitration under the UNCITRAL Arbitration Rules or before ICSID.

---

[1] Svitlana Romanova is a Partner in Baker & McKenzie's Kyiv office. Ms. Romanova routinely advises clients on various legal concerns involving natural resources, mining, oil and gas, as well as in related infrastructure and environmental projects. A member of the Ukrainian Bar Association, she has authored a number of publications on the regulation of the power and mining industries in Ukraine, and is a frequent contributor of articles on dispute resolution issues for major Ukrainian business publications.

[2] Olga Shenk is an Associate in Baker & McKenzie's Kyiv office, and a member of the Firm's Global Dispute Resolution, Energy, Mining & Infrastructure, IT/Communications, Mergers & Acquisitions and Employment Practice Groups.

[3] Kseniia Pogruzhalska is a Legal Clerk in Baker & McKenzie's Kyiv office and a member of the Firm's Dispute Resolution Practice Group.

The *Verkhovna Rada* ratified the ICSID Convention in 2000, and in 2006, the President of Ukraine adopted the decree *On Procedure for the Appointment of Representatives from Ukraine to be Included in the Conciliators' List and the Arbitrators' List of the International Centre for Settlement of Investment Disputes*.

Ukraine has also adopted separate laws on domestic and international arbitration, such as the law *On Domestic Arbitration*, dated 11 May 2004, and the law *On International Commercial Arbitration*, dated 24 February 1994 (the "Arbitration Law"). The Arbitration Law closely follows the UNCITRAL Model Law of 1985, except for the following two peculiarities. First, unlike in most Model Law countries, the Arbitration Law provides that the President of the Ukrainian Chamber of Commerce and Industry (the "UCCI") shall serve as the appointing authority when there is a failure to appoint an arbitrator. Consequently, the UCCI President is also the authority for challenging arbitrators. Second, the Arbitration Law establishes two arbitration institutions—the International Commercial Arbitration Court of the Ukrainian Chamber of Commerce (the "ICAC") and the Maritime Arbitration Commission of the Ukrainian Chamber of Commerce. At present, these are the oldest existing arbitration institutions in Ukraine.

A.2 Short Overview of Ukrainian Legislation regarding Arbitration

A.2.1. Arbitrability

The Arbitration Law provides that, upon agreement of the parties, the following disputes may be referred to international commercial arbitration:

- Disputes arising from contractual and other civil relationships in connection with foreign trade and other kinds of transactions, provided that at least one party is located abroad;

- Disputes involving companies with foreign investments, international organizations or associations, organized or incorporated in Ukraine, whether among themselves, between members of such organizations, or between such organizations and other Ukrainian entities.

Ukrainian legislation does not contain an integrated list of nonarbitrable disputes or a clear mechanism for determining a dispute's arbitrability. References to non-arbitrable disputes can be found separately in some international agreements and national laws. However, Ukrainian legislation does expressly define the following types of disputes as nonarbitrable:

- Disputes arising from corporate relations between a company and any of its current or former participants (i.e., founders or shareholders), or between the company's participants themselves, relating to the establishment, activity, management or termination of their company (pursuant to Article 12 of the Commercial Procedure Code of Ukraine);

- Disputes that, according to the Civil Procedure Code of Ukraine, are categorized as "non-contentious proceedings" (generally, such disputes relate to the establishment of legal facts, disclosure of bank secrets, restoration of rights for lost securities, etc.);

- Disputes concerning the invalidation of the acts of state authorities (pursuant to Article 12 of the Commercial Procedure Code of Ukraine);

- Disputes concerning the execution, change, termination and fulfillment of state procurement contracts (pursuant to Article 12 of the Commercial Procedure Code of Ukraine); and

- Disputes concerning the bankruptcy of a Ukrainian debtor.

Additional disputes may be defined as non-arbitrable in other legislation regulating specific areas of legal relationships. In 2005, the Ukrainian law *On Private International Law* was adopted to regulate the rules relating to choice of law and jurisdiction in disputes with a foreign element. However, the adoption of this law has not solved one of the most important problems — the scope of arbitrability of international commercial disputes. In fact, this law has caused more confusion in determining the arbitrability of disputes concerning immovable property, intellectual property and securities disputes. Article 77 of this law provides for the exclusive jurisdiction of the national courts of Ukraine over disputes concerning immovable property, intellectual property and securities disputes. Recent legal practice demonstrates that there is a tendency to apply this provision to avoid arbitrating these types of disputes.

A.2.2. Interim measures

Unless the parties agree otherwise, the arbitration tribunal, upon the request of any of the parties, may order interim measures against another party. The Arbitration Law also provides that parties may apply to state courts for the issuance of interim measures. At the same time, however, the applicable Ukrainian procedural law is silent about the court's authority to order interim measures in aid of arbitration, which leads to certain practical difficulties.

It should be noted that the Civil Procedure Code of Ukraine was amended in September 2011. Since then, interim measures may be ordered by the court at any stage of the proceedings for recognition and enforcement of an arbitration award upon the motion of a party and in accordance with general provisions regulating the issuance of interim measures, as foreseen by the Civil Procedure Code of Ukraine. However, no practical application of this new rule is available yet and thus we cannot comment on its impact.

The Commercial Procedure Code provides that interim measures may be obtained before the claim is filed in court. In such cases, the claim must be filed within five days following the ruling of the relevant court granting the interim measure. A motion on an application for interim measures may also be filed at any stage of the court proceedings if there are grounds to believe that the enforcement of the judgment would be jeopardized. The court must decide whether to grant interim measures within two days from the date it receives the motion and the resulting order has immediate effect. An order granting interim measures may be issued *ex parte*.

The powers of Ukrainian courts to grant interim measures are generally more limited than those available in common law jurisdictions. However, the following types of interim measures may be granted: (i) sequestration of the property or funds of the defendant; (ii) restraining orders prohibiting the defendant from performing certain actions; (iii) restraining orders on third parties prohibiting certain actions relating to the subject matter of the dispute; (iv) suspension of enforcement actions carried out unilaterally on the basis of an enforcement document; and (v) suspension of the sale of seized assets in disputes concerning the recognition of ownership of assets and removal or release of the seized assets' seizure.

Ukrainian commercial courts are expressly prohibited from issuing the following forms of injunctive relief:

- Prohibiting shareholders' meetings or other meetings of the owners of a commercial enterprise and hindering the issuance of decisions at these meetings;

- Prohibiting provision of the registry of privileged shares or information about shareholders or other owners of a commercial enterprise by the issuer of the shares, the registrar, the custodian, or the depositary for the purposes of holding general shareholders' meetings; or

- Prohibiting shareholders or owners of a commercial enterprise from establishing the legal capacity of the general shareholders' or other meetings.

Court assistance in taking evidence

The Arbitration Law expressly allows arbitral tribunals and parties to request assistance from relevant state courts in the gathering of evidence for arbitral proceedings, but such evidence must be gathered in accordance with court rules established for taking evidence in Ukrainian court proceedings.

A.2.3. Setting aside arbitral awards

Under the applicable legislation, district courts of common jurisdiction at the place of arbitration have jurisdiction to set aside arbitral awards. Previously, only appellate courts of common jurisdiction could consider applications to set aside an award. This change has brought additional opportunities to appeal a court's decision to set aside an award and, consequently, significantly prolong the proceedings. Moreover, traditionally, judges of common jurisdiction courts have little experience in commercial disputes and very limited knowledge of arbitration, which has resulted in an increase in the number of appeals concerning arbitration.

A.2.4. Recognition and enforcement

Ukraine recognizes and enforces arbitral awards only if issued in member countries of the New York Convention. Otherwise, recognition and enforcement is possible only on the basis of reciprocity.[4]

The procedure for the enforcement of foreign judgments, including foreign arbitral awards, is set forth in the Civil Procedure Code of Ukraine, according to which the interested party must file a motion for recognition and enforcement of the award with the competent Ukrainian court. The motion for the recognition and enforcement of the foreign arbitral award must be submitted to the court of common jurisdiction at the location of the debtor's domicile or assets within three years of entry into legal force of the arbitral award. Generally, the decision on the enforcement of an arbitral award should be taken within two months, with a possibility to extend this time period. The court's decision on the enforcement and recognition of an arbitral award is subject to an appeal on general grounds, as identified by the Civil Procedure Code of Ukraine. Upon recognition of a foreign arbitral award by the competent Ukrainian court, the ruling on enforcement is transferred to the state enforcement authorities. The procedure for such enforcement is governed by the Ukrainian law *On Enforcement Procedure*, dated 21 April 1999.

A.2.5. Insolvency issues

Bankruptcy proceedings in Ukraine are regulated by the Ukrainian law *On Restoration of a Debtor's Solvency or Recognition of Debtor as Bankrupt*, dated 14 May 1992 (the "Bankruptcy Law").

---

[4] Under the provisions of the Civil Procedure Code of Ukraine, such reciprocity exists by default, unless otherwise established.

If bankruptcy proceedings are commenced by the state commercial court against a party to a pending arbitration proceeding, a creditor must apply with its claims to the court considering the bankruptcy case within a period of 30 days from the date of official publication in the press of the initiation of the bankruptcy proceedings. The court will dismiss claims filed after expiration of this period and will consider as discharged the debtor's liabilities to the defaulting creditor.

Once the debtor is recognized as bankrupt, all active enforcement proceedings initiated against the bankrupt debtor are closed and enforcement documents are sent to the liquidation commission. Therefore, any recovery of the debt in favor of the creditor will be carried out within the bankruptcy proceedings, and the creditor's claims will be satisfied from the liquidation pool of the debtor's assets in the order of priority in accordance with the Bankruptcy Law.

Where a Ukrainian debtor's bankruptcy is initiated after issuance of the final arbitral award, the creditor must apply with its claims to the state court considering the bankruptcy case within the same period, providing the court, in particular, with a certified copy of the arbitral award translated into Ukrainian, as well as a court's resolution on its recognition and enforcement.

All creditors whose claims matured after initiation of the debtor's bankruptcy proceedings are considered to be the current creditors and have a special status in bankruptcy proceedings, as they are entitled to apply to the court with their claims against the debtor and recover the debt outside the pending bankruptcy proceedings. Ukrainian bankruptcy legislation is silent regarding the effect of bankruptcy proceedings on a pending arbitration regarding the same claims made by the creditor. However, pending bankruptcy proceedings do not *per se* terminate, postpone or otherwise suspend the arbitration of the dispute.

A.3 Recently Adopted Ukrainian Legislation regarding Arbitration—Corporate Disputes May Not Be Subject to International Commercial Arbitration

In 2009, the Ukrainian Parliament adopted changes to the Commercial Procedure Code of Ukraine that prohibited the arbitration (domestic or international) of any disputes arising from corporate relations between a company and its current or former participants, or between the company's participants themselves, relating to the establishment, activity, management or termination of their company. All of these disputes must now be submitted to the commercial courts of Ukraine, which have exclusive jurisdiction to consider them.

This amendment was passed in order to address corrupt practices of certain local Ukrainian arbitration institutions in considering corporate disputes, and to formalize the positions expressed in *Recommendations of the Supreme Commercial Court of Ukraine* (Presidium No. 04-5/14 of 28 December 2007) and *Resolution of the Supreme Court of Ukraine* (Plenum No. 13 of 24 October 2008). As a consequence of these legislative changes, any arbitral award concerning these types of corporate disputes will run counter to the new provisions of the Commercial Procedure Code of Ukraine and, as such, will not be enforceable in Ukraine.

A.4 International Commercial Arbitration Court of Ukrainian Chamber of Commerce ("ICAC")

While Ukraine was still a part of the USSR, it did not have its own arbitration institution. Instead, there was only one Arbitral Tribunal and Maritime Arbitration Commission at the Chamber of Commerce and Industry of the Soviet Union. After Ukraine became an independent state in 1992, the Ukrainian Chamber of

Commerce and Industry established the ICAC. According to the ICAC's statistics, during the period 1992-2009, ICAC resolved cases involving parties from 105 countries. From 2004 to 2010, the number of resolved cases reached 2,346. According to the Report of the ICAC, published in January 2011, there were 689 cases pending before the ICAC in 2010. This number increased since 2009, when, according to the ICAC, it considered 651 cases. The ICAC arbitrators' list includes arbitrators from Ukraine, Azerbaijan, Austria, Belarus, Bulgaria, Croatia, Czech Republic, Finland, France, Germany, Great Britain, Hungary, Latvia, Macedonia, Moldova, the Netherlands, Norway, Poland, the Russian Federation, Serbia, Slovakia, Slovenia, Sweden and the USA.

According to the ICAC, the average timeframe for a case is three months in 60% of its cases; six months in 35% of its cases and more than six months in 5% of its cases. On 11 September 2010, the ICAC celebrated its 18th anniversary and elected a new President—Mr. Mykola Selivon, a former judge of the Constitutional Court of Ukraine and Ambassador Extraordinary and Plenipotentiary of Ukraine to the Republic of Kazakhstan. The former President of the ICAC, Mr. Igor Pobirchenko, will continue his work as Honorary President of the ICAC.

B. CASES

B.1 Investment Disputes

Since Ukraine obtained its independence, and especially after the Orange Revolution, the amount of foreign investment in the Ukrainian economy has increased significantly. At the same time, however, Ukraine is frequently mentioned as a party to investment disputes before ICSID. To date, Ukraine has participated in the following concluded ICSID cases: *Joseph C.*

Lemire v. Ukraine (Case No. ARB(AF)/98/1), *Joseph C. Lemire v. Ukraine* (Case No. ARB/06/18), *Generation Ukraine Inc. v. Ukraine* (Case No. ARB/00/9), *Tokios Tokeles v. Ukraine* (Case No. ARB/02/18), *Alpha Projektholding GmbH v. Ukraine* (Case No. ARB/07/16), *Western NIS Enterprise Fund v. Ukraine* (Case No. ARB/04/2), *GEA Group Aktiengesellschaft v. Ukraine* (Case No. ARB/08/16) and *Global Trading Resource Corp. and Globex International, Inc. v. Ukraine* (Case No. ARB/09/11).

It is a party in two cases that are currently pending before ICSID: *Bosh International, Inc. and B&P, LTD Foreign Investment Enterprise v. Ukraine* (Case No. ARB/08/11) and *Inmaris Perestroika Sailing Maritime Services GmbH and others v. Ukraine* (Case No. ARB/08/8).

Except for the obligation to pay USD 2,979,232 under the award rendered in Case No. ARB/07/16, Ukraine has not lost any other concluded ICSID cases, and two of them were settled. However, while considering *Joseph C. Lemire v. Ukraine* (Case No. ARB/06/18), the ICSID tribunal found in its preliminary decision that Ukraine violated the fair and equitable treatment provision of the Agreement between Ukraine and United States of America on Promotion and Mutual Protection of Investments on several occasions, and dismissed the investor's other claims. Nonetheless, on 28 March 2011, the tribunal issued an award on the determination of damages, obliging Ukraine to pay compensation to the claimant in the amount of approximately USD 9,500.

The Ministry of Justice of Ukraine received a notice seeking the pre-trial settlement of a dispute between Transportation Investment Limited ("TIL") and the Government of Ukraine, with the term for such settlement to be agreed within three months starting from 2 July 2010. The dispute arose from a treaty on the promotion and mutual protection of investments between the Government of Ukraine and the Government of Great Britain and Northern Ireland, signed on 10 February 1993. Ukraine is accused of causing significant losses (in the amount of over USD 1 billion) to TIL, arising from the construction by its subsidiary, PE Ukrtranscontainer, of a container terminal in Illichivsk port. Ukraine rejected the terms of settlement proposed and, therefore, TIL was entitled to submit the dispute to trial. However, no further information regarding the status of this case is available.

B.2 Arbitration Disputes against Ukraine

On 24 July 2010, the Ministry of Justice of Ukraine published the official list of disputes pending before foreign courts (including arbitration institutions) involving Ukraine as a party. Apart from the abovementioned investment disputes before ICSID, the list also included the following disputes:

Naftrac Limited (Cyprus) v. the National Agency for Ecological Investment

On 25 November 2009, Naftrac Limited applied to the Permanent Court of Arbitration in the Hague seeking to charge Ukraine for quotas on greenhouse emissions of almost 20 million AAU (Assigned Amount Units) under the Kyoto Protocol and USD 185 million in compensation for projects not completed in Ukraine. The matter concerns agreements, in particular those of Naftrac, with regional Ukrainian gas companies that envisaged modernization projects. Cypriot companies were to install energy saving technologies at Ukrainian enterprises in exchange for greenhouse emissions quotas. Upon the formation of an arbitration tribunal on 8 April 2010, Naftrac requested interim measures, which the tribunal refused. The parties made a number of submissions during 2010-2011, with the last being the plaintiff's rejoinder, dated 1 April 2011. The oral hearings were scheduled for the period 2-5 May 2011.

OSJC Tatneft (Russia) v. Ukraine

On 21 May 2008, the Russian party Tatneft filed a notice of arbitration and a statement of claim with an *ad hoc* arbitration tribunal created under the UNCITRAL Arbitration Rules. Tatneft accused Ukraine of violating its rights as a shareholder of Ukrainian CJSC "Uktatnafta" (an entity controlling the Kremenchuk oil refinery). Paris is the place of arbitration.

Tatneft increased its compensation claims to USD 2.4 billion due to indirect losses caused by the sale of those shares. After the rejection of Ukraine's objections to the jurisdiction of the tribunal on 28 September 2010, a further schedule of submissions and hearings on the matter was approved on 29 November 2010. Accordingly, the parties' first submissions were to be provided by 1 September 2011. A number of other submissions will also need to be made in 2011 and 2012, followed by oral hearings on the merits.

Vanco Prykerchenska Ltd. (British and Virginia islands) v. Ukraine

This dispute was initiated by Vanco Prykerchenska, Limited ("Vanco") in April 2008 after the Ministry of Environmental Protection of Ukraine annulled a special permit issued to Vanco for exploration of the Prykerchenska part of the Black Sea shelf. Consequently, the Cabinet of Ministers of Ukraine ("CMU") unilaterally withdrew from the production sharing agreement earlier concluded with Vanco, which at a later stage assigned the CMU's contractual rights to Vanco. The arbitration was filed on 16 July 2008 at the SCC.

While this dispute was pending, Vanco tried to approach the Ukrainian government with proposals to resume cooperation under the production sharing agreement. In particular, on 1 October 2009, the company officially submitted a work program and budget in the amount of USD 57 million for the purposes of implementing the first phase of the development of the Prykerchenska part of the Black Sea shelf in 2010, as provided for in the agreement. On 12 May 2010, the Government of Ukraine proposed an amicable agreement. The parties started negotiations in July 2010 and the arbitration proceedings were suspended. In order to sign an amicable agreement, the parties agreed to extend the postponement of the arbitration process until April 2011. On 11 April 2011, the CMU reported that the project was approved by Ruling No. 627-r. However, it remains unclear whether an amicable agreement was signed by the parties because Vanco denies having agreed to any of the agreement's envisaged projects.

Torno Global Consulting Spa and Beta Funding SrL (Italy) v. Ukrainian Transport and Communications Ministry and the State Automobile Road Service of Ukraine

In September 2009, Italian-based Torno Global Contracting S.P.A. and Beta Funding S.R.L. filed a claim at the ICC against the Ukrainian Transport Ministry and the State Road Service. The amount claimed is approximately EUR 45 million. The claimants accuse the Ukraine Government of violating the conditions of a general agreement on cooperation during the reconstruction and operation of the Kyiv-Odessa highway, signed on 9 October 2008.

The schedule of submissions and hearings on the case was approved in March 2011. Accordingly, a number of submissions are scheduled to be made throughout 2011 and 2012; oral hearings are to be held in March 2012.

B. Cases

Laskaridis Shipping Co. Ltd., Lavinia Corporation, A. Laskaridis and P. Laskaridis (Greece) v. Ukraine

This arbitration was filed on 7 November 2007 with an *ad hoc* arbitration tribunal created under the UNCITRAL Arbitration Rules. The amount claimed is approximately USD 9 million.

Remington Worldwide Ltd. (UK) v. Ukraine

This arbitration was filed on 25 September 2008 with the SCC. Ukraine was accused of violating the Energy Charter Treaty, ratified in 1998. The amount claimed was over USD 33 million. The final award, rendered on 28 April 2011, obliged Ukraine to compensate only USD 4.5 million instead of the amount claimed by Remington, as Ukraine was found to be violating only one provision of the Treaty.

In addition to the above disputes, on 8 June 2010, an SCC tribunal ordered NJSC "Naftogaz" to return 11 billion cubic meters of gas to RosUkrEnergo (a gas supply company owned by the Russian Gazprom and Ukrainian individuals). In addition, the tribunal ordered that RosUkrEnergo receive a further 1.1 billion cubic meters of gas from Naftogaz instead of receiving entitlement to penalties for breach of contract. The award was recognized and enforced by the decision of a court of first instance (Shevchenkivskiy District Court of Kyiv City) on 13 August 2010 and was upheld by a ruling of the Appellate Court of Kyiv City on 17 September 2010. On 24 November 2010, the Supreme Court of Ukraine refused to satisfy the cassation complaint of Naftogaz, upholding the decisions of the lower courts.

B.3 Shares Sale and Purchase Agreement Is Not a "Corporate Relationship" under Ukrainian Law

In 2010 a tribunal, acting under the Rules of Arbitration of the International Arbitral Centre of the Austrian Federal Economic Chamber ("the Vienna Centre Tribunal"), resolved a dispute pertaining to the validity of several agreements to transfer ownership rights to the shares of a Ukrainian company (the "Transaction Agreements") to a non-resident company. Notably, prior to commencement of the arbitration, the respondent, a former shareholder of the Ukrainian company, initiated several proceedings in Ukrainian courts seeking to invalidate the transaction agreements with subsequent restitution.

Given the fact that the dispute arose between a non-resident company, at the time a shareholder of the Ukrainian company, and a Ukrainian respondent, a former shareholder of the same Ukrainian company, the latter objected to the jurisdiction of the Vienna Centre Tribunal by referring to the nonarbitrability of the dispute. Reference was made to Article 12 of the Commercial Procedural Code of Ukraine, which provides that disputes arising from corporate relations between a company and its current or former participant, or between the participants themselves, relating to the establishment, activity, management or termination of their company, are not arbitrable.

However, the tribunal dismissed these arguments and recognized its jurisdiction over all disputes arising out of the transaction agreements for the following reasons: (i) the transaction agreements were governed by Austrian law, and, therefore, the issue of arbitrability should be governed by Austrian law, and (ii) the claim in the dispute was of a contractual nature and, therefore, did not concern any corporate relations between the parties within the meaning of Article 12 of the Commercial Procedural Code of Ukraine.

The Vienna Centre tribunal resolved the arbitration dispute in favor of the claimant. The claimant then applied to a Ukrainian court for recognition and enforcement of the arbitral award. The respondent, in turn, filed objections to the recognition and enforcement of the arbitration award, making reference to an alleged breach of public policy. The procedure for recognition is currently under review at the court of first instance.

B.4 Refusal to Recognize and Enforce an Arbitral Award against a Ukrainian Debtor for Failure of Notice

An American company, Sea Emerald S.A. Panama (the claimant), applied to a Ukrainian court for recognition and enforcement of an arbitral award regarding the collection of a debt (the "Enforcement Request") owed by a Ukrainian company, Sudnobudivnyi Zavod im. Komunara (the respondent).

In the proceeding, the respondent stated that it was not duly informed about the arbitration proceedings. According to the claimant, the arbitral tribunal informed the respondent of every procedural action in the arbitration by e-mail and by facsimile. The respondent, however, argued that it had no officially registered e-mail addresses and that, unless the claimant could prove otherwise, the arbitral award should not be recognized and enforced in Ukraine for this reason.

Thus, although the respondent (during its performance of the terms under the contract) used certain e-mail addresses and facsimile numbers, the claimant could not prove that such contact details were officially registered in connection with the respondent's name. As a result, the Ukrainian court dismissed the claimant's request for recognition and enforcement of the arbitral award against the respondent.

B.5 Ukrainian State Enforcement Service Refused to Enforce Arbitral Award against a Ukrainian Debtor Due to Technicality

A German grain trading company filed an application for recognition and enforcement of an arbitral award rendered under the Rules of the Grain and Feed Trade Association in London with the Percherskyi District Court for the City of Kyiv. The award was rendered against the Ukrainian grain company (the debtor) and provided for the collection of a debt. The Ukrainian court granted the application to enforce the award, and thereafter, the company filed an enforcement order with the State Enforcement Service. However, the State Enforcement Service returned the application to the German company, stating that the enforcement order did not provide for clear enforcement measures, such as collection of a debt. Despite the fact that Ukraine's legislation provides that enforcement authorities can take any actions prescribed by Ukrainian courts, it is clear that these authorities are merely using formal excuses to obstruct the enforcement of foreign arbitral awards.

C. PUBLIC POLICY IN INTERNATIONAL ARBITRATION

C.1 Scenarios of Reliance on Public Policy

The procedure for invoking public policy considerations in the sphere of arbitration in Ukraine is regulated under the New York Convention, the Ukrainian Law on Arbitration, and the Civil Procedure Code of Ukraine.

As a general rule, according to the Law on Arbitration, public policy considerations may be invoked within the procedure for recognition and enforcement of an arbitral award in Ukraine.

Thus, as outlined in Article 36 of the Law on Arbitration, the recognition and enforcement of an arbitral award may not be granted if such an award is found to be in violation of the public policy of Ukraine. The rules that constitute "public policy" will be specifically addressed in paragraph C.3 below.

In the meantime, the Civil Procedure Code of Ukraine foresees that the state court may refuse to grant recognition and enforcement if such enforcement threatens the interests of Ukraine. The notion of the "interests of Ukraine" is vague due to the lack of legislative efforts to clearly define it. However "national interests" are defined in the Ukrainian law *On the Fundamentals of National Security of Ukraine* dated 19 June 2003 as including the vital material, intellectual and mental values of the Ukrainian nation, which bear sovereignty and are the only source of power in Ukraine, as well as the determinative needs of society and the state, the fulfillment of which guarantees the sovereignty and progressive development of the Ukrainian state.

It is worth indicating that the Law on Arbitration also provides the parties with the possibility to request the cancellation of an arbitral award on the grounds of public policy violations, on the sole condition that the place of arbitration was Ukraine. Otherwise, arbitral awards cannot be reconsidered on their merits and, therefore, foreign arbitral awards cannot be cancelled with reference to public policy considerations. Consequently, as foreseen by Ukraine's arbitration law, a party can rely on public policy mostly at the stage of the recognition and enforcement of foreign arbitral awards in state courts, invoking it as a defense. The court, in turn, is entitled to refuse recognition and enforcement of the arbitral award on these grounds.

C.2 Modes and Limitations of Reliance on Public Policy

The procedure for recognition and enforcement of an arbitral award is commenced by a motion on recognition and enforcement, which can be filed by the interested party with the court of general jurisdiction, as discussed in detail in paragraph A.2.4. In addition to the New York Convention, the procedure is regulated under the Civil Procedure Code of Ukraine, according to which the court shall notify the debtor within five days of the filing of such motion, simultaneously inviting the debtor to file its objections, if any. The debtor may proceed with such objections or refuse to do so within one month of the court's notification. As was indicated in paragraph C.1, when objecting to the motion on recognition and enforcement of an arbitral award, the debtor may invoke public policy considerations in its request for the court to refuse recognition and enforcement of the arbitral award.

It is noteworthy that Ukraine's arbitration legislation does not set forth any specific requirements for reliance on public policy at the enforcement stage. It is for this reason that there is no necessity to prove, in particular, that the public policy defense was previously invoked but rejected by the arbitral tribunal that considered the parties' dispute on its merits. Moreover, according to the Arbitration Law, the court shall refuse recognition and enforcement of an arbitral award if the award had not been declared binding on the parties or was vacated, or if its enforcement was suspended by the court at the place of arbitration or a court applying the law used by the tribunal in its consideration of the dispute.

C.3 Rules that Constitute "Public Policy"

The term "public policy" is not clearly defined in Ukraine's legislation. It is debatable whether a broad legal category with such specificity and varied dynamics can ever be strictly defined by the law. However, the concept of "public policy" is viewed by the Supreme Court of Ukraine as the legal order of a state, encompassing the leading principles and foundations that constitute the basis of its social order (e.g., those provisions concerning the independence, integrity and immunity of the state, or its main constitutional rights, freedoms and guarantees).

There is no legislative distinction between "domestic" and "international" public policy. Theoretically, such a division can be made. However, as regards international commercial arbitration, the legislative rules developed thus far refer solely to the concept of "public policy of Ukraine," i.e., "domestic public policy." Given the absence of legislative definition, a party may invoke any breach of public policy as a defense, which must, however, fall within the parameters provided by the Supreme Court of Ukraine. Therefore, the alleged violation of fundamental principles of national public law, basic constitutional rights, freedoms, or guarantees of the rights of individuals and legal entities, including their procedural rights, may serve as a defense against recognition and enforcement of an award.

Ukrainian courts in turn tend to interpret the concept of "public policy" broadly, a tendency that can be demonstrated by court practice. Thus, the Shevchenkivskiy District Court of Kyiv City, through its ruling of 28 November 2008, cancelled the arbitral award rendered by the ICAC in a dispute between the parties to an arbitration agreement, according to which all disputes should have been referred to the Arbitration Court at the Kyiv Chamber of Commerce and Industry. Due to the existence of only one arbitration court within Ukraine, located in Kyiv (the ICAC), the latter accepted this case for consideration.

The state court treated ICAC's acceptance of jurisdiction over the dispute as a breach of the fundamental principles of Ukraine concerning legislatively-adopted rights on court defense, and therefore, proceeded to cancel the award on the basis that a breach of the public policy of Ukraine had occurred.

Another ICAC award was cancelled by a state court on the basis of a breach of the requirements as to the identity and admissibility of court evidence. The court ruled that the award contradicted the constitutional principle of competitiveness and thus breached the public policy of Ukraine.

In conclusion, the concept of public policy may be broadly invoked by a party and is rather broadly interpreted by the Ukrainian state courts, an approach which provides for the possibility to refuse the recognition and enforcement of awards on a relatively large scope of grounds not yet specifically defined and delineated by Ukrainian legislation.

C.4 Review of Alleged Breaches of Public Policy

Alleged breaches of public policy may be considered *ex officio,* as no express reliance on them by the affected party is required. Accordingly, a court may establish a breach of public policy on its initiative while considering the motion on recognition and enforcement of the arbitral award as defined in Article 36 of the Arbitration Law, which corresponds to the relevant provisions of the New York Convention.

At the same time, there may not be a need for a *révision au fond,* as demonstrated by Ukrainian court practice. In this regard, the Supreme Court of Ukraine, in its Ruling No. 12 of 24 December 1999, clarified that "the court shall consider motions on recognition and enforcement of arbitration awards within given limitations and cannot discuss the correctness of such awards on their merits or make any amendments to the latter."

This suggests that a state court must not consider the case on its merits, but instead only examine the possible consequences of the recognition and enforcement of an award and, specifically, whether such enforcement will contradict "domestic" principles that constitute public policy in Ukraine.

UNITED KINGDOM

Edward Poulton,[1] Kate Corby,[2] Fiona Lockhart and Katherine Wilde[3]

A. LEGISLATION, TRENDS AND TENDENCIES

International arbitration in England and Wales[4] continues to be governed by the Arbitration Act 1996 (the "Arbitration Act"), to which no legislative amendment was made in 2011.[5]

---

[1] Edward Poulton is a Partner in Baker & McKenzie's London office. He practices all forms of dispute resolution and specializes in international arbitration. His experience ranges from contract and M&A disputes to claims in the banking sector and investment treaty claims.

[2] Kate Corby is a Senior Associate in Baker & McKenzie's London office. She regularly represents clients in international arbitrations, often in the construction and natural resources sectors.

[3] Fiona Lockhart and Katherine Wilde are Solicitor-Trainees in the Dispute Resolution Department of Baker & McKenzie's London office.

[4] England and Wales are two of the four countries that make up the United Kingdom. They have a common legal system, whereas the other two countries in the United Kingdom (Scotland and Northern Ireland) have separate systems. For the purposes of the current publication we intend only to refer to the laws of England and Wales. Any reference to "England" or "English" in this section should also be taken to include "Wales" or "Welsh."

[5] *See also* Civil Procedure Rules and Practice Direction, Part 62; Arbitration Act 1996 (Commencement No. 1) Order 1996 SI 1006/3146; High Court and County Courts (Allocation of Arbitration Proceedings) Order 1996 SI 1996/3 125; The Unfair Arbitration Agreements (Specified Amount) Order 1996 SI 1996/3211; Arbitration Act 1950, Part II Enforcement of Certain Foreign Awards.

B. CASES

B.1 Legality of Arbitration Agreements

B.1.1. *Jivraj v. Hashwani* [2011] UKSC 40

The English Supreme Court has overturned the decision of the Court of Appeal (reported in the 2010 edition of this publication) by ruling that a requirement in an arbitration clause that arbitrators must be from the Ismaili Muslim community was not unlawful. The Supreme Court held that an arbitrator is not an employee within the meaning of the Employment Equality (Religious and Belief) Regulations 2003 (the "2003 Regulations") and that, even if the 2003 Regulations *had* been applicable, the requirement would have fallen within the "genuine occupational requirement" exception in regulation 7(3) of the 2003 Regulations. There had been a fear amongst the international arbitration community that the Court of Appeal's decision, if upheld, could potentially have wide-ranging consequences because its reasoning might also apply to nationality, which is a ground for unlawful discrimination under the Equality Act 2010. However, the Supreme Court's decision confirms that arbitrators are not employees for the purposes of employment anti-discrimination laws. The Supreme Court also recognized that requirements of nationality or religion in arbitration clauses can be an integral part of arbitration, and that parties need to be confident in the ability of the arbitrators to take into account particular cultural or ethical considerations.

B.1.2. *Fulham Football Club (1987) Ltd. v. Sir David Richards and The Football Association Premier League Ltd.* [2010] EWHC 3111 (Ch)

This case confirms that unfair prejudice petitions can be referred to arbitration, thereby expanding the scope of arbitrable claims arising under shareholder agreements.[6] The English Court of Appeal upheld the decision of the High Court that a petition issued by Fulham Football Club ("FFC") on the grounds of unfair prejudice to the company's members should be stayed on the basis that the petition concerned matters that fell within the scope of an arbitration agreement.

The parties were in dispute over allegations that the chairman of the Football Association Premier League Ltd. (the "FAPL") had breached his fiduciary and general duties as a director of FAPL and had acted as an unauthorized agent by interfering in negotiations concerning the transfer of a well-known player, with the result that FFC lost out on the transfer. FFC wanted to obtain an injunction to restrain the chairman from acting as an unauthorized agent or from participating in any way in future player transfer negotiations, or in the alternative, that he cease to be chairman of the FAPL. The arbitration agreement that both FFC and FAPL were subject to under the rules of the FAPL and the rules of the Football Association did not allow for such relief. FFC therefore issued an unfair prejudice petition under Section 994 of the Companies Act 2006 in the High Court that, if successful, would allow the court to make any order it thought fit.

The chairman sought a stay of the unfair prejudice proceedings under Section 9(1) of the Arbitration Act[7] on the grounds that the matters fell within the terms of the arbitration agreements. In response, FFC argued that as arbitrators could not grant the relief

---

[6] Under Section 994 of the Companies Act 2006, shareholders have a right to petition the court on the ground that the company's affairs are being or have been conducted in a manner that is or would be prejudicial to the interests of some or all of the company's members.

[7] Section 9(1) of the Arbitration Act allows a party to an arbitration agreement against whom court proceedings are brought on matters under the agreement to apply to the court for a stay in the proceedings relating to that matter.

that FFC sought, it could not have been agreed that unfair prejudice proceedings were to be arbitrated. The High Court granted a stay in the unfair prejudice proceedings on the basis that the matters in the claim fell within the scope of arbitration. FFC appealed.

The Court of Appeal unanimously dismissed the appeal and held that there was neither an express nor an implied provision or reason why the unfair prejudice claim could not be arbitrated. The petition did not involve the binding of any third parties and was distinguishable from a class remedy. The court further held that the unfair prejudice claim did not necessitate state intervention nor was it of sufficient public interest to warrant judicial supervision. It therefore held that arbitrators could make an order against the chairman preventing him from acting as an agent for any club in the future and could also order him to resign as chairman of FAPL.

B.2   Anti-Suit Injunctions

B.2.1. *AES Ust-Kamenogorsk Hydropower Plant LLP v. Ust-Kamenogorsk Hydropower Plant JSC* [2011] EWCA Civ 647

This case demonstrates that where an arbitration clause provides for arbitration in England, a party does not need to commence arbitration proceedings to restrain foreign proceedings against it. It can, instead, rely on the arbitration clause to seek declaratory and injunctive relief from the English courts to restrain those proceedings using Section 37 of the Senior Courts Act 1981 (the "SCA 1981").

In 2004, in proceedings between the parties' predecessors, the Kazakhstan Supreme Court made a ruling that the arbitration clause in the concession agreement at issue was void because, contrary to Kazakh public policy, it sought to refer tariff disputes to arbitration. The concession agreement was governed by

Kazakh law but contained an arbitration clause that provided for arbitration in London under the ICC Rules. In 2009, the Ust-Kamenogorsk Hydropower Plant JSC (the "defendant") brought a claim against AES Ust-Kamenogorsk Hydropower Plant LLP (the "claimant") in the Kazakh courts for further information about the value of the concession assets. The claimant applied to dismiss the claim on the basis that the parties were obliged to arbitrate in England. The Kazakh Economic Court rejected the claimant's application on the basis of the 2004 ruling that the arbitration clause was void. The claimant therefore filed a claim in the English Commercial Court seeking: (a) a declaration that the defendant was bound to submit disputes to arbitration; and (b) an anti-suit injunction to restrain the Kazakh proceedings. The Commercial Court granted a final anti-suit injunction and declaration, and the defendant appealed.

Neither party wished to commence arbitration proceedings to resolve the dispute over the validity of the arbitration clause, and it was undisputed that, as there was no actual or intended arbitration, the English court had no jurisdiction to grant a declaration or an anti-suit injunction under Section 44 of the Arbitration Act. As a result, the question arose whether the court could nevertheless have jurisdiction. Another question was whether it could intervene even though Section 1(c) of the Arbitration Act provides that the court "should not intervene except as provided by this Part." The Court of Appeal held that the Arbitration Act did not apply where there was no arbitration in prospect. The court therefore concluded that Section 1(c) of the Arbitration Act did not prevent the court from intervening and that in such circumstances, there is no statutory or principled objection to the English courts' jurisdiction under the SCA 1981.

Turning to the merits of the application, it was undisputed that the English court, under Section 32(3) of the Civil Jurisdiction and Judgments Act 1982 (the "CJJA 1982"), had discretion to recognize the judgment of the Kazakh Supreme Court on the validity of the arbitration clause. In exercising such discretion, the Court of Appeal held that the Kazakh Supreme Court's interpretation of the concession agreement was incorrect. Under those circumstances, therefore, there was no reason why the judgment should be recognized or enforced.

Finally, in relation to the defendant's argument that the claimant had submitted to the jurisdiction of the Kazakh courts in the 2009 proceedings, the Court of Appeal held that the claimant had at all times challenged the Kazakh court's jurisdiction on the grounds of the arbitration agreement, but found that it had no choice but to argue the merits after the Kazakh court refused to decline jurisdiction. The court held, however, that even if the facts did amount to submission, the judgment of the Kazakh court should not be recognized by the English courts and there was nothing in the CJJA 1982 that required this.

B.2.2. *Excalibur Ventures LLC v. Texas Keystone Inc. and Other Companies* [2011] EWHC 1624 (Comm)

In this case, the English Commercial Court granted an injunction restraining the claimant from pursuing arbitration proceedings in New York, because it had already commenced substantive proceedings in the Commercial Court. The claimant and the first defendant, Texas Keystone, had entered into a collaboration agreement to acquire petroleum blocks in Iraqi Kurdistan. The agreement contained a clause referring disputes to arbitration under the ICC Rules in New York. The other three defendants (the "Gulf companies") argued that they were not parties to either the collaboration agreement or the arbitration agreement, and therefore applied for an injunction restraining the arbitration proceedings.

The Commercial Court held that the English courts have jurisdiction to grant injunctions restraining foreign arbitrations although that power should only be exercised in exceptional circumstances, and with caution. Such circumstances include where there is an issue over whether the parties consented to the arbitration. Applying *Dallah*,[8] the Commercial Court held that it was a matter for the English court to decide whether there was an agreement to arbitrate. Furthermore, the claimant had clearly submitted to the jurisdiction of the English court by itself stating that the circumstances of the case were "substantially connected to England and Wales." The court further held that the Gulf companies had not submitted to the jurisdiction of the ICC, and at all times had made it clear that they did not accept its jurisdiction. The court considered the *AES* case referred to above and held that, although in that case the Court of Appeal was not dealing with a foreign arbitration, the judgment clearly supported the proposition that in circumstances such as exists in *Excalibur*, the English court has jurisdiction to decide whether an arbitration agreement exists.

Having established that the court had jurisdiction to grant the injunctions, the court then considered whether it was appropriate to grant them. It held that in the circumstances, it was appropriate to do so and, in particular, pointed to the fact that:

(a) the Gulf companies had a strong, arguable case that they were not party to either the collaboration agreement or the arbitration agreement; (b) none of the three defendants had any connection with the ICC or New York; (c) the claimant had commenced substantive proceedings in the Commercial Court but had not made any substantive applications with the ICC; and (d) it would be vexatious to force the defendants to defend proceedings relating to the same issues in two different jurisdictions.

---

[8] *Dallah Estate and Tourism Holding Company v. The Ministry of Religious Affairs, Government of Pakistan* [2010] UKSC 46 (*see* summary in the 2010 edition of this publication).

B.3 Enforceability of Declaratory Award

B.3.1. *African Fertilizers and Chemicals NIG, Ltd. (Nigeria) v. BD Shipsnavo GmbH & Co. Reederei KG* [2011] EWHC 2542 (Comm)

In this case, the Commercial Court held that a declaratory award is enforceable under Section 66 of the Arbitration Act. A dispute arose between the parties in relation to a bill of lading, which incorporated the terms and conditions of an underlying voyage charter containing an arbitration clause referring disputes to arbitration in London. Prior to the London arbitration, African Fertilizers commenced arbitration and court proceedings in Romania. The English High Court granted BD Shipsnavo an injunction restraining African Fertilizers from continuing arbitration proceedings in Romania. It also issued an interim declaration that the arbitration clause was binding on African Fertilizers and that the Romanian arbitration and court proceedings were in breach of the agreement to arbitrate in London. The London arbitral tribunal then granted a declaratory award in favor of BD Shipsnavo that the arbitration clause was validly incorporated into the bill of lading and was binding on African Fertilizers, and that they had jurisdiction over all disputes arising out of the bill of lading.

BD Shipsnavo remained concerned that African Fertilizers could obtain judgment in its favor in the Romanian court and then seek to have the judgment recognized and enforced in England. BD Shipsnavo therefore sought, and was granted, an order for enforcement of the arbitral award under Section 66 of the Arbitration Act. African Fertilizers applied to have the order giving BD Shipsnavo leave to enforce the award and to enter into a judgment on its terms set aside. The application was based on the grounds that enforcement was not possible under Section 66 of the Arbitration Act and that a judgment under

Section 66 of the Arbitration Act did not constitute a judgment within the meaning of Article 34(3) of Regulation 44/2001 (the "Brussels I Regulation"). This, African Fertilizers argued, was because such a judgment did not involve any consideration by the court of the issues between the parties but was simply a mechanism for summary enforcement.

The Commercial Court refused African Fertilizer's application to have the order set aside. It confirmed that the arbitral award could be enforced under Section 66 of the Arbitration Act and the common law remedies in an action to enforce the award included a declaration that an award was valid. It further held that a judgment under Section 66 of the Arbitration Act falls within the meaning of judgment for the purposes of the Brussels I Regulation.

C. PUBLIC POLICY IN INTERNATIONAL ARBITRATION

C.1 Scenarios of Reliance on Public Policy

Under the Arbitration Act, parties may submit all arbitrable issues to an arbitral tribunal for determination, although the parties' freedom to decide how their disputes are to be resolved is subject to "such safeguards as are necessary in the public interest."[9] Although a contract will be void *ab initio* if the making of it is expressly or impliedly prohibited by statute or is contrary to public policy,[10] the doctrine of separability[11] provides that an arbitration agreement is separate from the underlying or

---

[9] Arbitration Act, s.1(1)(b).

[10] *Archbolds (Freightage) Ltd. v. S. Spanglett Ltd.* [1961] 1 Q.B. 374.

[11] As established by case law, a statutory codification of which is set out in the Arbitration Act, s.7.

principal contract. It is therefore extremely rare that an arbitration agreement itself will not be upheld, and the fact that the underlying contract may be void is not generally sufficient to prevent an arbitral tribunal from having jurisdiction to determine the parties' disputes.[12] However, the English courts have recognized that there may be "illegal or immoral dealings"[13] that are, from an English law perspective, incapable of being arbitrated, as an agreement to arbitrate them would be contrary to English public policy. One example is a clause providing for the arbitration of disputes arising from placing of bets, which was held to be void on the ground that any contract or agreement by way of gaming or wagering was void under the Gaming Act 1845.[14]

After an award has been issued, a party to arbitral proceedings seated in England may make an application to the court to challenge the award on the basis that a serious irregularity affecting the tribunal, the proceedings or the award has caused, or will cause, substantial injustice to the applicant. One situation that may meet this test is where the award, or the way in which it was procured, is contrary to English public policy.[15] A successful challenge on this ground is likely to require "some form of

---

[12] Although the courts distinguish between disputes as to the existence of the arbitration agreement, which are likely to be determined by the courts, and disputes as to the validity of the arbitration agreement, which should be determined by the tribunal wherever possible.

[13] *Soleimany v. Soleimany* [1999] Q.B. 785, per Waller L.J. at 797. This case concerned an agreement to arbitrate a dispute arising out of a claim for an account of the proceeds from the sale of carpets, which had been smuggled out of Iran illegally. The arbitration agreement was found to be valid, although Waller L.J. suggested that, had the parties been seeking to arbitrate how to split the proceeds of a joint venture that had as its object the commission of offenses in Iran, the court would have been inclined to find that the arbitration clause was invalid.

[14] *O'Callaghan v. Coral Racing Ltd.*, [1998] All E.R. (D) 607.

[15] Arbitration Act, s. 68(2)(g).

reprehensible or unconscionable conduct,"[16] such as illegality, fraud, bribery or corruption.[17] The English courts have, for example, set aside permission to summarily enforce an award made in England where the award referred on its face to an illegal object and was therefore found to be contrary to public policy.[18]

Finally, recognition or enforcement of a New York Convention award may be refused by the English courts on the grounds that "it would be contrary to public policy"[19] to do so. However, the English courts are predisposed to favor the enforcement of awards. Indeed, even where such grounds are established, the English courts have limited discretion to recognize or enforce an award.[20] However, the exercise of any such discretion is likely to be restricted to circumstances where, despite the original existence of such grounds, "the right to rely on them had been lost by for example another agreement or estoppel,"[21] or where there are circumstances "which might on some recognizable legal principles affect the *prima facie* right to have an award set aside arising in cases listed in s.103(2)."[22]

---

[16] *Profilati Italia SrL v. Paine Webber* [2001] EWHC Commercial 24, [17]; *Cuflet Chartering v. Caroussel Shipping* [2001] 1 All E.R. (Comm) 398.

[17] *Westacre Investments Inc. v. Jugoimport-SPDR Holding Co. Ltd.* [1999] Q.B. 740.

[18] *Soleimany v. Soleimany* [1999] Q.B. 785, in which the arbitral tribunal had found a contract to smuggle carpets out of Iran to be illegal under Iranian law.

[19] Arbitration Act, s.103(3).

[20] *China Agribusiness Development Corporation v. Balli Trading* [1998] 2 Lloyd's Rep 76.

[21] *Yukos Oil Co v. Dardana Ltd.* [2002] EWCA Civ 543, [8].

[22] *Ibid.* at 18. *See also Svenska Petroleum Exploration AB v. Lithuania (No.1)* [2005] 1 Lloyd's Rep. 515.

C.2 Modes and Limitations of Reliance on Public Policy

The Arbitration Act provides that a party to arbitral proceedings may not raise an objection, *inter alia*, that there has been a serious irregularity affecting the tribunal or the proceedings on the grounds of breach of public policy (or otherwise) if it took part, or continued to take part, in proceedings without immediately[23] making that objection. The only exception is if the party is able to show that at the time it took part in the proceedings, it did not know, and could not have discovered, the grounds for the objection.[24] In addition, an application to challenge an award on the grounds of serious irregularity may only be brought once the applicant has exhausted any available arbitral process of appeal or review, and must be brought within 28 days of the date of the award or, where such arbitral process of appeal or review occurs, within 28 days of the date when the applicant is notified of the result of such process.[25]

Under the Arbitration Act, the courts may refuse to recognize or enforce a New York Convention award where the party that alleges it proves that the award has not yet become binding on the parties or has been set aside or suspended by a competent authority of the country in which, or under the law of which, it was made.[26] Furthermore, where an application has been made to such a competent authority to set aside or suspend a New York Convention award, and such application is pending, the court has discretion to adjourn its decision regarding recognition

---

[23] Or within the appropriate timeframe as may be set out by the arbitration agreement, the tribunal or the Arbitration Act.

[24] *Ibid.* s.73(1).

[25] *Ibid.* s.70(2).

[26] *Ibid.* s.103(2)(f).

or enforcement of the award.[27] It has also been held that the English courts possess an inherent jurisdiction to stay the enforcement of an English award overseas where Article V of the New York Convention applies.[28]

C.3 Rules that Constitute "Public Policy"

Public policy has been described by the English courts as a "very unruly horse, and when once you get astride it you never know where it will carry you."[29] As a consequence, the English courts have repeatedly warned that its application should be approached with extreme caution.[30] Although considerations of English public policy can never be exhaustively defined, in order to rely on such a ground it must be shown that there is some element of illegality, or that the enforcement of the award would be clearly contrary to the public good or, possibly, that enforcement would be "wholly offensive to the ordinary reasonable and fully informed member of the public on whose behalf the powers of the state are exercised."[31] However, when considering whether to refuse to enforce an award on the grounds of public policy, the English courts seek to balance the need to discourage activities that are contrary to public policy with the strong English public policy considerations in favor of giving effect as far as possible to the finality of international arbitration awards.

As a ground for refusal of enforcement of an award, public policy is, for the purposes of the English courts, confined to the

---

[27] *Ibid.* s.103(5).

[28] *Apis AS v. Fantazia Kereskedelmi KFT* [2001] All E.R. (Comm) 348.

[29] *Richardson v. Mellish* (1824) 2 Bing 229, DC, per Burrough J. at 252.

[30] *See, e.g., Deutsche Schachtbau — und Tiefbohr-Gesellschaft m.b.H. v. Shell International Petroleum Co. Ltd.* [1990] 1 A.C. 295.

[31] *Ibid.* at 316.

public policy of England as the country in which enforcement is sought.[32] However, a distinction is drawn between English public policy and public policy in the context of enforcement of international arbitration awards. The English courts have held that there are some rules of public policy that, if infringed, would lead to non-enforcement by the English court whatever their proper law, and wherever their place of performance, for example, concerns regarding drug trafficking. However, enforcement of contracts that violate rules of public policy based on purely domestic concerns and that are not performed within the jurisdiction of the English courts will not be refused on the grounds of English public policy.[33] Where enforcement of an award would result in a breach of England's treaty obligations, then the English courts will not enforce such an award on public policy grounds.[34]

C.4 Review of Alleged Breaches of Public Policy

Although the Court of Appeal has suggested that it may be possible for an English court to re-open an arbitral tribunal's findings where the tribunal has already ruled on the issue of public policy,[35] in a number of subsequent cases, the courts have reached the opposite conclusion.[36] Case law suggests that in the

---

[32] *IPCO Nigeria Ltd. v. Nigerian National Petroleum Corp.* [2005] EWHC 726 (Comm).

[33] *Westacre Investments Inc. v. Jugoimport-SPDR Holding Co. Ltd.* [1999] Q.B. 740, referring to *Lemenda Trading Co. Ltd. v. African Middle East Petroleum Co.* [1988] 1 Q.B. 448, applied in *R v. V* [2008] EWHC 1531 (Comm).

[34] *Eco Swiss China Time Ltd. v. Benetton International BV* [1999] 2 All E.R. (Comm) 44.

[35] *Soleimany v. Soleimany* [1998] 3 W.L.R. 811.

[36] *Westacre Investments Inc. v. Jugoimport-SPDR Holding Co. Ltd.* [1999] Q.B. 740, applied in *R v. V* [2008] EWHC 1531 (Comm).

majority of cases where a public policy defense is raised at the challenge or enforcement stage, the English courts will restrict themselves to reviewing the reasoning of the arbitral tribunal, rather than reviewing the underlying facts.

Although the court may consider public policy issues regardless of whether such issues are raised by the parties,[37] in the context of enforcement of a New York Convention award, the burden of proving that enforcement would be contrary to public policy rests on the party seeking to rely on such grounds.[38]

---

[37] *Beresford v. Royal Insurance Co. Ltd.* [1938] A.C. 586, *Yukos Oil Co v. Dardana Ltd.* [2002] EWCA Civ 543.

[38] *Minmetals Germany GmbH v. Ferco Steel Ltd.* [1999] C.L.C. 647.

UNITED STATES

Donald J. Hayden,[1] Jose A. Avila,[2] Ethan A. Berghoff[3] and Karen Sewell[4]

A. LEGISLATION, TRENDS AND TENDENCIES

A.1 Legislation

Since its passage in 1925, the Federal Arbitration Act ("FAA") has undergone only five amendments, most recently in 1990. Two of those five amendments were to implement the New York and Inter-American Conventions. In general, the FAA has grown stronger over time and held to its original purpose of promoting a strong national policy in favor of arbitration.

Since 2007, however, a bill has been floating around Congress that seeks to significantly narrow the scope of the FAA and exclude most forms of consumer disputes from arbitration. The bill is known as the Arbitration Fairness Act ("AFA"). It has taken various forms over the years and was re-introduced in

---

[1] Donald J. Hayden is a Partner in Baker & McKenzie's Miami office. His practice involves primarily cross border disputes being resolved through litigation and arbitration. He leads Baker & McKenzie's Dispute Resolution Group in Miami and is a member of the Steering Committee of the Firm's Global Arbitration Group.

[2] Jose Avila is an Associate in Baker & McKenzie's Miami office. His practice focuses on commercial litigation, international arbitration, and white-collar criminal matters.

[3] Ethan Berghoff is a Partner in Baker & McKenzie's Chicago office. He represents clients in a broad range of international matters, including distributorship and supply agreements, power, fuel supply and construction contracts as well as post-acquisition disputes. He has also appeared before ICC, LCIA and ICDR arbitration panels around the world.

[4] Karen Sewell is an Associate in Baker & McKenzie's Chicago office and focuses her practice on cross-border business disputes.

Congress in May 2011.[5] This most recent version provides that "no predispute arbitration agreement shall be valid or enforceable if it requires arbitration of an employment dispute, consumer dispute, or civil rights dispute."[6] The bill would also mandate that "a court, rather than an arbitrator," determine the validity of a contract containing such an arbitration clause.[7]

In addition, a group of congressional Democrats introduced another bill, the Consumer Mobile Fairness Act, in the Senate.[8] This one reads much like the AFA, except that it invalidates only those pre-dispute arbitration agreements between a cellphone user and the cellphone service provider.

Over the course of the FAA's existence, dozens of laws have been proposed in an attempt to limit the FAA's reach, often in the consumer context. But none of them have ever had sufficient congressional support to become law. Given the trajectory of the AFA and its prior failed attempts, commentators are not confident that this time will be any different.

Aside from the FAA, there are a number of federal laws that contain provisions relating to the availability of arbitration or other dispute resolution procedures to settle disputes arising under those laws. Among these, the Patent Law was amended in 2011 to allow arbitration of newly revised patent derivation proceedings.[9]

---

[5] H.R. 1873 – Arbitration Fairness Act of 2011, sponsored by Rep. Henry Johnson (D-GA) on May 11, 2011 in the House of Representatives, and, on May 12, 2011, S. 987 – Arbitration Fairness Act of 2011, sponsored by Sen. Al Franken (D-MN) in the Senate.

[6] *Id.*

[7] *Id.*

[8] S. 1652, sponsored by Sen. Richard Blumenthal (D-Conn.), along with Sens. Franken and Sheldon Whitehouse (D-R.I.) on October 4, 2011.

[9] Patent Reform Act of 2011 (America Invents Act) 35 U.S.C. §135(f). The American Invents Act, introduced as H.R. 1249, was signed by President Obama on Sept. 16, 2011 and became Public Law No. 112-29.

A.2 Trends and Tendencies

The re-introduction of the AFA came on the heels of the U.S. Supreme Court's decision in *AT&T Mobility LLC v. Concepcion* (discussed below in Section B) and typified the major trend in U.S. arbitration in 2011: the interplay between the strong tradition in the United States in favor of class actions, on the one hand, and the strong national policy in favor of arbitration on the other. Other issues analyzed in the courts included arbitrability, confirmation of awards, public policy, and judicial review, among others, but no one issue was as recurrent or prominent as class action waivers. These cases are described in more detail below in Section B.

B. CASES[10]

B.1 Supreme Court, Others Uphold Class Action Waivers in Consumer Arbitration Agreements

***AT&T Mobility LLC v. Concepcion*, 563 U.S. ____, No. 09-893 (Apr. 27, 2011)**

The Supreme Court issued a 5-4 decision in *AT&T Mobility LLC v. Concepcion*, 563 U.S. ____, No. 09-893 (Apr. 27, 2011), ruling that arbitration agreements containing class action waivers are valid and enforceable. The Court's ruling in *Concepcion* takes a bold swipe at putative class action plaintiffs who seek friendly state laws to aid their escape from contractual arbitration clauses. Previously, under the Court's *Stolt-Nielsen*[11] decision, it

---

[10] The authors would like to thank the contributors of Baker & McKenzie's *North American International Litigation and Arbitration Newsletter* for the case summaries used in this report.

[11] *Stolt-Nielsen v. AnimalFeeds Int'l Corp.*, 559 U.S. ____, No. 08-1198 (Apr. 27, 2010).

was established that parties generally cannot be compelled to resolve disputes under class action procedures, whether in arbitration or in court, where they have contracted to arbitrate disputes and have not consented to class procedures. *Concepcion* develops the interplay between class action and arbitration procedural law one step further, establishing that parties can enter into arbitration clauses that expressly opt out of class actions and opt exclusively for bilateral arbitration.

In *Concepcion*, the plaintiffs challenged a consumer contract provision that mandated arbitration and waived class-action dispute resolution. Plaintiffs contended that such class waiver violated California law—established in *Discover Bank v. Superior Court*, 36 Cal. 4th 148 (2005)—under which collective-arbitration waivers in consumer contracts of adhesion were deemed unconscionable if individual damages were "predictably small" and the plaintiff alleged a "scheme to cheat consumers."[12]

The Supreme Court held that AT&T could not be compelled to engage in class-wide arbitration under the *Discover Bank* rule where the arbitration agreement at issue provided only for bilateral arbitration. *Concepcion* is regarded as a significant victory for businesses and a stinging defeat for the plaintiffs' class action bar, which has been attacking class waivers under state law for years. It also signals greater court scrutiny of state laws that disproportionately invalidate arbitration clauses while purportedly applying *universally* to any contract clause.

The Supreme Court addressed the question of whether § 2 of the FAA (the "savings clause"), which requires that arbitration agreements be enforced except "upon such grounds as exist at law or in equity for the revocation of any contract," preempted

---

[12] *AT&T Mobility LLC v. Concepcion*, 563 U.S. ____, No. 09-893, slip op. at 12 (Apr. 27, 2011).

California's *Discover Bank* rule.[13] The lower courts had each held that, because the *Discover Bank* rule was based on California's unconscionability law, which is a ground for the revocation of any contract, it fell within the ambit of § 2's savings clause. The Supreme Court signaled that the lower courts' construction of § 2's saving clause was overbroad. Noting California courts' frequent reliance on the *Discover Bank* rule to strike down arbitration agreements on unconscionability grounds, the Court explained that "[a]lthough § 2's saving clause preserves generally applicable contract defenses, nothing in it suggests an intent to preserve state-law rules that stand as an obstacle to the accomplishment of the FAA's objectives."[14]

Having squarely teed up the preemption question, the Court held that California's *Discover Bank* rule flew in the face of the FAAs § 2. The Court began by noting that the overarching purpose of the FAA "is to ensure the enforcement of arbitration agreements according to their terms so as to facilitate streamlined proceedings."[15] Accordingly, the Court noted, parties are free to craft arbitration clauses so as to specify what topics are subject to arbitration and the procedures to be utilized in arbitration.[16] However, the *Discover Bank* rule would essentially invalidate any arbitration clause that did not provide for class arbitration procedures.[17] This type of forced class arbitration, the Court held, was inconsistent with the purpose of the FAA.[18]

---

[13]   *Id.* slip op. at 5.

[14]   *Id.* slip op. at 9.

[15]   *Id.*

[16]   *Id.* slip op. at 10-11.

[17]   *See id.,* slip op. at 9, 12.

[18]   *Id.* slip op. at 13.

The Court also addressed the dissent's primary contention—that the *Discover Bank* rule "does just what § 2 requires, namely, puts agreements to arbitrate and agreements to litigate 'upon the same footing.'"[19] According to the Court, "States cannot require a procedure that is inconsistent with the FAA, even if it is desirable for unrelated reasons."[20] In addition, the Court "f[ound] it hard to believe that defendants would bet the company with no effective means of review, and even harder to believe that Congress would have intended to allow states to force such a decision."[21]

The Court's emphasis in *Concepcion* that arbitration agreements must be enforced according to their terms leaves open the question of the extent to which other notions of "unconscionability" may be used to invalidate arbitration provisions. In *Green Tree Financial Corp.-Ala. v. Randolph*, 531 U.S. 79 (2000), the Court indicated that a party seeking to invalidate an arbitration provision as being prohibitively expensive in relation to the claim bore the burden of showing the likelihood of prohibitive costs. Lower courts construed *Green Tree* to authorize them to invalidate certain arbitration provisions on this basis.[22] This ruling may now be open to attack. It is apparent that the arbitration agreement in *Concepcion* was drafted to deflect allegations of prohibitive expense.[23] But given that conceptions of unconscionability through expense or procedural inequality invariably affect arbitration differently than litigation, the *Concepcion* decision may provide fertile

---

[19]   *Id.* slip op. at 5 (Breyer, J., dissenting).

[20]   *Id.* slip op. at 17.

[21]   *Id.*

[22]   *See, e.g., Kristian v. Comcast Corp.*, 446 F.3d 25, 54 (1st Cir. 2006).

[23]   *Concepcion*, 563 U.S. __ slip op. at 2.

ground for resisting efforts to avoid arbitration based on such claims of unconscionability.

Litman v. Cellco P'ship, No. 08-4103 (3d Cir. Aug. 24, 2011)

Plaintiffs in this putative class action lawsuit were cellular phone customers of defendant Verizon Wireless ("Verizon"). Plaintiffs asserted violations of the New Jersey Consumer Fraud Act as well as claims for breach of contract and unjust enrichment, all in connection with Verizon's alleged practice of assessing unauthorized administrative fees on plaintiffs' cellular phone bills. Verizon moved to compel individual arbitration of plaintiffs' claims pursuant to the class waiver in the arbitration clause of plaintiffs' contracts with Verizon. Plaintiffs opposed the motion on the ground that the class waiver violated New Jersey public policy as stated in a 2006 decision of the New Jersey Supreme Court.

The district court granted the motion to compel arbitration, finding that the Federal Arbitration Act ("FAA"), 9 U.S.C. § 1 *et seq.*, as interpreted by recent Third Circuit case law, preempts the 2006 New Jersey decision. The court of appeals reversed. It reasoned, on the basis of an even more recent Third Circuit decision, *Homa v. American Express Co.*, 558 F.3d 225 (3d Cir. 2009), that because the 2006 New Jersey case provided a public policy-based defense against all waivers of class-wide actions— not just waivers that compel arbitration—it was not contrary to, and thus not preempted by, the FAA. Verizon then timely filed a motion to stay the court's mandate pending the filing of a petition for writ of certiorari to the Supreme Court. On May 2, 2011, the Supreme Court granted the writ, vacated the court of appeals holding, and remanded the case back to the court of appeals in light of the Court's recent decision in *AT&T Mobility LLC v. Concepcion.*

On remand, the court of appeals found that *Concepcion* preempted plaintiff's state law-based argument and affirmed the decision of the district court compelling individual arbitration of plaintiffs' claims. The court of appeals understood the holding of *Concepcion* to be unequivocal: any state law invalidating a class-arbitration waiver was inconsistent with, and thus preempted by, the FAA, regardless of whether class arbitration is desirable for other reasons. Further, the court interpreted *Concepcion* to apply equally to any law that invalidates a class-arbitration waiver, irrespective of whether the law would also invalidate a class-litigation waiver, as the 2006 New Jersey Supreme Court case would do. The court concluded that *Concepcion* absolutely bars plaintiffs' state law-based argument and affirmed the district court's order compelling individual arbitration of plaintiffs' claims in accordance with the terms of the arbitration agreement.

Cruz v. Cingular Wireless, LLC, No. 08-16080 (11th Cir. Aug. 11, 2011)

Plaintiffs were cellular-phone customers of defendant Cingular Wireless LLC (now AT&T Mobility, LLC). Each signed a service contract with defendant agreeing to arbitrate any disputes arising out of the contract, and to waive all rights to bring any claims as a class or in a representative capacity. Notwithstanding this "class-action waiver," plaintiffs filed a putative class action lawsuit in the U.S. District Court for the Middle District of Florida, alleging that defendant violated the Florida Deceptive and Unfair Trade Practices Act ("FDUTPA") by charging them fees for a "Roadside Assistance Plan" that they never ordered, hiding such fees in their bills without notice or warning, and refusing to refund the fees even after plaintiffs canceled them.

Defendant successfully moved to dismiss the complaint and to compel arbitration based on the class action waiver in the arbitration agreement. In granting the motion, the district court observed that Florida law will invalidate an agreement to arbitrate on public policy grounds only when the agreement would defeat the remedial purposes of the statute at issue, in this case FDUTPA. The district court concluded, however, that the class-action waiver embedded in the arbitration agreement did not defeat FDUTPA's remedial purposes, and was thus valid and enforceable, because (1) it did not limit plaintiffs' substantive remedies under FDUTPA, (2) it provided for the recovery of attorneys' fees, (3) it imposed no confidentiality rule restricting plaintiffs from disseminating information about their claims to other potential claimants and (4) it required that defendant bear the costs of the arbitration.

Plaintiffs appealed, contending that the district court failed to consider that the class-action waiver "functionally exculpated" defendant from liability, and thus defeated the remedial purposes of FDUTPA in violation of Florida public policy. In particular, plaintiffs argued and presented statistical evidence to support their claim that, because the dollar amount of each individual claim was so small, potential claims were numerous, and many customers may not know about or pursue potential claims absent the availability of class procedures; the net effect of the class action waiver would be to ensure that the majority of claims would go unprosecuted and would thus insulate defendant from liability.

While the case was pending on appeal, the Supreme Court issued its decision in *AT&T Mobility LLC v. Concepcion*. Applying *Concepcion* to plaintiffs' claims, the court found that plaintiffs' "functional exculpation" argument was preempted by the FAA. The court noted that the Supreme Court had considered, and rejected, the very same argument in *Concepcion*. Specifically, the Supreme Court held that even if class proceedings were necessary to enable consumers to bring small-value claims that would otherwise go unprosecuted, and even if a waiver of class proceedings would prevent consumers in such instances from vindicating their statutory rights, any state rule invalidating such a class-action waiver would conflict with the FAA's objective of enforcing arbitration agreements according to their terms. Thus, the court held that, to the extent Florida law would invalidate the class action waiver on public policy grounds, the FAA preempted Florida law on the issue.

The court also rejected plaintiffs' attempt to distinguish *Concepcion* as inapplicable to the facts of this case. Plaintiffs contended that *Concepcion* preempts only "inflexible" state law rules, like California's, that invalidate class waiver provisions in an entire category of cases. Plaintiffs argued that Florida law, in contrast to the pro-consumer California rule, invalidates class-action bans only when the individualized facts demonstrate that the waiver would functionally deprive a litigant of the ability to vindicate his or her statutory rights. The court disagreed. It found that plaintiffs' argument merely restated in different terms its public policy-based argument—namely that the class-action waiver is "functionally exculpatory" because it strips consumers of the ability and financial incentive to bring small-value claims. Moreover, the court found that, contrary to plaintiffs' assertion, applying Florida's public policy rule would result in the invalidation of nearly as many arbitration agreements as would applying the California rule, as both rules are based on the unconscionability doctrine and both rules would, in practice, "encompass the field of small-value consumer fraud claims."[24]

Thus, in light of *Concepcion*, the court affirmed the district court's order dismissing plaintiffs' class-action complaint and compelling arbitration of plaintiffs' claims.

---

[24] *Cruz v. Cingular Wireless LLC*, No. 08-16080, slip op. at 20 (11th Cir. Aug. 11, 2011).

B.2 Supreme Court Holds Arbitrability of Some but Not All Claims Still Requires Arbitration of Those Claims Parties Agreed to Arbitrate

KPMG LLP v. Cocchi, 565 U. S. ___, No. 10-1521 (Nov. 7, 2011)(per curiam)

In a recent unanimous, unsigned (*per curiam*) opinion generally reserved for non-controversial matters, the U.S. Supreme Court ruled that trial courts may not issue a "blanket refusal" to compel arbitration solely on the ground that some of the claims involved in a dispute are not subject to the arbitration clause, nor can appellate courts affirm such decisions.

The proper approach, explained the Court, is for trial and appellate courts to review all of the claims alleged in the complaint and determine if any are within the scope of the arbitration clause, and if there are any, refer them to arbitration. The opinion, issued without a hearing, was based on the parties' briefs for and against Supreme Court review, and did not include merits briefing. The Court simultaneously granted KPMG's petition for review and vacated a Florida Court of Appeal ruling that affirmed a trial court's refusal to compel arbitration based on a determination that two out of four claims alleged in the complaint were not covered by the arbitration agreement.

In this case, nineteen investors in three limited partnerships that invested with Bernard Madoff sued the funds, the companies that managed them, and the auditor KPMG to recover large investment losses. They alleged that the accounting firm failed to use proper accounting standards, which led to "substantial misrepresentations" in the partnership financial statements about the health of the partnerships.[25] The investors asserted four

---

[25]   *KPMG LLP v. Cocchi*, 565 U.S. ___, No. 10-1521, slip op. at 2 (Nov. 7, 2011)(per curiam).

claims: negligent misrepresentation, violation of Florida's deceptive trade practices act, professional malpractice, and aiding and abetting a breach of fiduciary duty. KPMG moved to compel arbitration based on the arbitration clause in the audit agreement between it and the fund managers. The arbitration clause stated that it extended to "any dispute or claim involving any person or entity for whose benefit the services in question were or are provided."[26]

The trial court denied KPMG's motion and the Florida Court of Appeal affirmed. First it determined that only derivative claims (i.e., claims based on services KPMG performed under the audit agreement) could be arbitrated because none of the investors had expressly agreed to the audit agreement or the arbitration clause. The appellate court determined that the causes of action for the negligent misrepresentation claim and the statutory claim were not derivative claims, but it drew no conclusions about the other two causes of action. It then affirmed the trial court's refusal to compel arbitration.

The Supreme Court concluded that Florida's Court of Appeal "failed to give effect to the plain meaning of the Act and to the holding in *Dean Witter*" by not addressing whether the arbitration agreement would apply to the professional malpractice and breach of fiduciary duty claims.[27] *Dean Witter* states that the FAA "leaves no discretion by a district court, but instead mandates that district courts *shall* direct the parties to proceed to arbitration on issues as to which the arbitration agreement has been signed."[28]

Therefore, the Supreme Court vacated the judgment and remanded the case back to the Florida appeals court to determine

---

[26]   *Id.*

[27]   *Id.* slip op. at 4.

[28]   *Id.* (quoting *Dean Witter Reynolds Inc. v. Byrd*, 470 U.S. 213, 218 (1985)).

whether the remaining claims were covered by the arbitration agreement.

B.3   New York State Appellate Court Holds That Debt Owed to Foreign Party Can Be Attached in Anticipation of an Arbitration Award against the Foreign Party, Even Where There is No Jurisdictional Connection to New York

Sojitz Corp. v. Prithvi Information Solutions, Inc., No. 602511/09 (N.Y. App. Div. 1st Dep't, Mar. 10, 2011)

Petitioners alleged they were owed over USD 40 million dollars from respondents under a contract containing an arbitration clause naming Singapore as the forum. Petitioners moved *ex parte* for, and were granted, an order of attachment for the amount allegedly owed in anticipation of arbitration. Upon a showing by respondents that they did not have sufficient contacts with New York to be subject to the personal jurisdiction of the New York courts, the New York Supreme Court vacated the USD 40 million order of attachment but upheld the attachment of approximately USD 18,000 owed to respondent by a New York customer, which money was located in New York. Respondents appealed.

The First Department upheld the attachment of the lesser amount under Section 7502(c) of the New York Civil Practice Laws and Rules, which allows the Supreme Court to grant an order of attachment in anticipation of an arbitration award in a foreign jurisdiction if the petitioner can show that "the award to which the applicant may be entitled may be rendered ineffectual without such provisional relief."

The court noted that respondent did not challenge the showing that the award may be rendered ineffectual without the relief. Therefore, the only question was whether it was appropriate to attach a debt owed by a party lacking contacts with New York under the federal rules on personal jurisdiction. As the court recognized, this issue had not previously been addressed by any court.

The court examined U.S. Supreme Court precedent on this issue, and particularly the decision in *Shaffer v. Heitner*, in which the U.S. Supreme Court remarked in *dicta* that minimum contacts over a defendant were not necessary where a court sought to attach property located in the state "as security for a judgment being sought in [another] forum."[29] The Appellate Division decided that the instant case fell within this exception, and therefore upheld the attachment of the debt owed to respondent and located within New York.

B.4 D.C. Circuit Holds that a District Court May Not Extend the Time Limit under the Federal Arbitration Act for Serving Notice of Motions to Vacate or Modify an Arbitral Award

Argentine Republic v. National Grid Plc, No. 10-7093 (D.C. Cir. Mar. 11, 2011)(per curiam)

On November 3, 2008, an arbitration panel sitting in Washington, D.C. found appellant Republic of Argentina ("Argentina") liable to National Grid plc ("National Grid") for approximately USD 53 million, concluding that Argentina violated a bilateral investment treaty between Argentina and the United Kingdom by taking certain emergency measures during its financial crisis. On November 13, 2008, Argentina received a copy of the arbitral award, triggering the three-month deadline under the Federal Arbitration Act ("FAA") to serve notice of a motion to vacate, modify or correct an arbitral award.[30]

---

[29] 433 U.S. 186, 210 (1977).

[30] *See* 9 U.S.C. § 12.

On February 6, 2009, Argentina filed a motion to vacate the award with the U.S. District Court for the District of Columbia ("Motion to Vacate"). National Grid cross-moved to confirm the award. On February 10—three days before the February 13 deadline for serving process of the Motion to Vacate—Argentina filed a motion seeking to extend the time for service ("Motion for Extension"), claiming that timely service would be impossible because, under the Hague Convention on the Service Abroad of Judicial and Extrajudicial Documents in Civil or Commercial Matters ("Hague Convention"), proper service in the U.K. required using a central governmental authority. As the legal basis for its motion, Argentina relied on Fed. R. Civ. P. 6(b)(1), which provides in part:

> When an act may or must be done within a specified time, the court may, for good cause, extend the time: (A) with or without motion or notice if the court acts, or if a request is made, before the original time or its extension expires.

On February 19, before the district court ruled on either motion, Argentina and National Grid filed a joint stipulation in which National Grid agreed to accept service of process notwithstanding the Hague Convention. The stipulation provided, however, that National Grid reserved all defenses "including but not limited to defenses based on the timing of service." As a result of the stipulation, the district court dismissed the motion for extension as moot. The district court then issued a final judgment denying Argentina's motion to vacate as untimely and granting National Grid's cross-motion to confirm the arbitral award. Argentina appealed.

On appeal, the D.C. Circuit Court of Appeals affirmed the judgment in its entirety. As a threshold matter, the court rejected Argentina's assertion that National Grid had waived its timeliness defense: the court held that, in fact, National Grid expressly preserved this defense in the stipulation. On the merits, the court rejected Argentina's claim that the district court erred in dismissing the motion for extension and in denying its motion to vacate as untimely. As to the motion for extension, the court agreed with "[e]very court to have considered the question" that Fed. R. Civ. P. 6(b) "may be used only to extend time limits imposed by the court itself or by other Federal Rules, but not to extend time limits imposed by statute."[31] The court acknowledged that the 2007 revision to the Federal Rules eliminated the language in Rule 6(b) that specifically stated it applied only to other Federal Rules and court orders. The court explained that the 2007 revision was meant to be stylistic only, meaning the pre-2007 text remains relevant to interpreting the Rule. The court also cited Rule 6(a) as further evidence that Rule 6(b) cannot be used to enlarge statutorily prescribed time limits. Rule 6(a), which governs methods for computing time, expressly applies to statutes as well as to other rules and court orders; Rule 6(b) by negative implication should apply only to rules and court orders. Finally, the court emphasized that it would be "incongruous" for courts to extend statutory timelines based on Rule 6(b) when courts routinely prohibit such extensions on equitable grounds.

Thus, the court concluded that because Rule 6(b) cannot be used to extend statutory time limits, the district court could not have extended the three-month notice provision set forth in the FAA. For that reason, the district court did not abuse its discretion in dismissing Argentina's motion for extension as moot. Thus, because Argentina presented no evidence of timely service, the court affirmed the district court's order denying Argentina's motion to vacate the arbitral award.

---

[31] *Argentine Republic v. National Grid Plc*, No. 10-7093, slip op. at 4 (D.C. Cir. Mar. 11, 2011)

Argentina also argued that the district court erred by granting National Grid's cross-motion to confirm the award, claiming the district court did not afford it an opportunity to raise defenses available to it under the New York Convention. The court disagreed. It stated that confirmation proceedings are summary in nature and that Argentina carried the heavy burden of demonstrating that the award suffered from one of the specific defects enumerated in the New York Convention. Argentina, however, had failed to raise any such defect in its opposition to National Grid's cross-motion. Therefore, the court affirmed the district court's order granting National Grid's cross-motion to confirm the arbitral award.

C.   PUBLIC POLICY IN INTERNATIONAL ARBITRATION

As a signatory to the New York Convention as of 1970, the United States recognizes the public policy exception to the enforcement of foreign arbitral awards. Under Article (V)(2)(b) of the Convention, a competent U.S. court can refuse to recognize and enforce a foreign arbitral award if the recognition or enforcement of that award would be contrary to the public policy of the United States.[32] Despite its availability, this exception has rarely been invoked successfully in the United States.[33]

---

[32]   9 U.S.C. § 201; Convention on the Recognition and Enforcement of Foreign Arbitral Awards, Art. V(2)(b), 21 U.S.T. 2517.

[33]   As for enforcement of arbitration agreements, 9 U.S.C. § 2 obligates the U.S. to refer a dispute subject to the Convention to arbitration upon the request of one of the parties to the agreement, unless the court finds that the agreement is null and void, inoperative, or incapable of being performed. Attempts to read into that provision a public policy exception to the enforcement of the arbitration agreement itself have been largely unsuccessful, and courts have been even more reluctant to refuse to enforce an agreement than to refuse to enforce awards on

Chapter 2 of the FAA institutes the New York Convention. Section 203 of the FAA grants jurisdiction to federal district courts to hear cases to recognize and enforce foreign arbitral awards and Section 205 authorizes the removal of such cases from the state courts.[34] Recognition and enforcement under the New York Convention through the FAA must occur within three years after an arbitral award falling under the Convention is made.[35] The court from which confirmation is sought must confirm the award unless the court "finds grounds for refusal or deferral of recognition or enforcement of the award specified in the said Convention."[36]

Article V of the Convention contains an exclusive set of grounds for refusal by a court of competent jurisdiction in the U.S. to recognize and enforce a foreign arbitral award. Unlike the Geneva Convention which preceded it, the New York Convention circumscribed the universe of available defenses to those enumerated in Article V and it "clearly shifted the burden

---

public policy grounds, or otherwise. *See M/S Bremen v. Zapata Off Shore Co.*, 407 U.S. 1 (1972); *Scherk v. Alberto-Culver Co.*, 417 U.S. 506, 516 (1974) ("A contractual provision specifying in advance the forum in which disputes shall be litigated and the law to be applied is . . . an almost indispensable precondition to achievement of the orderliness and predictability essential to any international business transaction. . . Such a provision obviates the danger that a dispute under the agreement might be submitted to a forum hostile to the interests of one of the parties or unfamiliar with the problem area involved"). Therefore, the remaining sections will deal instead with the body of U.S. law dealing with the New York Convention's Article V(2)(b) exception to award enforcement. *See Lindo v. NCL (Bahamas) Ltd.*, 652 F. 3d 1257, 1281 (11th Cir. 2011) (Article V, including the public policy defense contained therein, applies only at the arbitral award-enforcement stage and not at the arbitration-enforcement stage).

[34] 9 U.S.C. § 203; 9 U.S.C. § 205.

[35] 9 U.S.C. § 207.

[36] *Id.*

of proof to the party defending against enforcement."[37] As the case precedent summarized below reflects, while the public policy exception is available under controlling law, the exception has little or no utility to parties seeking to defend against recognition and enforcement in the U.S. of arbitral awards rendered against them in a foreign forum. Consistent with the Convention's basic thrust to liberalize procedures for enforcing foreign arbitral awards, U.S. courts have been hesitant to breathe much life into the public policy exception. Federal courts have almost uniformly enforced foreign arbitral awards despite claims that the enforcement of the very substance of the award would violate U.S. public policy. Moreover, there has been little, if any, success in invoking the public policy defense in connection with attempts to demonstrate procedural infirmities with the arbitrations in which the disputed awards were rendered.

Parsons & Whittemore Overseas Co. v. Societe Generale de L'Industrie du Papier (RAKTA),[38] was one of the first U.S. cases to interpret the exception and it created a very narrow threshold for denying confirmation of foreign awards based upon the public policy exception. In *Parsons,* the Second Circuit Court of Appeals affirmed a New York district court's confirmation of a foreign arbitral award in favor of an Egyptian corporation, rejecting plaintiff's argument that the award violated U.S. public policy. Plaintiff sought an expansive reading of the public policy exception by arguing in effect that U.S. public policy should include consideration of U.S. foreign policy. The contract underlying the arbitral dispute contained a *force majeure* clause, which the American plaintiff argued should have been triggered when the U.S. government severed its relations with Egypt and

---

[37] *Parsons & Whittemore Overseas Co. v. Societe Generale de L'Industrie du Papier* (RAKTA), 508 F. 2d 969, 973 (2d Cir. 1974).

[38] 508 F. 2d 969 (2d Cir. 1974).

withdrew financial backing for the incomplete project in dispute. Plaintiff's failure to complete construction of the project pursuant to the contract terms occurred in the wake of the Six Day War in 1967, during which U.S.-Egyptian relations were cut.

The historical context in which this case arose dramatically demonstrates the legitimacy the reviewing court was prepared to grant the new world arbitral regime, and the general pro-enforcement bias emphasized in the Convention and the domestic arbitration laws giving it effect. Despite the United States' official foreign policy stance towards Egypt at this time, the Second Circuit rebuffed plaintiff's attempts and held that "[t]o deny enforcement of this award largely because of the United States' falling out with Egypt in recent years would mean converting a defense intended to be of narrow scope into a major loophole in the Convention's mechanism for enforcement." [39] The court reasoned that concluding otherwise, and reading the public policy defense expansively, "would vitiate the Convention's basic effort to remove preexisting obstacles to enforcement."[40]

Parsons significantly circumscribed the exception and laid the groundwork for the subsequent line of federal cases similarly limiting the relevance of the public policy exception. The court concluded, in an oft-cited statement, "that the Convention's public policy defense should be construed narrowly. Enforcement of foreign arbitral awards may be denied on this basis only where enforcement would violate the *forum state's most basic notions of morality and justice.*"[41]

Subsequent cases dealing with the public policy exception have reaffirmed the *Parsons* court's narrow reading of that

---

[39]   *Id.* at 974.

[40]   *Id.*

[41]   *Id.* (emphasis added).

exception. In *Waterside Ocean Navigation Co. v. International Navigation, Ltd.*,[42] the reviewing court held that the admission and consideration of inconsistent and allegedly false testimony on an issue material to the arbitration, did not meet the high threshold for vacating the award under the public policy exception. Appellant argued that confirmation of the arbitration award would be contrary to "this nation's public policy against granting relief on the basis of sworn testimony directly contradictory to prior sworn testimony, and in favor of the sanctity of the oath and maintenance of the integrity of the judicial system."[43] Despite acknowledging an inconsistency in the testimony, the court concluded that "the assertion that the policy against inconsistent testimony is one of our nation's most basic notions of morality and justice goes much too far."[44] Similarly, in *Avraham v. Shigur Express, Ltd.*, the court noted that it was well settled that the admission of evidence in an arbitration that might be precluded in a U.S. court of law does not sufficiently undermine or make illegitimate an award, unless the mistake is so gross as to amount to fraud or misconduct.[45] The District Court of Delaware went even further on this point, noting in *National Oil Corp. v. Libyan Sun Oil Co.* that even in instances of actual fraud by a witness in an arbitral proceeding, "courts must be slow to vacate an arbitral award on the ground of fraud" so as to protect the finality of the arbitration process.[46]

---

[42]   737 F. 2d 150 (2d Cir. 1984).

[43]   *Id.* at 151.

[44]   *Id.* (internal marks and citations omitted).

[45]   No. 91 Civ. 1238 (SWK), 1991 U.S. Dist. LEXIS 12267, *7-8 (S.D.N.Y. Sept. 3, 1991).

[46]   733 F. Supp. 800, 814 (D. Del. 1990); *See also Newark Stereotypers' Union No. 18 v. Newark Morning Ledger Co.*, 397 F. 2d 594, 600 (3d. Cir. 1969) (perjury

U.S. courts have consistently refused to apply the public policy exception to invalidate awards when evidence is excluded in an arbitration that would have been admissible in a U.S. court. In *Generica Ltd. v. Pharmaceutical Basics*, the U.S. District Court for the Northern District of Illinois enforced an award in favor of a licensor of a drug against the licensee notwithstanding claims that the award violated U.S. public policy due to the arbitrator's failure to allow adequate cross-examination, refusal to accept rebuttal evidence, and refusal to require the licensor to disclose the basis for its damages claim.[47] The court noted that "[t]he arbitrator is not bound to hear all of the evidence tendered by the parties: however, he must give each party an adequate opportunity to present its evidence and arguments."[48] More importantly, "absent exceptional circumstances . . . a reviewing court may not overturn an arbitration award based on the arbitrator's determination of the relevancy or persuasiveness of the evidence submitted by the parties."[49] The *Generica* decision is an example of the great hesitancy of U.S. courts to import U.S. procedural rules into a public policy defense to confirming an arbitral award.

Despite the strong presumption in favor of enforcement of foreign arbitral awards, U.S. courts have been unwilling to enforce awards that are penal in nature. In *Laminoirs-Trefileries-Cableries de Lens, S.A. v. Southwire Co.*, the court found that the use of the French legal rate of interest in the award was permissible, and not usurious, but rejected the provision in the award increasing the interest rate awarded to 14.5 and 15.5

---

does not justify vacating an arbitral award if it relates to issue remote from the question to be decided).

[47]   No. 95 C 5935, 1996 U.S. Dist. LEXIS 13716 (N.D. Ill. Sept. 16, 1996).

[48]   *Id.* at *10 (internal quotation marks omitted).

[49]   *Id.* at *22 (internal quotation marks omitted).

percent if the award was not satisfied by a certain date.[50] The increase was rejected as a penalty, which the court noted "the law does not lightly impose."[51] The court articulated the distinction between an allowable award of interest and an unenforceable penalty. In this case where the interest awarded had no "reasonable relation to any probable damage which may follow," the interest award would not be enforced. [52]

The decision in *Sea Dragon, Inc. v. Gebr. Van Weelde Sheedvaartkantoor B.V.* presented an unusual situation where the U.S. court was asked to confirm an arbitration award that conflicted with a foreign court decree. In *Sea Dragon*, the court declined to enforce a foreign arbitration award against the charterer of a vessel in favor of the owner because a foreign court order obtained by a creditor of the charterer of the vessel prohibited the charterer from paying its debt to the owner.[53] The court noted that "[t]he public policy exception to the enforcement of arbitration awards is not available for every party who manages to find some generally accepted principle which is transgressed by the award. Rather, only when an award is so misconceived that it compels the violation of law or conduct contrary to accepted public policy is the defense available."[54] The court concluded that the arbitration award, by requiring the charterer to pay the freight due the owner notwithstanding the order of the Dutch court to the contrary, exposed the charterer to the dilemma of conflicting orders – whether to pay as the panel ordered or to retain the funds as decreed by the Dutch court – and that it amounted to a

---

[50] 484 F. Supp. 1063 (N.D. Ga. 1980).

[51] *Id.* at 1069.

[52] *Id.*

[53] 574 F. Supp. 367 (S.D.N.Y. 1983).

[54] *Id.*

violation of public policy to expose the charterer to such a choice. More to the point, the court stated that the "doctrine of comity founded on diplomatic respect for valid foreign judgments militat[ed] against disregard of the Dutch order since comity is to be accorded a decision of a foreign court so long as the court is a court of competent jurisdiction and as long as the laws and public policy of the forum state are not violated."[55] While the owner of the vessel claimed that the Dutch order was fraudulently obtained because the charterer colluded with its creditor, the owner provided little evidence of fraud to the arbitrators and such claim should in any event have been made before the Dutch court. The court found that the owner did not challenge the jurisdiction of the Dutch court nor demonstrate that the award violated U.S. law or policy, remarking that in the absence of any evidence to the contrary it was the firm and established policy of American courts to respect a valid foreign decree.

In line with the general direction of the cases in this body of jurisprudence, a misapplication of foreign law was found not to amount to a violation of U.S. public policy such that the reviewing court in *Ukrneshprom State Foreign Economic Enterprise v. Tradeway, Inc.* was empowered to refuse to recognize and enforce the arbitral award.[56] There, defendant Tradeway also asserted that the award should not be enforced due to its being contrary to the public policy of the United States. Specifically, Tradeway argued U.S. public policy would be violated by enforcing an award resulting from a misapplication of the chosen law of the arbitration, which in this instance was Ukrainian law. The court, however, held that misapplication of Ukrainian law regarding, *inter alia*, the statute of limitations in arbitral claims does not amount to a violation of the United

---

[55]   *Id.* at 371.

[56]   95 Civ. 10278 (RPP), 1996 U.S. Dist. LEXIS 2827 (S.D.N.Y. Mar. 11, 1996).

States' most basic notions of morality and justice, and again reaffirmed the intended narrow scope of the defense.[57]

In a more recent case, *Steel Corp. of the Phil. v. Int'l Steel Serv.*, the Third Circuit Court of Appeals held that the pendency of a motion to vacate an arbitral award in a foreign jurisdiction does not prevent a U.S. court from recognizing and enforcing the same disputed award, and that confirmation in that context would not be in contravention of the United States' most basic notions of morality and justice.[58] The party seeking vacatur of the award, ISSI, argued that enforcing the award while proceedings were ongoing in a foreign country would violate the fundamental principles of *res judicata* and judicial comity, thus running contrary to the public policy against forum shopping in the U.S.[59] Despite these arguments, the court confirmed the award, holding that "parties may bring suit to enforce awards notwithstanding the existence of ongoing proceedings elsewhere."[60]

In *Karaha Bodas Co., L.L.C. v Perusahaan Pertambangan Minyak Dan Gas Bumi Negara*, defendant Pertamina asserted that the arbitral award confirmed earlier by a U.S. district court triggered the public policy exception because it violated the international law doctrine of abuse of rights.[61] The court noted

---

[57]   *Id.* at *16-18.

[58]   354 Fed. Appx. 689, 695 (3d Cir. 2009).

[59]   *Id.* at 694.

[60]   *Id.*

[61]   364 F. 3d 274, 305 (5th Cir. 2004) ("An action violates the abuse of rights doctrine if one of the following three factors is present: (1) the predominant motive for action is to cause harm; (2) the action is totally unreasonable given the lack of any legitimate interest in the exercise of the right and its exercise harms another; and (3) the right is exercised for a purpose other than that for which it exists.")

that this international law doctrine is not established in U.S. law, but nonetheless considered the factors under the doctrine and went on to make the finding that the record developed from the arbitration did not support Pertamina's argument that enforcing the award would penalize obedience to a governmental decree.[62] An interesting aspect of this decision is the Fifth Circuit Court of Appeals' willingness to consider international law in the context of a public policy exception challenge to an arbitral award, highlighting that U.S. public policy need not be exclusively drawn from domestically operative laws. The *Karaha Bodas* court, however, true to form, refrained from overruling the lower court's confirmation of the foreign arbitral award. The court described the public policy exception as a "steep threshold."[63]

In 2003, in *Aasma v. Am. S.S. Owners Mut. Prot. & Indem.*, a federal district court excluded the so-called "American Rule" regarding the award of attorney's fees from the body of public policy to be afforded recognition for purposes of Article V(2)(b).[64] Plaintiffs in the case "characterize[d] the award of costs and fees as exorbitant and immoderate, punitive in nature, and issued by an unsympathetic arbitrator in a foreign land."[65] However, as the court provided:

> Though under the American Rule parties normally bear their own costs of litigation, parties are free to contract regarding the apportionment of fees. In the instant action, the parties' arbitration agreement was silent as to the award of fees, thus implicating the default provisions of the Arbitration Act of 1996. Costs of arbitration are routinely awarded under the

---

[62] *Id.* at 305-306.

[63] *Id.* at 306.

[64] 238 F. Supp 918, 922 (N.D. Ohio 2003).

[65] *Id.* at 922.

Act, and Plaintiffs were presumably aware of this fact but nonetheless chose to pursue the arbitration . . . [66]

In light of the liberal nature of arbitration, an arbitral award is not required to comply with the domestically operative rule regarding attorney's fees in order to receive confirmation in the United States. The *Aasma* court, therefore, concluded that the American Rule is not integral to the most basic notions of morality and justice of the American justice system. Underlying this, and other decisions previously seen, is a push to preserve the flexibility of international arbitration. An expansive public policy exception would undermine this liberalism and limit freedom of contract by imposing too many mandatory provisions, both procedural and substantive, that parties contemplating U.S. award enforcement would need to strictly respect.[67]

In sum, U.S. courts have consistently limited the application of the public policy exception of the New York Convention when confirming and enforcing foreign arbitral awards. We see little or no movement from the position first reflected in the *Parsons* decision 38 years ago: while available, the public policy exception to enforcement is rarely, if ever, invoked as a legitimate basis for not recognizing a foreign arbitral award.

---

[66]   *Id.* at 922-23.

[67]   *See Mitsubishi Motors Corp. v. Soler Chrysler-Plymouth, Inc.*, 473 U.S. 614 (1985) (the Supreme Court indicated that international comity, respect for the capacities of foreign tribunals and the need for predictability in the resolution of international commercial disputes require enforcement of foreign arbitration agreements, even assuming that a contrary result might be reached in a domestic context).

VENEZUELA

Henry Torrealba,[1] Edmundo Martínez,[2] and Gabriel De Jesus[3]

A. LEGISLATION, TRENDS AND TENDENCIES

Commercial arbitration in Venezuela continues to be governed by the Law on Commercial Arbitration ("LCA"), published on April 7, 1998 in Official Gazette No. 36.530. This law is based on the UNCITRAL Model Law. The LCA introduced commercial arbitration in Venezuela, and distinguished between "institutional" and "*ad hoc*" arbitration. According to LCA Article 2, institutional arbitration is "conducted through the arbitration centers to which this Law refers, or those that may be created by other laws," whereas *ad hoc* arbitration is "governed by rules agreed by the parties, without intervention of the arbitration centers." If the parties elect institutional arbitration, all matters will be governed by the provisions in the arbitration regulations of the arbitration center to which the parties have submitted the controversy. The LCA is not limited to regulating internal or domestic commercial arbitration. Its provisions may also be applied to international commercial arbitration. Some

[1] Henry Torrealba L. is a Partner in Baker & McKenzie's Caracas office. He heads the Civil, Commercial and Criminal Litigation Department of the office. He has acted as president of arbitral tribunals and sole or co-arbitrator in several arbitrations before the Arbitration Center of the Caracas Chamber of Commerce.

[2] Edmundo Martínez is a Partner in Baker & McKenzie's Caracas office. He is a member of the Civil, Commercial and Criminal Litigation Department of the office. He is also a member of the Trademark and International Arbitration Practice Groups of the Firm's Global Dispute Resolution Practice Group.

[3] Gabriel De Jesus is a Partner in Baker & McKenzie's Caracas office. He is a member of the Civil, Commercial and Criminal Litigation Department of the office and a member of the Firm's Global Dispute Resolution Practice Group.

commentators draw this conclusion based on the historical background of the LCA.

LCA Article 1 provides that the LCA governs commercial arbitration without prejudice to the application of international treaties currently in force in Venezuela. In substance, this provision is similar to Article 1 of the Law on International Private Law. Article 62 of the Law on International Private Law states that all matters related to international commercial arbitration are governed by the special rules, save for the provisions of Article 47 *ejusdem*. Article 47 sets forth the three cases in which Venezuelan jurisdiction cannot be derogated by agreement, namely: (a) when the matter refers to disputes over title to real property located in the territory of the Republic; (b) "when dealing with issues not admitting settlement"; or (c) when the matter affects the essential principles of Venezuelan public order.

B. CASES

The following is a summary of case law developments in Venezuela for international commercial arbitration and investment arbitration involving state-owned entities.

Following is an analysis of the issues of (i) the admissibility of arbitration, (ii) consent to arbitration, and (iii) enforcement of the awards in cases involving Venezuelan state-owned entities. These are the three most difficult areas in conducting international arbitration with Venezuelan state-owned entities.

B.1 Admissibility of Arbitration

Article 258 of the Venezuelan Constitution states that the law will promote arbitration. This is an order addressed not only to legislators but also to all public powers.[4] This provision should encourage the entities of the Venezuelan state to favor arbitration, including international arbitration. However, in theory, Articles 1 and 151 of the Constitution are opposed to arbitration. Additionally, the LCA allows arbitration with state-owned entities, albeit submitting it to special authorization requirements (Article 4) and excluding it in controversies directly related to the powers or functions of the state or of public law persons or entities (Article 3.b).

Article 1 of the Constitution lists immunity among the inalienable rights of the Venezuelan nation, along with sovereignty and national self-determination. Article 151 states the domestic variation of the Calvo Doctrine in the following terms: "In contracts in the public interest, unless inapplicable by reason of the nature of such contracts, a clause shall be deemed included even if not expressed, whereby any doubts and controversies which may arise concerning such contracts and which cannot be resolved amicably by the parties, will be decided by the competent courts of the Republic, in accordance with its laws, and may not by any cause or reason give rise to foreign claims."

The apparent contradiction between these two provisions and, therefore, the apparent obstacle for international arbitration for the state-owned entities, was dismissed in a judgment of February 11, 2009 issued by the Constitutional Chamber of the Supreme Court.[5] This judgment stated that "from such rules

---

[4]   *See* Hernández-Bretón, "Arbitraje y Constitución: El Arbitraje como Derecho Fundamental, en Arbitraje Comercial Interno e Internacional, reflexiones teóricas y experiencias prácticas," Academia de Ciencias Políticas y Sociales (2005). Caracas.

[5]   *See* Judgment No. 97, Case File No. 08-0306, F. Toro *et al.*, www.tsj.gob.ve/decisiones/scon/Febrero/97-11209-2009-08-0306.html.

(Articles 1 and 151 of the Constitution) derives a harmonic relationship that can in no circumstance deny the sovereignty or contradict the principle of self-determination of the Bolivarian Republic of Venezuela."

This judgment ratified the criteria stated in the October 17, 2008 judgment of the Constitutional Chamber,[6] which confirmed and broadened the criteria of the August 17, 1999 judgment of the former Supreme Court in Full Accidental Chamber.[7] Let us now examine the details of these two decisions.

In the judgment of August 17, 1999, the Supreme Court admitted that Article 151 of the Constitution (equivalent to Article 127 of the 1961 Constitution) adopted the criterion of relative immunity of jurisdiction. However, Venezuelan state-owned entities often invoke Article 151 to reject the possibility of international arbitration. Certain judicial precedent also rejects the arbitrability of controversies with state-owned companies merely for being related to national public interest agreements.[8]

---

[6]   *See* Judgment No. 1541, Case file N° 08-0763, *Petition for Interpretation of Article 258 of the Constitution and Article 22 of the Law for Promotion and Protection of Investments*, www.tsj.gob.ve/decisiones/scon/Octubre/1541-171008-08-0763.html.

[7]   *See* Ramírez & Garay, "Venezuelan Judicial Precedents," Volume CLVII 1999 August, Judgment 2096-99, pp. 606-622, Oil Opening Case.

[8]   *See Venezolana de Televisión, C.A. v. Elettronica Industriale SpA*, Supreme Court, Political Administrative Chamber, Judgment No. 855 of April 5, 2006, Case file N° 2001-100, www.tsj.gov.ve/decisiones/spa/Abril/00855-050406-2001-0100.htm. In this regard, *see* Alfredo de Jesús O., "Cronica de Arbitraje Comercial: Cuarta Entrega," in *Revista de Derecho, Tribunal Supremo de Justicia*, N° 29, 2008, Caracas, pp. 141-162; also *Minera Las Cristinas v. Corporación Venezolana de Guayana*, Tribunal Supremo de Justicia, Sala Politicoadministrativa, Judgment No. 832 of July 15, 2004, Case No. 2002-0464, www.tsj.gov.ve/decisiones/spa/Julio/00832-140704-2002-0464.htm; Alfredo de Jesús O., *Crónica de Arbitraje Comercial –No. 3*, in *Revista de Derecho, Tribunal Supremo de Justicia*, No. 23, 2006, Caracas, pp. 125-155, esp. pp. 140-155; and

Notwithstanding this precedent, the judgment of October 17, 2008, in allowing international arbitration with Venezuelan state-owned companies, made some important determinations, which we will henceforth discuss. The Constitutional Chamber considered that international arbitration is an instrument that promotes foreign investment. It stated in this regard:

> from these general conditions, which encourage and allow foreign investment, results a practice that is common and agreeable to the majority of the investors: the need to submit potential differences arising from the development of the corresponding economic activities to a jurisdiction that, in the opinion of the interested parties, does not tend to favor the internal interest of each state or of individuals involved in the controversy.

Nevertheless, and notwithstanding this favorable opinion, the Chamber immediately clarified that it continued to view the arbitral institution with reservations, stating:

> It does not escape either from the analysis of this Chamber, that the transfer of the jurisdiction from ordinary courts to arbitration courts, in many cases, is due to the fact that the resolution of conflicts will be carried out by arbitrators that in a considerable amount of cases find themselves to be affiliated with and tend to favor the interest of transnational corporations, rendering themselves an additional instrument of domination and control of national economies, due to which it is barely realistic to merely present an allegation of the impartiality of arbitral justice to the detriment of the

---

Victorino J. Tejera Pérez, "La norma electa una via, *non datur recursus ad alteram* en el marco jurídico venezolano de protección y promoción de inversiones," *ibidem*, pp. 359-395, esp. pp. 384-395.

justice of the ordinary courts, to justify the acceptance of the jurisdiction of the general interest agreements.

Then, after formulating the above explanation, the Constitutional Chamber proceeded to outline and confirm the mechanism to determine the scope and contents of Article 151 of the 1999 Constitution. With regards to this, it stated that such a determination should be made:

> under the existing circumstances of international commerce, which cause the convergence of the (opposed) interests of the states, in developing projects or generating favorable economic situations that guarantee the achievement of their goals, whether by means of *developing projects that serve the public interest* or by the adoption of policies promoting the productive investment of foreign capital, as well as of the investors participating in businesses or economic activities that generate the largest amount of economic benefits for them.

According to the judgment, there is need for a "pragmatic approach to the situations" that reinforces "the need to allow in our constitutional juridical laws, that, in agreements for the general interest, the State have the possibility to submit the conflicts derived from such agreements to the arbitral jurisdiction and thus make viable the international economic relationships needed for the development of the country."

It is on the basis of these criteria that one must understand the phrase "if it was not acceptable pursuant to their nature" in Article 151 of the Constitution. Such an expression "should not be understood as relative to a formal or doctrinal distinction between public or private law agreements." As a consequence, arbitration will be admissible if it "allows the effective possibility to develop a given economic activity or business related to public interest matters."

Based on the above, the Constitutional Chamber concluded that within the framework of the 1999 Constitution and, as concerns the determination of jurisdiction, it is "impossible to sustain a theory of absolute immunity or state in general terms the unconstitutionality of arbitration clauses in agreements relating to the public interest; on the contrary, to determine the validity and extent of the respective arbitration clauses, one must refer to the appropriate, particular juridical system."

After the Constitutional Chamber has admitted the possibility of international arbitration, it becomes the responsibility of the state to "determine the scope, opportunity and convenience of submitting certain matters to an arbitration proceeding or other means of alternative dispute resolution."

B.2 Consent of the State to International Arbitration

Having resolved this first difficulty and having stated that the recourse to international arbitration is a matter of convenience for the state and its entities, and that it is not constitutionally excluded, we will examine the question of consent of the state to international arbitration. For this purpose, we will refer to the judgment of the Constitutional Chamber of the Supreme Court of October 17, 2008, cited *supra*. This judgment discussed whether Article 22 of Decree No. 356, with the rank and force of the Law Establishing the System for Promotion and Protection of Investments (Official Gazette of the Bolivarian Republic of Venezuela No. 5.390 Extraordinary, of October 22, 1999), constituted an open offer of international arbitration and, fundamentally, whether it constituted a unilateral offer of the Venezuelan state to arbitrate controversies pursuant to the ICSID Convention to which Venezuela is a party.

The judgment states that "it is well-established in Venezuelan law that the will manifested by the state to be submitted to arbitral jurisdiction must be stated in writing, because it must be express and it must be perfectly clear on which matters or issues [this jurisdiction] may decide, which assumes . . . that such written formalization is free and unequivocal." Thus, in the case of the LCA it is required, as a general rule, that the arbitration agreement is evidenced in a document or documents that set on record the will of the parties to submit to arbitration. A reference made in an agreement to a document containing an arbitration clause will constitute an arbitration agreement, provided such agreement is in writing and the reference implies that such clause is a part of the agreement. For adhesion agreements and for normalized agreements, the will to submit to arbitration must be stated expressly and independently (Article 6 of the CAL).

If consent is stated by means of an arbitral agreement or clause, the consent of the State must be express, in writing, unequivocal and particular "because it cannot refer in general terms to any juridical relationship—but to a given one, which, once defined, may be established in broad or restricted terms, it being necessary that it be express and unquestionable." The court made these statements based on the text of Article II of the New York Convention, to which Venezuela is a party (Approbatory Law published in the Official Gazette of the Bolivarian Republic of Venezuela No. 4.832 Extraordinary of December 29, 1994). Pursuant to the text of this rule, the juridical relationship may or may not be contractual and it is not required that the consent of the interested parties be stated in one document. Neither the Convention nor the judgment clarify how the judicial relationship to which the arbitration refers must be determined (or individualized). This is a matter left to the autonomy of the interested parties. The effects of the arbitration clause are limited to the contracting parties and, according to the relationships between them, it may happen that the consent to arbitration must be reviewed within the context of the whole contractual relationship of the parties and not limited to a particular document; therefore, the arbitration may be applicable to the whole transaction.

Under the assumption of the consent stated in a bilateral or multilateral treaty, the arbitration clauses established in treaties for promotion and protection of investments or BITs acquire special importance. The court accepts that the consent to arbitration may be stated through the BITs and that, in any case, the analysis of such a consent must be made on a case by case basis. The court does not state, however, whether the above-mentioned parameters must also be satisfied in this case. With the wide array of BITs and other treaties, it is possible that the parties (the investor and the state) will search for the forum of their convenience ("forum shopping"). This conduct is admitted as legal so long as a "true fraud" has not been committed, such as the behavior of the parties once the controversy or dispute has arisen, it being necessary in this case to apply the criterion of rationality, according to which "the potential plaintiff does not end up subject to a forum to which it did not reasonably expect to be submitted."

The third assumption, consent via a national law, is the most relevant for the court's analysis, because, behind the appearance of an exercise in constitutional interpretation or revision, it actually sought to examine whether Article 22 of Decree No. 356, with the rank and force of Law Establishing the Regime for Promotion and Protection of Investments, constitutes the consent of the Venezuelan state to international arbitration.

The Court recognizes the possibility of consent to arbitration via national law, as accepted by the arbitral judicial precedent set by the case *Tradex Hellas SA v. Albania*, ICSID Case ARB/94/2, of December 24, 1996, or as contained in the controversial decision in *Southern Pacific Properties (Middle East) Ltd. v. Arab*

Republic of Egypt, ICSID Case ARB/84/3 of November 27, 1985. In the first case, the court states that "it was determined that Article 8 of the so-called "Albany Law of 1993" contained a statement of written will sufficiently unequivocal as to be subsumed under the assumptions of Article 25 of the Convention on the Settlement of Investment Disputes between States and Nationals of Other States," while in the second, it was determined that "the structure and contents of Article 8 of the so-called "Law of Investments of Egypt" did not require from the conflicting parties a statement of will other than the one already contained in the above-mentioned rule."

The court considered that Venezuelan law "does not contain in itself a unilateral statement of submission to international arbitration" governed, *inter alia*, by the ICSID Convention, "but that it turns to the contents [of the applicable treaties] to determine the legitimacy of the arbitration, . . . a situation which does not apply in the case of Article 25 of the ICSID Convention. . . " That is, the court considered that the applicable treaty itself must have established arbitration as compulsory, so that a national law would become irrelevant and even redundant. In this manner, the court drained Article 22 of its importance. It came as no surprise, then, that the court concluded that Article 22 has the nature of an "enunciative rule" that "governs the terms according to which the State may submit the controversies relating to the object of the mentioned law to the system of international arbitration."

In deeper analysis, the court stated:

> The same conclusion must be reached from a comprehensive reading of Article 22 of the Investment Promotion and Protection Law, because when the rule states that 'Any disputes arising. . .shall be submitted to international arbitration under the terms provided for in the respective

treaty or agreement, should it so provide,' a phrase which indicates, when subject to a literal, teleological and rational interpretation of the rule, that the will of the legislator refer expressly and unequivocally to the internal contents of the respective agreements or treaties. Therefore, given that the Convention on the Settlement of Investment Disputes between States and Nationals of Other States does not contain in itself any statement of will for submission to the arbitral system, any argument in this vein must be dismissed, except if it contradicts the abovementioned jurisprudential doctrine and the contents of Article 25 and the preamble of the mentioned Convention ...

According to the court, another approach may be to admit "*the alleged will in matters of arbitration, which is unacceptable under any law...*" (emphasis added). Once again, the court does not recognize any function to Article 22, considering it a useless law.

B.3 Enforcement of Awards against State-Owned Entities

Having already analyzed the constitutional admissibility of international arbitration with entities of the Venezuelan state and having examined the means for such entities of expressing consent to the arbitral process, we will examine the final question of our analysis: the enforcement of arbitral awards against entities of the Venezuelan state. This is the third area of difficulty that parties face when seeking recourse against entities of the Venezuelan state through international arbitration.

With regards to this matter, it is important to refer once more to the judgment of the Constitutional Chamber of October 17, 2008, confirming the statements in its judgment of July 15,

2003,[9] pursuant to which foreign awards (including ICSID and other awards) were not to be enforceable in Venezuela if they violated the domestic constitutional public order.

In the judgment of the *Chavero Gazdik* case, the court stated that the

> national sovereignty cannot be relaxed because of Article 1 of the Constitution, which establishes as inalienable the following rights of the nation: independence, freedom, sovereignty, territorial integrity, immunity and national self-determination. Said constitutional rights are *inalienable*, are not subject to be relaxed, except if expressly stated by the Constitution, jointly with the mechanisms that enable them (i.e., Articles 73 and 336.5 of the Constitution) (emphasis in the original).

For the Constitutional Chamber, the "consequence of the above statements is that, in principle, the enforcement of the judgments of the Supranational Courts cannot threaten the sovereignty of the country or the fundamental rights of the Republic." Immediately thereafter, the Chamber warns, "the decisions concerning the matter decided may become binding, creating international responsibility for non-fulfillment (for example, Article 87.7 of the Law Approving the Statute of Rome of the International Criminal Court), but never lessening the rights contained in Article 1 of the Constitution, diminishing or weakening the exclusive competences of the national entities to which the Constitution grants certain competences or functions."

In the case of international arbitral tribunals, the Constitutional Chamber clarified that "they are not entities that are superior to

---

[9]   *See Rafael Chavero Gazdik, Supreme Court, Constitutional Chamber,* Judgment No. 1.942, Case File No. 01-0415, www.tsj.gob.ve/decisiones/scon/Julio/1942-150703-01-0415.htm.

the Sovereign States, rather, they are at their same level because, although the judgments, awards, etc., can be enforced in the territory of the signatory States, that is done through the courts of that State and 'according to the rules on enforcement and judgments that are in force in the territories in which such enforcement is intended' (as stated by Article 54.3 of the Law Approving the Convention on the Settlement of Investment Disputes between States and Nationals of Other States)."

In summary, according to the Constitutional Chamber, "the only advantage contained in the decisions of these entities that resolve disputes involving a state is that, for the enforcement of a decision in the territory of that State, a previous *exequatur* is not necessary, the result being that the enforcing judge is rendered the controller of constitutionality."[10]

---

[10] *See* Victorino J. Tejera Pérez, "La Ejecución de Laudos Arbitrales ICSID en contra de la República: Referencia a la Sentencia No. 1.942 del 15 de julio de 2003 de la Sala Constitucional del Tribunal Supremo de Justicia," ("The enforcement of the ICSID Arbitration Awards" in Fernando Parra Aranguren (editor), *Temas de Derecho Procesal, Colección de Estudios Jurídicos,* (Issues of Procedural Law, Collection of Juridical Studies), No. 15, Supreme Court, Caracas, 2005, pp. 467- 483, esp. 473-483).

VIETNAM

Fred Burke,[1] Chi Anh Tran,[2] and Andrew Fitanides[3]

A.   LEGISLATION, TRENDS AND TENDENCIES

A.1   Background and Overview of the Applicable Law

Vietnam has a growing economy and an improved investment regime. In 2007, Vietnam acceded to the WTO and the United States granted it permanent normal trade relations. These developments have made Vietnam an attractive destination for foreign investment, and increased investment will lead to more disputes. Historically, arbitration has not been a popular means for resolving disputes in Vietnam, particularly those involving foreign and foreign-invested enterprises. This year, however, reforms contained in the Law on Commercial Arbitration[4] that replaced the often-criticized 2003 Ordinance on Commercial

---

[1]   Fred Burke is the Managing Partner of Baker & McKenzie's Vietnam offices, which he helped to establish in the early 1990s following postings in New York and Shanghai. His commercial and property practices involve a regular stream of contentious matters, often involving influential state-owned, foreign or local government entities. A member of the Prime Minister's Advisory Council on Administrative Reform since 2008, his work on numerous legislative drafting projects involving Vietnam's main commercial and investment laws gives him insights when provisions of these laws come up in cross border disputes.

[2]   Chi Anh Tran is an Associate in Baker & McKenzie's office in Ho Chi Minh City and a member of the Dispute Resolution Practice Group. Her principal practice areas include dispute resolution, compliance and competition law.

[3]   Andrew Fitanides is an Associate in Baker & McKenzie's Ho Chi Minh City office and a member of the Dispute Resolution Practice Group working primarily in commercial litigation.

[4]   Law No. 54/2010/QH12 on Commercial Arbitration adopted on 17 June 2010, effective on 1 January 2011 ("Law on Commercial Arbitration").

Arbitration[5] have greatly improved Vietnam's arbitration regime, suggesting arbitration will increase in popularity going forward.

Vietnam is a signatory of the New York Convention;[6] however, Vietnam is not a party to the ICSID Convention. The Bilateral Trade Agreement between Vietnam and the United States[7] allows for settlement by binding arbitration of certain disputes between natural and juridical persons of diverse nationality. However, Vietnam's arbitration law is still developing and remains quite different from the UNCITRAL Model Law, the basis for the arbitration laws of other jurisdictions in the region.[8] Although litigation remains the most common dispute resolution mechanism in Vietnam, commercial arbitration offers important advantages, including faster resolution due to simplified procedural and evidentiary requirements, greater flexibility regarding the confidentiality of proceedings and greater predictability.

Some uncertainty remains as to whether a given dispute may be resolved by arbitration. Under the Law on Commercial Arbitration, arbitration may only be used to settle disputes: (1) arising out of commercial activities; (2) where one of the involved parties engages in commercial activities; or (3) other

---

[5]   Ordinance No. 08/2003/PL-UBTVQH11 on Commercial Arbitration, adopted on 25 February 2003, effective on 1 July 2003 (the "Ordinance"), superseded by the Law on Commercial Arbitration.

[6]   *Available at:* http://www.uncitral.org/uncitral/en/uncitral_texts/arbitration/ NYConvention_status.html.

[7]   The Bilateral Trade Agreement was ratified on 18 October and 7 December 2011 by the President of the U.S.A. and the President of SRV respectively, taking effect from 10 December 2001.

[8]   Please note that some provisions of the Law on Commercial Arbitration such as Articles 47, 48 and 50 incorporate elements of the UNCITRAL Model Law.

disputes stipulated by law.[9] Under Vietnamese law, commercial activity is broadly and vaguely defined, introducing the risk that an arbitration award may be set aside if a Vietnamese court holds the dispute to be non-commercial in nature.[10] The Law on Commercial Arbitration also limits the application of arbitration to disputes involving consumers.[11] For example, consumers of goods and services have the right to refer their disputes to court, even if they have entered into a valid arbitration agreement.

Additionally, significant obstacles remain to the efficient and equitable recognition and enforcement of foreign arbitral awards under Vietnamese law. These practical issues are discussed in detail below with reference to specific cases.

A.2 Arbitration in Vietnam

The Law on Commercial Arbitration introduces important improvements concerning the appointment of arbitrators, choice of law, language of the proceedings and available interim relief measures. It also allows for the creation of foreign arbitral institutions in Vietnam. In order to appreciate the significance of these reforms, it is important to understand the overall framework of Vietnam's arbitration regime.

---

[9]   Article 2 of the Law on Commercial Arbitration. Note that the phrase "other disputes stipulated by law" is not defined.

[10] Law No. 36/2005/QH11 on Commerce defines commercial activity as "activity for profit-making purposes, comprising purchase and sale of goods, provision of services, investment, commercial enhancement, and other activities for profit making purposes."

[11] Article 17 of the Law on Commercial Arbitration.

A.2.1. Disputes involving a "foreign element"

Vietnam employs a bifurcated arbitration regime that distinguishes between domestic disputes and disputes involving a foreign element. "Dispute involving a foreign element" is indirectly defined as a dispute that arises out of a civil relation involving a foreign element, as provided in the Civil Code of Vietnam.[12]

Under the Civil Code, a civil relation involves a foreign element if:[13]

- at least one of the parties is foreign; or

- at least one of the parties is a Vietnamese national residing overseas; or

- the basis for establishment, modification or termination of such relation was the law of a foreign country or such basis arose in a foreign country or the assets involved in the relation are located overseas.

As explained below in greater detail, parties generally have more options in disputes involving a foreign element than in purely domestic disputes.

A.2.2. Arbitration centers

The Law on Commercial Arbitration provides for the establishment and operation of domestic arbitration centers. The Law also permits foreign arbitration centers to operate in Vietnam through branches or representative offices, although arbitral awards issued by these bodies remain foreign arbitral awards for the purpose of enforcement in Vietnam. There are currently no foreign arbitration centers in Vietnam.

---

[12] Civil Code No. 33/2005/QH11, adopted on 14 June 2005, effective on 1 January 2006 ("Civil Code").

[13] Article 758 of the Civil Code.

There are six well-known domestic arbitration centers in Vietnam.[14] The best known of these, the Vietnam International Arbitration Center ("VIAC"), is a non-governmental body established by the Chamber of Commerce and Industry of Vietnam. Although the Law on Commercial Arbitration and VIAC's rules allow the center to employ the parties' choice of arbitration rules, in practice VIAC refuses to apply any arbitration rules other than its own, on the basis that other rules could be viewed as contrary to Vietnamese law.

Arbitration Procedures

1. Appointment of Arbitrators

Significantly, the Law on Commercial Arbitration now allows non-Vietnamese citizens to qualify as arbitrators. This is a promising improvement from the perspective of foreign or foreign-invested enterprises because of the perceived greater expertise and impartiality of foreign arbitrators.

The appointment of arbitrators is conducted according to the arbitration center's rules. For example, unless the parties have agreed that their dispute will be heard by a single arbitrator, under VIAC rules, a three-member arbitration panel will be created. Each party has the right to select an arbitrator from VIAC's list. The two members thus selected will then nominate a third arbitrator to serve as chair of the arbitration panel.

Although *ad hoc* arbitration was allowed under the Ordinance, it is not known to have ever been used. However, recent reforms make *ad hoc* arbitration a viable option. Under the Law on

---

[14] These are, the Vietnam International Arbitration Center ("VIAC"); the Hanoi Commercial Arbitration Center; the Ho Chi Minh City Commercial Arbitration Center ("TRACENT"); the Can Tho Commercial Arbitration Center; the Asian International Commercial Arbitration Center ("ACIAC"); and the Pacific International Arbitration Center ("PIAC").

Commercial Arbitration, *ad hoc* arbitration is conducted by a panel of three arbitrators, unless the parties have agreed otherwise. Where the parties are unable to agree on the appointment of arbitrators, a competent court may appoint arbitrators to hear the dispute.

2. *Role of Vietnamese Courts in Domestic Arbitration*

Either party may petition a court of first instance to set aside the award of a domestic arbitration center. This decision may be appealed. A domestic arbitration award may be set aside for a variety of substantive and procedural defects.[15]

A.3   Enforcement of an Arbitral Award

Award from Domestic Arbitration Centers

A valid domestic arbitral award is equivalent to a final decision of a Vietnamese court. Where an award debtor refuses to honor an award, and has not sought to set it aside, the prevailing party may request the assistance of the civil judgment enforcement authorities.

Award from Foreign Arbitration Centers

In principle, foreign arbitral awards are enforceable in Vietnam. The Civil Procedure Code[16] provides for the recognition and

---

[15]   Article 68 of the Law on Commercial Arbitration. The grounds for setting aside a domestic arbitral award are: absence of a valid arbitration agreement; defects in the forming of the arbitral panel or in arbitral proceedings that run contrary to the agreement of the parties or the Law on Commercial Arbitration; lack of subject matter jurisdiction for the center to hear the dispute; forged evidence or material benefits to an arbitrator which produces a conflict of interest; or the arbitral award is contrary to basic principles of Vietnamese law.

[16]   Civil Procedure Code No. 24/2004/QH11, adopted on 15 June 2004, effective on 1 January 2005, amended by the Law No. 65/2011/QH12, adopted on 29 March 2011, effective on 1 January 2012 (the "CPC").

enforcement in Vietnam of any award from a nation that is a signatory of a relevant international convention, (*inter alia*, the New York Convention) or, otherwise, on the basis of reciprocity. However, a foreign arbitral award must be recognized and approved for enforcement by a Vietnamese court before it becomes the equivalent to a legally effective decision of a Vietnamese court or domestic arbitration center. Court approval also allows assets derived from enforcement to be transferred abroad.

The three-judge panel hearing an application for the recognition and enforcement of a foreign arbitral award may not review substantive issues of the dispute, only the basis for the recognition and enforcement of the award in Vietnam. Recognition may be denied if the:

- parties lacked the capacity to sign the arbitration agreement or arbitration clause;

- arbitration agreement is invalid under applicable law;

- respondent did not receive sufficient notice of the appointment of arbitrators or the arbitration proceedings;

- award was validly set aside, revoked or suspended;

- award was not binding on the parties;

- subject matter of the dispute is not capable of settlement by arbitration under Vietnamese law; or

- court deems it as contrary to the basic principles of Vietnamese law to allow recognition and enforcement.

Other Issues

1. Choice of Law

In a dispute involving a foreign element, the arbitral tribunal will apply the law chosen by the parties without regard to its variance from the basic principles of Vietnamese law.[17] However, the parties should be mindful that any award may be set aside or rendered unenforceable at a later stage if Vietnamese courts hold that the application of foreign law was "contrary to the basic principles of Vietnamese law."

2. Language

Under the Law on Commercial Arbitration, where the parties have not agreed on the language to be used, the arbitral tribunal may, in its own discretion, choose the language of any arbitration involving a foreign element.[18] Where no foreign element is present, arbitral proceedings must be conducted in Vietnamese, except for disputes in which at least one party is a foreign-invested enterprise.

3. Interim Relief

The Law on Commercial Arbitration empowers arbitral tribunals to grant interim measures not previously available under the Ordinance.

A.4 Trends and Tendencies

The success of the new Law on Commercial Arbitration will depend on the willingness of the Vietnamese courts to recognize and give effect to the arbitral process. However, Vietnamese

---

[17] Article 14 of the Law on Commercial Arbitration.

[18] Article 10 of the Law on Commercial Arbitration.

courts have a history of ambivalence towards arbitration, fueled by the broad discretion of Vietnamese courts to set aside arbitral awards. As the following cases demonstrate, awards have been set aside for invalidity of the arbitration agreement, procedural defects, ambiguity in the terms of the arbitration clause, and general public policy reasons.

B.   CASES

The little that is known about (normally confidential) arbitral proceedings comes from the very few available decisions of Vietnamese courts on set-aside petitions. The following cases provide a glimpse of some of the more noteworthy issues raised by Vietnamese courts when considering petitions to set aside domestic arbitral awards or recognize foreign arbitral awards.

B.1   Lack of Capacity to Enter Arbitration Agreement

Ben Thanh Corporation ("Sunimex") v. Recofi S.A. Company Limited ("Recofi")

On 25 October 1996, Sunimex and Recofi contracted for the sale and purchase of wheat flour from France. The contract's arbitration clause specified resolution of disputes by the ICC in France.

Following Sunimex's breach, the dispute went to the ICC in France, which held that the arbitration clause failed to identify the ICC International Court of Arbitration ("ICC Court") as the arbitral authority, and persuaded the parties to sign a new arbitration agreement based on the model ICC arbitration clause. An ICC tribunal heard the case, and, in March of 1999, issued an award in favor of Recofi.

Recofi petitioned the People's Court of Ho Chi Minh City for the recognition and enforcement of the award. On 24 April 2001, the court refused recognition of the award, holding that it was invalid because Mr. Vuong Cong Minh, who executed the arbitration agreement on behalf of Sunimex, was not authorized to do so.[19]

Under Article 16.1(a) of the Ordinance on Recognition and Enforcement of Foreign Arbitral Awards, a foreign arbitral award shall not be recognized or enforced in Vietnam if the parties to the arbitration agreement lacked the capacity to sign the agreement in accordance with the law applicable to each party. For international contracts, this results in a significant risk of non-enforceability because it may be difficult for a foreign party to confirm whether the Vietnamese signatory is authorized under the entity's internal regulations to execute such agreements. In *Sunimex v. Recofi*, the Vietnamese court interpreted the relevant statute narrowly to invalidate the arbitration agreement, without regard to the relationship of the parties or their commercial dealings.

Best practices, therefore, require that parties to an arbitration agreement obtain proof that the individuals executing the agreement are authorized to do so—regardless of whether the arbitration is conducted at a domestic or foreign arbitration center.[20] A domestic arbitral award may be set aside at the request of either party if the arbitration agreement is invalid.[21]

---

[19] Decision No. 78/QD-XQQTT.

[20] Article 18.2 of the Law on Commercial Arbitration.

[21] Article 68.2(a) of the Law on Commercial Arbitration.

B. Cases

B.2 Violations of Arbitration Proceedings

PT Badega Agri Abadi Company ("PT") v. Soon Chi Co., Ltd. ("Soon Chi")

The Indonesia National Board of Arbitration heard a dispute between PT (Indonesia) and Soon Chi (Taiwan) and issued an award in favor of PT on 1 November 2006. PT petitioned the Ministry of Justice of Vietnam ("MOJ") for recognition and enforcement against Soon Chi's assets in Hung Yen Province. Recognition and enforcement was decided by the People's Court of Hung Yen Province ("Hung Yen Court").

PT was unable to satisfy the Hung Yen Court's request to provide original copies of certain legal documents,[22] including the sale and purchase contract between PT and Soon Chi and the award. Soon Chi subsequently disclaimed that it had entered into a contract with PT, and requested that the court rule based on the non-original documents PT had previously provided to the Hung Yen Court. Soon Chi also introduced evidence that PT was never an established juridical entity.

On 10 August 2007, the Hung Yen Court issued a decision refusing to recognize the award on the basis that there was insufficient evidence to prove that the signatory of the contract (and therefore the arbitration agreement) was the legal or authorized representative of Soon Chi at the time of execution, or that the representative of Soon Chi present at the arbitration hearing was the legal or authorized representative of Soon Chi.[23]

The Hung Yen Court also noted that Article 10 of the contract provided for disputes to be settled according to the rules of Badan Arbitrase Nasional Indonesia ("BANI"). Pursuant to

---

[22] Publicly available information does not specify which documents were requested.

[23] Decision No. 03/2007/ST-KDTM.

BANI's Rules, the award should have been forwarded to the relevant parties, and two copies sent to BANI for delivery to the relevant district courts for registration. Based on this procedural defect, combined with PT's inability to provide original copies of the relevant documents to the court, the court denied recognition of the award for failure to comply with the arbitration rules.[24]

This case demonstrates that a foreign arbitral award may only be enforced in Vietnam where the arbitration proceedings complied with the arbitration rules and, to some extent, the laws of Vietnam in terms of arbitration procedures.[25]

B.3   Unspecified Dispute Resolution Body

Jackson Mechanical Industrial Co., Ltd. ("JMIC") v. Dai Dung Metallic Manufacture Construction & Trade Co., Ltd. ("Dai Dung")

The People's Court of Ho Chi Minh City ("HCMC Court") refused JMIC's petition to set aside a 17 June 2009 arbitral award of Ho Chi Minh City Commercial Arbitration Center in favor of Dai Dung.[26] JMIC had argued that the award should be set aside because the Vietnamese and Chinese versions of the arbitration agreement identified different dispute resolution bodies—the Ho Chi Minh Commercial Arbitration Center and the People's Court of Ho Chi Minh City, respectively. On 11 September 2009, the Ho Chi Minh City Court ruled that because JMIC had not objected to the authority of Ho Chi Minh Commercial Arbitration Center during the arbitration, it had assented to resolution by that body.[27]

---

24   Article 370.1(a), (c) and (dd) of the CPC.

25   Article 370.1(dd) of the CPC.

26   Decision No. 04/2009/QD-TT.

27   Decision No. 2637/2009/KDTM-QDST.

This case was decided under the Ordinance, which provides that an "arbitration agreement shall be invalid if it fails to specify, or to specify clearly, the subjects of the dispute or the arbitration organization authorized to resolve disputes, and the parties have failed to enter into any supplementary agreement."[28] Nevertheless, the HCMC Court overlooked this defect in the arbitration agreement, finding that JMIC assented to arbitration by the Ho Chi Minh Commercial Arbitration Center. Under the Law on Commercial Arbitration, the failure to specify an arbitration body no longer renders an arbitration agreement invalid. Furthermore, an agreement to arbitrate may be established between parties through a variety of communications, including "telegrammes, faxes, telexes, [and] electronic mail."[29]

B.4 Public Policy Objections

Tyco Services Singapore Pte. Ltd. v. Leighton Contractors (VN) Ltd.

Tyco Services Singapore Pte. Ltd. (Singapore) ("Tyco") entered into a joint venture contract ("JVC") with Leighton Contractors (VN) Ltd. (Vietnam) ("Leighton") to construct a hotel in Vietnam. The JVC dispute resolution clause stated: "Any dispute between the parties shall be finally settled by an independent arbitrator according to a request of a party and this arbitrator is appointed by the Chairman of the Australian Institute of Engineers. The arbitration will take place in Queensland according to the law of Queensland." Various disputes arose during the performance of the JVC and were submitted to an arbitration center in Queensland, Australia ("Queensland Arbitration"). The Queensland Arbitration issued awards in favor of Tyco for USD 1,865,342.37 and AUD 789,961. Leighton

---

[28]   Article 10.4 of the Ordinance.

[29]   Article 16.2 of the Law on Commercial Arbitration.

refused to pay and Tyco petitioned the MOJ of Vietnam to recognize and enforce the award in Vietnam.

Recognition and enforcement was decided by the HCMC Court at the first instance level. Leighton argued that the award should not be recognized because the JVC was itself invalid since it had not been approved by the Ministry of Planning and Investment and because Tyco was not licensed as a foreign contractor (as required by Vietnamese law) when it formed the JVC with Leighton. The HCMC Court rejected Leighton's argument on the invalidity of the JVC on the grounds that it was a substantive issue that could not be revisited, and upheld the two arbitral awards issued by the Queensland Arbitration. Furthermore, the HCMC Court ruled that at most, the JVC only suffered a defect in formality that made it voidable, not void, under the Civil Code. The HCMC Court reasoned that Leighton should have requested the court to declare the JVC invalid within the period prescribed by law; as it had not done so, the JVC remained valid.

Leighton appealed to the Supreme People's Court of Vietnam on the same grounds it had argued before the HCMC Court. On 21 January 2003, the Supreme People's Court of Vietnam reversed the decision of the HCMC Court, rejecting the recognition of the foreign arbitral award on the basis that to do so would run "contrary to the basic principles of Vietnamese law"[30] because Tyco had entered into the JVC in Vietnam without a license as a foreign contractor. The Supreme People's Court of Vietnam considered the contract a violation of Vietnamese law impacting the national interest and, therefore, found that Tyco should not benefit from recognition or enforcement in Vietnam.

---

[30] The Supreme People's Court based its decision on Article 16.2(b) of the Ordinance on the Recognition and Enforcement of Foreign Arbitral Awards which was replaced by the CPC. However, the same provision has been restated under Article 370(2)(b) of the CPC.

C. PUBLIC POLICY IN INTERNATIONAL ARBITRATION

C.1 Scenarios of Reliance on Public Policy

In principle, recognition and enforcement of foreign arbitral awards in Vietnam may be permitted (i) if the award is from a country which has signed or acceded to a relevant international convention, or (ii) on the basis of reciprocity.[31] In the first instance, a foreign arbitral award may be recognized and enforced in Vietnam according to the New York Convention to which both Vietnam and the country of arbitration are generally signatories.

Nonetheless, Article V of the New York Convention provides that: "Recognition and enforcement of a foreign arbitration award may also be refused if the competent authority in the country where recognition and enforcement is sought finds that: (a) The subject matter of the difference is not capable of settlement by arbitration under the law of that country; or (b) The recognition and enforcement of the award would be contrary to the public policy of that country." The CPC incorporates this provision in a slightly different form, changing the wording from "contrary to public policy" to "contrary to the basic principles of the laws of Vietnam."[32]

The substituted language is comparable to the laws of other signatories where public policy denotes fundamental legal principles.[33] Other signatories have made similar distinctions

---

[31] Article 343.2 and Article 343.3 of the CPC.

[32] Article 370.2(b) of the CPC.

[33] For instance, Switzerland, Germany, Canada: *Law and Practice of International Commercial Arbitration,* Alan Redfern and Martin Hunter with Nigel Blackaby and Constantine Partasides, 4th Edition, Sweet and Maxwell.

between domestic and international public policy, causing uncertainty in the enforcement of foreign arbitral awards, which eventually led to a narrower interpretation of "public policy," such as: "fundamental rules of natural law, principles of universal justice, *jus cogens* in public international law, and the general principles of morality."[34]

C.2 Rules that Constitute "Public Policy"

Unfortunately, because Vietnamese law does not define "public policy" in the context of arbitration, decisions hinge on the nebulous wording "contrary to the basic principles of the laws of Vietnam."[35] At the request of either party, a Vietnamese court may use its discretion, supported by this vague definition, to invalidate an arbitration clause, set aside a domestic arbitration award, or refuse the recognition of a foreign arbitral award. As seen in *Tyco Services Singapore Pte., Ltd. v. Leighton Contractors (VN) Ltd.*, failure to obtain a required license or virtually any other violation of law by the award creditor could be interpreted by Vietnamese courts as sufficient grounds to refuse recognition of a foreign arbitral award. In the absence of official guidance, the catch-all term "basic principles" has led to the indiscriminate and inconsistent application of public policy objections by the Vietnamese courts.

---

[34]   *Ibid.*

[35]   Article 68.2(dd) of the Law on Commercial Arbitration.